WAR, SCIENCE
and
TERRORISM

WAR, SCIENCE
and
TERRORISM

From Laboratory to Open Conflict

Jacques G. Richardson

With a Foreword by
Kenneth Macksey

FRANK CASS
LONDON • PORTLAND, OR

First published in 2002 in Great Britain by
FRANK CASS PUBLISHERS
Crown House, 47 Chase Side, Southgate
London N14 5BP

and in the United States of America by
FRANK CASS PUBLISHERS
c/o ISBS, 5824 N.E. Hassalo Street
Portland, Oregon, 97213-3644

Website: www.frankcass.com

British Library Cataloguing in Publication Data

Richardson, Jacques G.
   War, science and terrorism: from laboratory to open
   conflict
   1. Military research 2. Research – Finance 3. Science – Social
   aspects 4. Terrorism
   I. Title
   355'.07

ISBN 0-7146-5312-8 (cloth)
ISBN 0-7146-8269-1 (paper)

Library of Congress Cataloguing-in-Publication Data

Richardson, Jacques
   War, science, and terrorism: from laboratory to open conflict/Jacques G. Richardson
      p. cm
   Includes bibliographical references and index
   ISBN 0-7146-5312-8 (cloth) – ISBN 0-7146-8269-1 (paper)
      1. Military research. 2. Military–industrial complex. 3. Terrorism. 4. World
   politics–21st century. I. Title.
   U390 .R53 2002
   355'07–dc21

2002067627

Typeset by 11/12.5 Palatino Light by Cambridge Photosetting Services
Printed in Great Britain by MPG Books Ltd, Bodmin, Cornwall

To Erika for her ideas, dedicated help and patience,
Mi-chan for her professional assistance, and
Pam for her perennial encouragement

Contents

List of Figures and Tables

FIGURES

TABLES

Foreword

The purpose of this intriguing study of war by Jacques Richardson is to examine the interaction of scientific research on the art of war and its effects on society. In other words, how scientists, technologists and industry obtain employment and profits from the presence and activities of the armed forces, whose leaders and staffs seek advice, ideas and assistance from the intelligentsia. And also to what extent their joint contributions to the armed forces do stimulate and benefit society – or contrariwise, presumably.

This is a well-developed, scholarly, analytical work founded on historical research that aims to explore original military concepts in order to challenge entrenched beliefs, guesses and, possibly, hardware. It does so by analysing specially chosen periods in the evolution of science and technology, starting with the invention of long bows and arrows and proceeding through naval, land, air, chemical, biological and nuclear weapons to electronic weapon systems. It also seeks to demonstrate how, through the ages, the flourishing volume and power of weapons has increased the magnitude of their destructive power to do more than obtain simple means of offensive or defensive advantage in the strategic and tactical arena in combat or theatres of war. Without pause, suggests Richardson, these have in the past usually helped achieve victory through the psychological application of terror. And today leaders attempt to focus on this principle by the development of controversial, complex methods of simulation of strategy, operations and tactics. This notion seems to come close to that repudiated theory, the strategy of indirect approach, which emerged as a psychological doctrine in the 1930s, whereby destruction of the enemy's morale/production potential is preferable to unacceptably high casualties among one's own forces. The theory was proven impractical long before it was on the verge of burial at the start of the Second World War.

Personally, even as a young officer, I never was convinced by the arguments supporting the strategy of indirect approach as a way of minimising casualties and destruction. And so I am pleased to read that Richardson does not fall into the traps that are baited by mere speculations and hypotheses. That is, those semi-plausible propositions that are quite frequently floated by ambitious inventors and entrepreneurs on the make, whose vivid conjectures are designed to show, for example, that some wizard, high-technological simulations can be trusted to solve the problems of how to understand the roots of armed disputes.

Nevertheless, it does emerge in this book, quite fascinatingly in some detail in Part III and its closing chapters, with what success top-flight scientists of the past managed to estimate the shape of military things to come. Or the number of times they failed completely, of course. Be that as it may, right or wrong, we should not permit speculations to be adopted without remembering how fallible we are in the present as well as likely in our guesses about roles in future war. Not that we should be dismissive of carefully presented propositions suggesting that wars can be won relatively economically by new weapons and methods. Anybody who is in the slightest bit involved with today's scientists and technologists, who have at their fingers tips the latest techniques and machinery, will be aware that the vast facilities and financial support that can be placed at the disposal of the armed forces are capable (by judgement or luck) of pulling all sorts of rabbits out of hats that can bring with them astonishingly revolutionary ideas that, even only momentarily, can have decisive, war-winning effects.

I applaud Jacques Richardson's very apparent disquiet at what terrors the future holds for society. He is aware that an increasing proportion of the brilliant young people being recruited into various nations defence establishments are, as a matter of policy, starting younger and younger. For, clever though these 'fast-track' young men and women may be, it should not be overlooked that, with all their enthusiastic inventiveness and persuasive intellectual abilities, they can generate and then, in all their inexperience, manage cleverly to sell horribly dangerous weapon systems to the supposedly experienced decision-makers, who find themselves confused by the complexities of un-desirable and costly products that contain unimaginable, maybe uncontrollable, lethal power.

KENNETH MACKSEY
June 2002

Preface

'It is possible to live long and to travel far, without being once reminded, by any martial sight or sound, that the defence of nations [has] become a science and a calling.'

Lord Macaulay

The symbiosis between science and war and the latter's surrogate, terrorism, is multifaceted. Books abound on fighting and its technologies – past, present and future – yet few have probed the extensive research lying behind the tools created for the combatant. So the story that evolves in this volume is really a triple account.

The first concerns what science offers to the military as the product of research, given that the military have become the largest sustained funder of laboratory work and test-bench development. This raises intriguing questions. If the military had not been there, would science have progressed as rapidly as it did in the twentieth century? Another, graver in consequence: is science now promoted in large part by the impulsions of armed conflict? And graver still, are hostilities today and tomorrow extensions of the scientific endeavor?

The second facet of our story, happily benign, is a survey – interwoven throughout the text – of the advantages accruing to society as a result of the military sponsorship of scientific investigation. This is one thing I proposed to accomplish when I began this book. Let me explain.

A group of specialists met at the International Council of Scientific Unions (ICSU)[1] in Paris, in 1988, to plan a global symposium on the theme of International Science and its Partners. As we began our work, we had to determine the completeness of both *science* and *partners*. 'Do we include the social sciences?' we asked. 'Yes, some of them.' 'Do we deal with the contributions of industry through its technical research?' 'Of course', responded everyone. 'Do we include the military as generators of scientific research?' Pause, with a puzzled silence. Then all but one of us expressed the view that, clearly and without doubt, the military are responsible for originating and funding a significant share of the research effort in many countries.

The one dissenter on our team, a distinguished neuroscientist, resisted elegantly but with conviction and force. A civil institution such as ICSU, he maintained, could not admit the military into the province of research. It was irrelevant and perhaps indecent, he claimed, to include armed forces among science's 'partners'. The consensus of the men and women in our group carried the day, however, and our working document included a section on the role of the military in research.

Two years after that symposium, the *International Social Science Journal* asked me to prepare an article for an issue on the theme of innovation. There I reviewed the contributions of military research to the world's awareness of how human beings derive new technologies for defense and even aggression from developments in scientific knowledge. A well-known military historian read the published piece, and his immediate comment was, 'You must make this a book.'

The third aspect, as perplexing as it is complex, is why – despite scientific–military advance – terrorism has spread during the same period of scientific progress and left governments and populations so vulnerable to the scourge. Terrorism a century ago was usually a single, simply armed protester who assassinated an empress or a king, archduke, prime minister or president. Today, enraged malcontents act in growing numbers, use new technology and even scientific knowledge to advance their aims.

The result of this threefold impetus is the story of how part of the human species uses its accumulation of the knowledge of nature to immobilize, maim, kill or otherwise 'do in' adversaries. The enemy is sometimes only temporary, and hostile acts often leave permanent results, some of which ironically can be of social or cultural value.

To make these uneven parts of the story coherent, I have grouped them in major sections, each element introduced very briefly as we go along. The first part, 'Preparation for Conflict', sets the tone, explaining some of the science-based fundamentals that participants in conflict need to take into account before taking action. The second, 'Warfare and Its Management', explores the variety of challenges, problems and obstacles confronting those making the commitment to use arms. 'Behind the Action, and Wars to Come' is the third section; this concentrates on who contributes to using science for warmaking or for terrorism, and what their future may be.

In large measure because the United States administration 'finally achieved its goal of allocating 50 per cent of the R&D (research and development) budget to civilian research',[2] total military spending worldwide in 1999 was rather lower than when the Berlin Wall fell ten years earlier. Besides specifying what the world of science has created for those resorting to arms, sometimes at extraordinary cost, I show also that a good proportion of this innovation serves the everyday world as well. The ordinary citizen engaged in peaceful pursuits has no use – obviously – for a biological or chemical weapon, a nuclear bomb, or costly transport engineered to meet requirements demanded by environment and abuse. Yet many of the products and processes now commonplace around the world are the fruit of conceptions, designs, mechanisms and services devised originally to satisfy military needs.

This *dual purpose* is far more widespread than most of us realize, and some inventions might not take form at all if institutional authority did not exist.[3] The exploration here, if not encyclopedically complete, will be as comprehensive as possible. I have tried to cover the scientific waterfront without overloading the reader with history, by including the social and environmental as well as the so-called 'hard' sciences. And I trespass, admittedly, several times beyond that which is strictly scientific.

Two areas looked into only summarily require justification: aircraft and surface navies. The military's role in the genesis of aviation, reviewed in Chapter 1, was minimal until the First World War. The idea of a working dirigible came to Count Ferdinand von Zeppelin during his service as a volunteer during the American Civil War. Twenty years later, two French officers made a successful prototype. Once innovation-minded military officers had grasped the significance of the novelty, the material sponsorship they offered incited further development. After the First World War, the German military bypassed post-Versailles restrictions on the development of powered aircraft, using sports clubs to push the development of unpowered aircraft and engineers to devise the missile.

The Wright brothers of Ohio, bicycle dealers with virtually no scientific experience, analyzed the flight of birds so thoroughly as to achieve controlled and *sustained* flight of a heavier-than-air machine in 1903. Their achievement came to fruit in the great scientific tradition of exploiting and improving what their predecessors had done.[4] But the design and mechanics they applied, their reasoned exploitation of aerodynamics and pursuit of simple aeronautical engineering were the Wrights' own work. The two brothers 'were scientists, craftsmen and also test pilots. [They] set in motion the basis for the way we build airplanes today', according to the airman directing the reconstruction of the original plane for the Wright Brothers centenary in 2003.[5]

The First World War brought aeronautics directly to the battlefield, and war rose to the sky. Aerial reconnaissance, the first real application of air power, expanded rapidly, quickly proving its value in enabling commanders on the ground and at sea better to 'read' the battle. Comprehensive air-defense systems, non-existent in 1914, 'had to be organized wherever air attack threatened, [they] were yet another stimulus to invention and industrialization, a further drain upon resources to the traditional fighting arms and a stage in the deeper involvement of an entire nation in the war'.[6]

After the 1920s, aviation thrived and new protective systems, civil and military, emerged from a second great war. Yet highly refined defensive systems failed to prevent, in the first year of the twenty-first century, the use of commercial aircraft by irregular fighters against unprotected non-military targets and unsuspecting civilians.

Navies as well as ground and then air forces invested heavily in the systematic development of airframes and propulsion. This has been so in the United States, the major economies of western Europe, the former Czechoslovakia (now two countries), Poland, the former Soviet Union, pre-1946 Japan and, more recently, in the European Union, Brazil, Indonesia, China and again Japan. The Pacific War and the later world events of 2001–2 resulted (as it happens) directly from aggressive use of aircraft, creating entirely new problems of social organization against adversity.

More scientifically, continuing exploratory work in manned flight concerns the resolution of certain elemental problems. Difficult research challenges now include detecting clear-air turbulence via laser instead of by radar; discovering in adequate time the 'microbursts' of fast-moving air that are at the origin of wind shear; and combating or avoiding the corkscrew-type turbulence generated at the wingtips that perturb the flight of airplanes caught in the wake of larger craft (the possible cause of the American Airlines disaster of November 2001 in New York). These hazards to life, limb and material property affect both civilians and the military, and they constitute challenging scientific and engineering puzzles.

'Are manned flights always necessary?' is a question equally applicable to space vehicles and atmospheric craft. Drone aircraft are replacing piloted reconnaissance planes and some bomber fleets. Farther out in space, we shall continue for some years to explore Mars without human beings before our species is ready for live reconnaissance.

Athough I have avoided discussion of naval architecture and its supporting armaments in the evolution of warfare on the sea's surface, there is a notable exception: detection of an adversary's (invisible) presence, both on the surface and below. Detection is a field in which innovative technology resulting from knowledge of things lurking or moving in water has been paramount. The struggle of humans to live and work under water – a hostile environment, both socially and technically – represents, on the other hand, the scientific side. Hence, as readers may agree, the fairly detailed nature of Chapter 3. In the cases of both aerial and naval warfare, incidentally, the literature extant is impressive in quantity and authoritative in quality. I have not sought to compete with such excellence.

For the future, sound governance and public security must remain attentive to how we dispose, for example, of unwanted nuclear machinery and spent fuel. Current efforts by the Russian government to interest nearby states (Norway, for one) in helping to cope with this enormous environmental hazard may prove to be the only viable means to clean up the 'nuclear polygon' in and around the Arctic islands of Novaya Zemlya and the other nuclear graveyards dispersed far and wide in the former Soviet Union.

Something will be done about such unacceptable conditions, and wise efforts in this direction include full ratification and implementation of the START (Strategic Arms Reduction Talks) series of international agreements, together with continuing respect for the Nuclear Test-Ban and Comprehensive Test-Ban Accords. The quintuple nuclear tests claimed by each side in the India–Pakistan face-off of 1998 were violations of the spirit of such accords – although neither country was a signatory. If such acts help avoid hostilities in the region, however, they may also encourage 'nuclearizing' states to abandon their plans voluntarily. So much the better.

The future will probably see repetitions of the science-based terrorism practiced in 1995 against the citizens of Japan and in 2001 against the United States and elsewhere. The activities of Aleph Shinrikyô in Tokyo and of religious extremists striking the United States, the work of a few people energized by the belief that the only world acceptable is their own, will recur. A credo that justifies technologically trained plotters to attack society in the most destructive ways leaves governments and the public, temporarily, almost helpless to cope.

So the commentators on arms-based terrorism stress that they may recur. To strengthen public precautions and rationalize our fear of the evil that can emerge from scientific minds and laboratories as criminal assaults on society, all of us need to learn to communicate better with potential adversaries: more tolerance, a better effort to perceive others' aspirations, and more patient negotiation to urge peaceful resolution of disputes.

While nations are not likely to reduce military research appreciably in the coming decades, we can hope that advantages of unforeseeable value to many people will continue to flow from military R&D. A companion effort, peace research – in which both scientists and the military are deeply engaged – exists and moves ahead, but the subject is beyond the scope of this book.

Finally, a word on the sources. I have avoided for the most part military publications, already myriad around the world and of good quality, as most of them are. Instead interviews, conference excerpts, scientific papers, manuals and other books have been harvested, and I have added original research. If the reader is surprised at the call made on mass media, this is because I have followed the precept that today's news is tomorrow's well-known first draft of history, information that may take years – and often does – to find its way into our permanent annals.

Linear measure and speed are expressed according to normal civil and military usage: in the metric system for land, in the imperial system for sea and most air references. The metric *tonne* is specified when it should be differentiated from the English *ton*.

Critical as some passages may seem of scientists, of the military, or of government, I prefer to avoid denigration of the military in the science–war rapport. A research scientist, who earned his living from defense contracts once explained, 'I enjoy working with the military. They know what they want, and they have the means to pay.' I explore, therefore, just what the military have wanted and obtained from science, what they seek today, what may be the relationship between defense establishments and the research community in the years to come, and something of what all of it costs society, including sustenance of the new terrorism.

NOTES

1   The International Council of Scientific Unions is a nongovernmental organization founded in 1931. Now the International Council for Science (but still ICSU), it occupies the vintage Hôtel de Noailles in western Paris.

2   'Half of US Budget Goes to Civil R&D', *Outlook on Science Policy*, April 1999, pp. 44–5, reporting the American budget for the fiscal year 1999–2000. The headline refers to one-half the US science budget.

3   The first dual-purpose innovation recorded may be the sound-based writing invented by scribes among the Semitic mercenaries of Egypt's Middle Kingdom. Its remnants, dating from about 1850 BC, were discovered in 1993–94 among graffiti found at Wadi-el-Hol near Thebes by archeologists John C. and Deborah Yarnell of Yale University.

4   The Wrights' achievements are described in Harry Combs (with Martin Caidin), *Kill Devil Hill: Discovering the Secret of the Wright Brothers*, foreword by Neil Armstrong (Boston, MA, Houghton Mifflin, 1979).

5   Ken Hyde, interviewed by Michael E. Ruane, 'Redoing the Wright Brothers, from Scratch', *International Herald Tribune* (hereafter *IHT*), 13 September 2000, p. 2.

6   Kenneth Macksey, *Technology in War: The Impact of Science on Weapon Development and Modern Battle* (London, Arms & Armour, 1986), p. 85.

… die Not ist groß!
Die ich rief, die Geister,
Werd' ich nun nicht los.

… the need is great!
I cannot now rid myself
Of the spirits I summoned.

Goethe, *Der Zauberlehrling* (The Sorcerer's Apprentice)

Part I:

Preparation for Conflict

Perceiving nature and the universe beyond, and how they work, then using this knowledge to advantage: these are the processes we recognize as science and technology. Although human beings have been dedicated since earliest times to putting knowledge to use, the application of scientific knowledge in its modern form is only a half-millennium old.

Today, the utility of science translated into technology for military ends may make it as sensitive as a diplomatic secret. New research must also be paid for, whether by universities, firms, not-for-profit laboratories, national military establishments, even international consortia. In the spiraling economies of the 1960s to 1990, the governments of the principal powers had money to spend handsomely in support of science emanating from educational institutions, public and private enterprise, foundations, and national and international institutes. Much of the funding came from military budgets, making defense the sponsor of sometimes more than 60 per cent of the money spent on research. When budgets become strained, it is often the military who remain relatively free to spend and thus stimulate research.

We may thus ask: 'Is war an extension of science by other means?' A reply requires some understanding of the basic nature of the research–military relationship, so first we need to review some origins of armed conflict. Then we must examine how the teaching of science and technology spreads, and how proficiency evolves in the conception and deployment of weapons. Certain civil uses of science and technology, furthermore, are themselves dominated by the military.

Throughout, I strive to make a distinction between science (knowledge from research) and technology (its applications): the aim is to stress how science comes to the aid of the sailor, airman, soldier or terrorist in need of solutions to specific operational needs – and how these often also benefit – outside the realm of terrorism – many of the rest of us. We like to believe that adequate defense is a sound insurance policy safeguarding our societies and their institutions, much in the manner of a community preparing adequately for its needs in education, public health, and protection against fire or flood, crime and terrorism.

The origins of societal defense may lie rather (anthropologists and psychologists are not sure) in an aggressive posture. Our ancestors sought to use fire or explosion 'to get their way' with neighboring families, clans, or competitors of different cultural characteristics. As the human race mastered the use of new and different tools, so it adapted them to increasingly varied and complex applications.

Some of the most difficult challenges posed by the environment include moving about and working under water and in space, or how to make use of the atom's nucleus both for peace and for war. Harnessing nuclear fission and taking space walks, now routine, were not among the realities of life known to our great-grandparents. Such ventures are technically and culturally complicated, given that the human being's perception of nature was from the outset what eyes, ears, nose, touch and taste could tell. Analyzing and understanding, then experimenting with and applying accumulated knowledge, came incrementally. Step by step, we learned how to use nature's alien facets to our advantage.

Experience under water is about four centuries old, everything previously having been haphazard – and hazardous – exploration. The working submarine is only a century old. It is the military who have developed perhaps 90 per cent of submarine science and technology. So we usually think that, in its military configuration, the underwater boat was perfected with naval tasks in mind.

Yet, at the beginning of the twenty-first century, we remain ignorant of the extent of its civil usefulness. A growing curiosity about the sea floor, its riches and its dangers, combined with an astonishing ability to detect nuclear blasts at a distance, leads to new understanding of seismic disturbances both on land and under seas. International treaties on non-proliferation and other nuclear controls, some dating from the 1960s, help us reap other rich harvests in the geosciences – with the encouraging bonus that most of the data are free of state-controlled secrecy, a feature that we still cannot claim in all of science's realms.

Secrecy, military advantage and national prestige have driven the space race thus far, although increasing transparency set in with the collapse of the Soviet Union in 1991. Here space exploration is treated in a special way, pointing out the remaining barriers to spaceflight (manned and unmanned) and some of the most significant scientific advantages emerging from expeditions beyond the Earth's atmosphere, to the Moon and (perhaps some day) to all the planets and farther.

The nucleus of the atom and its wonders are a story in themselves. Humankind is the author of violent interactions among atomic particles

– and, moreover, among the atomic nuclei of only a few of the elements. Our theoretical understanding of the atom saw its breakthrough during the exploration of radiation in the 1890s, at the close of the first century of truly experimental science. With the discovery of the atom's electron in 1897 came the new domain of nuclear physics, ever expanding.

The pathfinding that characterized the first decades of the last century opened all sorts of laboratory doors, leading quickly to the first controlled explosion of a nuclear device – the atom or fission bomb. I shall contrast how military scientists working in totally different political settings conducted their research and trials, and how they accomplished this work in record time. As a consequence, war at its worst is now irrevocably identified with scientific research.

These chapters close with a glimpse at the minds and wills constituting the military services. Besides those of the men and women in uniform, there are also those of specialists outside who help improve the selection of candidates for military–technical vocations. Psychologists and psychometrists assisted the military, early on, to construe recruitment and military education in special ways. We shall see how the armed services continue to exploit novel concepts in human-resources management. The military help the psychologists, too, to improve their own methods and skills.

One result has been a constantly better rapport between both managers and the managed. In a world today distancing itself from mass conscription, reliance on the completely prepared military man and woman is increasingly the norm in most industrial democracies.

The armed forces are thus adjusting their sights on new targets assigned to them by their governments amid sometimes fast-changing political, economic, cultural and military conditions around the world. Among these is international terrorism, perhaps the identifying phenomenon of an entirely new age.

1

From Bows and Arrows to Missiles and Aircraft

'We may find a practical philosophy by means of which, knowing the force and action of fire, water, air, the stars ... we can in the same way employ them in all those uses to which they are adapted'
René Descartes, *Discourse on Method*

'Are scientists present in governance', asks historian Suzanne Citron, 'only to justify decisions made by political leaders on H-bombs ... and the like?' Does war extend science by other means? This paraphrase of Carl von Clausewitz's remark about war related to governance (a continuation of politics by other means)[1] will be a major preoccupation in the chapters ahead.

A contemporary of Clausewitz, Swiss-born General Baron Antoine Henri de Jomini, in *The Art of War* (1830), divided the total military endeavor into strategy, grand tactics (today's operations), logistics, engineering, small-unit tactics and diplomacy. To these the ensuing history forces us to add the dimension of science. This helps explain where and how science fits into societal conflicts, enabling us to peer into the different disciplines of research that have accelerated the severity of armed clashes and terrorism.

Invoking Clausewitz's dictum runs the risk of reverting to anachronism, however, in view of the non-combat actions imposed on the military since the Cold War's end. The famed German military scientist's sweeping relativity between politics and war was reinforced by his explanation that armed dispute is 'an act of violence intended to compel our opponent to fulfill our will',[2] especially after other means have failed. Most analysts have perceived territoriality or its expansion as the main impetus to violent conflict, to which in the 1990s the al-Qaeda organisation added imposed theocracy.[3]

LOW-TECH WEAPONS BUT HIGH KILL RATES

In the evolution of military tools and techniques, the Hundred Years War between England and France bridged the fourteenth and sixteenth centuries. The conflict joined what would become a new era of science-based technology of war to the simple weapons of past centuries: the arms race of the period.

A transitional weapon of the time was the longbow, used with deadly efficacy by Edward III's English troops against French King Philip II at Crécy in 1346 and, later, by England's Henry V also against the French. The troops – most of them on foot – marshaled by Sir Thomas Erpingham at Agincourt against the cavalry and infantry of Charles VI of France proved near-invincible against a politically demoralized enemy on a sunny October morning in 1415. Henry V was determined to win, to enforce his territorial claims in France.

The empirical 'science' of bow and arrow reaches back to the late Ice Age, probably 20,000 years before Agincourt. The English bow was made of ash, elm, witchhazel or the rare yew; its length measured between 180 and 260 centimeters. Its arrow was 75cm long, iron-tipped – the metallic projectile made it a subject of moralizing about the ethics of using certain weapons.[4] A bow string of linen (not vine or gut or thong), when properly greased and drawn, propelled its arrow at 180km/h (112mph) over a 200-meter course. The missile slowed to 35 m/sec (75mph) at the moment of impact. A normal arrow weighed 60gm (grams, 2 ounces), three times the weight of an arrow used by today's sporting archers. Its iron-jacketed head permitted the penetration of oak planks as much as 10cm thick, so that it could pierce the skin, bone and internal organs of human or animal targets.

British infantry favored the longbow from its demonstrated success by Edward I against William Wallace at Falkirk, Crécy and Poitiers, a preference over the short bow (and even the crossbow) used on the continent since the Crusades. Tests of the metals used at the time of Agincourt were made late in the twentieth century at the University of London and the Royal Armaments Research and Development Establishment in Great Britain by, respectively, Peter Pratt and Peter Jones. They found that when the longbow's arrow landed, it could pierce armor typically 1.5mm thick and, blunted by its passage through metal, made a mess of things beyond.[5] If hemorrhage and death did not follow, infection or gangrene set in to dispatch the victim.

The longbow and its arrows were not the only factors in the defeat of the French. The English longbowmen had been trained to reload and fire about ten arrows each minute, for minutes at a time: these archers were the commandos of their age. Five thousand English at Agincourt thus dumped volleys of about 800 arrows per second on the 22,500 French fighting on home soil. Laurence Olivier's film of 1945, *Henry V*, depicted authentically the clouds of English projectiles.

The longbowmen were arrayed in 'banners', each some 200 men strong and commanded by a banneret (a battalion or squadron commander). Remarkable logistics backed the infantry and cavalry. Besides armorers and gunners, there were blacksmiths and saddlers, wheelwrights and wagoners, carpenters and cordwainers, physicians and surgeons, chaplains and clerks – and fletchers and bowyers to ensure the supply of longbows and arrows. Until it could eat off the land, the invading force brought its own bread, oats and nuts; beef, pork and poultry; cockles, eels, mussels and sturgeon; grapes and assorted fruit; water, beer and wine.

The combat at dew-soaked Agincourt was a pitched struggle lasting three hours. A small, determined group of intruders decimated a domestic force much larger in strength but lacking the longbow. The English took 15 or more enemy lives to each one of their own lost.[6] In the wars of the nineteenth and twentieth centuries, losing sides would be far less overwhelmed, with a loss of one-third considered by that time the basis of complete defeat. (At the battle of the Somme in July 1916, the rapid decimation of the First Newfoundland Royal Regiment caused its disbandment.[7])

Agincourt's arrows would find a different sort of martial honor during Japan's early feudal centuries, when shafts were fashioned from the hard, fibrous stems of *yatake* bamboo – a natural resource so precious that it was outlawed for use by anyone not serving the samurai of Nippon's southern clans. This ban was similar to that governing oak wood from western Europe after the Renaissance, wood reserved almost exclusively to build fighting ships.

GAS BAGS BECOME BALLOONS

Although aviation had its origins within the domains of the paper-making and textile industries during the Age of Enlightenment, military necessity inspired at least one conceiver of manned flight. In autumn 1782, a Frenchman was musing over a print hanging in his sitting room that showed the Spanish investiture of the fortress at Gibraltar. He and his brother, Etienne Montgolfier, had just completed the lofting of the first balloon, made of paper, by hot air generated by a fire suspended in a basket.

As Joseph Montgolfier, a papermaker, studied the plight of the British troops surrounded by Spanish forces at Gibraltar, he let his imagination stray. He concentrated on the chimney fire that bore ash bits in its updraft. 'Surely the force that carried particles of smoke up the flue', relates historian Charles C. Gillispie, 'could be confined and harnessed to lift conveyances and float men above the surface of the Earth.'[8]

An early military use of the phenomenon took place in 1861 at Cloud's Mill, Virginia, during the American Civil War. Thaddeus S. C. Lowe developed a balloon filled with hot coal-gas. The balloonist aboard Lowe's gas bag was assigned the task of observing, for the Union (Northern) forces, artillery pieces deployed by the Confederate (Southern) side. Afterwards, President Abraham Lincoln appointed Lowe 'chief aeronaut' of his army.[9] Field commander Major-General George B. McClellan went aloft himself to observe his opponent's deployment.[10] Nine years later, balloons were used extensively for observation in the Franco-Prussian conflict, especially around besieged Paris.

The earliest years in the development of heavier-than-air craft (1867–1902), especially the glider experiments done by Otto and Gustav Lilienthal in Germany and Octave Chanute in the United States based on earlier concepts formulated by Britain's Sir George Cayley, lay almost exclusively beyond military concerns, as had been the case a century earlier when trials on lighter-than-air vessels were conducted in France. A working dirigible was inspired, as noted in the Preface, by Count von Zeppelin's study of a tethered balloon. French army captains Charles Renard and Arthur Krebs then built a prototype in 1884. These innovators operated mainly in the civil sector but, once receptive military officers grasped the significance of their work, material sponsorship urged further development.

AIRCRAFT AND OPERATIONS RESEARCH APPEAR

Wilbur and Orville Wright, bicycle tradesmen without scientific training, analyzed the flight of birds and accomplished the first sustained flight of a heavier-than-air machine. The design and mechanics used, the reasoned use of aerodynamics, together with rudimentary aeronautical engineering, were purely the Wrights' work. Their labor combined empiricism with new scientific understanding: how air 'lifts' an airfoil (wing) in order to sustain a body in flight using the forces of *drag* and *thrust*.

The determination of the Wrights 'to defy gravity and conquer the wind', says Bill Gates, led the brothers to build their own wind-tunnel to test airfoils 'and measure empirically how to lift a flying machine into the sky … [T]hat obsessive kind of world-changing belief is a force that drives you to solve a problem, to find the breakthrough.'[11]

After these pioneering ventures into the sky, the military took interest in 1907 when a firm order was passed by the government in Washington for the construction of a flying machine. This order gave birth to an 'aerial fleet' for the United States. Since then progress has been essentially technological, with much of the R&D funded – in, ultimately, a score of countries – by defense establishments through the financing of experimental and prototype designs. Building aircraft often produces, consequently, civil as well as military configurations.

At the end of the twentieth century, military planners in Washington re-adopted the lighter-than-air balloon, reinforced by sensitive electronic detectors, as a reasonably inexpensive but now *unmanned* means to thwart attacks by adversary cruise missiles. 'For around $50 million any nation can purchase either a very few fighter aircraft, about four attack helicopters or fifteen ballistic missiles. But the same amount buys hundreds of cruise missiles – what the Army calls a "poor man's air force"'[12] or many more balloons. Today rigid dirigibles and non-rigid blimps are experiencing a comeback in the on-and-off evolution of airships for military or civil use.

The Second World War inspired the application of mathematics to the solving of practical, and pressing, problems of direct concern to the managers of the air forces involved. Physicist Freeman Dyson recounts in *Disturbing the Universe* one of these urgent concerns, the loss of too many air crews, during his assignment as a 20-year-old civil employee of Britain's Royal Air Force (RAF). Dyson was one of a small group among the expanding '"operations researchers" or "operations analysts"'.[13] Some attribute the origins of this methodology to Benjamin Franklin who calculated that the £3 million spent by the British in the North American colonies' struggle for independence meant that the Crown treasury had spent £20,000 for each of the 150 American rebels killed until 1775.[14] Later, during the First World War, Commander Reginald Henderson brought statistical analysis and ensuing operational decision to Britain's Royal Navy, when he pressed for armed convoys to protect merchant shipping. As a result, merchant tonnage lost to submarines dropped from 869,000 tonnes in April 1917 to less than 300,000 tonnes a year later, despite an increase in the number of German submarines.[15]

In the Second World War, RAF commanders were becoming familiar with *creepback*: progressive, linear withdrawal from the intended target zone as air crews became more experienced and defensive, and as promised periods of rest and recuperation approached or were delayed. Creepback continued to be a phenomenon of increasing concern to the air strategists of the Western Allies trying to assure target saturation.

The operations analysts (whose other work is explored in Chapter 12), by taking the time necessary and profiting from their distance from combat, quickly perceived one of creepback's causes. The maelstrom of the *flak*-infested skies over German ground-targets incited, in terms of group psychology, flight crews to drop their bombs prematurely or not at all. With the aggravation of creepback, the British, Canadian, American, French and Polish air forces inadvertently saved some crews. This did not prove to be a severe handicap in the bombing of Japan, however, whose naval and air-force defenses by 1944 were so reduced as to be marginal. Japan's vulnerability to attack by incendiary bombs was, on the contrary, increased and exploited by the US squadrons overhead.

To give a thumbnail sketch of operations research (OR), it differs from system engineering in that analysis of *how* a system works, or fails to work, normally excludes human performance as a variable factor. To assess a system's performance, it is necessary to identify and define the objectives of the process, and then attribute numerical values to them, although time may cause these to evolve. Change and re-identification may be needed. To know the system, then, analysis is required: first, determining the aims to be accomplished; next, how these are fed back to the organizing or controlling entity; then, how data related to the system's requirements are fed back; and finally, indication of the action to be taken, with what resources, and for how long. All this information is usually represented on a flow chart, a diagram enabling investigators to understand the variables and how they affect operation.

Aerial bombing, for instance, does not always destroy targets by blast or fire. A spectacular 'dam-busting' raid in May 1943 by the RAF's 617 Squadron of 19 Lancaster bombers intended to exploit water stored in a series of dams above the Ruhr river valley – one of the world's densest industrial zones – to play havoc with highly productive communities downstream. The leader of the raid on the Ruhr dams was Wing Commander Guy Gibson. The raid's designer was Barnes Neville Wallace, later to become chief of aeronautical R&D at the British Aircraft Corporation.

Using a newly developed, low-flying technique of skip-bombing, the Lancasters broke two dams, causing a titanic deluge of nearly half a billion tonnes of water that pushed 15-meter-high walls of water rapidly downstream. This flood wrecked power plants, factories and bridges (without speaking of human beings) on a route of ruin 150 kilometers long. The RAF's losses numbered 53 of 133 crewmen and eight of the Lancasters, but the damage to Germany's wartime economy took weeks to repair. The dams were still not properly functional 18 months later.

ROCKETS AND MISSILES

Three months after the Western Allies had disembarked on the French coast in June 1944 to open an additional front against the Axis forces in Europe, the first German A4 (or V1) rockets came crashing down on London and Paris from launch sites in the Netherlands. The German missile better known now as the V2 was descended from the first small rockets designed and developed after 1936 at the Peenemünde proving ground. There, Wernher von Braun worked with Walter Dornberger to implement the concept of chemically propelled projectiles different from anything fired in anger before.

The first airborne tests of the V2 took place in June–October 1942 at Peenemünde, whence the test-firings of the V1 'buzzbomb' had been made earlier. (The V1 was the prototype of cruise missiles, together with a 'proof of concept' realization developed in 1944 by the Blohm & Voss submarine builders of Hamburg.[16]) Weapons of this variety had not been foreseen in the German armaments that the Treaty of

---

BOX 1 PARADOX OF THE MODERN ROCKET

Konstantin E. Tsiolkovskiy, Russian schoolteacher and amateur researcher on aerospace questions, published *Exploring Space with Reactive Devices* in 1903. He theorized that the absence of oxygen beyond the Earth's envelope of air could be overcome by loading a rocket with hydrogen and oxygen (both in liquid form) as propellants, thereby overcoming a physical obstacle: the absence of something to 'push against' once away from Earth. Physicist Robert Goddard of the United States pursued the theory, and in 1926 tested a rocket lifted by gasoline mixed with liquid O_2. A grant from the Guggenheim Foundation allowed him to test new rockets throughout the 1930s in New Mexico.

German scientists showed the most interest in Goddard's trials, yet in 1939 the American army politely turned down his offer to collaborate with the military. (There were no funds.) German Hermann Oberth took out a patent on a rocket, launching it in 1931. He pursued rocket development in his country with enthusiastic military partners, leading to the V1 and V2 in 1944. After the Second World War, Soviet and American authorities each commandeered about half the German rocket specialists. In the Soviet Union, Sergei P. Korolev and his team developed the engine that launched *Sputnik 1* (1957) as the Americans were elaborating *Explorer 1* (1958).

Versailles proscribed in 1919. Dornberger had, in fact, begun his research work on rockets in the 1920s under secret orders of the Wehrmacht. This military R&D was disguised, in part, by a civil designation, Elektromechanische Werke GmbH, Katslhagen, adjacent to Peenemünde.

The V2 was to have been succeeded by the A9, the first two-stage missile ever, with a range of 700 kilometers. Although the war's end canceled these plans, Germany was producing 5,000 V1s by August 1944 and firing them off at both military and civil targets. The devastated and labor-short German economy managed to turn out more than 2,500 V2s. Half of these fell on Antwerp, a fifth on London, and the rest near Ipswich, Norwich, and communities in the Netherlands, Belgium and France.[17]

THE BIRTH OF THE COMPUTER

J. Presper Eckert, a young researcher at the University of Pennsylvania in 1943, joined a mentor named John W. Mauchly to build the *e*lectronic *n*umerical *i*ntegrator *a*nd *c*omputer (ENIAC). Its concept was based on a design of 1937–40 by John Vincent Atanasoff, professor of physics and mathematics at Iowa State College. The 30-tonne machine built by Mauchly and Eckert contained 18,000 vacuum tubes and handled data a thousand times faster than electrical counting machines. Yet a single one of today's silicon chips alone has more computational power than had the ENIAC monster.

ENIAC's purpose was to calculate firing tables for army artillery.[18] This work was completed in February 1946, five months after hostilities ended. The two inventors founded, in the same year, the Eckert-Mauchly Computer Corporation, a firm bought by Remington-Rand in 1950 and renamed successively Sperry-Rand, Univac, and Unisys. Competitors joined the race to exploit the new technology – born of the applied mathematics required by artillerymen – most profitably. The priority of invention, incidentally, was not awarded to Atanasoff until the epochal decision by the Minnesota Federal District Court of October 1973;[19] this resulted from a suit to establish priority filed in 1967 by Sperry-Rand and Honeywell, each against the other.

An entirely new age of numeration and literation thus arrived midway through the twentieth century, with applications transcending by far the in-flight behavior of artillery projectiles. Futurists Alvin and Heidi Toffler call the advent of the computer the 'third wave' of civilization – the first and second waves having been, respectively, agriculture about ten millennia ago and the age of steam, beginning about 1750.[20]

GUNS AND CIGARETTE MAKERS

When the Lockheed U-2'spy plane'of the United States Air Force was shot from Soviet skies on 1 May 1960, it was felled by a new Soviet rocket designed by a scientist. Petr Grushin devised, in all, 14 kinds of anti-aircraft missiles that the USSR used in the Middle East and Vietnam and sold to nearly 40 countries. It was his model V-750 that downed the U-2, striking it at an altitude of around 90,000 feet or 27.5 kilometers.

The U-2, later redesignated the SR-71, was indirectly a development based on the principle that lighter-than-air craft can rise high into the stratosphere while their propulsion units still 'breathe'. As an aide and subsequently deputy director of the Central Intelligence Agency responsible for covert activities, Richard Bissell, Jr, 'guided the agency's clandestine program for building the high-flying [U-2] and the first orbiting spy satellite, called Corona'.[21] One of the functions of an intelligence service is to provide some of the knowledge, methods, technology and evaluation required to satisfy information needs established by military intelligence (see Chapter 9). The U-2, as long as it could operate beyond public view, proved to be a productive response to this need. Corona, never in the public awareness,'steadied the resolve of American presidents … [making] an extraordinary contribution to world stability'.[22]

One of the specialists claiming to have devised countermeasures to the American Stealth aircraft is Oldrich Barak, a former Czech major-general who had directed procurement for the ground forces of Czechoslovakia's army. After the Czech and Slovak republics split in 1993, Barak retired and became president of a firm called High Technology Transfer, which then merged with a company known as Tesla Paradubice (TP). TP owned the TAMARA radar system, co-invented by Barak.[23]

In 1987, Czechoslovakia was selling 3 per cent of its national output as arms for export. Between 1989 and 1993, TP reduced its work force from 6,000 to 3,500 because lessened demand had lowered its production by 70 per cent. By winter 1997–98, the entire Czech economy suffered a severe setback, a major recession (causing the resignation of Prime Minister Vaclav Claus) attributable in part to the diminished Czech arms industry.

Czech military production fell in monetary value, between 1987 and 1992, from 30 million to 4 million koruna. TP applied to Prague for permission to sell six TAMARA systems to the Iranians but, after pressure exerted by the West, the Czech government refused approval. In June 1993 the Czechs created a corporate entity called the Research,

Development and Production Group, a dual-purpose firm of 180,000 employees whose subsidiaries manufacture cigarette-making equipment as easily as nuclear reactors, and have remodernized Soviet-era T-72 tanks.

SKY INTRUDERS

Countermeasures to rockets and missiles, as well as to aircraft, imply detectability. Between 1960 and 1974 the United States maintained a system designed to detect intruders, with part of the widely dispersed equipment placed on the rooftops of American diplomatic installations. The system also detected low-frequency shock waves generated by meteoric explosions in the atmosphere, a bonus for astronomers, although experts believe that only one-tenth to one-hundredth of the air bursts that took place were recorded by the detection system.

One of the registered disturbances, occurring early in the process somewhere between South Africa and Antarctica, was believed at first to result from a thermonuclear weapon exploded by the Pretoria government. The explosion probably came, however, from the entry into the atmosphere's upper layers of a spatial body measuring some 20 meters across; it took the form of a monstrous detonation equaling a half-million tonnes of TNT – or 500 times more than the Hiroshima bomb of 1945.[24] To compare, the meteorite that struck Siberia's Tunguska region in 1908 (before the notion of detection systems existed) probably had a diameter of 30 meters, weighed 1,000 tonnes, and heated surrounding atmospheric gases to 25,000°C. It released some 15 megatonnes of TNT-equivalent energy 10km above the Earth.

Three other explosions by meteors near the global surface were detected by the American missile-detection system. On 16 April 1988 a meteor crashed through the atmosphere above Indonesia (5,000 TNT-equivalent tonnes), a second of 2,000 equivalent tonnes entered the atmosphere north of Australia on 1 October 1990, and a meteoroid disintegrated above the Arctic Ocean on 4 October 1991. Colonel Simon Worden of the US Ballistic Missile Defense Organization pointed out in *Sky and Telescope* (February 1994) that, if the Australian intrusion had taken place over Kuwait during the Gulf War, the Allied side could have understood its natural origins but not the Iraqi side. 'Impact specialists', noted *Sky and Telescope*, 'hope [that] the release of the previously classified records represents the first step in a long-term partnership with the surveillance community'. This proved to be the case, as Colonel Worden (an astronomer) was instrumental in the declassification of much of this detection activity.

THE PERPLEXITIES OF MISSILE DEFENSE

The Strategic Defense Initiative (SDI or 'Star Wars') of the United States, inaugurated by President Ronald Reagan in 1983, was intended to become the antiballistic missile system *par excellence*. The science-based scheme using platforms deployed in space envisaged using laser beams to detect and halt incoming ballistic missiles launched against American territory. In one of its conceptions, X-ray lasers aboard satellites would intercept hostile ICBMs (intercontinental ballistic missiles) at the moment of launching. The adversary of the time could only have been the USSR. During the 1980s, however, scientists and military strategists realized that a space-based program was probably unreliable and prohibitively costly. In 1991, Congress passed the Missile Defense Act, a law enabling the improvement of land-based defenses against limited attacks.

There was opposition from the scientific establishment at home and abroad, and the scheme risked foundering. Many physicists, engineers and applied mathematicians, among others, construed the aims of SDI as unrealizable – not to speak of their objections and those of much of the public to the cost of the undertaking. Reactions from the USSR were strong, and to be anticipated in view of the estimated 25–33 per cent of its own budget already dedicated to defense. China's Deng Xiaoping wrote in the authoritative journal, *Liaowang*, 'The space arms race signals the qualitative escalation of the US–Soviet arms race' and 'will go completely out of control [without] reducing the danger of war.'[25] Europeans viewed the US project with serious reservations.

In 1984, the Office of Technology Assessment, an independent body (now defunct) created ten years earlier to advise the United States Congress in a non-partisan way of the socioeconomic implications of new scientific developments, published an appraisal of SDI:

> The prospect that emerging 'Star Wars' technologies, when further developed, will provide a perfect or near-perfect system, literally removing from the hands of the Soviet Union the ability to do socially mortal damage to the United States with nuclear weapons, is so remote that it should not serve as the basis of public expectation or national policy.

The author of this paper, Ashton Carter, hardly ingratiated himself with the political leadership of the time; during the Clinton administration, Carter became a high official in the Department of Defense.

A decade after its inauguration, when the Initiative's scientific-technical constraints had been identified more or less precisely, the program was rethought and renamed (1993) the Ballistic Missile Defense Organization. There were no changes in the budgeting of the program. But new thought was given to the possibility of developing – with one or more like-minded nations – 'theater missile defense' (TMD). This approach found impetus in the experience of United States and Israeli defensive measures during the brief Iraq–Kuwait conflict, when a primary concern became the defense of field troops against the short-range SCUD missile,[26] used in the Gulf War as a surface-to-surface weapon.

Within two years the Phillips Laboratory in New Mexico and the Massachusetts Institute of Technology were developing an infrared laser mounted aboard a Boeing 747 for use against the famed SCUD, built by Raytheon Corp. The weapon thus contrived is known as a COIL (*c*hemical, *o*xygen, *i*odine, *l*aser) a device using chemical reactions, instead of physical ones, to create light. The COIL combines the reactive effects of water with chlorine and potassium hydroxide to spew an oxygen jet, the oxygen mixing with iodine in order to create considerable light. The 2 megawatts developed by a COIL in combat readiness should pierce a SCUD missile's covering in short order; an aircraft so equipped should be able to destroy 40 missiles as far away as 200 kilometers. This is the theory, but one of several critical factors in perfecting the new matériel will be the accuracy of aim that can be brought to bear against individual targets.[27]

The events of 11 September 2001 and the use of unorthodox missiles against American cities will affect the follow-on of Star Wars, National Missile Defense (NMD), one way or another – either realization or abandonment. Deployment of new American missiles should remain problematic, beset by political and diplomatic complications as well as basically technical obstacles. The ABM (Anti-Ballistic Missile) treaty is one of these (prohibiting mobile defenses), so that weapons cannot be installed on naval vessels offshore. Another is the detection of diverted commercial flights. And what if newly nuclear nations threaten? And what is the capability of so-called 'rogue' states? An alternative to NMD is Theater Missile Defense (TMD). The US Army's Theater High-Altitude Air Defense (THAAD) system or the US Navy's Ship-Based Area and Theater-Wide (NTW) system are practicable TMDs; THAAD, for example, could be operational by 2006–7, assuming 'adequate funding'.[28]

Meanwhile managers of orbiting weapon systems will benefit from the great advances being made in repair and replacement, by remote control, aboard strictly civil craft. The experience in repositioning solar panels on *Mariner 10* (a Venus and Mercury probe dating from 1973), in rescuing *Voyager 2* (launched in 1977 towards Jupiter and Saturn), in fixing the main antenna of the Jupiter-bound *Galileo* probe, as well as the spectacular rehabilitation of solar observer *SOHO* (1998) are contributions to spatial exploration that the military can exploit (see Chapter 2).[29]

TO BE IN SPACE OR NOT TO BE

Star Wars and the Internet, the global positioning system (GPS), the *Clementine* space craft (a US Navy project described in Chapter 9), and 'Project Keyhole' were conceived of as activities not for public disclosure. Their R&D was funded in part or in whole by undivulged budgets, sometimes without the knowledge of the United States Congress. Project Keyhole evolved into the Hubble astronomical telescope, a program conceived originally to manage satellites of the downward-looking kind: platforms intended to improve by orders of magnitude the target-selection capability of US military forces. The facilities of Keyhole, to select but one example of its accomplishments, were put to noteworthy use during the Iraq–Kuwait conflict and its information shared with allies within the United Nations Coalition.

GPS was the first of these, initially secret, activities to pass into the public domain. Its satellites were intended to operate from intermediate orbit, providing sophisticated transmissions for the clients of Defense and less refined signals that managed, none the less, to render civil navigation far more accurate than ever before. The US Congress wished to turn over management of GPS to NASA (National Aeronautics and Space Administration), but external consultants resisted for fear that the latter's capability 'to wield the vital tool of systems management' was deficient.[30] The military were considered, in other words, efficient in comparison with their civil counterparts.

Returning to the TMD strategic concept, this coincided with Japan's arrival among the nations possessing capability in space: launching capacity to deliver into orbit large satellites for telecommunications or Earth observation. In February 1994, Japan's National Space Development Agency launched the H2 rocket, purely Japanese science-and-technology that took ten years to realize, costing US$2.4 billion). The 50-metre-long H2 placed in geosynchronous orbit a satellite weighing 2,000kg or, in a low orbit of 250km above the Earth, a 10,000kg payload. A scientist who once headed Japan's Space Activities Commission, Saitô Shigebumi, justified Japan's first large-scale space event to the *New York Times*: 'If we have no [space] vehicle, it is like a navy without ships.'

ACADEMIC 'GIGANTOMANIA'

As the twentieth century ended, the United States and the former Soviet Union were the only countries to have succeeded in sending human beings on space voyages. Doubters wondered if Russia and its formerly associated states had ever *seriously* projected putting human beings on the Moon.

According to Alain Dupas and John M. Logsdon, two space observers, there had been an early intention on the part of the Soviets to put men and women on the Moon. Professional jealousy, political rivalry and a struggle to command resources among the leading designers of spaceflight – Sergei P. Korolev, Valentin P. Glushko, Vladimir N. Chelomei and Nikolai D. Kuznetsov – contributed to poor progress in the USSR in placing a cosmonaut on the Moon by the original Soviet target year of 1968. Korolev died unexpectedly in 1966, and his successor, Vasily Mishin, had neither the managerial ability nor the political standing of his predecessor. The Americans quickly revised their Apollo program, made available a supplementary Saturn Vl launching vehicle, and beat their competitors to the lunar surface.[31] This was confirmed to the author by American astronaut 'Buzz' Aldrin of the history-making Apollo 11 mission of July 1969. 'The Soviets shifted their goals in the mid-1960s', said Aldrin, 'there is little doubt about that.'[32]

The shifting of Soviet science continued in other ways. In 1988, the American journalist Flora Lewis interviewed the director of Moscow's Institute for Space Research, Roald Sagdeev (who was later to emigrate and marry the granddaughter of Dwight D. Eisenhower). Fifty-five years old at the time, the atomic physicist analyzed the state of research in the Soviet Union on the occasion of the launching of a probe to the Mars, meant to land two unmanned vehicles on its Phobos moon.

Sagdeev disparaged the seriousness of the Soviet Academy of Sciences, 'just another bureaucratic ministry with a political rather than a scientific agenda'. In the very midst of Mikhail S. Gorbachev's era of *glasnost* and *perestroika*, Sagdeev branded science in the USSR an endeavor thoroughly ridden by bureaucracy, lack of contact between researchers and students,

> gigantomania, 'mafia' groups that keep Jews out of universities and dominate the direction of learning, and stifling centralization that favors showy projects and starves creative individuals of needed equipment … The … soldiers in the army of science are left without even simple means, like personal computers or pure chemicals.[33]

THE EYES OF SPOT

Science plays tricks on even the most studied of its military applications. The B-2 Stealth bomber of the United States Air Force, a national investment of $45 billion for 21 exemplars of this supersophisticated, long-range aircraft – that is, $2.14 billion each – turned out to be vulnerable to water, other humidity and extreme climatic conditions. The radar-defying treatment of the aircraft's surfaces proved to be unusually sensitive and only briefly exposable to the atmosphere – so much so that each flight resulted in the need afterwards to house the aircraft in special, climate-controlled hangars. Plans for deployment outside the United States were canceled.

Another sequel to the Cold War's end is the ostensibly reduced need by the military of high-precision optical systems mounted aboard satellites. Some manufacturers have turned to the development of civil clienteles previously unexploited except by the French firm, SPOT. SPOT has been concerned mainly with mapping and land-use exercises. In the late 1990s in Colorado a company called Earthwatch Inc. advertised American-made orbiting devices as aids to oil exploration, disaster relief, urban and regional planning, and law enforcement. An Earthwatch pamphlet explained that 'Vacationers will plan exotic sailing cruises along foreign coasts. Small retail businesses will have a better understanding of demographics.' More and more dual use and spin-off. And if the police, too, broaden their call upon satellites for law enforcement, so too might private detective agencies.

More scientifically, the end of the twentieth century witnessed the appearance of new theories and concepts that could find practical use in the design and flight of transport above the terrestrial surface and on the seas. Nonlinear dynamics, for instance (the so-called 'theory of chaos', first popularized in the 1980s), took on proactive characteristics in fields ranging from fine control over how air passes over and under an airfoil, or regulated control of flame and smoke, or the slipping of water past a ship's hull, to potential clinical regulation of epileptic seizures.

Chaos theory also provides us with the means to observe phenomena nominally controlled by the laws of science: how clear weather becomes a storm, how and when a liquid boils, and so on. During the 1990s, imaginative researchers began thinking of how to control the violent instabilities in aerial flight caused by surges in air flow (by 'commanding' minuscule hairs coating a navigational surface to stand or cling); dampening the flickering of reactants fed into catalytic reactions (by finely altering the rate of feed-in of these reactants); and fine-tuning electrochemical flows in the body's brain and cardiac muscle. The mastering of chaos, in other words, became feasible.

ATMOSPHERIC DISTURBANCES

The emerging approach to this domination of dynamics is based on the mathematical idea of phase. In phase space,[34] the patterns that swirl in what appears to be random motion (such as flames in the fireplace) are mathematically describable. If these patterns could be delineated within a system, they might be poked and guided to yield stability in what otherwise seems to be total instability (for example, hi-fi speakers unable to cope with a sudden audio overload), much as one strives to regain one's balance after stepping off a merry-go-round. The applications, apparently endless, are sufficiently of dual purpose to attract researchers in military establishments such as the US Naval Surface Warfare Research Center in Maryland. Research of this kind holds the promise, indeed, of a dual-purpose future for aircraft, projectiles, moving ships and many other moving systems.[35]

Lest the reader conclude that such research lies mainly on the western side of the Atlantic Ocean, the EU (European Union) manages to keep pace. A report prepared in the late 1980s, intended to consolidate European armament policy in terms of its overall thrust during the 1990s and to exploit regional strengths in electrical engineering and robotics, recommended cooperation in defense technology increased by an order of magnitude. Financing was scheduled to begin with 200 million ecu (today's euro) per year, building gradually towards 500 million euro by the year 2000.[36] This did not happen, although the EU's revised attitudes towards defense, external policy and protection against terrorism will probably bring this about during the decade ending in 2010.

The dual nature of much aircraft design, a military–industrial truism dating from before the First World War, made possible the discovery of a type of lightning previously unknown. With knowledge accumulated since Benjamin Franklin studied lightning at the end of the eighteenth century, specialists were aware that lightning bolts shoot earthwards or laterally across the horizon, have an electromotive force of several hundred million volts, and turn portions of the atmosphere white hot at temperatures of more than 27,700°C. Two centuries after Franklin, it seemed we knew all that there was to know about celestial fireworks.

Then, thanks to exploration done in the 1990s aboard high-flying aircraft, researchers found that lightning can depart *upwards* from cloud masses. Photographs show flashes in colors of dark blue, pink and red – the last associated with strong bursts of radio waves and reaching as high as 100km – at the upper limit of the middle atmosphere, that is, between the mesopause and the ionosphere. Satellites in orbit have found potent bursts of gamma rays emanating from thunderheads. Russian and American scientists continue to study these extraordinary phenomena. Indeed, NASA has a special program on flash studies, managed by Richard J. Howard. The significance of this high-level lightning in terms of climate and weather are, as yet, unknown.

A bane of pilots, military and civil, has always been clear-air turbulence (CAT): air seemingly devoid of strong variations in pressure that can cause an aircraft suddenly to drop like a stone hundreds of meters, without warning. Military research costing $30 million has enabled a Pentagon contractor, Coherent Technologies, Inc., to develop LIDAR (*li*ght, *d*etection, *a*nd *r*anging), originally intended to detect enemy aircraft or ships. With this technique a beam of 5–10cm in diameter is emitted that, ongoing tests reveal, may be effective at distances of 10–16km ahead to detect reflections from the solid and liquid particles normally suspended in air (air itself does not reflect a laser beam). If translatable into an easily used device, LIDAR could make it possible for aircraft commanders to have a half-minute warning before entering a CAT zone.

An alternative approach is to devise a 'virtual microphone', one also using a laser beam, but to detect at a distance both natural and aircraft-generated sounds of turbulence. In this case, because laser beams move more slowly as air becomes denser, the instrument would measure shifts in air density. Refinement is needed, however, so that it becomes possible to distinguish noises produced by engines, by air swirling past wings, and by the turbulence present in aircraft wakes. This technique is called 'Socrates' and is being developed by a Connecticut firm, Flight Safety Technologies, Inc.

AND WHEN TO MARS?

In a bid to facilitate travel to Mars, Carlo Rubbia seeks to attenuate the punishing ratio of 280:1 representing the weight of fuel relative to payload.[37] His booster would be fueled by the element americium-242 (a transuranic substance found in the wastes produced by nuclear reactors), disposed in a thin film 1 micron thick. One kilogram of this element can produce 500 megawatts of energy. Fragments from the americium would heat hydrogen, ejected as plasma from the space vessel at extremely high speed – thus ensuring a continuous ramjet effect, the push of the propulsion unit against the atmosphere compressed behind. Because such speed would enable spacecraft to avoid the usual elliptical path, or Hohmann orbit (more about this orbit in the next chapter) that exploits the Sun's attractive force, the flight to

Mars would be almost direct. What would otherwise be a round-trip of three years could be reduced to two months.

The world of rocket boosting needs more experience, furthermore, in protection from meteoroid impacts on orbiting objects. About 25 per cent of the hundreds of packages currently in orbit around the planet are military, but their surveillance is considered critical. US Space Command announced that it had re-oriented (turned out of the way, or temporarily reduced the electrical power flowing through) satellites during the 33.25-year cycle of the 55P/Tempel-Tuttle comet on the occasion of the Leonid meteor showers of November 1998. This was to minimize electrical problems resulting from impacts caused by meteoric dust. Little damage occurred in 1998, although it is not impossible that entire satellites (when there will be more of them in motion) could be knocked out during the next Leonid showers in February 2032.

Back on Earth, the rockets that became aircraft also created a major industry of the twentieth century and, through this transport sector, contributed in large part to the globalization process that began with the spread of aerial transport during the Second World War. Boeing, a major designer of military and civil aircraft, was by 1998 the chief contributor to US exports: $27 billion in that year. Building large, safe and profitable passenger aircraft became a strategic industry employing scores of thousands of highly trained staff, with Boeing, before the end of the century, in a neck-and-neck race with the European Airbus conglomerate.

Aircraft showed their acute vulnerability to shock terrorism, the attacks in the United States of 11 September 2001 foremost among these. Public confidence in this means of transport was severely affected, reaching into the labor economics of this industry as tens of thousands lost their jobs. The events also reinforced new R&D on fuel combustibility and its potential for havoc: a kilogram of kerosene-like jet fuel has potentially ten times the energy of TNT, so that the heavy Boeings targeted against the Twin Towers slammed into their objectives with more than 170,000kg[38] of prepackaged, assured destruction aboard. We need no reminder of the ensuing cost in lives, property and public confidence.

NOTES

1 '[W]ar is not merely a political act, but also a real political instrument, a continuation of political commerce, a carrying out of the same by political means.' Clausewitz's thesis is questioned by recent authors such as Martin van Creveld, *On Future War* (London, Brassey's, 1991); see also note 4.

2 Carl von Clausewitz, *On War*, trans. J. J. Graham (London, Routledge & Kegan Paul, 1966), sec. 24 of ch. 1, bk 1.
3 See, for example John A. Vasquez, *The War Puzzle* (Cambridge, Cambridge University Press, 1993), pp. 123–52.
4 Adrian Gilbert contrasts massive slaughter in battle with the (often random) work of the lone marksman, as became apparent almost daily at Sarajevo during the war of 1992–95. See Gilbert's *Sniper: The World of Combat Sniping* (New York, St Martin's Press, 1995).
5 Peter Evans and Gareth Rees of the Scott Polar Research Institute, 'Science Now', BBC Radio 4, 4:30 p.m., 11 June 1993, pp. 15–19 of their script.
6 See also Christopher Hibbert, *Agincourt* (London, Batsford, 1964), pp. 34–5. In his re-revised English version of *Histoire de France*, André Maurois puts the French losses at 10,000 killed. See this version, *A History of France*, trans. Henry L. Binsse, with additional chapters by Gerard Hopkins (London, Methuen/University Paperbacks, 1964, 3rd rev. edn), pp. 90–1.
7 Martin Middlebrook, *The First Day on the Somme* (London, Allen Lane, 1971); the British expended 23,000 tonnes of projectiles during a week's softening up, 230 times more than Napoleon used at Waterloo.
8 Charles Coulston Gillispie, *The Montgolfier Brothers and the Invention of Aviation, 1783–1784* (Princeton, NJ, Princeton University Press, 1983), p. 16.
9 Herman Hattaway, *Shades of Blue and Gray: An Introductory Military History to the Civil War* (Columbia, MO, and London, University of Missouri Press, 1997), p. 56.
10 President Lincoln considered McClellan a good organizer but too hesitant as a field commander, and relieved him of combat duty.
11 Bill Gates, 'The Wright Brothers' (Time 100 series), *Time* (Europe edn), 29 March 1999, p. 40.
12 Daniel G. Dupont, 'Up, Up and Away: The US Military Brings Back the Balloon', *Scientific American*, June 1996, p. 28.
13 In Operations Research's earliest moments in Britain, Solly Zuckerman sought to apply to human beings his knowledge of the reactions of primates in conditions of stress.
14 Stafford Beer's definition of OR: 'the attack of modern science on complex problems' combining 'men, machines, materials and money in industry, business, government and defense to predict and compare the outcomes of alternative decisions, strategies or controls', *Decision and Control: The Meaning of Operational Research and Management Cybernetics* (Chichester, John Wiley, repr. 1995), p. 92.
15 Kenneth Macksey, *Technology in War: The Impact of Science on Weapon Development* (London, Arms & Armour, 1986), p. 88.
16 Project BV 246, 1944; the author thanks engineer Florian Windischbauer of BGT Bodenseewerk for bringing this to his attention, 7 August 2001.
17 Martin Middlebrook, *The Peenemünde Raid: The Night of 17–18 August 1943* (London, Penguin, 1988): a concise account of the German missile program.
18 Niccolò Tartaglia, mathematician and civilian, developed in his *Nova Scientia* (1537) the first calculating tables for firing cannon. He invented ballistics, part of mechanical engineering.
19 A complete account of this tale of professional rivalry is found in Lee Loevinger, 'The Invention and Future of the Computer', *Interdisciplinary Science Reviews*, 21 (1996), pp. 221–34.

20 Alvin and Heidi Toffler, *The Third Wave* (New York, Bantam, 1980). See also the Tofflers' *Creating A New Civilization* (Atlanta, GA, Turner, 1995).

21 A detailed report on the Corona program of 1959–71 is Albert D. Wheelon, 'Corona: The First Reconnaissance Satellites', *Physics Today*, February 1997, pp. 24–30.

22 Wheelon, 'Corona', p. 30.

23 The Czech arms story appeared in numerous media in 1993: cf. 'Czech Arms: Buyers, Please', *The Economist*, 6 November 1993, p. 92. An interpretation of the stealth factor found in early American naval architecture is Roger Archibald, 'Six Ships that Shook the World', *American Heritage of Invention and Technology*, Fall 1997, pp. 26–37.

24 Jean-Luc Nothias, 'Les bombardements extraterrestres longtemps classés "Secret défense"', *Le Figaro*, 29 January 1994, p. 8; J. Kelly Beatty, 'Impacts Revealed', *Sky & Telescope*, February 1994, pp. 26–7.

25 See Bonnie S. Glaser and Banning N. Garrett, 'Chinese Perspectives on the Strategic Defense Initiative', pamphlet (Washington, DC, United States Information Agency, 1986), pp. 28–44.

26 'The Empire Strikes Back', *The Economist*, 25 March 1995, p. 117.

27 A fuller description of the infrared laser device is 'Lasers on the Stun' in the Science & Technology section of *The Economist*, 16 December 1995, p. 101.

28 John Deutch, Harold Brown and John P. White, 'National Missile Defense: Is There Another Way?', *Foreign Policy*, Summer 2000, pp. 91–100.

29 See, for example, 'The Long Arm of the Celestial Repairman', *The Economist*, 17 October 1998, pp. 105–6.

30 Eric J. Claisson, '*Clementine*, Keyhole and Cosmic Rats', *Scientific American*, December 1994, p. 96. Claisson is the author of *The Hubble Wars* (New York, HarperCollins, 1994).

31 John M. Logsdon and Alain Dupas, 'Was the Race to the Moon Real?', *Scientific American*, June 1994, pp. 16–23.

32 Conversation in Paris with the author, on the occasion of the 25th anniversary of the *Apollo 11* flight, June 1994.

33 Flora Lewis, 'A Scientist Talks Like Gorbachev', *IHT*, 11 July 1988, p. 4.

34 A phase space is a hypothetical configuration, one having as many coordinates as required in order to define the state of a given system or substance.

35 See James R. Gleick, *Chaos: Making A New Science* (New York, Viking, 1987); 'Balancing Broomsticks', *The Economist*, 25 June 1994, pp. 95–6; and Stuart Kauffman, *At Home in the Universe* (New York and Oxford, Oxford University Press, 1995), pp. 26–9, 79–80, 103.

36 Ernst A. van Hoek, 'The Development of the EUCLID Programme', *Deuxième Symposium EUCLID* (held at the French State Secretariat for Research, Paris, 26–7 November 1996, p. 1.

37 A payload of 200 tonnes destined for the planet 300 million km from Earth would require a booster of 60,000 tonnes – the mass of the Empire State Building.

38 See 'NewsScan', *Scientific American*, November 2001, p. 10.

2

The Real Stakes in the Space Adventure Are Military

'The Soyuz and Shuttle successes have indicated the feasibility of deploying military personnel and weapons in space.'

General Accounting Office of the US Congress[1]

The twentieth century witnessed the ascendancy of the telephone, automobile and radio; then television and computers, as well as growing control over most epidemic scourges. We also began to understand theoretical physics, a new cosmology, and the molecular basis of life. We first left the Earth's surface in powered machines built for the purpose, and progress in research hastened the translation of new knowledge into more and more innovative technology. The century staged, also, the most devastating wars in history and nearly globalized terrorism; we are still counting all their dead.

THE FEATS OF DEVELOPMENT AND HUMAN SECURITY

Here we take up the relationship between science and aerospace exploration: what science gives and what science gets, strongly under the sponsorship of military preparedness almost from the outset. 'We are convinced that a complete mastery of the art of rockets', wrote Wernher von Braun immediately after Germany's capitulation in 1945, 'will change conditions in the world ... as did the mastery of aeronautics ... [T]his change will apply to both the civilian and military.'[2] The United States proceeded to send half of Germany's rocket experts to the United States, while the Soviet Union transferred the other half to its own territory.

'The Cold War', space observer William E. Burrows emphasizes, became 'the great engine ... that sent rockets and their cargoes far above Earth and worlds away.'[3] As the Germans had done, the Soviet Union and then the United States created a relationship between the defense authority and the non-military research establishment. The tie-up worked, and is likely to continue.

What follows is divided roughly into two parts: first, a cursory account of the evolution of the missile and, second, the problems to be overcome in spaceflight, both manned and unmanned. In the first section, the missile's development comprises propulsion: destination-defined locomotion; materials for rocket construction and maintaining the operation of space vessels; and guidance, or steering the space vehicle through space both near and far. In the second part, we treat the security of manned spaceflight. This embraces improving our understanding of animal physiology (for life support) and behavioral science, together with the protection of human beings against radiation. Added to these is the need for surety of communication between astronauts and their Earth-bound bases.

A few remarks may be helpful at this point, since space research has been as much the object of serious criticism as it has of praise and admiration since its debut on a large scale during the 1950s.

FROM POLITICAL WILL TO RISK EVALUATION

Critics of humanity's venture into the stratosphere and extra-atmospheric space, and they are many, use persuasive arguments. The main objections are:

- Exploration is out of balance with more basic public needs; the money spent could be better used for social purposes.
- Much 'research' will surely continue, but spaceflight is really more engineering, navigation and logistics than science.
- The research and engineering involved are nothing more than a bid for new forms of military supremacy.
- The Russians and Americans made space exploration a political race; putting a human being on the Moon was a definitive lap in this contest.

The space endeavor thus serves as poorly disguised neck-and-neck competition in military preparedness: setting up potential armament systems based in space, together with the accompanying observation and surveillance systems by each 'side' of the other's developing resources. This argument was particularly valid, at any rate, as long as the Cold War lasted. Now new contestants have thrown their hats in the ring: China, Japan, India, Pakistan and Brazil among them and, ultimately, perhaps the New Terrorism.

The superpowers of the United States and the former USSR insisted, all along, that their programs were civil undertakings. But the reality was transparent, from the selection of astronauts/cosmonauts/spationauts[4] to the refinement of both robotic and manned vessels in orbit or on their way to the planets and (someday) the stars. This is why here we interpret the space efforts of the two major actors of the Cold War as militarily-prompted undertakings, while trying to measure at the same time some of the truly scientific rewards of the effort.

All of the justifications used for or against aerospace exploration are correct in their own way, one is forced to admit. This chapter supplements, therefore, the arguments of *Realpolitik's* space story by adding a few essential considerations that may not be readily evident. Thus far these have been:

- political precaution and foresight on the part of the two superpowers' leaders;
- political willingness to commit resources: financial, material, human;
- remarkable ingenuity on the part of designers, engineers and builders;
- individual determination of the most visible participants – most astronauts are experienced test pilots, therefore a pre-handpicked group: dynamic, resilient and resourceful;
- persistence in the face of repeated, costly failure (e.g. the frustrations of the Americans to out-*Sputnik* the Soviet accomplishments in the late 1950s);
- successive debacles by the Soviets between 1960 and 1967 (trying to place instrument packages on Mars and Venus);[5]
- inherent anomalies in *Soyuz/Mir* and the international Space Station *Alpha*;
- permitting the political agenda to override the astronomical calendar of 'windows of opportunity' for the optimal launching times of interplanetary vehicles.

SUPERSONICS

The evolution of the rocket is more sophisticated than the simple extrapolation of a new device from ancient Chinese fireworks. The father of theoretical spaceflight, much influenced by the writings of Jules Verne and other nineteenth-century enthusiasts of space travel, was Konstantin E. Tsiolkovskiy, born in 1857 in Russia. Tsiolkovskiy believed in the potential of space voyages from an early age, and began publishing articles on what manned trips would require. He took the trouble to calculate carefully the thrust-to-weight relationship between the fuel required and the object to be moved in order to leave

Earth's gravity at 'escape' velocity: almost 500km per minute or 30,000km/h – data he published in the same year (1903) as the Wright brothers' successful heavier-than-air flight. Tsiolkovsky envisaged a multistage rocket or booster, each stage being released from the rocket after its fuel was consumed in a combustion compartment. The non-working load (capsule) and its disposal thus became a principle of launching design *before* the machinery itself was realized – and this was the engineering design finally adopted.

Astronomers Giovanni V. Schiaparelli of Italy and James Percival Lowell of the United States did much at the close of the nineteenth century to popularize the nature of the Martian surface, leading to a common belief in the existence of canals there. This further whetted the public's curiosity about spaceflight and whether it could be realized. In 1917, when part of the Austro-Hungarian Empire's fate was being decided along the Alpine valleys of northern Italy, a 19-year-old medical student in Vienna named Hermann Oberth proposed to the Austro-German defense authorities the development of a liquid-propelled missile to supplant limited-range artillery and help end a disastrous war on Earth.

The innovative idea was disregarded by the strategists and logisticians, but the notion was picked up in 1921 when the young USSR created a development laboratory to explore the possibilities of powder as a rocket propellant, an idea advanced by chemist Nikolai I. Tikhomirov. This became the Gas Dynamics Laboratory of the Red Army; its work encouraged the Soviet Union to create, in 1924, the Central Bureau for the Study of Rocketry Problems – the first official sanction given to rockets by any government. At about the same time, Oberth shifted his studies in Austria from medicine to engineering and became the first rocketeer in the German-speaking world.

Hermann Sänger, an Austrian, was the first to envisage an 'aerospace' vehicle resembling heavier-than-air craft – what ultimately would take form as the space shuttle. Yet another Austrian, Friedrich Schmiedl, constructed small rockets (up to 30kg in total weight) and, during test flights, transported mail within his country. Schmiedl failed to win a contract with the post office, but he continued to build experimental rockets, both clustered and multistaged.

EARLY FLIGHTS

In post-First World War Germany, shrewd military staff officers hit upon research on rockets as a way of circumventing the bans on arms design and procurement. Aircraft, for example, were prohibited by the

Treaty of Versailles. Gliding clubs provided some of the camouflage necessary: their members' main interest was, ultimately, jaunts through extra-atmospheric space. In 1932, a young Prussian engineer, the civilian Wernher von Braun, joined Captain Walter Dornberger and other military engineers who had been assigned specific goals. Working on solid-propellant rockets and devising navigational mechanisms, they labored behind the screen provided by the forests of Brandenburg around Berlin.

Their program expanded as Hitler took power; it included testing fuel mixtures of alcohol and liquid oxygen. These activities grew exponentially as a test facility was established on the Baltic Sea, at Peenemünde, as we saw earlier. Their production resulted, by the end of the Second World War, in the military V1 and V2 missiles. These were the propulsion prototypes for the launching of increasingly heavy pay-loads – the explosive packages intended for delivery to the enemy – today's 'cruise' and intercontinental ballistic weapons.

An American, Robert H. Goddard of Massachusetts, encountered ridicule in the press in 1919 when he declared that it was possible to put a rocket on the Moon. In the following year, Goddard who was interested in the real nature of the lunar and Martian faces, submitted a long paper to the Smithsonian Institution in search of a research grant. He sought to launch an exploration rocket that would exceed the 30km altitude to which balloons were limited. Goddard did not receive the funds he sought, and the military were not forthcoming at all; but he continued his applied research.

Goddard and Oberth began an exchange of research results, and interest in rockets expanded. Money in the United States came from nongovernmental sources, and Goddard moved his test site from New England to ranchland in New Mexico. Oberth's publications in the 1920s, including his 423-page *Wege zur Raumschiffahrt* ('The Roads to Space Travel') 'did more to spread the concept of going to space than any other scientific work to that time'.[6] Oberth and Goddard drew plans, experimented – exploring both liquid and solid fuels and com-binations of these – and involuntarily exploded (imperfect) models. It was Goddard, using a liquid propellant of gasoline and oxygen, who launched first. A 4.5kg device, two metal cylinders connected by tubes, rose to almost 14 meters over a distance of nearly 60 meters. This inaugural flight of mechanical-chemical rockets took place in March 1926 in Massachusetts. In 1928, Arturo Crocco, a general in the Italian air force doing secret work with solid propellants, launched his own miniature missiles.

ENGINE DEVELOPMENT

Britain's Frank Whittle and Germany's Jans J. Pabst von Ohain developed respectively turbojet and jet engines, both men going into service with their countries' air forces in 1944. In the same year jet aircraft first became operational. Industry, after equipping fighters and reconnaissance aircraft for flight faster than the speed of sound at the end of the Second World War, became intrigued by supersonic flight possibilities for the world of commerce. The Franco-British *Concorde* offers deluxe service for clients of British Airways and Air France (a catastrophic accident in 2000 notwithstanding), while a Soviet equivalent in the Tupolev series failed certification. Despite the *Concorde*'s civil livery, this supersonic transport 'is a military aircraft, all right. This is very clear', insists a French military engineer.[7]

Tsiolkovskiy, Schiaparelli, Lowell, Goddard (and, of course, H. G. Wells) were all influenced by Jules Verne's science fiction. Fact steadfastly replaced fiction, however, and the space pioneers began building their escalator to the stars. Sergei P. Korolev (or Korolyov), an engineer from Ukraine who commanded the USSR's second generation of rocket developers, reintroduced the idea of grouping rockets together to obtain more thrust. He and his colleagues worked on cluster configurations between 1948 and 1955, when testing began at the new Tyuratam launch pads near the Aral Sea. The Americans did much the same thing, launching from space centers in Florida and California, and the western Europeans developed the Eurospace/Ariane effort with launchings from Kourou in French Guyana. Today, improvements in basic metallurgy, pumping equipment and the selection of propellants constitute a highly refined engineering process with far more successes than failures.

The engines propelling rockets are, as in the first Benz motor car or aboard jet aircraft, internal-combustion devices. Much of the energy they generate is lost as heat, so their designers are confronted with the same problems of raising mechanical advantage (or relative efficiency) as apply to other power plants. The fuels they burn need to be handled with a maximum of safety and efficacy. The liquid oxygen or hydrogen or hydrogen peroxide whose combustion can be switched off, or even the solid fuels used (when thrust is a less critical requirement), are bulky and need special handling and insulation while in transit or loading. All combustibles must be consumed with optimal efficiency, of course, and their combustion chambers must be resistant to very high temperatures.

MATERIALS AND RELIABILITY

The construction materials and workmanship involved necessitate attention to the smallest detail, even if official contracts go to the lowest bidder, by designers and builders.

From the outset of rocket research, there has been technical preoccupation with the selection and improvement of materials used to build both propulsion components and the spaceborne vessels they lift – from the metallurgy of nozzles through which flame, heat and violent turbulence must pass to how an orbiting body reacts to extremely cold or high ambient temperatures, radiation and stress-and-strain forces at work on manmade structures.

Because of the need to overcome gravity, weight is a critical constraint in the selection of materials to build space vehicles on Earth or 'on site' high in the sky and in optimizing their powered stages, heating and cooling systems, and communication equipment. Research continues on the behavior of complex fluids and solids in low-gravity conditions, from the design of nuclear-power systems to untested extraterrestrial construction materials and methods. Little scientific research is involved in these areas, it is true, but much basic technological research is demanded and should continue indefinitely.

There are problems even among the long-lasting probes. Ten years after *Galileo*'s launch (1989), it continued to function superbly, sending rewarding images to Earth of what it 'sees'. The probe's controllers noted that, in *Galileo*'s proximity to Jupiter and Jupiter's moon Io, radiation from the huge planet combined with the satellite's own radiation to leave the onboard computers in temporary inactivity.

Reliability – the hoped-for infallibility – of guidance systems absorbs the detailed attention of designers. Tsiolkovsky, Oberth and Goddard were all aware of the complexities that would face the directing of space vehicle A from point X to point Y, especially when Y is situated beyond the Earth's atmosphere. A, X and Y embody what is known in applied mathematics as the three-body problem: computing the movements of three objects, each somewhere in the universe, moving in response to gravitational attraction.

Newtonian mechanics made such calculations possible, but as Newton's physics was subject later to modification by the new geometry of Georg Riemann, and then by the relativity physics of Einstein and at least the theoretical implications of the quantum mechanics of Planck–Bohr–Heisenberg, would-be space travel could be confronted with humanly incalculable navigational trajectories. Such computing requires tiresome numerical manipulation (of orbits, for example). Manual or logarithmic mathematics also requires pencils, much paper and time. The first punch-card systems facilitated the calculation task,[8] electromechanical machines later shortened the computing time, and microprocessor-equipped computers now work ever and ever faster.

But to go back to Earth's surface, it was Robert Esnault-Pelterie, a French airman, who was the first to imagine that the firing of a rocket along a ballistic curve (similar to the trajectory of artillery) could cause real havoc at the receiving end, more effectively and economically even than clouds of piloted aircraft. Esnault-Pelterie's musings in the 1920s became reality in less than two generations with the advent of the intercontinental ballistic missile: controlled destruction of life and property at great distances, leaving very little time for proper defense.

The predicament stimulated the cry for 'missile shields' and science-fiction-like systems of reaction to sudden, silent attack. This quest for such protection is likely to continue, as we saw in the last chapter, whether it be publicly declared or not – much as the German engineers found it possible in the 1920s to circumvent restrictions imposed upon research by developing the non-existent rocket.

Another problem accepted early on was the need for a means to get a rocket on its way by overcoming the Earth's gravity. The municipal engineer of the industrial city of Essen and a would-be space voyager, Walter Hohmann, thought up in 1925 the 'kick' system of moving an object from our own globe to another spatial body. The idea was to have the departing space vehicle leave Earth in the same direction as our planet's rotating movement and arrive at its destination in the same sense as the receiving body's rotation.

This 'transfer orbit' is known today as the Hohmann maneuver. It is the method used for manipulating long-range space probes: using the attractive force of the inner planets, and even Jupiter or Saturn or both, to move a space vessel to remote points. One such space probe is *Cassini*, the NASA 'bird' launched in 1997, flying by Venus twice and Earth once, each time profiting from the 'gravity assists' received by *Cassini* on its way to a Jupiter fly-past. *Cassini*'s mission is to learn if Jupiter has more moons than the 18 now known. The flight was pro-gramed for the end of the year 2000, well before the probe's arrival among Saturn's rings in 2004. Here we have an excellent illustration of how vital science is to navigation, and how navigation can repay science – despite what seems to some a caricature of costly ways to count a planet's natural satellites, big and small.

THE HUMAN BEING IN SPACE

Now to the second portion of this chapter, the problems of the human being engaged in travel through zero gravity, in weightless space, surrounded by a highly radiated but virtual void outside the spacecraft.

The requirements of spaceflight with living passengers aboard introduces serious questions of life support and wear-and-tear of anatomy and physiology, combined with the problem of foreseeing behavioral reactions. In anticipation of the day when human space-flight would become possible, Tsiolkovskiy's first book, *Free Space* (1883), explained the probable sensations:

> There is neither up nor down ... because 'down' is in the direction in which bodies move at accelerating speeds ... Just as the Moon hovers above the Earth without falling down to it, so a man there can hover over a chasm which would be frightening to earthlings. He is not, of course, suspended by ropes but hovers like a bird; or rather, like a counterpoised aerostat, since he has no wings.[9]

Not bad for a theorist, especially one with no means to test his hypothesis.

Before man could be lobbed into space, work thus needed to be done on animals. Laika, the little female mongrel that the Soviets sent aloft in 1957, inhabited a small, pressurized cubbyhole. She was supplied with food and drink automatically dispensed, and equipped with a bag to collect her bodily wastes. Sensors read her blood pressure, pulse and breathing rate – all radioed back to ground control. But little Laika would not be long for this world, or any other. Occupying an un-recoverable craft, she was given a lethal injection robotically after a week of flight. Subsequent tests sent more animals into space, and all their reactions were methodically interpreted.

Men and women ineluctably took the place of test animals, eventu-ally using diver-like space suits equipped with autonomous breathing gear for their 'walks' – working visits outside spacecraft. Here the designers of space suits benefited enormously from the experience of navies with a diversity of rigs and self-contained breathing gear for divers. (A Russian male holds the record for endurance aloft, with well over a year spent in the Soviet/Russian space laboratory.) Many space voyagers had difficulties, largely anticipated: nausea, dizziness, cardiac irregularities, irregular sleep, fantasizing. Ninety-nine per cent of the 279 American astronauts in flight between 1988 and 1995 suffered malaise or illness. Some still complain of lasting anomalies of different sorts.

Ten or more astronauts/cosmonauts perished because of accidents at takeoff or at the moment of recovery; the figure is imprecise because the total of Soviet fatalities is unknown. The human being proved, as a consequence, a relative success in space despite the lasting criticism – most often by scientists – that his/her presence is not required, that robots and scientific instruments can just as easily and more economically be the surrogates for vulnerable human operators, and that human beings are susceptible to the vagaries of ambient no-gravity. Artificial gravity is technically feasible, but impracticable at the present time.

THE BOGEYMAN OF RADIATION

There is another serious problem attending spaceflight: radiation. The main radiation to which astronauts and equipment are exposed is that of cosmic rays, or certain nuclei (including those of iron) and electrons traveling at almost 88 per cent of the speed of light, both within the solar system and beyond in our galaxy. The Sun emits some of these rays, but most originate in sources beyond the Milky Way. Satellite observations in the early 1990s revealed – this is a clear case of space exploration feeding scientific knowledge – that gamma rays, although produced by cosmic-ray interaction, are not extragalactic in origin. They 'almost surely [derive] from the most energetic events that take place in the galaxy', the explosions of supernovae.[10]

While the human body and other objects receive most of this radiation without adverse effect because of the protection afforded by Earth's natural magnetosphere, excessive doses can be harmful. In the case of astronauts working in space stations or engaged in extravehicular activity, the risk of exposure to dangerous levels of cosmic and other radiation peaks every 11 years when a maximum of sunspot activity occurs. The solar 'max' can also be the cause of radio blackouts, power failures, and the virtually indiscriminate zapping of unmanned satellites by the various radiation sources. The British medical journal *The Lancet* reported in December 2000 the findings of Danish researchers that leukemia incidence was higher than average among 3,700 (commercial) pilots and aircrew members flying more than 5,000 hours.

Safeguarding against radiation is also needed in the case of radioisotope thermoelectric generators (RTG). An RTG uses the heat of the radioactive decay of plutonium dioxide, a compound based on plutonium-238, to produce electricity on board space vessels. Pu-238 is 280 times more radioactive than its 239 isotope – present in the fallout from nuclear bombs – and every use worries environmentalists in case of failed launchings or other mishaps. The RTG is scheduled to be replaced in 2003 by the advanced radioisotope power system (ARPS), powering the *Europa Orbiter* with 5 kg of plutonium instead of the 33 kg fueling the RTG.[11]

What sort of 'people containers' would astronauts occupy, even properly prepared against radiation, the absence of gravity, and the lack of ambient oxygen to breathe? An early Austrian designer of manned vehicles, civil engineer Hermann Potocnik, published in 1929 his idea of a very large lived-in wheel, the *Wohnrad*. His wheel combined huge mirrors to collect solar radiation, an observatory for crew use, and the crew's quarters. The centrifugal force of the slow spin of the wheel would provide the necessary artificial gravity. Such a wheel does not yet exist (despite the magnificent opening sequence this concept provided for the film *2001: A Space Odyssey*) but, if manned space-flight is to continue, it is only a matter of time before its components are built, lofted and assembled.

COMMUNICATION REFINED AND EXPANDED

While communication, especially over long distances, is but another form of radiation, it is literally vital between space travelers and those supporting flight from the ground. Telecommunications were already advanced when the space programs began in the 1950s, so that both crews and ground-control bases benefited enormously from existing technology. Psychologically as well as physiologically speaking, both groups needed to learn patience for the delays in responses between correspondents. On the projected Mars expeditions, as much as 40 minutes will be required to direct a message to Mars and receive the reply.[12]

One type of communication less important to astronauts than to data-amassing scientists on Earth is that derived from the aerial photography discussed in Chapter 9: today's space imagery. This advanced technology combines the photochemical-electrotechnical processes with the transmission of their results via electronic flow. The earliest large rockets flown by the Soviets and Americans quickly showed that their onboard image-producing equipment was yielding more and better images, by far, than normal aerial photography could produce at increasingly high altitudes and across dynamic weather obstacles. Just how accurate such images have become continues to be held under military wraps, but we have some idea (from the commercial services available) of the resolution and definition of satellite images received on Earth. From an altitude of nearly 700km, for example, an observing instrument can pinpoint street intersections and even 'zero in' on vehicle registration plates. The degree of resolution can only improve with time.

The French-owned SPOT program was the first to make high-quality images of the planet's surface available to the public. Space Imaging, a firm based in Colorado, then built its own spacecraft to transport photo-imaging equipment capable of reproducing with accuracy painted lines 1 m wide. Besides military applications (for example, detecting preparations for nuclear testing underground), the product of 'sky-spy' activities mounted by NASA and the European Space Agency (ESA) is of enormous use to environmental researchers, water planners and glaciologists, forest and desert ecologists, forest-fire spotters, oceanographers, polar scientists and other investigators engaged in strictly civil regional planning and land use. With time and experience, the accuracy of imagery also can be expected to improve further.

In the gadgets and gimmicks department, manned spaceflight has generated devices comparable to those of the earthbound consumer. One such object was prompted by the overwhelming busy-ness experienced by astronauts tied down with scientific chores, engineering tasks and repairs, hygiene and other self-maintenance, and the bodily exercises required by flight conditions. This is a grapefruit-sized robotic helper called a personal satellite assistant (PSA). The PSA's fate is to be propelled through the weightlessness of a manned spaceship by tiny electric fans, hovering near each occupant, and responding to vocal commands. Equipped with diminutive speakers, cameras, microphones and other sensors, the PSA will be another set of eyes and ears as well as a nose for astronauts. The PSA has been developed under the leadership of engineer Yuri Gawdiak of NASA's Ames Research Center in California.

TECHNOLOGY, NAGIVATION, SUPPLIES

Although we have covered our two main points – the rocket's evolution and some problems of spaceflight – there remain other important issues in space R&D. That the engineering, navigational requirements and logistics associated with spaceflight are fraught with complexity is not disputed. The spells of failed productivity of the various space programs have repeatedly irritated both the public and legislators, the combined purveyors of funds. What are some of the most problematic challenges involved, including those of complexity, scale and cost, and rivalry facing spatial R&D? And how do the field's pioneers respond?

Take the case of the Lockheed Martin firm. Boosters exploded, engines performed improperly, satellites failed to reach their intended orbits. A *Titan IV* launching costs just under $400 million. After six failed launches (including a military *Titan IV* and the first high-resolution, commercial observation satellite) over a nine-month period, the firm appointed a team of outside experts in 1999 to review its technical practices.

Lockheed Martin's chief operating officer, Peter Teets, assigned the outsiders the task of thoroughly reviewing the experience of its staff, the adequacy of test programs, 'robustness' and reliability in its manufacturing processes, and other key elements. *The New York Times* noted editorially during the same year a shortage of engineers and technicians, exactly at a time when the industry was responding to pressure to fly more rockets, and more economically, to match foreign competitors. 'It's [a matter of] manufacturing and quality control', one private expert contended. 'Not a lot of this is real rocket science.'[13] Only such analysis of technical management can correct systemic deficiencies, whether at Lockheed Martin or elsewhere, in this multifaceted and costly military–industrial relationship.

The human species made scientific breakthroughs to develop aerial flight and to shatter the atom's nucleus (see Chapters 4, 5). Humankind did the same again, this time with the push of governmental determination, to enable its departure from the Earth's surface to explore what exists beyond. Purists may contend that the investigation of space is little more than a continuation and application of astronomy and astrophysics, but what removes space travel from the realm of purely civil science is the preponderant role of the military. This has been especially so in Russia and the United States, although cosmic adventure enjoys strong support in member countries of the ESA and in China.

If the effort is primarily the result of military pull, of course, a probing question to raise after five decades of aerospace R&D is: why did the Soviet Union lag so markedly in the race to the Moon and planets? The USSR certainly had the technical advantage and was leading the rocket race, until the late 1960s. T. A. Heppenheimer, an observer specializing in the evolution of aerospace systems, maintains that the Soviet Union led the space race because it lagged in developing and building nuclear arms. There were insufficient resources to do both equally well. The cutting of economic corners that was forced upon the Soviets came in the development stage. 'Faced [in 1968] with the challenge of a lunar landing by the Americans, Moscow proved bankrupt as it would so often in … later years.' This resulted in insufficient and inadequately rigorous testing – an engineering deficiency, in other words, and 'Moscow would build no monuments to failure.'[14] Funds were increasingly short, a situation that finally broke the entire Soviet economy.

SLIP-UPS AND OVERRUNS

Yet the rewards are not always to be heaped upon the technologically strongest. The United States-originated *Seasat* was a radar system sent aloft in 1978 to bounce radio waves off the globe's surface, yielding revealing images of what it 'saw'. Among the objects seen were minute traces of vestigial wake from surface ships, undersea vessels, and even fairly deep-roving submarines. *Seasat* managed also to 'distinguish signs of deep turbulence from the regular froth and heave of the sea'. After 100 days of exploitation of this keen detective in 1978, the radar satellite fell unexplainedly silent. Nineteen years later an American scientist was charged with having turned over the system's technical and performance data to a foreign power (China),[15] although this act is not presumed to be the reason that *Seasat* failed. China, today an expanding maritime power, can be expected to apply the acquired *Seasat* information to its own design and construction of submarines as well as to adapt the system to its commercial aircraft or satellites in order to locate other countries' submarines.

Costs and the risks of grievous loss, whatever the latter's form, are a nagging worry of governmental policy makers and budgeteers every-where. Between 1959 and 1981 (the eve of the launching of the Strategic Defense Initiative), for instance, the spending of the United States on military research over civil research in space was rather con-sistently about 7:5, but costs increased suddenly in 1980 to a ratio of 9:4, or a rise from about 140 per cent more, to 250 per cent more, military than civil research.[16] The increased tempo of the Cold War justified such a rise at the time but one wonders if such R&D money could not have been better invested for social gain.

In ballistic-missile defense, a heatedly debated and yet continuing application of space knowledge, the main concern of the US National Missile Defense (NMD) is how an adversary could 'beat the system'. This is what Richard Garwin, weapon designer and now an investigator at IBM's Thomas J. Watson Research Center, has to say in appraising the problem:

> It is a big effort to analyze every plausible option and choose the best. In a small program it is often better to choose an approach that gets the job done and avoids the cost and delay of a universal analysis ... A realistic assessment is necessary before a decision is made to build a

defensive system and before large expenditures lock in a system that might be ineffective, to the detriment of approaches that are less susceptible to countermeasures.[17]

Complementing Garwin's remarks are the conclusions of another specialist in weapon development, Gregory Canavan of the Los Alamos National Laboratory: 'If rogue missiles gain the ascendancy, it is likely they will succeed … If defense gains the ascendancy, the US and its allies could maintain sanctuaries [e.g. orbiting space-based lasers capable of firing downwards upon launched missiles] from which to provide a stabilizing effectiveness'.[18] The comment applies equally, of course, to the possible ascendancy of terrorism.

These and other reservations lay behind the decision of President Bill Clinton to declare, four and a half months before his departure from office, to defer any decision concerning NMD to his successor. In 2001, however, the future evolution of NMD remained in doubt, given the extraordinary budgeting required by the terrorism of 11 September. But, today, NMD is an active program.

Technical uncertainty is by no means limited to the military camp. Science can be a loser. The *Cassini* exploring spacecraft is a large and complicated device powered by electrical generators using plutonium as fuel. Today it is hurtling along a 1.3 billion-km track to a Saturn rendezvous in July 2004. The six-tonne probe was launched in October 1997 on a trajectory slinging it past Venus twice and Earth once, then picking up another gravity-assisted kick from the planet Jupiter in 2000. The scientific yield – this one strictly civil – should include much new data about Saturn, its rings and its huge Titan satellite. Some Earth-bound environmentalists feared in 1999, however, a burn-out of the spaceship as it passed our globe (at less than 1,200km), a menace that could have dispersed its plutonium throughout the atmosphere. And James van Allen, the Nobel Prize-winning physicist, reminds us that 'there is no [other] practical source of electrical power for space-craft that go to the outer planets'.[19]

Deep-space exploration, manned or not, will depend on the evolution of propulsion devices. Today's chemical fuels, heavy and voluminous aboard boosters, may be replaced in an intermediate stage by magneto-plasmic rockets propelled by plasmas heated to hundreds of millions of degrees Kelvin. Intermediate? Here again, the ultimate power plant would be a controled fusion rocket, one capable of yielding between 10 and 100 gigawatts.[20] But this is not for tomorrow. The longer a manned flight, the more the bone and muscle of the human body will be stressed and weakened and the immune system affected by cosmic radiation. Is Mars, therefore, a realistic destination of human beings?

ENVIRONMENTAL CHANGE AND SCIENTIFIC PROGRESS

Closer to home and our daily lives, one of the problems inherent in the efforts to determine climate change – in what ways, how much, for how long, and with what effects? – is the need to establish and maintain local observations.

Although we account sufficiently for nuclear tests and for the production of emissions hostile to the health of the atmosphere, we tally far too inaccurately the defensive emissions of nature itself. The climate models used thus far are not specific and focused enough, the experts say, to provide the accurate data needed for an assets-and-liabilities type of bookkeeping on atmospheric evolution. Freeman Dyson stresses that these models 'still use fudge-factors rather than physics to represent important things like evaporation and convection, clouds and rainfall'.[21] An extra effort is now essential, therefore, to accumulate and audit such data, and it is here that measurements from space should prove especially constructive.

An ongoing climatological project deserving mention is the European Space Agency's GOME-2 scanning telescope and spectrometer, the updated global ozone-monitoring experiment that is now funded (with 38.3 million euros) until the year 2019. This activity, a component of the EUMETSAT Polar System, targets the ozone and certain trace gases contained in the atmosphere and helps improve weather forecasts.[22] GOME-2 will not reduce the ozone hole over Antarctica, however: only concerted political decisions regarding toxic emissions can do that. Such decisions remain to be taken.

An ambience of microgravity aboard space vessels helped inspire the notion that certain crystals could be 'grown' aboard orbiting vessels. Considerable investment was made, consequently, in attempts to grow protein crystals aboard both the US Shuttles and the Russian *Mir* space station. In 1998, the American Society for Cell Biology cautioned NASA that the efforts could prove fruitless, and a year later there was a false report through NASA of a 'flu drug' developed in space. The National Research Council in Washington undertook an investigation of its own, and in 2000 announced that the effects of space-grown crystals on structural biology were 'extremely limited'. Because crystal-growth experiments were foreseen aboard the planned Space Station *Alpha*, the Research Council recommended a marked de-emphasis of attempts to grow crystals.

These vagaries notwithstanding, science should continue to benefit from space exploration. Of this there need be little doubt. Humanity would not know what it does now about near space and the farther firmament if the lavish military funding of a half-century had not been available. Large-scale experimentation is extraordinarily costly to the public treasury, but the footing of the bill by the public has not stopped, and promises to continue with remarkable willingness.

As a final example of space-research funds well spent, an unusual aid to improve our climatological and weather knowledge is a joint undertaking of ESA and NASA, the *SOHO* solar probe. One of the surprising missions of *SOHO* is to detect sunspots on the invisible, opposite side of the Sun. This was accomplished thanks to the Michelson Doppler imager (MDI) aboard the space probe, applying a technology called helioseismic holography. This analysis decodes seismic waves detectable on the Sun's visible side. In practical terms, space investigators – satellite operators, astronauts – and terrestrial power-network managers whose operations are often affected by solar eruptions should gain a week's notice of 'bad weather' coming up on the Sun.

At the same time, responsible professionals are querying the diverse 'moralities' involved in spatial exploration, especially the multiple connotations of manned spaceflight. See, for example, physician Alain Pompidou's *The Ethics of Space Policy*, published in 2000 in behalf of two major intergovernmental organizations.[23] The concerns of these bodies, the United Nations Educational, Science and Culture Organization (Unesco) and ESA, are particularly germane at a time when some space experts deem that 'the weaponization of space may be inevitable', that the space race is 'on a collision course with the point of no return: warfare in space'.[24]

A concrete change in US strategic policy was formalized – almost predictably – in May 2001 when the Secretary of Defense reminded Congress and the public that 'space issues are complex and merit a new focus'. Donald Rumsfeld added that the creation of a distinct military space force 'will help [us] to focus on meeting the national-security space needs for the 21st century'. There should thus be funds in the future for more space exploration, much as the rich governments find few obstacles to funding research under the sea.

NOTES

1 From a report of 1982 cited in James Canan, *War in Space* (New York, Harper & Row, 1982), p. 180.

2 Wernher von Braun, 'The Survey of Development of Liquid Rockets in Germany and their Future Prospects' (report), prepared at the direction of British and American military authorities at Garmisch-Partenkirchen, May 1945, cited in William E. Burrows, *This New Ocean: The Story of the First Space*

Age (New York, Random House, 1998), p. 118. *This New Ocean* is a complete, popular account of the development of the space age.

3 Burrows, *This New Ocean*, p. 147.

4 Respectively, the English-, Russian- and French-language terms used world-wide, in the chronological order in which they were coined. The alternative French *astronaute* first appeared, however, in the 1920s.

5 The United States' Mars Climate Orbiter, after a nine-month trip over 666 million km, crash-landed on the 'red planet' in September 1999 without communicating data that might have indicated there was once life on Mars. The mishap resulted from confusion among teams calculating in both the metric and imperial systems. Three months later, possible mechanical failure befell the Mars Polar Orbiter – a water seeker – and seriously retarded NASA's planning and financing of unmanned probes.

6 Burrows, *This New Ocean*, p. 51.

7 Daniel Estournet of the French Defense Ministry, speaking to a group of researchers at the Centre National de la Recherche Scientifique, Paris, 26 October 1999.

8 Punch cards used for calculations were devised for the United States Census Bureau by mining engineer Hermann Hollerith, based on the perforated cards used decades earlier to operate Jacquard looms in France. In 1896 Hollerith founded a computing firm that soon afterwards became International Business Machines Corporation (IBM).

9 As cited in Burrows, *This New Ocean*, p. 38.

10 Reuven Ramaty, James C. Higdon, Richard E. Lingenfelter and Benzion Kozlovsky, 'Rain of Fire', *The Sciences*, November/December 1999, pp. 24–9.

11 Mark Alpert, 'The Fallout from Cassini', *Scientific American*, September 1999, pp. 11–2.

12 A revealing estimate of 'How sick can you get during three years in deep space?' is by Jerome Groopman, 'Medicine on Mars', *New Yorker*, 14 February 2000, pp. 36–41. Mars expeditionary problems are dealt with in detail in 'Sending Astronauts to Mars (Special Report)', *Scientific American*, March 2000, pp. 22–45.

13 Editorial, *New York Times*, 13 May 1999, p. A30.

14 T. A. Heppenheimer, 'How the Soviets Didn't Beat Us to the Moon', *American Heritage of Invention & Technology*, Summer 1999, pp. 10–18; see also James Schefter, *The Race: The Uncensored Story of How America Beat Russia to the Moon* (New York, Doubleday, 1999). Eugene Cernan, an astronaut, with Don Davis, gives a related, sometimes hilarious, account in *The Last Man on the Moon* (New York, St Martin's Press, 1999).

15 William J. Broad, 'US Loses Hold on Submarine-Exploring Technique', *New York Times*, 11 May 1999, p. A6.

16 David Baker (with foreword by General George Keegan), *The Shape of Wars to Come* (Cambridge MA, Patrick Stephens, 1982), p. 80, graph.

17 R. L. Garwin, 'Technical Aspects of Ballistic-Missile Defense', *Physics & Society*, 28, 3 (1999), p. 4.

18 Gregory H. Canavan, 'Missile Defense in Modern War', *Physics & Society*, 28, 3 (1999), p. 7.

19 Robert L. Park, *What's New?* (American Physical Society), 20 August 1999, p. 1.

20 Franklin R. Chang Díaz, 'The Vasimr Rocket', *Scientific American*, November 2000, pp. 72–9.

21 Freeman J. Dyson, 'The Science and Politics of Climate', on the Back Page of *APS News* (American Physical Society), May 1999.
22 ESA media release no. 16–2000, 3 March 2000.
23 Alain Pompidou, *The Ethics of Space Policy* (Paris, Unesco and European Space Agency, 2000), 136 pp. and 11 technical annexes.
24 'Escalating Space Race', Stratfor.com (e-mail information service), 5 January 2001, p. 5.

3

Slipping the Warrior beneath the Seas

'Science has scored in a mission of destruction. What a marvelous adaptation of physics, pneumatics, and mechanics is displayed in a submarine, in which the highest standard of wholesale destruction is reached.'

Sir William Osler, 1915[1]

SILENCE, FIRST AND LAST

Geographer James Hamilton-Paterson recalls an exchange that occurred in the British House of Commons in 1961. Member of Parliament Hector Hughe was questioning Ian Orr-Ewing, Lord of the Admiralty, about recent experimental missions beneath the North Polar icecap by the submarines *Amphion* and *Finwhale*. Orr-Ewing replied that the revelation of details would not be 'in the national interest'. Thus clouded by military secrecy, their exchange was relegated to questions concerning the refrigeration physics of seawater.

> HUGHES: Can the hon. Gentleman say why the water under the North Pole does not freeze while the water on the surface does freeze? … Is the water under the ice kept warm by the heat generated from the center of the Earth?

> ORR-EWING: In view of the hon. and learned Gentleman's interest in bathing, I can understand his anxiety about where the ice forms. If he studies the physical tables, he will find that the water is most dense at 4 degrees centigrade and rises to the surface when it reaches 0 degrees centigrade and starts to freeze.[2]

This is typical of the code of submariners, well before and long after 1961. Theirs is one of the silent services, and their muteness extends to the public, of course, as Dan van der Vat maintains in his *Stealth at Sea* (1994).[3] The case can be made that the military submarine is the 'sea system' now indispensable to national defense, more so even than the aircraft carrier task-force and its logistical back-up: a technical arm affordable, in fact, only by major navies.

And why not? The ocean covers nearly 71 per cent of our globe's surface, and its water mass equals 1.4 billion cu km (cubic kilometers). Its average depth is about 3,700m yet, with submersibles that drop to 6,000m, about 97 per cent of the sea can be examined visually or with instruments, and its contents sampled for laboratory examination – a task perhaps infinite because of the sheer mass of seawater. Although there is no way to hide an aircraft carrier, a submarine can literally disappear into the sea and remain hidden: not only undetected, but dramatically undetectable.

During the Second World War, researchers operating sonar apparatus aboard an American surface vessel, USS *Jasper*, came upon a curious layer of water some 300–400m beneath the surface. As if it were a solid barrier, the layer reflected sonar signals. It was essential to exploit and protect this natural defense, eventually named the *deep scattering layer* (DSL). The DSL's existence was not revealed until after hostilities, lest the German–Italian–Japanese side exploit the situation by concealing its deployed submarines beneath the barrier.[4]

The DSL is one of several scattering layers formed by drifting biota moving up and down water columns in the sea at regular intervals. The masses of biota move upward at night, downward during daytime. Together with related organic strata in shallower waters, the DSL not only causes sound to rebound towards its origin; the layers tend to scatter sound as it impinges on these roughly horizontal layers of marine organisms. The DSL may also prove to be a new source of less-than-tasty food, such as lantern fish and some varieties of smelt, for industrial conversion into protein-rich fish flour.[5]

It is possible, despite the DSL and other secrets of the deep, to pierce these veils in order to understand what the modern submarine can do. H. G. Wells, an enthusiast of the politico-military possibilities of science, enjoyed doting on 'the abysmal failure of governments to understand the uses of weapons that science had provided'.[6] His prime example was the submarine.

HOW IT BEGAN

The first explorers of things in the sea were most likely people in search of edible mollusks and algae or elusive species of fish, or of sponge and pearl. Herodotus and Aristotle both envisaged humans working under water while breathing air from a tube to the surface.[7] The mariners of Alexandria are supposed to have used a primitive diving bell two millennia ago; Hamilton-Paterson names Alexander the Great as the occupant of a glass bell used there. Although possibly legend, this suggests that the Alexandrians understood the indispens-ability of air to human survival and that they accepted constrained mobility while working under water. Divers' bells were experimented with again, in Britain, between the sixteenth and eighteenth centuries: the earliest recorded concept of an undersea vehicle was an idea advanced in 1578 by William Bourne, a mathematician.

Bourne's idea was brought to reality by Cornelius van Drebbel, a Dutchman who in 1624 made a submersible boat operated by 12 oars-men. (A submersible is usually distinguished from a submarine by the former's lack of self-propulsion; a submarine has motive power that renders it theoretically autonomous. Today, the terms are interchange-able.) Drebbel's vessel was made of wood, encased in oil-soaked leather. How did these submariners breathe? As they were able to work their boat for several hours under water, they may have had a simple pipe connecting their cabin to the atmosphere.[8]

In 1776 a young American military officer, David Bushnell, motivated strongly by the struggle for independence from Britain, developed the *Turtle* or *American Turtle* in New Haven, Connecticut, as a consequence of his efforts to detonate gunpowder under water. This was a one-man, hand-propelled vessel equipped with ballast tanks and an explosive mine; the boat could remain below for 30 minutes. A pedal pump admitted or expelled water for descent and ascent. The state of Maine paid Bushnell a fee of £60 for his invention. (It was Bushnell who first called a submarine-borne charge of explosive powder a 'torpedo'.) The *Turtle* proved unsuccessful, however, when used against HMS *Eagle* and alternatively HMS *Asia* lying off Brooklyn, New York. The operator of the *Turtle* was one Ezra Lee, an army sergeant.

Bushnell, by then a captain of military engineers, thought better of his future and the prospects for the submarines, and turned instead to a career in medicine. Bushnell's work was not published until 1799, when the American Philosophical Society produced an article on the *Turtle*.

The Enlightenment and pre-revolution gave birth to a flurry of thought and action in France on exploration by undersea navigation. The medium offered the possibility of stealth in dealing with enemy surface ships, but it posed what must have seemed at the time insur-mountable scientific and technical problems. Besides an assured air supply, these included vision and communication outward from the vessel; maneuvering under water; marshaling energy sources; keeping explosives safe from flame, spark and excessive heat; and combating condensation and water leakage.[9]

The French designers Sillon de Valmer and Beaugenet conceived (1780) of armed undersea craft manned by crews of a half-dozen mariners ready to dive and then ascend to fire cannon or board men-of-war. Sillon even foresaw the potential of the submersible as a base for divers supplied with air from inside the vessel. When the threat of war between France and Britain continued severe in 1795–96, Armand Mazière and Jules Fabre advocated submarines to transport explosives. Going a step further, Louis Castera envisaged a tractor-submarine operating as deep as 10m (6.5 fathoms) below the waves, with other engines of war in tow. These inventors-on-paper emphasized, in particular, the havoc that the appearance of such devices was expected to wreak among the enemy.

The first sustained-operation underwater craft was the work of another young American inventor, Robert Fulton (1765–1815). Fulton showed more tenacity in his quest than Bushnell and the others. The British historian Paul Johnson calls Fulton 'the greatest military visionary of his age'.[10] Fatherless at the age of 10, Fulton was tutored in Lancaster, Pennsylvania, by jack-of-all trades Caleb Johnson. At the same time, a strong influence in the youth's life was another Lancastrian, William Henry, who served his community as both librarian and 'scientist-mechanic'.[11] In his teens Fulton was apprenticed to a silversmith in Philadelphia, where he applied his natural talents for drawing and other visual arts. Some typical 'scientists' of the era would have as little training in natural philosophy as Fulton, many far less.

Fulton did most of his thinking later in France, and the young man proved to be remarkably inventive and persistent. He went to Great Britain in the 1780s to pursue his study of painting, and stayed for a decade. While nominally a protégé of the American painter, Benjamin West, Fulton soon found new interests in ship-canal design and construction, and he began his first enquiries into boat propulsion by steam. By 1794 Fulton developed a method of presentation of technical projects using 'a calculated distortion of perspective outstanding for its clarity'. He was a pioneer in engineering drawing, having clearly perceived its merits because 'precise drawings easily read by fabricators were essential to successful implementation. His drawings as well as his verbal presentations convey an impression that his machines were already in operation'.[12] Fulton soon realized that he was capable of envisaging a complexity 'of many parts, to ferret out the social, economic and physical ramifications, and to integrate them into a continuously expanding system'.

FULTON THE ENTREPRENEUR

Fulton's approach, in its breadth and depth, was unique. His venture into the applications of mechanics, statics, hydraulics and hydrology made him, during his ten-year stay in England, an engineer. Except for the possibilities offered by France,[13] there was no way to gain the scientific foundation or the applied skills of the engineer except by committing oneself to learn empirically from the past and to practice refinement of old handicrafts. Scientist and engineer remained largely indistinguishable during much of the nineteenth century and their professional identifications were interchangeable.

Fulton went to France in 1797, during the menacing belligerency with Great Britain. Before long, he made contact with the Navy Ministry, whose portfolio was in the hands of the aged, one-legged Georges René Pléville-le-Pelley. Minister Pléville-le-Pelley was considered innovative, and he immediately grasped the deadliness implicit in Fulton's project for *Nautilus* – an ellipsoidal tube 6.5m long and nearly 2m in beam. The submersible had a windowed conning tower that served also as entry hatch. A periscope devised by Fulton provided surface observation. He was able to demonstrate, too, that a needle compass worked properly for navigational purposes under water. A keel-like iron tank beneath the hull provided enough permanent ballast, obviating the need to pump large amounts of water ballast for diving or surfacing. A manually operated horizontal screw supplied propulsion at about 1 knot. (As the momentum of an object under water increases per unit of speed, the power propelling the object must be cubed.)

A public demonstration of Fulton's *bateau poisson* (fish boat) took place on the Seine in Paris in June 1800. Fulton and principal assistant Nathaniel Sargent remained submerged in their sealed craft for more than 20 minutes, 'an extraordinary scientific and mechanical tour de force'.[14] What impressed observers most was that on the faces of Fulton and Sargent 'no alterations could be seen'[15] upon disembarkation. A test against British naval vessels not far from Rouen, farther down the Seine, proved unsuccessful, and Fulton again met disappointment.

The American inventor had the strong backing of Pierre Simon Laplace, astronomer, and Gaspard Monge, mathematician. These interceded on Fulton's behalf with Napoleon, who received Fulton at least once. Fulton's main economic argument was that a full-scale submarine, about 9m long, would cost the French government only 100,000 francs, whereas a major war vessel (which could be lost within a matter of hours after leaving port) cost at least 2 million francs.

Breathing remained the main life-sustaining problem for submariners, solved for Fulton by chemist Baron Louis B. Guyton de Morveau, who advocated either bottling oxygen for uncorking at strategic moments, or precipitating carbonic acid with lime, or precompressing air for storage in copper spheres. Guyton and Fulton calculated that 10 cu m would thereby sustain four crew members' and two burning candles', used for lighting, as long as three hours.

After interminable importuning and false starts, Fulton failed to sell or lease his device to the French or, a few years later, to the British fleets. Yet his experiments and developmental work would not be in vain for, in 1807, Fulton constructed and tested in the United States the world's first practical surface vessel operated by steam, the *Clermont*.

THE SPUR OF RESEARCH NEEDS

Improvements on surface vessels, however, are not our interest here. Mankind was increasingly curious about roving under the surface of the waves. Mapping coasts and harbors remained inadequate in the early nineteenth century, and knowledge of currents, the ocean's bed and much marine life was still elementary.

The evolution of seafaring folk as scientists, and of scientists as sea-going investigators, began with an international meeting of hydrographers in 1853. (This was also the year in which James Nasmyth obtained funds from the US Congress for a new submarine design.) Ten national navies organized the International Maritime Conference in Brussels. Their countries were already prime movers in the development of the mechanical chronometer and the floating compass and in advancing physical oceanography, coastal cartography and the preparation of manuals for use in ports and harbors. Ever since, naval directors (even those from closed societies such as the USSR) have been most influential in the founding of a handful of intergovernmental entities concerned with the world's ocean. While advancing science considerably, these initiatives have also improved understanding among nations.

The first International Meteorological Congress took place 20 years later in Vienna, creating what later became the World Meteorological Organization of the UN. This meeting activated the definition of weather phenomena and symbols, established weather charts, standard instruments and methods of observation, and invented international telegraphic codes for the exchange of weather data. Technical cohesion was strengthened in 1895 during a conference organized to estimate the future implications of the evolution of both electrical communication and the steamship in terms of improved cable-laying methods, mapping and commercial fisheries. All this was to prove invaluable not only to submariners, as well as to surface sailors, but to the world's economy.

The new research also significantly raised the effectiveness of inter-disciplinary and intergovernmental collaboration. This added value led to the creation in 1902 of the nongovernmental Council for the Exploration of the Sea (ICES), today an integral part of the International Council for Science (ICSU). The navies and their sub-marines benefited enormously from all of this investigative progress, and the efforts of the oceanologists culminated in the founding in 1960 of the Intergovernmental Oceanographic Commission (IOC), based in Paris.[16]

A specialized research program on the marine environment was established roughly at the same time as the IOC: the Marine Environment Laboratory (MEL) of the UN's International Atomic Energy Agency, with its base at Monte Carlo, Monaco. Derived indi-rectly from the original military enterprise to exploit atomic energy, MEL studies the effects of radioactivity on the oceanic environment. Its main thrusts at the beginning of the twenty-first century are in marine studies, radiometry and radioecology, and it works closely with both the IOC and the UN Environment Program.

Another defense-inspired study generates sound waves from the shores of California and Hawaii to detect ocean temperatures at long range, and receives the low-frequency signals at monitoring points scattered along the Pacific Ocean's rim. Because these sounds may interfere with the sensing of their environment by fish, seals and whales, the National Research Council in Washington produced a report (1999) evaluating these electronic transmissions on marine mammals in particular. The findings were that the signals do inter-fere.[17]

MILITARY ENCOUNTERS OF A NEW KIND

In February 1853 *Scientific American* reported the design of a sub-marine that was, in effect, a gigantic mortar shell submerged in a partially floating vessel. James Nasmyth had won the right, with an appropriation of $200,000 from the United States Congress, to have the Navy examine a 'torpedo boat' design. His floating mortar, as it was called (today, a mine), would be operated by a four-man crew, navi-gated into position alongside an enemy vessel and, using a percussive detonator placed in the bow, self-exploded. The explosive shell was described as being part of the vessel – meaning that the entire con-struction was intended to go up in flame, smoke and metallic debris. *Scientific American* did not specify how the contraption's crew would be saved from destruction.

Ironclad fighting vessels are not part of the submarine story, yet in the 1850s Swedish engineer John Ericsson thought that he could make a contribution in the form of a 'subaquatic system of naval warfare'. The British and French navies had already previously experimented by metal-plating the 'wooden walls' of their ships, so that Ericsson's *Monitor* was another step in the evolution of armored vessels.[18] This took definitive form in 1862 when the *Monitor* of the Federal fleet clashed with the South's *Merrimack* (renamed *Virginia*). The *Monitor* withdrew from the *Virginia*, its master's eyes peppered by iron splinters, with neither vessel beaten; but the encounter served to ensure the effectiveness of the Northern blockade and the continued neutrality of France and Britain regarding the American Civil War,[19] and signaled the end of wooden-wall ships.

During the Civil War, the Southern states were successful with the first submarine that took a visible toll on its Union adversary. In Alabama, the Confederate fleet built a boat almost 10m long called the *H. L. Hunley*. This vessel needed eight men to turn its propeller manually via a crankshaft (top speed 4 knots), its sole means of locomotion. In February 1864, during a night attack in Charleston harbor against the USS *Housatonic*, the *Hunley* planted a 42.5-kg mine against its hull. The Northern frigate blew up but, after its quarter-hour of glory, the *Hunley* was not seen again[20] for 131 years. Its wreck was found in a few fathoms of water not far from the seaward approach to Charleston's harbor – probably a victim of structural weaknesses. Specialists who examined the hulk estimated that the explosion that destroyed *Housatonic* loosened *Hunley*'s rivets, sinking the craft and drowning its crew.

The difficulty with the pioneering submarines, summarizes historian Herman Hattaway, was that they were unreliable, fraught with danger. Once submerged, 'all manner of things could go wrong and often did'.[21] Going down into the sea individually or in small numbers to see what might have gone wrong with a submersible posed problems of its own, related not only to breathing but to mobility and having sufficient lighting available. It was not until the end of the nineteenth century that a suitable scaphander or diving suit was developed in London by August Siebe. Fifty years later a French naval officer and naturalist, Jacques-Yves Cousteau, and a colleague developed the self-contained underwater breathing apparatus (SCUBA).

HUNTING THE HUNTER

Detecting the presence of submersibles did not become a significant challenge until the submarine threat posed by the German

Unterseeboot flotilla during the First World War. In the earliest moments of antisubmarine warfare, it was clear to Britain's Royal Navy that identification of different vessels in the German underwater force could profit from unorthodox methods. One technique depended on the human ear: 'the help of people with musical knowledge and perfect pitch was sought in order to classify the sounds made by submerged craft'.[22] From beyond the Admiralty came proposals

> to train seagulls to sit on periscopes or seals to bark at the presence of a U-boat [that] were no more ridiculous than those adopted by the Admiralty itself, such as issuing a picket boat with a canvas bag and hammer with a view to slipping the bag over the periscope before hitting it with the hammer.[23]

Desperate for solutions, the Admiralty's Board for Invention and Research asked a prominent composer and conductor, Sir Hamilton Harty, to classify the noises of propellers and hulls according to their 'most likely frequencies'. This identification was integrated into the mechanical procedures of sound detection under water, using earphones. Even Lord Rutherford – the New Zealand physicist who won the Nobel Prize in 1908 and was more at home with problems of cosmic time and elementary particles – played a part in the war effort. In the Firth of Forth, while Rutherford grasped the ankles of a friend who possessed perfect pitch, the friend stuck his head beneath the waves and identified the musical signature of a British submarine's engines. (The note was A-flat.[24]) During the Second World War, the US Navy enlisted musical conductor André Kostelanetz to make a similar musical contribution to the war effort. Musical analysis gave way, however, to serious study of the phenomenon of cavitation. In cavitation the high velocity of water passing over a ship's screw causes partial vacuum and throbbing, metal erosion (even of bronze), and distinctive hissing and jerking sounds that effectively give each vessel its own identity: hence, another tool in the detection box of search-and-destroy.

Yet the principles of 'tracking submarines and other objects underwater have, perhaps, surprisingly, remained largely intact'.[25] Between the two world wars, Germany developed an analogue computer for fire control of torpedoes: it provided direction and range instructions. These were embodied in the development of the *Ueberwasserzieloptik* (UZO) rangefinding binoculars, coupled with the *Vorhaltrechner* or 'aim-off' calculator for use aboard U-boats and – at one and the same time – the analogous torpedo data-computer (TDC) of the US submarine fleet.[26] Both instruments – analogue devices – prefigured today's digital computer.

During the Second World War the detection of submarines continued to evolve scientifically and technologically, but an even greater problem remained of reducing the 'kills' by German undersea craft wrought on the Western Allies' merchant shipping. This German effort was a modern *guerre de course* (pursuit of commercial ships) that threatened to choke off the British Isles from their sources of supply abroad. To help solve the problem, RAF Coastal Command had 16 scientists with no other task (1942–43) than devising defensive routing of trans-atlantic convoys and proposing the deployment of destroyers to protect them from the German undersea fleet.

Among the scientists was C. H. Waddington, who explained that his work was 'simply the general method of science employed to study [a] problem which may be of importance' to decision makers.[27] Operational or operations research, invented in 1937–38 by A. P. Rowe, was not simple. Yet on 23 May 1943, eight of the 22 German U-boats attacking convoys HX239 and SC130 were lost, a casualty so grave as to cause the overall commander of the German Navy, Admiral Karl Doenitz – a submariner himself – to recall the entire undersea fleet operating in the north Atlantic.

This painstaking world of analysis and anticipation by combining technical calculation and human factors would become the basis of *la prospective*, a discipline in France, studying the strategy of choosing among realizable options for future action. This is a proactive approach to analytical planning, refined during the 1980s and 1990s[28] – and applied more to civil than military tasks of 'analyzing the future'. (See also Chapters 7 and 12.)

By 1942, the Western Allies, despite a continuing shortage of long-range aircraft, had most of the science-based technology accessible, if not yet operational, that the Second World War offered to counteract the German submarine onslaught. This technology included high-frequency direction finding (HF/DF) by radio, capable of obtaining a fix on even the briefest radio signals emitted from U-boats by revealing them as points of light on the fluorescent screen of the 'huff-duff' device.

The Germans equipped their submersibles with receivers to detect huff-duff's meter-long waves, but the new microwave radars of the Americans and British pre-empted the German technique. The electro-magnetic war, back and forth, became a most intense kill-or-be-killed rivalry; it demanded the practice of radio silence too, a discipline that would become even more rigorous after the end of the war. The Cold War, as it was played out underseas for four and a half decades, became almost technically silent, introducing ever-better radio and radar detection that demanded more and more furtive deployment of the new nuclear submarines.[29]

Table 1:
Major Losses in Submarine Forces, 1939–45

	Crewmen lost at sea	*Percentage of force*	*Boats lost*
Germany	30,246*	75.4	790**
Japan	(not available)	(not available)	130***
Great Britain	3,144	not given	74
United States	3,505	14.5	50

Notes: *Another 5,338 were rescued from sinking vessels, made prisoners of war. *Doenitz,* a production of the Franco-German Arte television channel (1996), estimated the number of German submariners killed at some 28,000. This would reduce percentage of force from 75.4 to 71.9.
**Including boats sunk or scuttled at war's end.
***Total for the Pacific Ocean campaigns only.
Sources: Peter Padfield, *War Beneath the Sea, Submarine Conflict 1939–1945* (London, John Murray, 1995), pp. 461, 478–9; Royal Navy Submarine Museum; James F. Dunnigan and Albert A. Nofi, *Dirty Little Secrets of World War II* (New York, William Morrow/Quill, 1994), p. 340.

The advent of the nuclear submarine symbolized, together with the strategic air and missile forces of the two superpowers, the awesome military dimensions of the Cold War. While the stationary silos for the launching of strategic missiles by the United States or the USSR were vulnerable, this was never the case with the submarine forces' high mobility. This feature made the roving submarine all the more powerful in the minds of both military analysts and the public. Warfare in the nuclear age gave birth, in fact, to a new genus of science fiction, some of it dealing with war under the seas. One of the most impressive works in this category, dealing with a Soviet submarine tested in the 1980s, was Tom Clancy's *Red October.*

NEW BIOLOGY UNDERSEAS

Detection of submarines using hydrophones to pick up propulsion sounds and the 'signature' of each vessel's screws provided an unexpected peace dividend, after the Cold War, in marine geology. Sound detection led to identification in the 1980s of processes and events at the Juan de Fuca ocean ridge on North America's Pacific northwest coast near Seattle. There, instrumentation monitored the Earth's crust being formed by molten material surging from the globe's interior to create seabed 'dikes' of lava. Scientists from the National Oceanic and Atmospheric Administration and Oregon State University thus interpreted a rumble of low frequency they heard as arising from movements of magma emerging from the planet's crust.

These Pacific phenomena incited researchers from the University of Washington at Seattle to investigate the area, in 1993, aboard a submersible with a titanium hull permitting dives to 4,000m. There the scientists spotted not only lava fields but also giant towers of minerals precipitated from the chemical-rich hot brine spewing out of the erupting vents. For the first time human beings saw new crust being created and huge mats of bacteria that live on hot water and hydrogen sulfide, another big leap affecting the environment for many kilometers around. Only the gigantic pressures exerted by the ocean's mass above prevent these hot spots from boiling.

Vents were first observed, without being understood, in 1977 off the Galapagos Islands, and were identified in 1981 by John Baross of the University of Washington. They are related to the earliest forms of life known, an entirely new biological classification called the *archea*. Thomas Gold of Cornell University has suggested that these bacteria-like objects may constitute a deep biosphere that could surpass in volume the better-known biosphere at the planet's atmospheric–terrestrial interface. The lava layers under the sea could prove, in time, to yield resistant bacteriological enzymes useful to industry; their surrounding vents may be depositories of useful minerals.

Mineral fragments spewed at 315°C by the action of magma below the sea's floor turn black as they encounter seawater at 4.4°C, often piling up as spires that reach scores of meters high. The super-heated water welling from the vents generates local biota comprising bacteria, tubeworms, clams, mussels, snails, shrimp and some species of fish. Portuguese, French and American oceanographers, diving in 1997 near the Azores aboard the submersibles *Alvin* and *Nautile*, explored a vent 'forest' of more than 100 vents. Had submarine technology not developed to the point that submersibles can easily reach the depth explored by *Nautile* and *Alvin* off the Azores, some 2,480m, we would still be ignorant of the existence of these connectors between the Earth's top magma layers and the hydro-sphere.

DRIVING FORCES

The motivation, perhaps compulsion, of human beings volunteering to lead the unnatural life of the submariner is not easily explained. From the outset, the submersible was construed as a weapon – a special armament to be serviced by normal people trained to breathe and work in an abnormal milieu. Crew amenities were conspicuous by their absence, yet *comfort* is the ambient element most sought by the human animal. (The United States Navy was the first to introduce air conditioning aboard submarines, but not until a third of the way through the twentieth century.)

In his survey of the undersea war waged between 1939 and 1945, when the submarine reached its apogee of toll-taking of an adversary's resources, historian Peter Padfield offers an explanation.

> [Humans] were carried merely to serve the system, fitting in the spaces around the reload torpedoes and stores for the voyage, in most cases sharing bunks, 'hot bunking' with a shipmate from another watch and sleeping on unchanged sheets that became dirtier by the day. They were unable to bathe or shower, scarcely to wash hands and face, and frequently could not get dry after a wet spell on watch. There was often a queue for the fiendishly complex [toilet] in the heads, and even that could not be used when submerged below 70 feet because of the exterior pressure.[30]

Padfield describes the putrid air often breathed, the affliction of headaches and nausea, and the sometimes unbalanced rations eaten by submarine crews once fresh provisions are exhausted. Air supply in modern submarines is assured, on the other hand, by a combination of reprocessed air or oxygen circulated by pumps, combined with periodic fresh-air input during voyages that may last months. Padfield advises that one should not, in the psychological sphere, dwell on the consequences of 'incipient claustrophobia'.

How can one explain the motivation, perseverance and unflinching discipline among undersea crews? (See Chapter 6 for more on this discipline.) Morale, Padfield believes, depends on a strong sense of mutual responsibility, 'comradeship across barriers of rank', and commanding officers who can at all times be trusted by their crews.[31] The submarine, unlike the aircraft flight or infantry company, may be the one place where reciprocal confidence reigns supreme during the worst adversity.

Life in the cramped space of a submarine is thus anything but easy and relaxed: the vessels in today's underwater fleets were not laid out by designers of luxury yachts. The food provided, at least in navies such as those of the United States, France, Britain and Russia, is outstanding fare and indeed a perquisite together with premium pay. Submariners, both officers and crewmen, are handpicked and promised early retirement – because their subordination and the rigors of their tasks are best handled by the relatively young.

PERILS OF THE PROFESSION

What happens to men and equipment when a submersible meets disaster beneath the sea's surface? Some of us accustomed to living on *terra firma* can imagine the extremes of the claustrophobia native to us all, to one degree or another, when put to the test. But, given the total isolation of his working and living environment, a submariner's life may become harrowing.

In 1951 there occurred an accident involving a lone submarine moving along the seabed during peacetime. This was HMS *Affray*, lost in less than 100m of water near the Isle of Wight. She was on a training exercise, with a complement of 75 officers and men, equipped with sufficient escape material for everyone aboard. When the vessel failed to communicate with her base, a search was begun by military units of four nations. Three days after her disappearance, *Affray* was given up as lost. What happened?

When the submarine was found by an underwater television camera (a major success for this new technology), *Affray* seemed to be lying undamaged at 77m down, with her hydroplanes in position for resurfacing. But damaged she was: her hollow 'snort' or snorkel tube of 10m in height (allowing the craft's diesel engines to breathe during shallow submergence) had snapped off where it joined the hull. The hull valve inside was found in the OPEN position. The fracture was judged a consequence of design inadequacies. What may have ensued after the tube snapped, at only a few meters' depth, is related by James Hamilton-Paterson, based on accounts made by Captain W. O. Shelford, Royal Navy, who directed the search operations:

> Probably her commander had radioed his last message, dived, and the snort tube fractured on the way down. Even at a depth of only forty feet, water would have poured through the open valve at the rate of three quarters of a tonne per second … The water would have at once flooded the engine room and caused electrical short circuits followed by explosions, fire, and the release of noxious fumes … *Affray* was overwhelmed quickly and without warning … [B]y the time the alarm was raised her crew had already been dead several hours.[31]

On 30 March 1994 the officers and crew of the French nuclear attack-submarine *Emeraude* (Emerald) underwent another experience. *Emeraude* is one of a class of six undersea boats commissioned in France during the 1980s, vessels powered by nuclear energy but armed with 14 conventional torpedoes or, alternatively, the same number of SM-30 Exocet missiles. *Emeraude*, with a complement of nine officers and 57 other ranks, is powered by a 48-megawatt nuclear reactor capable of supplying energy for cruises of unlimited range. Its voyages are restricted in practice, however, to 45 days in order to resupply food.

The French submarine was engaged in normal maneuvers, somewhere in the Mediterranean between its Toulon base and the island of Corsica. The skipper was conducting a routine inspection of the steam-exchange compartment, a normally unoccupied area aft of the submarine's inhabited sections amidships. It was during this inspection that a defective pipe, channeling steam towards a turbine that powered an electrical generator, exploded.[32] Superheated steam filled the compartment, killing the captain, another officer and eight petty officers.[33] Although an analogous accident could have occurred aboard a surface vessel or in a nuclear electricity-generating plant ashore, the victims of *Emeraude* did not have a chance because of the enclosed and cramped volume they were inspecting. The vessel, commanded now by its executive officer, was able to return unaided to its base.

Far to the northeast, the Soviet naval ministry had been less fortunate when the nuclear submarine *Komsomolets* disappeared off the Norwegian coast in 1989. *Komsomolets* was a remarkable boat, capable of diving to 1,020m (560 fathoms), twice as deep as any other submarine; its hull combined titanium, aluminum, zirconium, vanadium, molybdenum and thallium. *Komsomolets* was built at incalulable cost, such concerns not being paramount in the Soviet Union of the Cold War. (Defense Minister Dmitri Ustinov called the boat unsinkable.[34]) Fire broke out aft of the reactor compartment while the vessel was at a depth of 340m. It sank, six months before the crumbling of the Berlin Wall.

Pollution of the northern seas increased with the loss of the Russian *Kursk*, a tactical submarine displacing almost 14,000 tonnes, when it exploded beneath the Barents Sea in August 2000. The twin-reactor, double-hulled craft suffered two or more detonations near its forward torpedo tubes. This caused massive flooding, killing the 118 hands aboard. Norwegian and Russian divers retrieved a few bodies, and most of the vessel was refloated a year later. Analysis of the accident remains to be revealed in full.

Some specialists attributed this sort of calamity to 'infrastructure decay', a generalized state in what remained of the former Soviet Union. There *could have been* another cause, however, given the advent (since 1977) of a missile capable of moving through seawater at several hundred miles per hour. These arms, typified by the *Shkval* (Squall), generate the phenomenon of supercavitation. Here a high-speed flow of fluid from a nose-mounted, flat-disk 'cavitator' develops a gaseous envelope around, for example, a torpedo. The projectile so wrapped overcomes friction as the bag increases its rate of displacement under water.[35] There are no countermeasures known.

CIVIL VERSUS MILITARY TASKS

The typical military submersible functions at an optimal depth of about 900m, the real figures being rigorously protected by the 'secret' stamp. So it is not military submarines that establish deep-diving records, as this is not an aim in the development of submarines operated by navies.

When compared with military exploitation, civil uses of the submarine have gained scant public attention. The limitations of appropriately suited and ventilated divers are strict. A SCUBA-equipped human being functions most comfortably and with minimal risk at about 40m, and a diver in a pressurized suit can go no deeper than 440m. So, throughout the maritime world, 'scientists [have] pleaded for money that would bring home knowledge of underwater currents, degrees of salinity, fish and plant life and sea-bottom topography that would benefit man. They got little attention or money for their pains.'[36]

Today this is no longer the case. Deep-submergence craft operated by research scientists – mainly in France, the United States, Japan and Russia – continue their civil investigations to depths equaling the heights of the peaks of our highest mountain ranges. The Japanese *Shinkai,* for example, has dropped to 6,500m (more than 21,300 feet) to explore some of the lowest depths found between the Japanese and Philippine archipelagos. The French submersible *Nautile* dives easily to depths of about 6,000m along the Mid-Atlantic Ridge, discovering structures such as dike complexes at 4,000m: geologic formations separating pillow basalt from gabbro layers.[37] (Gabbros are rock masses formed by the slow cooling of basalt.)

The robot *Jason,* launched from the ocean sled *Medea,* descended to 6,000m, while the total-depth record is still held by the non-maneuverable *Trieste* bathyscaphe which, in 1960, established the all-time record dive to 10,912m in the Mariana Trench's Challenger Deep. The Japanese robot *Kaiko,* exploring the Challenger Deep in March 1994, missed matching *Trieste's* record by exactly 1m. The depth reached equals an altitude exceeding Mount Everest's by 20 per cent.

The call for rigorous standards in the testing of underwater equipment, too, has a civil as well as a military clientele. Standards for breathing apparatus set by the Experimental Diving Unit of the United States Navy based in Panama City, Florida, are determined from physiological (neural and muscular) reactions combined with mathematical computation, as in the mixing of gases for respiration. Exacting standards are observed, through fallout, by non-military divers throughout North America and Europe, who have access to the list 'Authorized for Navy Use' by logging onto www.navsea.navy.mil/sea00c/pdf/anu.pdf on the Web.

Military and civil search conducted beneath the sea gave birth to the subdiscipline of marine biology, now thriving as the animal and plant arms of the life sciences of the ocean. Its discoveries range from the superheated hydrothermal vents already mentioned (found at 800 to 6,000m down) to the 5cm-long crustacean – called the amphipod – detected at 11,030m in the Mariana Trench. At such depths there is no natural light, and the water pressures are tremendous.

The expansion of marine biology made it possible, in turn, for scientists to establish that living organisms today fall into three categories instead of the previous two, bacteria and eukarya (everything from slime molds to animals). The new archaea classification includes biota found near thermal vents and *extremophile* microbes thriving in extreme conditions, including heat exceeding 100°C. Extremophiles may be alkali-loving (alkaliphilic) or salt-loving (halophilic) in addition to heat-loving (thermophilic, hyperthermophilic). Investigations are under way in North America, Germany and Japan to find industrial applications for the extremophiles, probably in pharmacology and food processing: uses comparable to those of enzymes.[38]

NEW ADAPTATIONS OF NATURE

One of the Cold War underwater mysteries remained unsolved until recently. In 1981, an undetected Soviet submarine went aground in Swedish territorial waters. Using refined detection methods, the Swedes and other Nordic states reported repeated intrusions in their national waters by unidentified underwater craft. In one case, the Swedish navy indeed flushed to the surface a Soviet submarine that found itself in acute mechanical distress. The Soviet Union denied any illegality.

It finally came to light that sound-detection apparatus operated by the Swedes was confusing sounds uttered by a species of sea otter, common to Sweden's boundary waters, with sonic fragments originating from submarines: a clear case of nature confounding advanced technology.[39] In 1995, the Stockholm daily *Dagens Nyheter* revealed a leak of information emerging from the Ministry of Defense. Sea-going mink and other aquatic mammals 'swishing and splashing as they searched for food', it said, were the sources of 'suspicious sounds' detected by Sweden's submarine-alarm system.[40] By 1999, the Norwegian Defense Research Institute found that groan-like signals emitted every 80 seconds by cod during the February–March mating season interfere with sonar waves originating with submarines.[41]

The work of the US Navy with dolphins is well known. Current efforts, such as those under way at the Naval Surface Warfare Center in Maryland, are meant to make manmade sonar perform more like nature's own sonar – already in use for millions of years. Animal sonar is not only good at finding objects by echo location, it also understands complicated shapes: forms that may reveal the exact nature of the thing detected. Speaking of shapes, the advent of nuclear submarines brought about changes in basic hull design, too. The old idea of shaping a submarine much like a shark, in order to overcome surface tension and raise speed, gave way – since, by definition, there is no 'surface' tension beneath the waves – to today's whale form.[42]

Less familiar are recent investigations to understand the electro-magnetic sensing and identification that certain fish are capable of, especially through experiments with the elephant-nosed *Gnathonemus petersii* of rivers in West Africa. Electrified fish are divided by researchers into:

- the *strongly electric* that find prey or repel predators by generating shocks of hundreds of volts, and
- the *weakly electric* that provide stimuli in terms of the fish's so-called electric sense by determining the form, location and conductivity of specimens nearby, challenging through electromagnetic recognition its own species, finding or tracking its own mates, and other com-portment vital to survival.

Scientists understand less well the strongly electric than the weakly electric – a category further subdivided into 'wave fish' and 'pulse fish', explaining the electromagnetic propagation of which they are capable. Both types generate their electrical output via a tubular organ running almost the length of the fish. This organ houses electrocytes (*electro* + *cells*), brain-controlled electromagnetic elements. These can have outputs of tens or hundreds of millivolts.

'New ocean sensors modeled after the exquisitely sensitive electro-receptors of sharks [should] be a boon to ocean researchers and to the military', according to Ingrid Wickelgrenn, reporting in *IEEE Spectrum*, journal of the International Institute of Electrical and Electronics Engineers. 'The military are also interested', she adds, 'in shark-style electric-field detectors that could pick up detailed information about passing ships and detect corrosion of their own.'[43]

An unexpected hazard to the natural sonar whales use for navigation and hunting is the collateral damage (military language meaning non-military casualties) caused by radar used under the waves. Alexandros Frantzis of the University of Athens has uncovered evidence that sub-marine-borne sonar may affect whalesong, the animals' own system of communication. According to this Greek researcher, writing in the weekly *Nature*, interference by manmade sonar seems to explain the faulty navigation of a few beaked whales, a species known as Cuvier's whale, and their stranding on shores around the world.[44]

SUBMARINES HELP US RELIVE THE PAST

The end of the Cold War caused a restructuring of defense industries everywhere (in the United States nearly half a million jobs were lost among the arms builders between 1990 and 1995). The firms involved in the heavy handling of metal – building artillery, armored vehicles and navy vessels – were affected seriously enough to leave only one builder of submarines. General Dynamics' Electric Boat Company survived because of its contract to build the *Seawolf*, an advanced, but essentially unwanted, nuclear submarine. The decision to proceed with this vessel's construction was based uniquely on the politically perceived need 'to keep the nation's submarine skills alive'.[45]

Despite a building scheme tapering off during the years 1990–2010, navies throughout the world continue to be concerned about accurate detection of opponents' vessels both at the surface and beneath the waves. A breakthrough in increasing this accuracy developed in 1996–97 with the innovation called the *atomic laser*. Wolfgang Ketterle's research team at MIT (Massachusetts Institute of Technology) upgraded the optical maser/laser created 40 years earlier by Charles Townes and Theodore Malman, which shot a stream of coherent microwave radiation in waves (and made possible, for example, the compact disk). The new atomic device fires a fine beam of matched waves of *matter*, and should improve magnetic-field detectors of petroleum deposits, surface vessels and submarines – as well as allow better nanotechnology, or microengineering. (Ketterle shared the Nobel Prize for Physics, 2001.)

In 1985 Robert Ballard, the American deep-diving ocean searcher who had previously found the remains of the Second World War battleship *Bismarck* 5km down, located the remains of the steamship *Titanic*, lying at a depth of more than 3km.

In 1993, Ballard and his associates took the submersible *Jason*, its robot *Homer* and the submarine *Delta* to a depth of almost 97m off the lighthouse near Kinsale in Ireland to scrutinize *Lusitania*, sunk by the German *U-20* submarine in May 1915. When the 'floating palace' was torpedoed by 30-year-old Walther Schwieger – commanding the *U-20*, and who had sunk three other British vessels only days before – the German government claimed that *Lusitania* was running the

German blockade of Britain as an armed merchant ship. Although the giant luxury liner was not armed, *Lusitania* indeed carried munitions and other wartime cargo. Ballard was not able to determine why the Cunard liner sank so fast, in 18 minutes; he speculated that an explosion of coal dust caused by flames spreading within the ship's fuel bunkers might have been the cause.[46]

Ten years after *Titanic*'s rediscovery, Ballard, profiting from a peace dividend offered by the US Navy, announced that he would use a fleet submarine for archeological research along the seabed connecting the Italian port of Ostia (near Rome) with ancient Carthage, in today's Tunisia. This trans-Mediterranean seaway was one of imperial Rome's main routes for commerce and transport of both military and slaves and, consequently, the resting place of countless shipwrecks. Yet, according to the *Journal of Roman Archaeology*, knowledge of Roman navigation undertaken during the Dark and Middle Ages remains poor.

Sea-floor surveys made by several nations during the 1970s and 1980s have left us many excellent 'road maps of the ocean bottom'.[47] Ballard's vehicle is the nuclear-powered *NR-1*, a deep-diver launched in 1969 for exploration and recovery; it is equipped with wheels, fore and aft, permitting the vessel to roll along the sea floor. Propulsion combines a nuclear reactor with twin screws, and forward thrusters permit tight maneuvering. Eleven sailors service the two scientific researchers aboard. *NR-1*'s special features include transparent openings in the hull, an extra-hull work module, sensors, cameras and lights, and especially strong manipulators for picking up debris and antiquities (dating from between the fourth century BC and the twelfth century AD) from North Africa, the eastern Mediterranean and the Italian peninsula.[48]

The end of the Cold War made possible reconnaissance of *Titanic* in August 1996 by the Institut Français de Recherche pour l'Exploitation de la Mer (IFREMER), which earlier collaborated with the Woods Hole Oceanographic Institution on *Titanic* investigations. The new exploration allowed Paul Matthias of Polar Imaging, Inc., to probe the sunken vessel with a sub-bottom profiler, an ultrasound scanner not dissimilar to that used by obstetricians. Matthias and his colleagues found that, contrary to belief since the sinking in 1912 that an iceberg had caused a major gash in her hull, in reality *Titanic* suffered six underwater tears in her plates of not much more than a square meter in total area.

AND THE PAST HAS ITS SECRETS

The exploit by Ballard with the sunken *Titanic* encouraged Paul R. Tidwell to probe nearly 5,200m below the sea's surface, locating and verifying the hulk of Japanese submarine *I-52*. *I-52* left Kure, Kyushu, on its first and last mission in March 1944 under instructions from Japan's silent service to execute highly unusual tasks. Carrying about two metric tonnes of gold,[49] the submarine put in to Singapore to load tin and other strategic raw materials. Wartime Germany was already critically short of many kinds of supplies, and Japan lacked the most up-to-date technology in weapons. The final load aboard *I-52* consisted of (besides gold) 54 tonnes of rubber, 228 tonnes of molybdenum, tungsten and tin, and three tonnes of quinine – the remedy then for malaria.

The vessel was under way again by late April 1944, sailing through the Indian Ocean, submerged during the day and surfacing at night for battery recharge. Its destination was the Nazi-controlled port of Lorient, France. *I-52* was larger than most submarines of the day: about 108m (357ft) in length, it housed a crew of 95 and 14 specialists from high-technology firms such as the Mitsubishi Instrument Co. The technicians were going to Germany to obtain technology not available in war-strained Japan. On 23 June *I-52* had a rendezvous with a German submarine in mid-Atlantic, more than 1,600km west of the Cape Verde Islands. The Japanese captain took aboard two German technicians, food and fuel, and a radar to help the submarine dodge Allied aircraft as it approached the naval base of Lorient.

I-52's mission proved futile because the Allies knew through cryptanalysis of its location, destination and cargo. A fighter-bomber from the carrier USS *Bogue*, piloted by Lieutenant-Commander Jesse D. Taylor, located the Japanese submarine after its nocturnal rendezvous. With the aid of flares, two 500-lb bombs, acoustic buoys and a single torpedo, Taylor and his crew sent *I-52*, fast losing its air to inrushing seawater, to a grave more than 5km below the waves.

A half-century later, the Cold War's thaw released to civil use many of the secrets of science-based underwater techniques developed by Americans and Russians, especially during the decades following the Second World War. Paul Tidwell and his colleagues were able to remove errors found in, and then reconstruct accurately, *I-52*'s original navigational plan. This exercise in precision charting enabled the fortune hunters to shave 32km from the site of the estimated sinking as it had been plotted during wartime by the US Navy. Working with Sound Ocean Systems, Inc., and Meridian Sciences, Inc., two private firms, the team was able to pinpoint with cameras and sonar dangled from cables the virtually intact *I-52* from aboard the Russian research vessel, *Yuzhmorgeologiya*. Once *I-52*'s gold is recovered, it should be worth millions to its finders and amortize the exploration's cost of nearly $8 million.[50]

TIME AND EFFORT SAVED

In terms of deep-water probing that exploits the full capacity of fiber-optic cables and computer-enhanced imaging by sonar, Robert Ballard reported in 1997 the greatest concentration of shipwrecks ever found on the sea floor. His discoveries, supplementing those of the *Titanic* and the *Bismarck*, took place at a spot in the Tyrrhenian Sea roughly half way between Sicily and Sardinia. Another aspect of the end of the Cold War – military secrets that suddenly become open information – was the revelation of innumerable hulks of vessels and their myriad spilled artifacts, all over the world.

Ballard's team used the US Navy-owned *NR-1* submarine and a crew of 13 to explore Mediterranean depths ranging from 2,740 to 6,000m. Ballard's chief archeologist, Anna Marguerite McCann of Boston College, has revealed that the compilation of a complete mosaic of electronic-camera views of a single hulk is now done in four hours. The same achievement, using the hand tools of traditional submarine archeology, previously took 11 years or more of painstaking effort.

Economy of time and effort can thus be another benefit of the transfer of military techniques to civil research and discovery. The major historical implication of the Ballard explorers' work is that we now understand that Roman merchant vessels were not coastal huggers: their captains braved the deep, well away from shore and often treacherous storms.

The yield from new seismic research, studies meant to sharpen detection of nuclear blasts at great distances, must not be omitted. Roger Jellinek, who for ten years edited the Lamont-Doherty ecological laboratory's *Newsletter* and *Yearbook*, has this to say:

> Much of modern Earth science is based on military objectives and military funding. The new paradigm of Earth tectonics would not have been established (after Alfred L. Wegener's enunciation of the theory of continental drift in 1912) without navy ships and navy money. The mapping of the seafloor … is proceeding with gravity and sonar techniques that were developed for missile guidance. The elaborate seismological networks were put in place as a direct bonus of nuclear testing. Ironically, the same science was also brought to bear *against* nuclear testing.

The geochemical measurements of ocean currents and the chemistry of the water column, and the interaction of ocean and atmosphere – all keys to climate change – were much paid for by the military who wanted to know where radioactive trace chemicals went after nuclear tests. Finally, environmental research, particularly research on global warming, is now perceived [in many countries] as a national-security issue.[51]

AND NOW, MECHANICAL FISH

Amazing progress is being made in our ability to simulate more realistically the workings of nature that permit human beings to adapt ever better to the undersea milieu. The first nuclear-powered submarine went to sea in the 1950s, with *Nautilus* setting a world record in 1959 by cruising a trifle more than 60,000 nautical miles – much of it while submerged under ice, on a single nuclear fueling.[52] Sixty thousand miles under water, incidentally, equal Jules Verne's 20,000 leagues.

Part of the progress is the theoretical and experimental work done by the Triantafyllou brothers, Michael of MIT and George of the City College of New York's Institute for Physicochemical Hydrodynamics. The Greek-born brothers have advanced the study of how a fish, as it swims, instinctively controls the size and force of the eddies generated by fins and tail. This movement allows a dolphin, for example, to crash through the waves at 23 knots (about 47 km/h). 'To capture energy from the vortices and boost its swimming efficiency', the Triantafyllous wrote in *Scientific American*, 'the fish instinctively times the flapping of its tail to create counterrotating whorls that meet and weaken' the encountered vortices.[53]

By judicious study of the 'Strouhal number' of different fish (the Strouhal number combines the frequency of the tail's flapping with the width of jet produced and the forward speed of the swimmer), the Triantafyllou team determined that the most effective number is between 0.25 and 0.35. Fish of all sizes swing their tails within this range. A concrete result of this analysis is the construction of a robotic, electric motor-operated 'tuna' made of Lycra and foam 'skin', aluminum hinges, pulleys and countless meters of wire and cable serving as tendons. There are six motors, positioned outside the 'fish', and this tuna 'swims' today at MIT's Ocean Engineering Test Facility.

What is the significance? The artificial tuna has been able to simulate, in a controlled test-environment, the flapping of real tails and fins. *Scientific American* surmises that 'boats and submarines may be next'. Much as the Wright brothers, nine decades earlier, successfully simulated the flight of birds, the Triantafyllous have opened the way for entirely synthetic vessels to replicate the coursing of fish under water.

THE FUTURE

The military undersea fleets are changing both operational concepts and strategy. Sweden considers its submarine force superfluous in today's military environment and in 2000 cut its fleet in half: six boats only. Australia is tinkering with its non-nuclear, 72-meter *Collins*-class (3,000 tonnes) boat, still considered noisy and equipped with an unreliable computerized combat system. The *Collins*, capable of remaining submerged for 70 days, will ultimately be a fleet of six craft – built for $3.2 billion, the country's single most expensive military outlay.

The United States, meanwhile, is advancing with its 115-meter *Virginia*-class, nuclear-powered boats set for launching in 2004. These craft (6,500 tonnes each) are designed to operate in continental waters offshore, equipped with videocameras as periscopes, and capable of weather analysis at night and during storms. Russia, erratically reported to be increasing its number of submarines, still has the world's largest tactical fleet, followed by the United States and China. Small North Korea has nearly 30 tactical submersibles.[54]

An investigator at the Monterey Bay Aquarium Research Institute, Marcia McNutt, summarizes the advances in ocean research as follows: 'The current format of oceanography … was largely an invention of the navy to meet its specific needs.'[55] That it was, indeed, this chapter has shown. The present, with its waves of new terrorism so far on land and in the air, gives every indication that ocean research will continue to meet naval needs.

NOTES

1 The noted physician wrote this in an essay, 'Science and War', *The Lancet*, 9 October 1915.

2 James Hamilton-Paterson, *The Great Deep: The Sea and Its Thresholds* (New York, Random House, 1992), p. 172.

3 Dan van der Vat, *Stealth at Sea* (London, Weidenfeld & Nicholson, 1994), *passim*.

4 The 2.6 million tons of merchant shipping lost off the American seaboards between January and August 1942 constitute the worst defeat inflicted on American sea power. See Gerhard L. Weinberg, *A World at Arms: A Global History of World War II* (New York, Cambridge University Press, 1994), pp. 365 ff. The severity of the merchant-shipping losses off the US East Coast remains controversial 60 years later. Weinberg and Peter Padfield, in *War Beneath the Sea: Submarine Conflict 1939–1945* (London, John Murray, 1995), attribute these losses to the poor defensive measures of the US Navy. Historian and former submariner Clay Blair, in *Hitler's U-Boat War: The Hunters, 1939–1942* (New York, Random House, 1996), claims, however, that only 1 per cent of Allied merchant fleets went to the bottom between December 1941 and August 1942.

5 Daniel Behrman, *The New World of the Oceans: Men and Oceanography* (Boston, MA, Little, Brown, 1969), p. 74.
6 Cited in Drew Middleton, *Submarine: The Ultimate Naval Weapon—Its Past, Present & Future* (Chicago, IL, Playboy, 1976), p. 35.
7 Irwin Stambler, *The Battle for Inner Space: Undersea Warfare and Weapons* (New York, St Martin's Press, 1962), p. 31.
8 The initial section of this chapter is based partly on J. G. Richardson, 'Submarine Exploration and the Tale of *SAGA*', *Impact of Science on Society*, no. 147 (1987), p. 278; see also his 'The Contract, Past and Future, between Scientist and Soldier', *International Social Science Journal*, 135 (1993), pp. 13–22, and Stambler, *The Battle for Inner Space*, p. 32.
9 Cynthia Owen Philip, *Robert Fulton: A Biography* (New York, and Toronto, ON, Franklin Watts, 1985), pp. 77–8.
10 Paul Johnson, *The Birth of the Modern: World Society 1815–1830* (London, Weidenfeld & Nicolson, 1991), pp. 13–6 and *passim*.
11 Biographical sources on Fulton are numerous; one of the most readable is Philip, *Robert Fulton*; see its p. 7 for the designation cited.
12 Philip, *Robert Fulton*, pp. 37–8.
13 The world's oldest engineering school is the Ecole Nationale des Ponts et Chaussées (National School of Bridges and Roads), Paris, established in 1747 by Louis XV's ministers in a pre-revolutionary effort to reform and improve the French kingdom's economy.
14 Philip, *Robert Fulton*, p. 97. Stambler, *The Battle for Inner Space.*, p. 39, states that the *Nautilus* remained submerged for six hours.
15 *American Historical Review*, 39, p. 492, as cited in Philip, *Robert Fulton*, p. 97.
16 The IOC is attached to Unesco. Its mission is to coordinate the world's marine-information exchanges and the training of developing-country talent in the marine sciences; see also Richardson, 'Submarine Exploration', pp. 13–22.
17 Summary of activities of the National Academy of Sciences for November–December: e-mail of 27 October 1999.
18 Two and a half centuries earlier Korea's Admiral Yi Sun Shin was the first to add plates of armor, studded with knife blades and spikes, to a ship's upper deck to protect crew below. Yi's 'turtle' ships (*kobukson*) engaged the Japanese when the latter invaded Korea several times, 1592–98.
19 Recounted in James Tertius de Kay (naval historian), *Monitor: The Story of the Legendary Ironclad and the Man Whose Invention Changed History* (New York, Walker, 1997).
20 Charles Eliot Morison, *The Oxford History of the American People* (New York, Oxford University Press, 1965), pp. 644–5; Frederic Golden, 'Probing a Sea Puzzle', *Time* (Europe edn), 19 June 2000, pp. 122–3.
21 Hermann Hattaway, *Shades of Blue and Gray: An Introductory Military History of the Civil War* (Columbia, MO, and London, University of Missouri Press, 1997), p. 196.
22 R. V. Jones in *Reflections on Intelligence* (1989), as cited by Hamilton-Paterson, *The Great Deep*, p. 114. Jones reveals elsewhere that in 1939 he was appointed 'to enquire into the organization of British Intelligence to discover why we knew so little about new German applications of science to warfare, and for this purpose I had been seconded from the Directorate of Scientific Research to the Air Section of MI6'. See 'A Sidelight on Bletchley, 1942', *Intelligence and National Security*, 9, 1 (1994), pp. 1–6.

23 Kenneth Macksey, *Technology in War: The Impact of Science on Weapon Development and Modern Battle* (London, Arms & Armour Press, 1986), p. 87.

24 Richard Rhodes, *The Making of the Atomic Bomb* (New York: Simon & Schuster, 1986), marvels at how Rutherford was able to work for the Royal Navy and keep the Cavendish Laboratory busy and productive.

25 Kyle M. Becker, 'Scanning Underwater Surfaces', *Scientific American*, August 1994, p. 80. The author proposes a homemade device to detect objects below the sea's surface, fish included, by measuring their electrical impedance and scattering strength.

26 Peter Padfield, *War beneath the Sea*, p. 43.

27 C. H. Waddington, *Operational Research in World War 2* (London, Elek, 1973), p. viii. Waddington later became professor of genetics at the University of Edinburgh. See also I. F. Clarke, 'World War II, or What Did the Future Hold?', *Futures*, 26, 3 (1994), p. 343.

28 For example, Thierry Gaudin, *2100: Odyssée de l'espèce* (Paris, Payot & Rivages, 1993). See also Fabrice Hatem, *Introduction à la prospective* (Paris, Economica-Gestion Poche, 1996), for a quick exposure to the discipline.

29 A little-remembered fact concerning the logistics required for the nuclear bombing of Japan is the fate of the USS *Indianapolis*, a heavy cruiser that delivered some of the bomb-related matériel from San Francisco to Tinian Island in July 1945. On 30 July, after completion of her mission, the *Indianapolis* was sunk by a Japanese submarine. Seventy-four per cent of its complement of 1,196 went to the bottom of the Pacific Ocean with their ship – one of the rare cases during the Second World War when a vessel's crew disappeared in such numbers.

30 Padfield, *War Beneath the Sea*, p. 14.

31 Ibid.

32 Hamilton-Paterson, *The Great Deep*, p. 135; Captain Shelford published his own account of HMS *Affray*'s disappearance in *Subsunk: The Story of Submarine Escape* (London, Harrap, 1960).

33 Jean-Paul Croizé, 'Drame dans un sous-marin nucléaire d'attaque', *Le Figaro*, 31 March 1994, p. 10.

34 For an unusual technological (not scientific) walk through a nuclear submarine, see Tom Clancy, *Submarine: A Guided Tour Inside a Nuclear Warship* (New York, Berkley, 1993).

35 Jacek Hugo-Bader, *Gazeta Wyborcza*, as reproduced in French, 'Le naufrage du *Komsomolets*: récit de la dernière grande catastrophe communiste', *Courrier international*, 15 July 1999, pp. 36–8.

36 See Steven Ashley, 'Warp Drive under Water', *Scientific American*, May 2001, pp. 62–71.

37 Middleton, *Submarine*, p. 68.

38 Françoise Praderie, 'The Dawn of Global Scientific Cooperation' (interview), *OECD Observer*, 187 (1994), p. 6; Enrico Bonatti, 'The Earth's Mantle below the Ocean', *Scientific American*, March 1994, pp. 29, 30–1.

39 Michael T. Madigan and Barry L. Marrs, 'Extremophiles', *Scientific American*, April 1997, pp. 66–71.

40 Telephone communication with an official of the Ministry of Defense, Stockholm, 9 September 1994.

41 The Associated Press reporting from Stockholm, 'Swedish Submarine Alert? Only Minks', *IHT*, 10 February 1995, p. 5.

42 'Faites l'amour, pas la guerre' (Make Love, Not War), *Courrier international*, 7 January 1999, p. 55, citing the *Independent*.

43 The author thanks William J. McCoy for bringing this fact to his attention: e-mail 28 November 2000.
44 Ingrid Wickelgrenn, 'The Strange Senses of Other Species', *IEEE Spectrum*, March 1996, pp. 32, 35.
45 As cited in 'Quiet, Please. Whales Navigating', *The Economist*, 7 March 1998, p. 109.
46 'Inside the Stockade', *The Economist*, 2 April 1994, p. 72.
47 Robert D. Ballard (with photographs by Jonathan Blair), 'Riddle of the Lusitania', *National Geographic*, April 1994, pp. 68–85
48 Robert Kunzig, *The Restless Sea: Exploring the World beneath the Waves* (New York, W. W. Norton, 1999), pp. 38, 59, 76.
49 William J. Broad, 'Sub to Scan Sea Floor for Roman Wrecks', *IHT*, 9 February 1995, p. 10.
50 With an average price of 63,000 French francs a kilogram during the 1990s, 2 tonnes of gold would be worth US$11 million or a little less – depending on exchange rates.
51 The first report of the *I-52* story is by William J. Broad, 'Salvaging Riches of Axis Sub', *IHT*, 20 July 1995, p. 10; see also Julie Dam, 'Striking Gold at Sea', *Time* (Europe edn), 31 July 1995, p. 41.
52 Roger Jellinek, personal communications with the author, 4 June and 9 October 1998.
53 Norman Polmar and Thomas B. Allen, *Rickover* (New York, Simon & Schuster, 1982), pp. 113–14; see also Gary Stix, 'Run Silent, Run (Not So) Cheap', *Scientific American*, October 1991, p. 14.
54 Michael S. and George S. Triantafyllou, 'An Efficient Swimming Machine', *Scientific American*, March 1995, pp. 40–8.
55 Mark Thompson, 'That Sinking Feeling', *Time* (Europe edn), 22 March 1999, pp. 46–7.
56 Marcia K. McNutt, 'Achievements in Marine Geology and Geophysics', in John Steele *et al.* (eds), *50 Years of Ocean Discovery* (Washington, DC, National Academy Press, 2000), p. 52.

4

The German and Anglo-American Race to Nuclear Armament

'We are in a completely new situation that cannot be resolved by war.'
Niels Bohr[1]

'The nuclear weapon was conceived by scientists,' summarizes French political scientist Pascal Boniface, 'given physical form [by them and] by engineers and technicians, and converted into a doctrine of use by strategists and politicians.'[2] How did this come about?

EARLY DETECTION OF RADIOACTIVITY

In December 1895, Wilhelm Roentgen, studying a fluorescing cathode-ray tube in Würzburg, Germany, discovered X-rays. The concept of radiating sources dates from three months later, when Antoine-Henri Becquerel of the Musée d'Histoire Naturelle in Paris stumbled on radioactivity. It was Maria Sklodowska-Curie of Poland who coined the term *radioactivité*, when she undertook her doctoral thesis in 1897, also in Paris, on the Becquerel phenomenon.[3] At the turn of the century Ernest Rutherford and Frederick Soddy in Britain developed the first theory of radioactivity. Then Vladimir Vernadsky, a mineralogist, told the Russian Academy of Sciences that, with the detection of radio-activity, 'new sources of atomic energy are opening up before us exceeding by millions of times all the sources of energy' envisaged by the human mind.[4]

The discovery of radioactivity in 1896 proved to be the initial step along a twisting road that would lead to R&D on nuclear weapons, the deliverers of 'death assured, an unthinkable reality'.[5] Some scientists were initially fascinated by the notion that the radiant activity of the atom could one day be controlled to both the advantage and the bane of humanity. Chemist George Pegram commented to the North Carolina Academy of Sciences (1911), 'Probably the most important problem before the physicist today is that of making the enormous energy [within the atom] available for the world's work.'

The following year Pegram invited Albert Einstein to lecture at Columbia University on relativity theory.[6] Einstein developed two major hypotheses, special relativity (1905), and general relativity (1915); in 1912 he was evidently in transit between the two. Niels Bohr, Werner Heisenberg, Erwin Schrödinger and such colleagues as Max Born and Wolfgang Pauli proceeded to elaborate quantum theory and quantum mechanics. These theories, together with quantum field theory, asserts Roger Penrose, were not 'independent of each other: general relativity was built on special relativity, and quantum field theory has special relativity and quantum theory as inputs'.[7]

Research on the electromagnetic phenomena manifested at the levels of the atom and its constituents broadened and deepened. During the 1920s Friedrich G. Houtermans in Germany and Robert Atkinson in Britain studied the production of energy in stars, and their joint paper on the subject incited studies in the 1930s of the carbon cycle in stars by Hans Bethe and Carl-Friederich von Weizsäcker.[8] German physicist Walter Bothe (described by Emilio Segrè as a 'physicist's physicist') and a student called Herbert Becker began examining the gamma rays produced by alpha-ray bombardment of light elements ranging from lithium and beryllium to aluminum, and of much heavier silver. They obtained radiation intensities almost ten times that of other elements investigated. Work on studying possible chain reactions remained for the future, as Bothe experimented with graphite (1940) and concluded that this substance absorbed too many neutrons to be able to sustain a chain reaction in natural uranium.[9]

After the surge in theoretical physics that marked the 1920s (with the efforts of Paul Dirac, James Jeans, Pauli, among others), the extent of the potential energy of atomic activity began to be suspected. The lithium atom was the first to be 'split', its nucleus bombarded with protons in a primitive accelerator built by students John Cockcroft and Ernest T. S. Walton at Cambridge University. The lithium nucleus was split into lighter particles – the helium isotopes, and protons and neutrons.

The energy balance (mass, plus energy before and after the collision) confirmed in the laboratory the Einsteinian equation, $E = mc^2$. In words, energy equals mass multiplied by the square of the speed of light. Cockcroft's and Walton's mentor, Lord Rutherford, described the phenomenon occurring in his students' jerry-built machine as 'a million volts in a soapbox'. Before he died in 1995, Walton voiced the hope that 'if an enlightened human race did not prevent the use of atomic discoveries in a war, a frightened [race] would':[10] psychological terrorism, in other words.

Einstein was quoted in 1934 by an American newspaper, expressing 'emphatic denial' of the notion that 'man might some day utilize the atom's energy'. The reporting journalist added his own interpretation: 'If you believe that man will someday be able to harness this boundless energy – to drive a great steamship across the ocean on a pint of water, for instance – then, according to Einstein, you are wrong.'[11] In the same year two Parisian researchers, Irène Curie (daughter of Maria Sklodowska and Pierre Curie) and her husband, Frédéric Joliot, announced that radioactivity could be induced in the laboratory.

So in a mere 40 years the world was introduced, step by sometimes highly publicized step, to the microcosm of natural and artificial radioactivity. The military were involved only when they showed up in science fiction's phantasmagoria.

COULD RADIOACTIVITY LEAD TO WEAPONS?

During the five years that followed, Lise Meitner, Otto Hahn and Fritz Strassmann experimented with uranium, challenged by bizarre results. It was only after Hahn and Strassmann separated a radioactive barium sample (using barium as a 'carrier' for radium) that Meitner and her nephew, Otto Frisch, were able to interpret the experiment in terms of Bohr's and John A. Wheeler's new liquid-drop model of the nucleus. Frisch dubbed this phenomenon *nuclear fission*, in analogy to cell fission in biology. Hahn and Strassmann published their analysis in *Die Naturwissenschaften* and *Nature* (January 1939), research results pointing strongly to the existence of fission of the atom's nucleus. At the instigation of Leo Szilard and Eugene Wigner, Einstein was prompted to sign a letter in the same year (August 1939), in which was communicated to President Franklin D. Roosevelt the suggestion that research on fission could lead to a powerful weapon.

Wolfgang Paul (not to be confused with the aforementioned Wolfgang Pauli), after obtaining a doctorate in physics and engineering in 1939, joined Hans Kopferman to work on particle physics. Competent physicists, in other words, were working on non-military physics in Germany during the 1930s, and the subdiscipline was of constantly widening scientific interest and was assuming inherently military implications. Yet thus far in Germany there was neither military sponsorship nor direct collaboration between the military world and this scientific domain. Although the work of Paul, Kopferman and their colleagues did not lead to the atomic bomb, Paul would later be awarded the Nobel Prize for physics in 1989.[12]

BOX 2 RUEFUL REGRETS IN RETROSPECT

Einstein would state, after the war, that the great mistake of his life was signing the text drafted by Leo Szilard and Eugene Wigner and sent to the American president. By 1957 Einstein would co-found the Pugwash Conferences on Science and World Affairs. 'Pugwash' is a major non-governmental organization dedicated to the elimi-nation of weapons of mass destruction. A young American sailor, almost in corroboration of Einstein and like-minded scientists, who entered Hiroshima several weeks after its bombing, declared that he 'felt jarred in the depth of my soul. I was witnessing the effects of a horror too terrible to imagine … The shock to my conscience registered permanently.'* The sailor became an American senator active in world affairs: Mark Hatfield of Oregon.

*Cited by Colman McCarthy, 'Let Us not Celebrate Einstein's "One Great Mistake"', *IHT*, 8 February 1995, p. 5.

The German *Heereswaffenamt* (Army Ordnance Bureau) neverthe-less became aware in April 1939 of the potential of nuclear fission, through physicists Paul Harteck in Hamburg and Kurt Diebner doing research on explosives at the Ordnance Bureau. Diebner showed Harteck's correspondence to Hans Geiger, 'who recommended pursuing the research. The War Office agreed',[13] decided to gather specialists to begin research on fission (September 1939), and for this work com-mandeered in October the Kaiser Wilhelm Institute for Physics in Berlin.

Thus, on the eve of the Second World War, there existed a fairly clear idea of the structure of the atom and of the energetic potential of its nucleus. It was accepted, for instance, that

- there are three basic constituents of the atom: proton, neutron and electron;
- the nucleus is composed of protons and neutrons and is surrounded by electrons – one negatively charged electron for each positively charged proton, so that
- the atom itself is electrically neutral;
- atoms emit, for each element, characteristic quantized radiation of many different frequencies – the most energetic being X–rays; and
- heavy nuclei spontaneously emit alpha particles (identical with helium nuclei), beta particles (identical with electrons) and gamma rays (particles similar to X–rays).

ENTER QUANTUM PHYSICS

Einstein's work on relativity theory had combined with the further understanding developed of quantum mechanics by Bohr and his Copenhagen school, the uncertainty principle advanced by Heisenberg, Dirac's mathematical hypotheses, and the later contributions of the 'Hungarian conspiracy' (as it became known in the United States): Szilard, Wigner, Edward Teller and John von Neumann, who all came from Budapest. The new theoretical work was enhanced mainly by the experiments of Enrico Fermi, Hahn and Strassmann, Frisch, Mark Oliphant at the University of Birmingham, and colleagues of the Rutherford school.[14] All this investigation gradually transformed itself into a firm mental grasp of how the atom's energy might one day be put to work.[15] Von Neumann's responsibility for the extensive mathematical calculations required to develop 'the bomb' led to his obsession with creating machines to do the work, thus helping stimulate the postwar computer industry.

Wigner, who died in 1995, was one of the first investigators to 'understand the complex actions of electrons … jumping from one quantum level to another … [He perceived] the deep symmetry involved in the balance of countervailing forces and particles, a perception that subsequently emerged as one of the guiding principles of 20th-century physics'.[16] He was able to apply mathematical group-theory to atomic spectra, and part of the scientific legacy of symmetry and order today includes 'Wigner energy', Wigner theorems, Wigner rule and Wigner crystals. A member of the faculty at Princeton University from 1930 to 1971 and winner of the Nobel Prize for Physics (1963) for his 'discovery and application of fundamental symmetry principles', the scientist contributed significantly to the advent of nuclear energy and the birth of the Bomb. Originally a chemical engineer, Wigner designed the production reactors at Hanford, Washington. It was because of his genius that the American plutonium project passed directly from laboratory to production without the usual intermediate stage of pilot plant.[17] Wigner was indeed 'a giant' of physics.[18]

Szilard's fascination with the potential of fission seems to have sprung, in part, from sources normally considered less rigorous than physics textbooks and laboratory experiments. Szilard and authors such as Richard Rhodes, I. F. Clarke, Warren Wagar and Bernard Cazes have linked the Hungarian's preoccupation with a moment (in 1932 or 1933) when Szilard read a German translation of either H. G. Wells' *The World Set Free* (1914) or *The Shape of Things to Come* (1932). Wells apparently had gleaned his ideas from an earlier popularization by the

British physicist Frederick Soddy, *Interpretation of Radium*. Szilard was impressed, too, by Harold Nicolson's *Public Faces*, political fiction involving an 'atomic bomb'.[19] All this could lead us beyond scientific reality, but the coincidences deserve mention.

A question arises: why was the new physics emerging largely from Germany? Is there perhaps a political parallel with the nascence of Marxism in the same country, and its failure to take hold there? One answer comes from the British popularizer of science and history, James Burke. In *The Day that Changed the Universe*, Burke remarks that

> Quantum physics ... developed in Weimar Germany in a social and intellectual environment that specifically encouraged a view of physics which did not naturally evolve [from] the previous physics structure. Quantum theory is to a great extent the child of Germany's military defeat [in the First World War].[20]

Some observers of the history of science may find this a *non sequitur* or perhaps irrelevant, yet Ruth Moore comments in *Niels Bohr: A Centenary Volume* that, in his political configuration, Bohr learned 'early that science cannot be separated from the world as it is'.[21]

THE PHYSICS OF WHOM?

After the Second World War there was a prolonged scientific debate, together with a security review, concerning the first public revelations of the discovery of atomic energy. And yet the rationale for the publication in *Die Naturwissenschaften*, under the editorship of Paul Rosbaud in 1939, and then in *Nature*, of the Hahn–Strassmann report was that an alert scientific editor in an established firm (Springer Verlag, Berlin) publishing *Die Naturwissenschaften* did nothing more than execute his work conscientiously.[22] (Natural, but rare, spontaneous fission occurs, it should be added, without benefit of external stimulus, as the result of the instability of heavy nuclei.)

Third Reich authorities in both the National Socialist government and the military soon put clamps on further publication of such material because of: (a) its relationship to Einsteinian and thus, in their minds, 'Jewish' physics – in opposition to traditional, pre-Einsteinian or 'German' physics deriving from the work of Newton, Maxwell, Planck, Poincaré, Mach and still others; and (b) its putative military applications both at home and by a possible adversary. Scientists and other intellectuals who could not accept such constraints joined the exodus from Hitler's Germany. Even Heisenberg considered emigration but, finally, overweening dedication to traditional German ideals seems to be what kept him at home.[23]

Concerned scientists in Britain, France and North America (Szilard, Fermi and Pegram foremost among them), aware of the atom's military potential, in effect conspired to withhold the publication of new results concerning uranium fission to prevent the information from reaching Nazi Germany. When the Soviet Union's Georgi Flerov sought in 1940 to have the American-based *Physical Review* publish his discovery of the *spontaneous* fission of uranium, for example, he evoked no reaction but silence.[24] (See Robert Oppenheimer's assessment, later in this chapter. In the following chapter there is more on Flerov's relations with Stalin.)

In the United States specifically, and as early as 1939 when Szilard and Wigner were composing the letter to Roosevelt, it was perhaps these two Hungarian-born researchers who were the most instrumental in agitating to keep from German eyes the growing knowledge outside Germany that emerged from experimental results on the atom's powerful potential.[25]

RAPPROCHEMENT BETWEEN PHYSICISTS AND THE MILITARY

In fairness to the combination of human effort involved in the 'Manhattan Engineer District' that culminated in the events on the United States' western desert (the Trinity test) and over Hiroshima and Nagasaki in July–August 1945, the first nuclear weapons were only in part American. Also involved were physicists, mathematicians and engineers from Great Britain, France, Italy, Canada, Denmark (Bohr and his Copenhagen school), Norway, Belgium and the Netherlands, together with still other countries – not to speak of the erudite expatriates from Germany and Austria.

The $2 billion cost of the main effort (something like $42 billion in 2002 values), together with the more than 100,000 technicians and laborers also involved, was paid by Washington. Because the Manhattan project did not evolve through the usual sequential stages – it could not, for reasons of urgency, political pressure and wartime secrecy – it is an early example of *concurrent engineering*: doing the conception and design, experiments and prototypes, delivering the quasi-finished product to the client-user in an all-in-one process that contravenes the customary orderliness of scientific engineering discussed in Chapter 3. In peacetime, on the contrary, concurrent engineering risks physical danger for the human beings involved, premature failure and prohibitive costs.

In a world that was moving science dramatically beyond the laboratory and classroom, the war of 1914–18 had begun to make clear to European leaders and military decision-makers how science-based technology could support the military effort. The American Congress and public experienced the first glimmerings of 'what a physicist was, made evident [by] the value of science to the development of technology, including especially military technology'. Official support and other financial aid to the institutions that are specific to the United States, as a consequence, were not long in coming. A sequel was that twice as many young students emerged as physicists in the United States between 1920 and 1932 (many of them finishing their studies in Europe) as during the six decades between 1860 and 1920. There were, in all, 2,500 physicists by 1932.[26]

An early contribution from research accomplished domestically by an American physicist, one that made it possible for the nuclear bomb to become reality less than a decade after his work, came from Alfred Nier of the University of Minnesota. Nier made some of the earliest studies on lead and uranium isotopes – helping science, in the process, to establish collaterally the first reliable estimates of the age of our planet. During a fellowship at Harvard University, 1936–38, Nier constructed a high-resolution mass spectrometer, an instrument invented earlier in Britain, enabling him to study isotopic structures. Mass spectrometers record, electrically, the mass-numbers of isotopes by passing streams of ions through electrical and magnetic fields that separate ions having different masses. Nier's spectroanalysis of lead and two principal isotopes of uranium, U-235 and U-238, would lead ultimately to development of the fission bomb.

There were no military subsidies to help finance studies of this kind in the 1930s, but Nier's work would implicate him later in the smooth operation of militarily financed gaseous-diffusion plants: devising portable mass-spectrometers to detect leaks in pipes and pumps.

THE HEAVY-WATER ROUTE

The first US military contact with nuclear fission came as early as March 1939 when Szilard prevailed on George Pegram to intervene with Charles Edison, under-secretary at the Navy Department. Edison not being available, Pegram was directed to an admiral named Stanford C. Hooper, a technical subordinate to the chief of naval operations. Nobel laureate Fermi, already a refugee in the United States, was elected to make a presentation before an *ad hoc* panel of army and navy representatives. Fermi's briefing did not, however, ring the necessary bells of operational plausibility with the military; he 'smelled condescension and cooled'.[27] The military, in Washington and elsewhere, would have to be 'sold'.

In September 1939, concurrently with the outbreak of war in Europe, Bohr and Wheeler published in *Physical Review* their all-inclusive theory of the fission of the nucleus, 'The Mechanism of Nuclear Fission'. This came immediately to the attention of German physicists gathered in Berlin for conferences on 16 and 26 September, with Heisenberg present at the second meeting. A significant outcome of these gatherings was the German government's decision to use heavy water as a moderator in any uranium-fission machine. The choice of costly heavy water, or deuterium oxide – its manufacture requiring much hydroelectric power – would prove to be one of the reasons why Nazi Germany did not achieve the construction of a reactor or realize atomic explosions. Deuterium, the heavy isotope of hydrogen, is virtually a non-absorber of neutrons.

Nine months later at the University of California at Berkeley, physicists Edwin McMillan and Philip Abelson showed that neutrons captured by U-238 are instrumental in the creation of 'transuranic' elements (those beyond uranium, the heaviest element occurring naturally), specifically neptunium and plutonium, or elements 93 and 94 on Mendeleyev's periodic table. By March 1941 the American physics community was able to confirm, essentially through the work of Glenn Seaborg and Emilio Segrè, that transuranic plutonium is fissionable and capable of being used as a weapon.[28]

Now that fission was a reality of nuclear physics, and knowing that neutrons were copiously emitted during fission, there remained only to calculate the quantity of uranium (or plutonium) needed to produce an explosive chain-reaction, the amount known as *critical mass*.

FIRST ESTIMATES OF DESTRUCTIVE POWER

The stage was set for an American decision to proceed with the elaboration of an atomic weapon. In June 1940, President Roosevelt created the National Defense Research Council (NDRC), later capped by the more powerful Office of Scientific Research and Development, (OSRD), naming at its head Vannevar Bush. Bush then brought in James B. Conant, president of Harvard and a chemist, as NDRC's chairman. As a young researcher during the First World War, holding a doctorate in engineering awarded jointly by Harvard and MIT, Bush had been involved in developing a magnetic detector of submarines – a hundred of which were built but never used against German U-boats.

BOX 3 HEAVY WATER AND GRAPHITE AS MODERATORS

A self-sustaining chain reaction using natural uranium and (natural) water as moderator is not possible. The hydrogen absorbs too
many neutrons.

There are two alternatives: using a less absorbing moderator, or
else uranium enriched in the fissioning isotope, U-235. Light nuclei
absorb fewer neutrons. Why *light*? The operator wants the moderating nucleus to carry away a substantial amount of the neutron's
energy in the elastic collision: if the moderating nucleus is too
heavy, the neutron simply bounces off. Less absorbing of neutrons
are carbon-12, oxygen-16, helium-4 and deuterium (really hydrogen 2). Deuterium oxide, or heavy water, is produced by electrolyz-
ing water. Norway and Canada have hydroelectric energy aplenty,
the latter using for power generation a heavy-water/natural uranium reactor known as CANDU.

Hyman Rickover's submarine reactor uses uranium enriched in
U-235 as fuel and pressurized water as both moderator and coolant.
The United States has much enriched uranium, and cost is a secondary consideration once the decision has been made to build
nuclear-powered submarines. Most American and French power
reactors are scaled-up models of the Rickover reactor. Britain has
built graphite-moderated, helium-cooled reactors. Alternative
designs have been proposed and a few experimental models built,
but the entry into industrial production of other designs will have
to await the 'second nuclear era', as Alvin Weinberg calls it.

Contributed by Berol Robinson, nuclear physicist

Bush would later recall[29] that this personal episode 'forced into my
mind pretty solidly the complete lack of proper liaison between the
military and civilian in the development of weapons in time of war'. The
creation of OSRD established fissile materials as part of the United
States' wartime arms menu, a potentially different weapon to be developed with the fullest imaginative and material capacities of the American
research and engineering communities, aided by foreign colleagues.

Francis Perrin, in Joliot-Curie's Paris laboratory, members of the
wartime scientific MAUD Committee[30] in London, and Arthur
Compton and George Kistiakowsky in the United States all studied
the question of critical mass. By the end of 1941, American specialists
had made notable progress. 'Compton calculated the critical mass of a
bomb heavily constrained in [a] tamper at no more than 3.4 kilograms;

Kistiakowsky debated whether a fission explosion would be as destructive in terms of energy produced as the explosion of an equivalently energetic mass of TNT'.[31] *Tamper* refers to a heavy, metallic substance (lead or even uranium) used to confine a chain reaction and to prevent the dispersion of the fission reaction, thus assuring a more powerful detonation.

The National Academy of Sciences in Washington, in a series of three closely held reports prepared in 1941, estimated that a kilogram of U-235 would produce an explosion of nearly 300 tonnes of TNT-equivalent (as contrasted with the MAUD Committee's earlier appraisal, six times greater). That was still vastly more than the detonating capacity of available explosives. The report noted, with concerned prescience, that the effects of radioactivity on living things 'may be as important as those of the explosion itself'.[32]

Thus were set the circumstances, goals and conditions for launching the largest and most intensive scientific-engineering project ever attempted. Its object was to create a weapon of previously unimagined force, and in this the program was an undisputed success. More than 50 years later (1998), the independent Brookings Institution in Washington released a report written by 11 scientists telling a story somewhat different from the publicly received version. Instead of the commonly accepted cost of $2 billion (in Second World War values), the Brookings specialists set a recalculated cost of $5,800 billion in 1996 dollars – a sum that amounts to a (weighted) figure 14 times that previously accepted. The report's authors questioned, furthermore, both the decision process used to create the huge nuclear arsenal and, in the subsequent geostrategic context, the faltering control of nuclear weapons once built, stored or deployed.[33]

The scientific knowledge necessary to accomplish this was systematically cultivated and reaped, and the full harvest would come with the brute engineering and massive technology devised by the Manhattan project, the nuclear weapons developed under the managerial supervision of the project's director, an army general of engineers named Leslie R. Groves (who had supervised completion of the Pentagon in the early 1940s – then the world's largest building), and under the scientific direction of J. Robert Oppenheimer.

This story – of how the atomic and hydrogen bombs were devised – is recounted magisterially by Richard Rhodes, Thomas Powers and several other chroniclers; and, in smaller increments, by the specialists involved – Oppenheimer himself, Robert Serber,[34] I. I. Rabi, Segrè, Frisch, Peierls, Abelson, Richard Feynman, Bertrand Goldschmidt, Arnold Kramish, Groves, Laura Fermi, and several dozen others.[35]

GOOD QUESTIONS, INADEQUATE REPLIES

We noted the role of Paul Rosbaud in selecting for publication, in *Die Naturwissenschaften* in 1939, the results of Hahn's and Strassman's research on the fission of the uranium atom. There were scientific precedents elsewhere in the research community for this editorial choice.

Nature of 22 April 1939 published the second of two papers signed by Frédéric Joliot, Hans von Halban and Lew Kowarski[36] on secondary neutrons emitted in uranium fission – meaning, in the words of the authors, that there were prospects for 'producing a chain of nuclear reactions'. Thus was born the concept of the chain reaction following neutron bombardment of a fissile nucleus. Word to this effect circulated quickly. We saw earlier that Diebner informed Hans Geiger (co-developer of the Geiger-Müller scintillation counter), who recommended – as we have already seen – that the German War Office commit itself to a study of the military possibilities implicit in the force of the nucleus.[37]

Just as promptly, the German government banned the export of uranium and established a supply of radium from the Joachimsthal mines in occupied Czechoslovakia, although the effort to build reactors and then to fabricate militarily usable explosives loomed as a costly challenge. The investment in reactors and weapons that might be needed forced the German military 'to ask questions that only scientists could answer: *how* expensive would they be? *how* long would they take?'[38] The same questions were raised by British and American officials, of course, the answers to which compelled President Roosevelt to proceed (autumn 1941) with the bomb project.

A week after the Joliot–von Halban–Kowarski report appeared in *Nature*, Bohr stated before an American Physical Society meeting in Washington that, according to a summary published by the *New York Times*,

> bombardment of a small amount of the pure isotope U-235 of uranium with slow neutron particles of atoms would start a 'chain reaction' or atomic explosion sufficiently great to blow up a laboratory and the surrounding country for many miles.[39]

By the time war broke out between Germany and Poland, the *Heereswaffenamt* organized a nuclear-physics investigating group at the Kaiser Wilhelm Institute, a research entity soon to be known as the *Uranverein* (Uranium Club).[40] Among the Club's charter members were Heisenberg and Carl-Friedrich von Weizsäcker. In a discussion in Leipzig between the two, Heisenberg told Weizsäcker that he was sure that Hitlerian Germany could not win the war. 'Hitler has a chess endgame with one castle less than the others', predicted Heisenberg, 'so he will lose'.[41]

AND STILL POOR ANSWERS

On 4 June 1942, a top-level meeting took place in Berlin among wartime Germany's managers concerned with industrial production, military logistics and scientific research. Key participants included Albert Speer, Hitler's favorite architect who had been assigned the economic portfolio after armaments and munitions minister Fritz Todt perished in an air accident. Also present were General Friedrich Fromm, responsible for the procurement of armaments; Generals Emil Leeb and Erich Schumann of the *Heereswaffenamt*; Marshal Erhard Milch of the *Luftwaffe*; two admirals; and about 20 research managers, including Heisenberg.

Speer and the military wanted to know how big an atomic bomb would be, and how soon they could expect it to become reality. To the first question Heisenberg replied, 'About as large as a pineapple.' To the second, according to Speer in his *Inside the Third Reich*, Heisenberg assured his interrogators that

> the scientific solution had already been found and that theoretically nothing stood in the way of building such a bomb. But the technical pre-requisites for production would take years to develop, two years at the earliest, even provided that the program was given maximum support.[42]

When Speer asked for an estimate of the cost of the needed infra-structure, Heisenberg cited the figure of 40,000 *Reichsmark*. Speer and the military interpreted this minuscule calculation as one that could come only from unrealistic, out-of-touch scientists. The bomb-research project was thus not able, then or later, to command top priority among wartime Germany's strategic and logistical directors, nor with Hitler himself – despite control over the program being transferred from army officers to the Reich Research Council. In late 1943 the program was placed under the management of Walter Gerlach, a physicist.[43]

Yet in the winter of 1942–43, Allied (especially British) military planners were deeply worried that German scientists were advancing in the development of an atomic bomb. Allied researchers knew that the Germans needed heavy water for their moderator in a reactor, and that Germany had only one source. Heavy water, as already defined cursorily, is D_2O: the hydrogen of mass 1 (^1H) is replaced in the water molecule, H_2O, by an atom of hydrogen of mass 2 (^2H), or deuterium (D). Besides its multiple uses in the laboratory, heavy water is used industrially for the sole purpose of moderating nuclear reactions because the deuterium nucleus absorbs very few neutrons when compared with hydrogen's nucleus. Oxygen also absorbs very little; its proton is a slightly more efficient moderator of neutrons than deuterium, but it gobbles the neutrons.

During the night of 27 February 1943, British forces parachuted a technically briefed Norwegian volunteer named Kurt Anders Haukelid, accompanied by a team of eight other commandos, in what was considered a suicide raid on the heavy-water plant at Rjukan in Norway's Telemark district. The Norwegians made their way furtively into the plant, blowing it up shortly after midnight. Daring as the mission was, no lives were lost[44] on either side, and the raid had little impact on the future of Germany's wartime atomic research. A later attempt to ship heavy water from Norway to Germany got no further than a Norwegian lake, where the ferry carrying numerous metal barrels of the substance was sent to the bottom (together with many innocent passengers) by another commando team sent by the Allies.

At roughly the same time as Speer's enquiry regarding costs, timing and size, British and American specialists were profiting fully from calculations made by German expatriate scientist (later Sir) Rudolph Peierls and his colleague, Otto Frisch. It was known that a nuclear explosion would require the assembly of much scarce uranium in order to permit the accumulation of critical mass. 'Much' meant something like 13 tonnes of uranium. But while working at Birmingham in 1940 Peierls and Frisch recomputed the quantity of the element needed and advised British military authorities. 'Not much more than a golf ball', Peirls decided. This estimate alone advanced the engineering perspective, making possible the detonation of the first nuclear weapons before the Second World War ended.

FAILURE AS QUANDARY

Ink in untold amounts has flowed since that war on why – and how – Nazi Germany did not develop an atomic weapon during the 12 years of the Third Reich. In November 1944, after Weiszäcker and other German academics had been established at the University of Strasbourg in occupied eastern France as a showcase of German education (the 'Reich University'), a military–scientific search mission co-headed by US Colonel Boris T. Pash and Dutch physicist Samuel A. Goudsmit looked for definitive indications in Strasbourg and elsewhere of nuclear progress by the Germans. Their group was known as the Alsos Scientific Intelligence Task Force, and its secondary purpose was to collect as many of the German scientists involved as possible.

Goudsmit and Pash found little in the way of evidence of progress. Goudsmit was thunderstruck, in fact, to learn that

> Weizsäcker worked only part-time on theoretical work for Heisenberg, that research was going on at many different laboratories with little coordination or even ordinary communication among them, and that nothing had proceeded beyond the experimental stage – as well as the many indications that 'energy production rather than an explosive is the principal German goal'.[45]

Boris Pash, Dr Goudsmit's military *alter ego* on the Alsos mission and whose personal mission was to find *all* the German atomic scientists (some of whom would fall into Soviet hands), does not offer an estimate of Heisenberg's research results in his published account. 'There remained [for later] the task,' he stated, 'of exploiting the Alsos wartime successes – work which fell to the scientists.'[46]

After the German capitulation, the British interned ten of the German researchers during the second half of 1945 in a country manor, Farm Hall, near Godmanchester. Unknown to the Germans, their quarters at Farm Hall were fitted with an electronic eavesdropping circuit, permitting their German-speaking British guardians to monitor their talk day and night. One of the custodians at Farm Hall was Major T. H. Rittner of the British Army. Rittner summarized part of a discussion in which Heisenberg, Walter Gerlach and Otto Hahn took part:

> Heisenberg stated that the people in Germany might say that [the German atomic-research team] should have forced the authorities to put the necessary means at their disposal and to release 100,000 men in order to make the bomb ... [H]e feels that if they had been in the same moral position as the Americans and had said to themselves that nothing mattered except that Hitler should win the war, they might have succeeded, whereas in fact [the German researchers] did not want him to win ... They [discussed] the feelings of the British and American scientists who had perfected the bomb and Heisenberg said he felt it was a different matter in their case as they considered Hitler a criminal.[47]

'What the Farm Hall transcripts show unmistakably', observes Thomas Powers, 'is that Heisenberg did not explain basic bomb physics to the man in charge of the German bomb program [Gerlach] until after the war was over.'[48]

Heisenberg, active in research and public life for three decades after his release from internment, addressed students at Göttingen University in July 1946. He spoke of the power that science can bring to human beings, 'a frightening aspect of our present-day existence'. Atomic and other superweapons confront 'the individual scientist [with] the necessity of deciding according to his own conscience ... whether a cause is good or even which of two causes is less bad'. The Nobelist reinforced his admonitions with a citation from Schiller, 'Woe to those who bestow the light of heaven on him who is forever blind; it sheds no light on him; it can but char and blacken lands and cities.'[49] And Schiller could not have foreseen the new terrorism of the twenty-first century.

INTELLECTUAL LOSS

What can be concluded about the efforts of Nazi Germany to realize a nuclear weapon? German-born Wolfgang Panofsky worked on the Trinity project at White Sands, New Mexico, in 1945 and then served as advisor on science and military strategy to Presidents Eisenhower, Kennedy and Carter. He was also director of the Stanford Linear Accelerator Center in Palo Alto, California. In reviewing Powers' book, *Heisenberg's War*, in 1993, Panofsky offered his own technical sketch as to why Germany had not proceeded beyond the pre-reactor stage:

> A nuclear reaction using natural uranium moderated by heavy water was begun, but fell far short of attaining a chain reaction. Isotope separation never left the laboratory. Work on a bomb was essentially nil ... Heisenberg said repeatedly that a nuclear reactor capable of producing power and therefore constituting a revolutionary source of energy could be built, but a nuclear weapon, even if possible, could never be built during the time that World War II was expected to last. Heisenberg ... knew that [plutonium-] 239 'bred' in a reactor was an alternative to isotopically pure U-235, difficult to separate, for raw material for a bomb.[50]

These remarks signify that wartime conditions were not conducive to the funds and painstaking R&D required. Panofsky might have added that German reliance on other super weapons – the V1 and V2, as we saw in Chapter 1 – by engineers, scientists and military-technical officers, and the incessant propaganda bluster of Hitler and Goebbels, were also contributing factors. The draining of Germany's and Austria's intellectual pool, including those tarred by the brush of 'Jewish' physics, was to contribute to the poor performance of atomic experimentation and engineering physics in the Third Reich.

MORE HOWS, OR MORE WHYS?

In a reminiscence imagined by British playwright Michael Frayn in his work *Copenhagen*, Niels Bohr wonders (in an encounter after their deaths) if Werner Heisenberg had envisaged using uranium to build weapons. Heisenberg replies in the affirmative. Bohr then expresses his horror to learn that Heisenberg arrogated to himself such a moral right.[51]

The *how and why* of the German scientists' performance level might be explained as follows.[52]

- When Bothe obtained the wrong 'cross-section' for carbon as a neutron absorber, this led the Germans to discard graphite as a relatively cheap and available moderator, in favor of the more costly heavy water not available in Germany.
- The German researchers limited their undertaking to the enrichment of uranium, for which they had adequate natural resources. Heisenberg failed to calculate accurately and estimate correctly the critical mass of uranium that would be needed.[53] He overestimated considerably.
- The German physicists failed, at the same time, to discover the relative virtues of plutonium because the chemical separation of elements is easier than the physical separation of isotopes.
- More abstractly, the German team seems to have been betrayed by inordinate self-confidence: if *we* cannot do it, then *no one else* can …
- On the scale of the national economy, the Third Reich did not have the necessary industrial base in view of the heavy calls made on war production for an army of more than 200 divisions, a hugely expanded submarine force and a persistently ailing air arm, and despite repeated propaganda promises of wonder weapons.
- The five major factors above combined to make Nazi Germany's adversaries, especially Britain and the United States, falsely appreciative of wartime Germany's R&D potential and her scientific-engineering capability to find a path requiring less brute force than nuclear arms – goading the Western Allies into a technical effort of colossal proportions.

An American theoretical physicist formerly associated with *Physical Review*, Jonothan Logan, also concludes that Heisenberg, as 'Germany's leading theorist', had come to an erroneous conclusion through faulty reasoning about whether an atomic weapon could be devised.[54] Friedwardt Winterberg, a German physicist who obtained his doctorate under Heisenberg in 1955, relates that 'little if any conversation about the German uranium project took place' in Heisenberg's institute after the war. 'I believe Heisenberg must have felt that Goudsmit's account of the German uranium project was not objective, in particular his downplaying Heisenberg's knowledge of bomb physics.'[55]

Another German physicist, Günter Herrmann at the University of Mainz, believes that Hahn and Strassmann were discouraged by the report published by the Americans McMillan and Abelson in *Physical Review* (1940) that the decay product, element 94 or plutonium, was not obtainable through experiment with element 93, neptunium; their wartime notebooks indicate that they did not even try.[56] Igor Fodor of Munich points out, furthermore, that the Americans bombed the uranium purification plant at Oranienburg near Berlin in March 1945 'to prevent the pure uranium stored there from falling into Soviet hands'.[57]

An additional point is that of the official fetters clamped on the scientific-technical community charged with exploiting the power of the atom. This applied both in Germany and among the Western Allies. For the first time on a large scale, scientific knowledge developed publicly was made an official secret to be protected by all its custodians. 'One of the things that worries us', confided Oppenheimer in a letter to Wolfgang Pauli (who was then in non-defense science at the Institute for Advanced Study in Princeton),

> is that none of the people in our field are publishing work in the *Physical Review* for the very good reason that they are not doing anything that can be published. It must be apparent to the enemy that we are finding good uses for our physicists and in some cases I think that this is in itself a piece of information on the nature of the work that we are doing.[58]

Security clearances were developed and imposed on far vaster technical communities than on those that had worked, for example, on submarines and ASDIC (from Anti-Submarine Detection Investigation Committee) during the First World War (see Chapter 3) or on radar at the beginning of the Second World War, as related in Chapter 10. 'What if a not dissimilar crisis arises in the future?' asks Daniel Patrick Moynihan. 'What if, this time, we opt for openness?'[59] The senator asked this question just before toxic sarin struck the Tokyo underground in 1995.

COUNTERACTING THE NUCLEAR THREAT

The nuclear heritage is diverse and complex, as well as disruptive and threatening. And, as in the domain of electronic warfare, nuclear 'measures' brought the anticipated 'countermeasures'. The most extensive of these was probably DEWS, the distant early-warning system, a $2 billion project approved during the presidency of Harry S. Truman (1949–52) to detect nuclear-headed missiles launched from the Soviet Union over the North Polar cap. Management of this system, a continental network of radar stations in the northern United States and Canada, was put in the hands of radiation physicist Albert G. Hill of the MIT's Lincoln Laboratory and it has functioned for many years.

There have been many results from the development of the bomb by the Western Allies, especially that coming directly from the Manhattan program and the weapon's practical engineering. Mass spectrometry, for example, which we have seen was already intro-duced in laboratories during the 1920s and 1930s, was perfected in wartime as a microanalytic technique – making possible analysis of even small quantities of isotope. Peierls and Frisch, working in Britain, estimated that a weapon powerful enough to obliterate an entire city could be made if U-235 could be separated as an isotope from U-238. Once isotope detection and separation improved, the production of massive quantities of separated isotopes for military and civil purposes became realizable. It was salient advances such as these that impelled the Manhattan project forward.

The techniques of mass spectrometry and kindred instrumentation, as refined by the Manhattan specialists, also made possible new studies in geochronology: work done by Harold C. Urey and others. One of Urey's students, G. J. Wasserburg, developed the accurate potassium-argon method as a tool used in archeological and paleon-tological dating[60] – a field having nothing to do with military needs. The method of using carbon-14 in archeological dating, devised by American chemist Willard F. Libby, is another spin-off: a technique that is valid for estimations reaching as far back as 30–50,000 years ago.

The American nuclear barrier may have been penetrated by espionage a second time, perhaps in the 1980s, when China may have gained access to computer data used to model the reliability of weapon design. Such modeling is used in place of real tests. The Americans and the French have resorted for decades to computer-simulated testing of nuclear 'explosions'.[61] In 1999, the US Department of Energy, responsible for classified work done at the Los Alamos, Lawrence Livermore and Sandia laboratories, closed down the computer networks linking these research centers and sent thousands of scientists and other specialists 'back to school' for a week to polish their computer security. When the Lawrence Livermore, incidentally, declassified in 1994 much of the laser technology it had used in the elaboration of nuclear arms, the lab began applying this same technology to cosmology. One of its ongoing astrophysical analyses is trying to understand star formation in the M16 or Eagle nebula, 7,000 light years from Earth: again, dual use.

In late April 1999 the United States' Director of Central Intelligence issued a statement on damage assessment in which he declared, 'We do not know whether any weapon-design documentation or blueprints were acquired'[62] by China. A laboratory head at Los Alamos, John Browne, expressed the usual paradox of security versus research effectiveness when he stated, 'We have to look at threats to information security from a risk–benefit standpoint', and then apply new procedures 'that make sense. We can't raise the bar so high that we can't get any work done. That affects national security, too.'[63]

When carbon-14 is used in place of other carbon atoms in the production and use of certain organic compounds, a powerful tool is present for the study of reactions in organic chemistry and biochemistry. The irradiation of food products – still not wholly accepted today because of public apprehension concerning anything bearing the label *radiated* – is another area that gained momentum from the studies of nuclear and particle physics advanced by the bomb's development.

Skepticism or outright rejection of radiation by the public has not been encountered, however, in the widespread irradiation today of surgical supplies (nor in the testing of anthrax-sprinkled mail). The patient never 'sees' or ingests such radiation. Nuclear *magnetic-resonance imaging*, too, is now a powerful diagnostic tool; but instead of NMRI, its designation was made acceptable to public opinion by de-emphasis of the first word in the terminology. The technique is called, simply, MRI, and many of us have been so scanned.

Other medical uses of radioisotopes in diagnosis and therapy have made it possible, for instance, to use a small dose of radio-iodine, administered orally, to measure thyroidal function or to diagnose its malfunction. A larger dose can be administered orally to destroy an enlarged thyroid gland, thus sparing the patient danger and discomfort and the expense of invasive surgery.

SOME APPRAISAL TECHNIQUES EMERGE

When scientists at Los Alamos faced the challenge of measuring how neutrons travel through materials of different kinds, mathematicians among them developed a model using simulations based on a series of random 'sample points'. The same technique was applied to study the rushing of rarefied air past high-flying experimental aircraft and, later, to modeling the aerodynamic flow experienced by space shuttles re-entering the atmosphere. Called Monte Carlo, the method found application in a domain distant from blackboards and laboratory benches, chain reactions and nuclear detonations: financial management, in order to establish the values of securities derivatives such as options. Somewhat slow, Monte Carlo was used nevertheless for this purpose over a period of 50 years. It was eventually supplanted, in part at least, by the Paskov-Traub 'faster valuation' method announced by the *Journal of Portfolio Management* in 1995. The spin-offs from military research can be curious.

Future uses of simulation include application of the American-conceived Caliope program, the R&D for which was developed by five different nuclear-research centers. Caliope stands for *c*hemical *a*nalysis by *l*aser *i*nterrogation *o*f *p*roliferation *e*ffluent. It makes possible the detection of chemical emissions as certain gases escape from uranium-enrichment or plutonium-processing operations on an adversary's territory.[64] In the first decade of the new century the Pentagon is studying the feasibility of low-yield nuclear weapons equipped with nose cones to attack underground command centers, with their attendant environmental risks – enabling the United States at the same time to reduce its stockpile of more potent warheads.

NOTES

1 Quoted by J. Rud Nielsen, writing in *Physics Today*, October 1963.
2 From an address given before the French section, Pugwash Conference on Science and World Affairs, 6 April 1994.
3 Maria (Marie) Sklodowska-Curie was the first woman scientist to win the Nobel Prize (1903).
4 David Holloway, *Stalin and the Bomb: The Soviet Union and Atomic Energy 1939–1956* (New Haven CT and London, Yale University Press, 1994), p. 29.
5 Philippe Delmas, *Le bel avenir de la guerre* (The Rosy Future of War) (Paris, Gallimard, 1995), p. 19 and *passim*.
6 Lee Anna Embry, 'George Braxton Pegram', *Biographical Memoirs of the National Academy of Sciences*, 41, (1970), p. 357, as cited in Richard Rhodes, *The Making of the Atomic Bomb* (New York, Simon & Schuster, 1986), pp. 293–4.
7 Stephen W. Hawking and Roger Penrose, 'The Nature of Space and Time',

Scientific American, July 1996, p. 46. The special theory of relativity holds that if two systems are in motion relative to one another, nothing can be determined about their motion except that it is *relative*. The general theory extends the special theory, dealing with (*a*) frames of reference that are accelerated instead of inertial and (*b*) gravitation. In quantum theory, radiant energy is transmitted in the form of *quanta* (discrete units). Quantum field theory hypothesizes that fundamental forces or *fields* are quantized, i.e. transmitted by quanta.

8 Thomas Powers, *Heisenberg's War: The Secret History of the German Bomb* (New York, Alfred A. Knopf, 1993), pp. 17, 84.

9 Rhodes, *The Making of the Atomic Bomb*, p. 159.

10 'Milestones', *Time* (Europe edn), 10 July 1995, p. 10.

11 Page 1 article (unsigned) in the *Pittsburgh Post-Gazette*, 29 December 1934, with the title, 'Atomic Energy Hope is Spiked by Einstein'; reproduced in *Scientific American*, June 1994, p. 88.

12 Obituary notice on Wolfgang Paul from the New York Times Service, *IHT*, 9 December 1993, p. 3.

13 Rhodes, *The Making of the Atomic Bomb*, p. 296.

14 'Others' included such scientific personalities as Hans Bethe, Robert Oppenheimer, Rudolph Peierls, Léon Rosenfeld and John Wheeler.

15 Rhodes, *The Making of the Atomic Bomb, passim*; Jeremy Bernstein, *Hitler's Uranium Club: The Secret Recordings at Farm Hall* (New York, American Institute of Physics, 1996), *passim*; Powers, *Heisenberg's War, passim*.

16 William J. Broad, 'Eugene P. Wigner Dies at 92, Key Figure in Nuclear Physics', *IHT*, 5 January 1995, p. 5.

17 A French science critic maintains that American success in developing the atomic bomb quickly was because the work was in the hands of engineers (mainly from DuPont), whereas development of Soviet superweapons was managed almost exclusively by scientists. Pap N'Diaye, 'Les ingénieurs oubliés de la bombe', *La Recherche*, February 1998, pp. 82–7.

18 Robert L. Park, *What's News* (American Physical Society), 6 January 1995.

19 Szilard, 1898–1964, studied electrical engineering and physics. 'He was imaginative, volatile and immodest … In 1934 he had taken the earliest patent on nuclear reactions, covering in general terms the use of neutrons in a chain reaction to generate energy, or an explosion.' D. I. J. and M. Millar, *The Cambridge Dictionary of Scientists* (Cambridge, Cambridge University Press, 1996), p. 309.

20 James Burke, *The Day the Universe Changed* (Boston, MA, and New York, Little, Brown/Back Bay, 1975, 1995), p. 333.

21 Ruth Moore, 'Niels Bohr as a Political Figure', in A. P. French and P. J. Kennedy (eds), *Niels Bohr: A Centenary Volume* (Cambridge, MA, and London, Harvard University Press, 1985), p. 253.

22 The rationale is summarized, perhaps in hyperbole, by Robert Jungk on p. 63 of his *Brighter than a Thousand Suns: A Personal History of the Atomic Scientists*, trans. James Cleugh (New York, Harcourt Brace, 1958).

23 Heisenberg's motives are contested, years after his death. The author prefers to accord the benefit of doubt to this outstanding physicist, following the reasoning developed further along in this chapter.

24 Berol Robinson, an American nuclear physicist, stresses this aspect of the story in private communications with the author, 11 April 1995, 18, 19, 24 August 1996 and 2 February 1997. Robinson believes that this episode was 'a conspiracy of silence, one which the Joliot-Curies, for example, refused to join.'

Flerov sniffed out the importance of fission in a Sherlock Holmesian manner. ("What was so peculiar about what the dog did at night? The dog did *not* bark.") Flerov noted that reports on fission suddenly ceased to appear in *Physical Review* towards mid-1940.' See also Rhodes, *The Making of the Atomic Bomb*, p. 501, and Rhodes, *Dark Sun: The Making of the Hydrogen Bomb* (New York, Simon & Schuster, 1995), pp. 60–1.

25 Rhodes, *The Making of the Atomic Bomb, passim*, esp. chapters 9 and 10.

26 Ibid., p. 142.

27 Ibid., pp. 293, 297.

28 Bernstein, *Hitler's Uranium Club.*, p. xxvii; Rhodes, *The Making of the Atomic Bomb*, pp. 352–4.

29 Vannevar Bush, *Pieces of the Action* (New York, William Morrow, 1970), p. 74.

30 Created in 1940, housed within the Ministry of Aircraft Production, to determine the practicability of a fission bomb using uranium.

31 Rhodes, *The Making of the Atomic Bomb*, p. 387.

32 Ibid., p. 386.

33 Brookings Institution, *Atomic Audit: The Costs and Consequences of US Nuclear Weapons* (report), (Washington DC, 30 June 1998); Irwin Goodwin of *Physics Today*,'Une victoire à 5,800 billion de dollars' (A 5.8 Trillion Dollar Victory), *La Recherche*, December 1998, pp. 42–5.

34 Serber, five years Oppenheimer's junior, served as the latter's first scientific officer and coordinated the research of physicists, mathematicians and ordnance officers. His and Oppenheimer's acquaintance with the United States' political far left, including members of the Communist Party, ultimately cost them their security clearances. Serber maintained, until his death at the age of 88, that he had neither regret nor remorse about his work on the bomb and its use against the Japanese.

35 After the war at a meeting called by UNESCO in 1950, Rabi proposed setting up a research center permitting European physicists to catch up with American scientists. Result: the creation in 1954 at Geneva of CERN, the European Laboratory for Particle Research – then as now devoted exclusively to civil research.

36 In postwar Europe, Kowarski (a French citizen of Russian birth) eventually headed CERN.

37 Rhodes, *The Making of the Atomic Bomb*, p. 296.

38 Ibid., p. 117.

39 Ibid., p. 297.

40 At various times during the early years of the Second World War, the Germans, Americans and British used dissimulations for their bomb-development units: respectively, *Uranverein*, Uranium Committee, TubeAlloys Ltd, and Manhattan District. TubeAlloys, through its affiliation with the umbrella Non-Ferrous Metals Research Association, was prey to the longest-served KGB foreign agent: Melita Norwood (born 1912), who spied for Moscow from the 1940s to the 1980s; see Michael Binyon's reports on the revelations made by ex-KGB archivist Vasiliy N. Mitrokin, *The Times*, 11, 13 September 1999, and later editions.

41 Weiszäcker, in an interview in 1988 with Powers, *Heisenberg's War*, p. 19, n. 24. See also David Cassidy, *Uncertainty* (New York, W. H. Freeman, 1992), who adds that 'the Nazi leaders hoped to use the secret of nuclear fission as a bargaining chip in negotiating a conditional surrender with the Allies' (p. 495).

42 Powers, *Heisenberg's War*, pp. 146–7.

43 Physicist/journalist Jeremy Bernstein states that Gerlach was 'senior physicist and chief administrator of German fission research beginning in 1944', *Hitler's Uranium Club*, p. 55.

44 Obituary of Haukelid prepared by the Associated Press, *IHT*, 12 March 1994, p. 5.

45 Powers, *Heisenberg's War*, p. 430. Bernstein, *Hitler's Uranium Club*, makes the point repeatedly that Weizsäcker in his intercepted conversations at Farm Hall seemed to champion the notion that 'We could have done it, we knew how to do it, but we didn't do it on principle', p. 129 and *passim*.

46 Boris T. Pash, *The Alsos Mission* (New York, Award, 1969), p. 248.

47 Bernstein reports this in *Hitler's Uranium Club* and it is also cited in Powers, *Heisenberg's War*, p. 443.

48 Powers, *Heisenberg's War*, p. 451; Bernstein, in his later book, *Hitler's Uranium Club*, makes the same point repeatedly.

49 Powers, *Heisenberg's War*, p. 475.

50 Wolfgang Panofsky, 'Uncertainty over Heisenberg: Hero or Pragmatist?' (book review), *IEEE Spectrum*, October 1993, p. 11.

51 Michael Frayn, *Copenhagen*, a two-act play first performed at the Royal National (Cottlesloe) Theatre, London, 1998–99, directed by Michael Blakemore. The passage cited is from Act One. The book was published by Methuen Drama, London, 1998; see pp. 36–7.

52 In formulating this recapitulation, the author is indebted to Berol Robinson, as the present chapter underwent much redrafting.

53 Paul Lawrence Rose reviewed critically the entire Heisenberg process in his *Heisenberg and the Nazi Atomic Bomb Project: A Study in German Culture* (Berkeley, CA, University of California Press, 1998).

54 Jonothan Logan, 'Critical Mass', *American Scientist*, May–June 1996.

55 Letter to editor, *Physics Today*, January 1996, pp. 11–13.

56 Ibid., pp. 13–14.

57 Ibid., pp. 14–15.

58 In a letter from Los Alamos dated 20 May 1943, reproduced in *The Sciences*, March–April 1980, p. 12.

59 The then United States senator from New York and chairman of the Commission on Protecting and Reducing Government Secrecy asked this question in the *Washington Post*, published 26 January 1995 in *IHT*, p. 8.

60 Frank Press and Raymond Siever, *Earth* (San Francisco, W.H. Freeman, 2nd edn, 1978), p. 45.

61 Since 1992 the United States has conducted no full-scale testing of nuclear devices, using instead simulations and partial testing. In autumn 1999 the media reported that the 'Oboe' test inside solid rock under Nevada's desert used chemicals to detonate a medallion-sized sample of plutonium. Purpose: to ensure the reliability and safety of the nuclear arsenal as a whole. Such tests do not violate the Comprehensive Test Ban Treaty.

62 As cited in *What's New* (American Physical Society), 23 April 1999, paragraph 3.

63 James Risen, 'US Halts Nuclear Lab Computers', *IHT*, 8 April 1999, p. 3.

64 Described by, *inter alia*, François Géré, in *Demain, la guerre: Une visite guidée* (A Guided Tour to the War of Tomorrow) (Paris, Calmann-Lévy, 1997), p. 221.

5

Russia and Other Powers Hurry to Catch up with the Nucleus

'… the Hungarian-born mathematician John von Neumann advocated that the bomb should be used to knock out the Soviet Union before the Russians developed their own. Fortunately, compassion prevailed over this cold reason, which would not have shrunk from killing millions for the crime of living under the wrong regime.'

Max Perutz, in *Is Science Necessary?*[1]

A NEW COUNTRY NEEDS SCIENCE

Shortly after the Bolshevik *coup d'état* against the Mensheviks in 1917, the new Soviet leadership quickly understood that the scientific community was a force to be nurtured politically and materially. Lenin grasped that science and technology were essential to economic development – and defense. The new government took every care to make the best use of scientists and technologists.

Russian science did its first work in radioactivity at this time, the winter of 1917–18. Two years later rumors flew between Petrograd (today's St Petersburg), Moscow and London crediting Dmitri S. Rozhdestvensky with sensational work. *The Nation* of London reported on 20 November 1920 that Rozhdestvensky 'had at last discovered the whole secret of atomic energy. If that were true', added the magazine, 'the man who held the secret could smile at our labours to extract coal and harness waterfalls'.

During the 1930s research at atomic and nuclear levels was conducted by Vladimir Vernadsky, Sergei Vavilov, Iakov Frenkel, Boris Vannikov, Petr Kapitza, Igor Tamm and Nikolay Dollelzhal – all born in the nineteenth century. To their work would be added the findings of Anatoly Aleksandrov, Georgi Flerov, Vladimir Fok, Yuli Khariton, Izaak Kikoin, Vyacheslav Malyshev, Lev Landau, Igor B. Zeldovich, Andrei Sakharov and Igor Kurchatov: all born in the twentieth century. In the 1940s, Kurchatov would be named, by Stalin and Lavrenti Beria, overall scientific manager of the nuclear-bomb enterprise. He held this post until his death in 1960, by which time the Soviet Union was firmly established as one of the world's two nuclear superpowers.

But there remained a distance to be traveled, scientifically speaking, before speculation, theory and experiment could become fact. Political purges in the 1930s, decapitating the armed forces and some of the Communist Party's own leadership, also deprived the upper scientific ranks of some of the best thinkers. As a consequence much of the creative and innovative power of the Soviet Union was immobilized. And yet, recalls Roald Sagdeev, 'the basic symbiosis between the military and science was established long before' the Second World War. 'In our history we had been taught to admire and praise military commanders. The bright young commanders of the Red Army, like Mikhail Tukhachevsky, were applauded as being men of vision … who promoted military-industrial innovations.'[2]

The launching of Operation *Barbarossa* against the Soviet Union, 22 June 1941, would make an extreme call upon the new nation's resilience, vision and stunted capacity for innovative work.

A NEW COUNTRY'S DEFENSE NEEDS

Barbarossa struck the Soviet leadership like a thunderbolt, from Stalin (who suffered a fortnight's nervous breakdown) downwards and in expanding circles throughout the USSR's power-and-prestige apparatus. On 22 June the presidium of the Academy of Sciences met in emergency session, several of its chemist members proposing that new measures were needed to bring scientists into the war effort. Stalin rallied and created the State Defense Committee on 30 June, with himself as chairman and Vyacheslav M. Molotov his deputy. In July the government decreed the formation of the Scientific-Technical Council, headed by Sergei V. Kaftanov. The Council's mission was to organize wartime research and evaluate all scientific and engineering proposals submitted.

An exodus of personnel and facilities began, evacuating critical establishments from Moscow, Leningrad and Kharkov. The Physics Institute, the Institute of Chemical Physics and other Academy of Sciences laboratories were moved to Kazan. The Ukrainian Physicotechnical Institute was shifted from Kharkov to Ufa and Alma Ata. Research on nuclear energy was not a priority, however, during the Great Patriotic War against Germany. Only the Potsdam conference of July 1945 and the immediately ensuing attacks on Hiroshima and Nagasaki confirmed to Stalin, whose spies had already reported on the progress made in the United States, the real potential of the new weapon and its strategic reach.[3]

Wartime training for promising young physicists got under way. A typical student at the Leningrad Polytechnic Institute, Yuri V. Novozhilov, was one of an entire class evacuated in 1942 from his besieged birthplace to Tashkent. There he continued his studies in aerodynamics and hydrodynamics. He earned his first university degree in 1945, anticipating doctoral work to be applied in industrial-aviation design.

'When the first atomic bomb exploded', recalls Novozhilov,

> two colleagues and I were put in experimental work called 'nuclear physics.' The courses were not very good and, instead of spending three years on doctoral work, we spent six months. Luck was with me, however: five of us were selected to study under Yakov I. Frenkel. My dissertation was on nuclear dipole resonance. Then, with our advanced degrees, members of our group were distributed to Arzamas-16 [see below], Leningrad where I returned, and the Kharkov Physicotechnical Institute. We were all sponsored by the State Committee for the Peaceful Applications of Nuclear Energy.
>
> I then went to the Institute of Electrophysical Apparatus in Leningrad, where all the Soviet reactors were built, as the theoretician concerned with how to separate uranium isotopes. In more than a year there, I was put to work on plasma physics and strong magnetic fields. By then, 1949, I was able to begin serious, advanced theoretical physics under Vladimir I. Fok.[4]

In addition to continuing his investigations, Novozhilov taught and became full professor at the University of Leningrad.

Later, Novozhilov served the UN's main scientific arm in Paris (he speaks English, French and German), returning to Leningrad. Today professor emeritus, Novozhilov still works part-time at the renamed University of St Petersburg, and he is vice-president of the Euro-Russian Society of Physics.

Unsure management in the early years succeeded in finding its way into the scientifico-military development of the Soviet bomb. Unlike the United States, the USSR failed to keep an official chronicle of its atomic project – even of its principal episodes.[5] The Cold War's end and the disintegration of the Soviet Union made it possible, nevertheless, to learn many details of the development of Soviet fission and fusion weapons. In 1996 the Pentagon commissioned a 2,000-page history, prepared under the supervision of theoretical physicist Aleksandr Chernyshev. Chernyshev supervised the work of some 200 contributors who described 715 nuclear tests extending over 41 years of Soviet history. The United States' Defense Special Weapons Agency paid $288,501 for the chronicle.[6]

A CRITICAL WEAPON: THE ATOM BOMB

Yuli Khariton, who was deputy to the developer of the first Soviet atom bomb – Igor Kurchatov, scientific director of the program (1943–60) – made it uncontestably clear that this first nuclear arm was a copy of the one manufactured in the United States.[7]

Khariton obtained his doctorate under James Chadwick at Cambridge University in 1932. It was Chadwick who discovered, the same year, 'radiation' of uncharged particles of protonic mass, 'neutrons',[8] while at New York's Columbia University. Harold Urey discovered, also in 1932, hydrogen's heavy isotope, deuterium: the heavy water capable of slowing neutrons to help assure a chain reaction. Khariton worked with Kurchatov and did pioneering research with Yakov B. Zeldovich on nuclear chain-reactions. Khariton was decorated Hero of Socialist Labor three times; he was named a member of the Soviet Academy of Sciences in 1953, and joined the Communist Party in 1956.

Kurchatov was known as research manager of what the Soviets termed the 'uranium problem', that is, R&D director of the entire nuclear program. The project's administrative head during its early years was the aforementioned Beriya, in addition to his role of minister of the interior responsible for the secret police, border troops and espionage. Kurchatov's research locus was Laboratory No. 2, later called the Laboratory of Measuring Instruments (Soviet Academy of Sciences), and still later eponymously the Kurchatov Institute. Today this is simply the Russian Science Center–Kurchatov Institute.

Khariton 'headed the bomb group at Laboratory No. 2 during the war, and he became the scientific director of the first Soviet nuclear-weapons center at Sarov, 400 kilometers east of Moscow in 1946'. His position corresponded to that of J. Robert Oppenheimer.[9] To confuse us further, this center also was numbered KB-11 among the Soviet 'design bureaus' but called 'the Installation' by Andrei Sakharov in his recollections – and known to still others as Arzamas-16 (or farcically, 'Los Arzamos', according to both Novozhilov and Holloway).

Khariton directed this laboratory until 1992. KB-11 was first established (1946) at Sarov at the former St Serafim monastery. The Communists had closed this Orthodox abbey in 1927, but it served during the Second World War as a factory producing Katyusha projectiles for rocket artillery. In 1992 the installation was redesignated the Russian Experimental Physics Research Institute.

THE ROLE OF ESPIONAGE

We have alluded to the role of Stalin's spies in regard to nuclear weapons. A word is necessary about Klaus Fuchs, a German who went to work for the British atomic program and later joined one of the Manhattan project's research teams. Fuchs was identified by the British and American governments as a conscience-motivated, voluntary passer of secret scientific information to the USSR.[10] He was tried and convicted by Great Britain after the war and spent most of the 1950s in prison, before his release to the East Germans.

There was civil–military rivalry endemic among the Western powers in the Fuchs and analogous cases involving espionage or (as the Robert Oppenheimer situation evolved at the end of the war and immediately after) alleged indiscretion, that is, association with individuals suspected of disloyalty. The civil point of view, generally, was to work in the traditional environment of international openness that characterizes science. The military preferred secrecy, requiring their own administrative apparatus. In the USSR there were no options open to civil or military scientific workers: one either conformed or became a resident of the Gulag, or worse.

The Fuchs account does not end here. *The New York Times* summarized the technical significance of Fuchs' revelations in an article published after the German physicist's death in 1988. Citing assessments by Western nuclear experts, the paper concluded that Klaus Fuchs 'had learned almost nothing of how to make the hydrogen bomb from the atomic bomb'.[11] This may explain the East German regime's boldness in the mid-1980s when it sought to rehabilitate Fuchs in Western eyes by proposing that he publish an article in a United Nations periodical commemorating the development of particle physics and quantum theory. The author of this book was at the UN end (at Unesco, in Paris) of this link. Only foot-dragging at Unesco, glossed over with diplomatic niceties, avoided publication of Fuch's text.[12] The correspondence is stored in Unesco's archives.

Besides exploiting spies who happened to have been born in Germany, the Soviet Union also gained access to members of the German nuclear-research group itself at the end of the Second World War – despite the pre-emptive Allied operation mounted by Samuel Goudsmit and Boris Pash, mentioned in Chapter 4. One of the German military scientists captured by Soviet troops was Manfred von Ardenne, who had helped develop a cyclotron in Berlin's Kaiser Wilhelm laboratories. From 1945 until 1955 von Ardenne worked in a research center on the Black Sea, elaborating a process to split isotopes in order to yield uranium-235. U-235 proved to be crucial in the efforts of the USSR to make its first nuclear bomb. Von Ardenne, who never joined a Communist party, stated that the first bombs developed by the Soviet Union helped bring parity to the race between the two superpowers, 'our contribution to atomic peace'.[13]

Another category of German specialist working with the Soviet bomb effort was represented by Nikolaus Riehl, a half-Russian, half-German radiochemist who invented the fluorescent tube while working with the Osram lamp firm in the 1930s. Riehl spent part of the wartime years extracting and purifying uranium for the German atomic project. At the conflict's end, with Berlin smoldering in rubble and human remains, he was sought by the Soviets, found and taken to the Soviet city of Elektrostal to develop a similar activity for Soviet atomic piles.

Riehl spent ten years in the Soviet nuclear R&D environment, living comparatively comfortably in an otherwise penurious economy, even earning awards such as Hero of Socialist Labor and the Stalin Prize. With his work completed in 1955, he left for the German Democratic Republic, and then made his way to the West. The English-language version of his *Zehn Jahre im goldenen Käfig* (Ten Years in a Golden Cage) was co-written with the eminent American physicist Frederick Seitz and published in 1996 by the American Chemical Society.[14] Alexei Kojevnikov of the California Institute of Technology compares Riehl's reconstruction with Andrei Sakharov's *Memoirs* (1990) as perceptions of 'an insider's situation and perspectives' within the workings of the Soviet nuclear program.[15]

'TORMENT OF SECRECY'

The tripartite Yalta conference held in February 1945 prepared the ground for the exploitation of nuclear energy as a weapon for the next half-century. Churchill, Roosevelt and Stalin represented their countries at this meeting, although Stalin was still five months away from learning of the bomb through intergovernmental channels. Yalta officialized, in geopolitical terms, the division of Europe in two spheres of influence, partitioning the East from the West, and setting the geostrategic stage for the Cold War. After hostilities ended in September 1945, the emerging tension between eastern Europe and the West exacerbated the race between the new superpowers to equip themselves with a maximum of nuclear armament and the capacity to deliver it.[16]

In broad retrospect, it cannot be forgotten that the American and, later, British and French nuclear programs were born of the wartime fear that Nazi Germany might develop this type of super-armament first. This fright, added to the specter of conquest and occupation by the Third Reich and its allies, was real, imperiling – and energizing.

The British program grew from what can only be called a paranoid refusal by the United States to accept the United Kingdom as full partner in the atomic enterprise, a plausible consequence of the Fuchs episode. The French program emerged, once the war had ended, in part from France's humiliation by defeat in 1940 and partly from its postwar insistence on being an independent, self-sufficient military power. There is more, later in this chapter, on the French nuclear undertaking.

In 1945, the State Defense Committee in Moscow created a special group to oversee 'all work on the utilization of the intra-atomic energy of uranium'. Two days later a signal was sent to the military-intelligence chief stationed in Ottawa, Colonel Nikolai Zabotin, to 'take measures to organize acquisition of documentary materials on the atomic bomb'.[17] These measures Zabotin set about to undertake most conscientiously.[18] Although Stalin may not have been convinced of the political utility of possessing nuclear arms until after the Americans' first use of the devices over Honshu Island, he corrected his aim and in winter of 1945–46 gave the Soviet program first priority.[19]

The military-intelligence cipher clerk at the Soviet Embassy who later conveyed the Zabotin information to Canadian authorities gave birth to the 'Guzenko case', the first major revelation of wartime and postwar espionage by the USSR against its collaborators in the Second World War and the direct cause of a new guardedness towards the Soviet Union by these Allies. Although the British, American and Canadian governments decided during the conflict with Germany, Japan and Italy not to share atomic secrets with the Soviet Union, scientific information was thus collected surreptitiously by the USSR for military purposes.[20] The Communist Party in the United States, furthermore, through a member named Rudy Baker, succeeded in penetrating the guarded facility at Los Alamos where his agents purloined the 'blueprint' for the first fission bomb – the weapon later duplicated by the Soviets.[21]

This was the known genesis of the Soviet espionage effort to gain secrets from the West's incipient nuclear arsenal until July 1995, when Washington released the first of 2,200 deciphered texts of messages exchanged between Moscow and agents in the United States. These communications, and more released later, were monitored and 'cracked' between 1943 and 1980, and are known as the Venona intercepts. They made it clear to a small number of initiates that the Soviet Union had sufficiently covered the bomb effort in Los Alamos and elsewhere to be able to duplicate the R&D undertaken during the war in Britain, Canada and the USA.[22]

As early as 1946 a cryptanalyst of the US Army's Signal Intelligence Service, Meredith Gardner by name, deciphered a message intended for Moscow that bore the names of the principal researchers involved in the Manhattan project. In order to protect its sources, Washington chose to keep this knowledge to itself. The silence would not last long; in 1948 an American cipher clerk transmitted 'knowledge of the knowledge' to the Soviets – and he was not unmasked until two years later. This back-and-forth game set in motion what the British sociologist Edward Shils has called the torment of secrecy. '[A] culture of secrecy took hold within the [American] government. Some saw conspiracy everywhere.'[23]

Suppose that Washington officials had opted to play the game openly, telling the US public that 'we know that they know that we know', and so on. Daniel Patrick Moynihan, long concerned with the fullest disclosure possible of governmental activities, tried to answer this question in an editorial comment written for the *Washington Post*. 'It is just possible', wrote Senator Moynihan, 'that we Americans might learn something from the Venona files. Had they been published in 1950, we might have been spared the soft-on-communism charge that distorted our politics for decades [and] the anti-communist stance that was no less helpful.'[24]

FIRST TESTS …

The Americans under Roosevelt and Truman, with the aid of some friends from abroad, had taken three years and nine months, from October 1941 (the time of Roosevelt's decision to proceed) until the first test in the desert, to perfect the bomb. With the Great Patriotic War over, and despite the staggering damage to its population and industry, the USSR took on the nuclear challenge as the priority of priorities. The Soviet leadership was convinced that nuclear energy had a future in the country's capacity to generate electricity – as Lenin had foreseen for hydro power – as well as serve its armamentarium. The Soviets took four years, from August 1945 to August 1949, to build their first atomic device.

The initial Soviet testing took place at the Polygon site, 3,000km east of Moscow, not far from Semipalatinsk in today's Kazakhstan. The test device went off on 29 August 1949 and, because no precautions had been taken to warn local populations, contaminated much of the neighboring Altai region of Russia proper. See Chapter 11 for some of the long-term health implications of the first Soviet 'bomb'.

The first trial with a thermonuclear weapon, one whose nuclear charge fuses instead of fissioning, occurred in the Soviet Union in November 1955. The test was a success, but on the same evening – during a banquet headed by Artillery Marshal Mitrofan Nedelin – physicist Andrei Sakharov uncovered the basis for his later dissidence. In the American edition of his *Memoirs* (p. 41), Sakharov remarks that, although he had not been a soldier in the struggle against Germany during the Second World War, he regarded himself 'as a soldier in this new scientific war'.[25] His boss Kurchatov, Sakharov added, occasionally signed memoranda and letters, 'Soldier Kurchatov'. Yet even eyewitness Kurchatov stated to physicist Anatoly Aleksandrov, 'That was such a terrible sight! The weapon must never be allowed to be used.'[26]

It was Aleksandrov who designed the graphite-moderated reactor later made famous by the power-plant explosion in 1986 near Chernobyl. Western specialists long maintained that the model was unsafe. Chernobyl proved, according to fellow physicist Yevgeni Velikhov and former vice-president of the Soviet Academy of Sciences, to be 'Aleksandrov's greatest tragedy, for which he largely accepted … blame'.[27] Ten years after the accident, however, Russian authorities stated that only 32 lives had been claimed after the fire in Chernobyl's reactor No. 4. At the same time the Ukrainian environment minister, Yuri Kostenko, declared that the concrete sarcophagus covering the plant's No. 4 reactor was insufficient in the long run and that the site was unsafe without removal of the radioactive fuel.[28] A consortium of Western democracies, willing to pay $3 billion in order to close all of Chernobyl's reactors in 2000, balked at footing a bill of billions more to extract the nuclear fuel and build a second sarcophagus.

… LEAD TO A NEW WORLD AGENCY

Igor Vasiliyevich Kurchatov, gradually disillusioned by the genie that he and his scientists had released from their laboratories, believed that the Soviet style of official and scientific secrecy inhibited the betterment of the Soviet physics community as a whole. He found that he had a part to play, therefore, as an informed actor in the first 'thaw' of the Cold War. Kurchatov, the human being, was able to impress Soviet authorities of the truly vital role of his teacher, Abram Yoffe. The elderly scientist had trained half the Soviet Union's physicists in his 'school', yet his accomplishments were eclipsed through Stalinist repression in 1950. He was made a Hero of Socialist Labor only on his 75th birthday, in 1955.

At Kurchatov's instigation too, the Academy of Sciences approved and the Soviet Union hosted in July 1955 an international meeting in

Moscow on peaceful uses of atomic energy. This preceded by a few weeks a broader international assembly in Geneva on the same topic. Soviet scientists announced that the world's most potent particle accelerator would soon go on-line at Dubna. Their behavior in Moscow and then in Geneva left, according to Enrico Fermi's widow Laura, a favorable impression on colleagues visiting from the West.[29]

Six months later Kurchatov, as a member of the Communist Party's Central Committee, told the 20th Party Congress that the world's science community gave high marks to researchers and engineers in the USSR. Thanks to its physicists (and implicitly to Kurchatov himself), science and technology in the Soviet Union were on the road to inter-national reintegration after a hiatus of two decades of Stalinist repres-sion. In a follow-up meeting, East and West proposed the adoption of nuclear safeguards to be established and applied internationally.

Khrushchev decided to have the research director accompany him on a mission to the United Kingdom in 1956, where British authorities permitted Kurchatov to visit and speak at nuclear research centers such as Harwell. Kurchatov spoke of Soviet experiments designed to produce nuclear fusion in high-temperature discharges in deuterium gas. This openness was received appreciatively in London and Washington. It led, shortly after, to the creation of the International Atomic Energy Agency, with headquarters in Vienna.

THE NEW PRIORITY OR PRIORITIES

The analogy of thought, word and deed between Kurchatov and Oppenheimer – the American who came early to question the morality of the nuclear weapons that he helped make possible – does not elude us today. It is reminiscent of an exchange of comments during the Second World War between Niels Bohr and Frederick Lindemann, shortly after the former's exfiltration from Norway by the British. During a dinner held at London's Savoy Hotel, Lindemann asked Bohr if the bomb represented a 'practical proposition'. Bohr's reply was that the bomb was indeed practical, adding, 'That is not why I came over here. What I am concerned with is the political problem of what is going to happen afterwards.'[30]

Only now can we appreciate fully the precocity of Bohr's thinking. Richard Rhodes, who made a name for himself as the star layman among chroniclers of the warlike applications of nuclear fission and fusion, tallies the account towards the end of his *Dark Sun: The Making of the Hydrogen Bomb*: '[H]ow to release nuclear energy introduced a singularity into the human world – a deep, new reality, a region where the old rules of war no longer applied'.[31] Rhodes went further in a prominent magazine article that he published shortly after *Dark Sun.* 'The Cuban missile crisis finally taught the superpowers', he wrote, 'the lesson that nuclear war would be suicidal.'The United States did not win the Cold War, the'world had won. Science ... revealed a limit to total war.'[32]

This limit might be expressed in other terms, those of the impact of scientifically wrought tools of destruction compared with nature's aggression against the planet that all of us share. Alan R. Hildebrand of the Geological Survey of Canada has made a computation of awesome proportions. If all the nuclear weapons that existed at the end of the twentieth century, estimates Hildebrand, were to be exploded at once, the energy released would be some 10^{31} ergs.[33]Yet this would be approximately equivalent to 'only' 1/1000th of all the energy released 65 million years ago when an unknown celestial object collided with the Earth at Chicxulub,Yucatán, Mexico.The cosmic visitor is estimated to have had a diameter of 16km, have left a crater 175km wide, and may have caused the demise of the dinosaurs.

NEVER A PRIORITY: TOXIC POLLUTION

The push to make the Soviet Union a nuclear power was part of an overall effort, emphasizes Sergei P. Kapitza of Moscow's Institute for Physical Problems,'aimed primarily at making an atom bomb'.The son of Nobelist Petr L. Kapitza, who on more than one occasion from his base at the same institute dared to defy Stalin, the younger Kapitza adds that in his country the scientific-technical leadership had'an utter disregard for human life'. He notes, furthermore, that his country's nuclear industry was operated by 'able, determined and ruthless managers who did not take human life into account – insofar as such concerns did not serve their immediate task. The terrible mess [they] left is the painful legacy of those attitudes.'[34]

The Russian biologist Zhorez A. Medvedev states that the Soviet nuclear effort, from the mining of uranium ore to the finished products and services,'required the forced labor of millions of prisoners held in secret, special camps'. The lack of respect for human life underlay the difficulties encountered by the Soviet military and civil nuclear-energy programs from their inception. Political prisoners staffed entire 'design institutes' (R&D centers). The *sharashka* (prison design-bureau) came into existence during the Great Patriotic War, with specialists such as aircraft designer A. N. Tupolev actually in charge of the *sharashka* to which he was assigned as a prisoner. The dissident author

Solzhenitsyn, trained as a mathematician and having served on the front as an artillery captain, was assigned at the end of the war to a *sharashka* devoted to development of secure telecommunications. (He recounts the story, somewhat fictionalized, in *The First Circle*.) Yet even Solzhenitsyn was unaware that the 'Gulag archipelago' used prisoner-scientists and engineers to mine or create logistical facilities for, or even develop, weapons of mass destruction.

In addition to uranium and related mineral mining in the USSR, Soviet authorities also arranged for extraction in Czechoslovakia (1945–50), Saxony in eastern Germany, Poland, Bulgaria and the then Soviet-occupied province of Xinjiang in China.[35] By 1999, eight years after the putsch against Gorbachev, the situation had gone from best to worst, with scientific and maintenance staff at the Tomsk-7 installation, for example, in desperate straits. Vladimir Matusha, holding a doctorate in nuclear physics, told French television that he and his colleagues had not been paid in months. Matusha explained that he resisted offers to work abroad 'in order to stay here and be able to feed my family'.[36]

The 'terrible mess' mentioned by the younger Kapitza could easily have included, in terms of weapons deployed, a ready-made nuclear power – the world's third largest – when Ukraine won its divorce from the former Soviet Union.[37] The Yuzhmash plant, the largest nuclear-missile assembly point in the former USSR, was at Dnepropetrovsk, 400km southeast of Kiev. Nevertheless, by the end of 1994 American defense contractors were working side by side with local engineers to dismantle 130 nuclear-tipped SS-19 and 46 SS-24 surface-to-surface weapons (once bearing 1,800 warheads), and vaporizing their rocket fuel.

This work was paid for by the United States and undertaken by the Morrison-Knudsen Corporation, a job scheduled for completion a year later. One of the Ukrainian specialists involved, Gennadiy Shevchenko, commented, 'As an engineer, I feel sorrow. A lot of brains, a lot of ideas, a lot of life was put into this. Destroying this is like cutting your heart, [but] as a citizen I understand.'[38] Irony reinforced paradox: Ukraine's president, Leonid M. Kuchma, was one of the engineers who had helped assemble the Soviet bombs.

MEANWHILE, ELSEWHERE

At the end of the Second World War, Japan destroyed virtually every record of its effort to master the atom's nucleus for military purposes.

BOX 4 A TALE FROM THE MUSEUM OF NUCLEAR NIGHTMARES

A few weeks after the Soviet air force shot down a South Korean commercial airliner, a Boeing on KAL flight 007 in 1983, the watch officer at Serpukhov-15 south of Moscow was 44-year-old Stanislav Petrov. A lieutenant-colonel serving in the Soviet air-defense system, Petrov was head of the 'graveyard' shift on the morning of 26 September, monitoring early-warning instrumentation aboard Soviet surveillance satellites. One of the satellites suddenly sent a signal indicating that a missile attack was being launched from the United States. What to do, *what to do*?

Petrov, a veteran of the satellite-borne system since its inception a decade earlier, knew the drill. He immediately read his computer's assessment of the signal: not static, but an attack on the way. He relayed this in real time to the warning system's command post, whence the message went, via the general staff of the armed forces' *Krokus* system, straight to the Soviet leader, Yuri Andropov, for a decision on retaliation.

The basic signal multiplied itself, finally showing five Minuteman missiles en route to Soviet targets. Petrov revealed years later that he and his colleagues were 'in shock'. But Petrov guessed that even five missiles could not possibly be the 'massive', single-assault wave that Soviet doctrine anticipated, and recommended that the signals be construed as transmission errors. After a thorough investigation of the incident by security personnel, Petrov was neither blamed nor praised. He eventually retired, forgotten, as he told the *New York Times*. But Petrov knew the drill.

David Hoffman, 'When the Nuclear Alarms Went Off, He Guessed Right', *IHT*, 11 February 1999, p. 2.

During the conflict Suzuki Tatsusaburo (born 1912), building on basic research in physics done at Kyoto Imperial University, managed a team of 50 scientists and engineers dedicated to building an atomic bomb to be targeted mainly against Pacific airbases used by the United States. The Japanese researchers lacked, among other resources, sufficient electromagnetic capacity to ensure the utility of their investigations. Some investigators used their meager sugar rations to make uranium hexafluoride for the extraction of its uranium. The scientists were even visited by members of the Imperial family, who were briefed on the work and sought to invigorate a team working with resources reduced by the exigencies of war.[39]

Five decades later Suzuki recalled,

> No one ever contemplated how terrible it would be. Towards the end of
> … the war, some experts thought it would take us about 100 years to
> develop the bomb. I was of the opinion that, if we spent 100 times more
> in research efforts, we would have developed the bomb in one year.
> After seeing [the destruction at Hiroshima and Nagasaki], I am [now]
> of the firm opinion that atomic weapons should not have been used.[40]

His view is supported by physicist Nambu Yoichirô, and an American
colleague, Laurie M. Brown. Brown and Nambu emphasize that the
isolation in which Japanese scientists found themselves during the
Second World War did not prevent them from competing 'in originality
and importance' with their Western counterparts.[41] Their resolution
to try to stay at the forefront of theoretical physics kept physics
alive, leading after the war to three Nobel Prizes in the discipline:
Yûkawa Hideki in 1949, Tomonaga Shinichirô in 1965, and Leo Esaki
in 1973.

There has been consensus, at least among the major powers openly
holding title to the bomb – the United States, Great Britain, Russia,
France and China – that the nuclear weapon must retain a dissuasive
role. It is not to be considered, in other words, as the superweapon it was
likened to, following the razing of Hiroshima and Nagasaki. Believers in
this dissuasionist school, recalling that the world's experience with
nuclear bombs remains limited to the two assaults of August 1945,
reckon that today's and tomorrow's nuclear weapon has two purposes:
to protect one's homeland or the alliance to which it belongs, and to
maintain a stable situation in short-of-war circumstances.

On the eve of the twenty-first century the president of the Republic
of South Africa announced that his country *possessed* – but *renounced
further development of* – the nuclear weapon. Israel has the bomb.[42]
India has it, Pakistan has it. Was the emergence in 1998 of India and
Pakistan as declared nuclear powers, therefore, a factor in the new
clash between the two countries, the following year, over hegemony
in Kashmir? General V. P. Malik, the Indian Army's chief of staff,
declared that this possibility 'was far, far away … [W]e're a responsible
nation, and a responsible military force. We understand the thresholds.'[44]
The thresholds are hardly fantasies; in the winter of 2000–1 Pakistan
created its Nuclear Command and Control System.

Syria, Iraq, Libya and North Korea appear to possess what is
necessary to develop their own nuclear resources. Brazil may be doing
the same, as the 'nuclear club' grows in membership *de facto* if not

through recognition by international law. Will organized terrorism be in a similar position in the years to come?

We need to draw a distinction between the availability of warheads and their live testing – perhaps little more than a mitigation of reality. We need to draw a distinction between the availability of warheads and their live testing – perhaps little more than a mitigation of reality. Table 2 summarizes the record of known tests made by the five 'official' nuclear power during the first half-century of the superbomb's existence, until the controversial series of tests held by France during the prolonged experimental period of 1995–96.

Table 2:
Known Tests Completed by the Nuclear Powers*

United States	1,051**
USSR–Russia	715
France	192***
Great Britain	45
China	42

Notes:
*SIRPA, French Ministry of Defense, September 1995, as quoted in *La Lettre de Matignon*, 486, 15 September 1995.
**Until December 1993, of which 204 were subterranean and 204 were kept secret.
***Until 1966 there were 17 tests held in the Sahara Desert, of which 4 were atmospheric and 13 underground. In the Pacific Ocean there were 175 tests (134 underground and, until 1974, 41 atmospheric).

The French tally stands somewhat apart from that of the other allies of the Second World War, suffering as it did from both defeat and occupation and a lack of access to its own laboratories. The occupying Germans controlled France's research centers, including facilities in Strasbourg that were put at the disposal of Werner Heisenberg and his colleagues (Chapter 4).

France caught up, however, when testing grounds in southern Algeria became available after the war, and exploded its first weapons there. Later the French moved tests to territories in the Pacific Ocean, but encountered difficulty in developing explosions attaining some 20 million °C. This obstacle was overcome, and France began a long series of underwater and subterranean testing on its atolls – to the dismay of the nations of Oceania.

AFTER FRANCE, CHINA

When China was on the threshold of possessing the bomb during the 1960s, Charles de Gaulle served his final years as French president.

With China on the verge of becoming an atomic power, France was still not fully a nuclear power and would not be until August 1968. The era was a frustrating one for France's nuclear strategists and weapon designers, constrained as they were by a defense establishment more interested in the development of conventional weapons than super-arms. Various accounts of how France finally engineered its first hydrogen bomb have appeared since that time.

The most likely story appears to have been a calculated divulging of state secrets between countries during the British premiership of Harold Wilson. At that time the scientific counselor to the Ministry of Defence in London, Sir William Cook, may have been instructed by his prime minister to pass nuclear information – related to the amount of fissile materials the French were using in their H-bomb trials – to Paris, in exchange for a halt in French protests against Britain's effort to join the Common Market (today's European Union). So states an article from an authoritative source published three decades later.[44] The story is probably true.

China acquired the bomb in 1964, but until then the government of President Lyndon Johnson seriously considered bombing conventionally (and even with nuclear weapons) the Lop Nor test installation to deny the Chinese the hydrogen arm. Documents released by the Department of State 34 years later indicate that there was torment at the federal level over this issue. Despite a positive expression of feasibility registered by the Joint Chiefs of Staff on 14 December 1964, the cooler heads prevailed and nothing more came of the proposal.

Thirty-five years after China acquired nuclear capability, the American specialized laboratories (Los Alamos, Lawrence Livermore, Sandia) were exchanging safety data with China's Institute of Atomic Energy. The Americans' purpose was to help protect nuclear facilities and safeguard supplies of fissionable materials, and their agenda in 1999 included new monitoring controls on nuclear reactors and the tightening of export controls. The congressional General Accounting Office, together with the National Security Military Procurement Subcommittee of the House of Representatives, however, viewed the contacts with alarm: they feared a give-away program, insecurely protected on the American side.

Richard Garwin and Wolfgang Panofsky, prominent physicists, spoke out against a report by Congressman Christopher Cox on reputed attempts by China to obtain data concerning advanced weapons. Cox claimed that China obtained information concerning the United States' W-70 neutron bomb as well as design material for the Trident missile's W-88 warhead developed in the early 1970s for launching from submarines. 'The technical community knows that

China tested a neutron bomb in 1988', stated the two American scientists,

> but there is no indication that China ever deployed such a device … Despite the China scare that the Cox report produced, [it] provides no answer about whether the alleged thefts… will affect US national security. We believe that the answer to both these questions is 'no'.[45]

This incident in Chinese–US relations remains unnresolved.

ARE SUPERWEAPONS REALLY NEEDED?

Aspirations to acquire nuclear arms embrace both (a) the strategic type: easily capable of demolishing cities, destroying a system of national defense, or disabling an entire nation's economy and social organization; and (b) the tactical kind: the so-called 'battlefield' weapons destroying mainly military units, their equipment and supporting services.

The specter of strategic weapons is by now near-universal. Although the threat may seem less perilous in the case of tactical arms, how can one be sure of the demarked radius of a surface-to-surface or a surface-to-air delivery of a nuclear charge? Much as in the case of some poison gases, the effects of blast could prove variable, as functions of terrain and weather, and the later results of exposure to radiation of civil populations nearby could remain incalculable, as at Chernobyl in 1986.

Nikolay A. Dollezhal, mentioned earlier in this chapter, was once director of the USSR's All-Union Design, Planning and Scientific Research Institute of Chemical-Mechanical Engineering and, later, chief designer of the first plutonium-production reactors. He sought to rationalize the use of a nuclear weapon as follows:

- the bombing of Hiroshima was a 'repulsive act of cynical anti-humanism';
- making a superweapon does not equate with using it against peaceful, urban areas. Targets should be selected by political and military leaders, not by scientists;
- possession of the bomb does not mean that such weapons will be used. As in the case of chemical weapons, the dread of retaliation would prevent their use.[46]

The rationale is not, however, good enough. In speaking of the nuclear road ahead, the director-general of the UN's atomic-energy agency foresaw in 2001 four goals. First, 'accelerated progress towards nuclear disarmament'; second, 'in parallel, the development of an alternative system of collective security that does not depend on nuclear deterrence'; third, the need for 'universal adherence to the non-proliferation regime, with a credible international verification system … adequately financed and unequivocally supported by the Security Council', and finally, effective national and international methods 'for the physical protection of nuclear material and the combating of illicit trafficking'.[47]

Nuclear arms originated as the work of scientists and technologists, as we were reminded by Pascal Boniface of the University of Paris, at the beginning of Chapter 4. Boniface interprets the continued existence of nuclear weapons in the twenty-first century as 'tools of diplomacy and military strategy'.[48] Richard Garwin – the nuclear physicist, arms designer and peace activist already cited – is even more succinct. He sees the 'core function' of nuclear weapons in the new century as one 'to deter their use by others'.[49]

Confirmed data are not available on how organized terrorism might be proceeding with plans to use nuclear energy surreptitiously; one can only assume that those involved will take pages from the military book.

NOTES

1 Max Perutz, *Is Science Necessary? Essays on Science and Scientists* (New York, E. P. Dutton, 1989), p. 97.
2 Roald Z. Sagdeev, *The Making of a Soviet Scientist: My Adventures in Nuclear Fusion and Space from Stalin to Star Wars* (New York, John Wiley, 1994), p. 45.
3 See R. Louis Benson and Michael Warner (eds), *Venona: Soviet Espionage and the American Response 1939–1957* (Washington, DC, National Security Agency and Central Intelligence Agency, 1997); Joseph Albright and Marcia Kunstel, *Bombshell: The Secret Story of America's Unknown Atomic Spy Conspiracy* (New York, Random House/Times, 1997); Robert Chadwell Williams, *Klaus Fuchs: Atom Spy* (Cambridge, MA, Harvard University Press, 1987).
4 Russian physicist Yuri V. Novozhilov, private communications and meetings with the author, 1994.
5 Yuli Khariton and Yuri Smirnov, 'The Khariton Version', *Bulletin of Atomic Scientists*, May 1993, p. 20.
6 David Hoffman, 'Russians Wrote Atomic History for Pentagon', *Washington Post*, 27 October 1996, pp. A1, A31.
7 See, in part, David Holloway, 'Soviet Scientists Speak Out', *Bulletin of Atomic Scientists*, May 1993, pp. 18–19.
8 W.F. Bynum, E.J. Browne and Roy Porter (eds), *The History of Science* (London, Macmillan, 1985), p. 304.
9 Holloway, 'Soviet Scientists Speak Out', pp. 18–19. Vyacheslav M. Molotov

claims in his memoirs that the Soviet Union had been working on atomic-energy research since 1943. 'I was in charge of it', according to Albert Resis (ed.), *Molotov Remembers: Inside Kremlin Politics, Conversations with Felix Chuev* (Chicago IL, Ivan R. Dee, 1993), p. 56. On p. 341 of the same work Molotov states: [Beriya] 'was a good organizer, a good administrator ... Regarding the bomb, that was his responsibility.'

10 The Anglo-Soviet Treaty of 1942 specified, however, an agreement to share openly secret technology and related military data between the United Kingdom and the Soviet Union.

11 William J. Broad, 'The Soviet H-Bomb: Spy's Role Revised', *IHT*, 4 January 1990.

12 The issue of *Impact of Science on Society* in question was meant to mark the centenary of Niels Bohr's birth in 1885. This multilingual quarterly is now known, in book form, as the biennial *World Science Report.*

13 Associated Press, obituary, *IHT*, 28 May 1997, p. 4.

14 Nikolaus Riehl and Frederick Seitz, *Stalin's Captive: Nikolaus Riehl and the Soviet Race for the Bomb* (Washington, DC, American Chemical Society, 1996).

15 In a review of the Riehl volume published in *Physics Today*, April 1997, p. 66.

16 Excellent background is found in Jean Laloy, *Yalta: Hier, aujourd'hui, demain* (Yalta Yesterday, Today, Tomorrow) (Paris, Robert Laffont, 1988). Laloy was present, as a young French diplomat, at Yalta. See also Alan Bullock, *Hitler and Stalin: Parallel Lives* (London, HarperCollins, 1991), pp. 959–67.

17 Holloway, *Stalin and the Bomb* (New Haven, CT and London, Yale University Press, 1944), p. 129. The paragraphs following are based largely on Holloway's detailed reconstruction.

18 See Christopher Andrew and Oleg Gordievsky, *KGB: The Inside Story of Its Foreign Operations from Lenin to Gorbachev* (New York, HarperCollins, 1990), p. 317.

19 Holloway, *Stalin and the Bomb*, pp. 116–49.

20 The case of Igor Guzenko is covered copiously in the open literature.

21 Harvey Klehr, Earl Haynes and Fridrikh I. Firsov, *The Secret World of American Communism* (New Haven CT, Yale University Press, 1995), *passim.*

22 Analysis of the thousands of Venona intercepts is expected to continue well into the twenty-first century. See also Joseph Albright and Marcia Kunstel, *Bombshell*, cited in Note 3 above.

23 Edward A. Shils, *The Torment of Secrecy: The Background and Consequences of American Security Policy*, (Chicago IL, University of Chicago Press, 1956), as cited by Daniel P. Moynihan (see Note 24).

24 Daniel P. Moynihan, 'When a Far-Reaching Culture of Secrecy Took Over America', *IHT*, 26 July 1995, p. 8.

25 Published in New York by Knopf, 1990; cited in Holloway, *Stalin and the Bomb*, p. 206.

26 Holloway, *Stalin and the Bomb*, p. 317.

27 Associated Press, obituary, 'Advocate of Chernobyl Reactor Dies', *IHT*, 5 February 1994, p. 3. A slightly different interpretation is Roald Sagdeev, *The Making of a Soviet Scientist*, pp. 66, 285–8 and 292.

28 The Chernobyl cataclysm released a record 12×10^{18} becquerels (12 trillion international units of radioactivity): International Atomic Energy Agency, *Ten Years after Chernobyl: What Do We Really Know?* (Vienna, 1996), p. 7.

29 Confirmed by Roald Sagdeev, *The Making of a Soviet Scientist*, pp. 69–76, a credible 'inside' account of the performance of the Soviet scientific delegation.

30 Michael W. Perrin (British intelligence officer who was present) to historian David Irving, cited in Powers, *Heisenberg's War*, p. 244.

31 Richard Rhodes, *Dark Sun: The Making of the Hydrogen Bomb* (New York, Simon & Schuster, 1995), p. 587.
32 Richard Rhodes, 'The General [Curtis LeMay] and World War III', *New Yorker*, 19 June 1995, p. 59.
33 For those with secondary-school physics far behind, one erg equals the work done by a force producing an acceleration of 1 cm/sec/sec on a 1 gm mass.
34 Sergei P. Kapitza, 'Lessons of Chernobyl: The Cultural Causes of Meltdown', *Foreign Affairs*, 72, 3 (1993), pp. 7–11.
35 Holloway, *Stalin and the Bomb*, pp. 176–7.
36 Seen on French television channel TF1's evening news with Patrick Poivre d'Arvor, 8 p.m., 6 October 1998.
37 An extensive review of the atomic 'mess', based on Soviet archives, is Paul R. Josephson, *Red Atom: Russia's Nuclear Power Program from Stalin to Today* (New York, W. H. Freeman, 2000).
38 Jane Perlez, 'New Partners Jointly End Ukrainian Nuclear Era', *IHT*, 10 December 1994, one of a series reported by Ms Perlez on the subject.
39 Involvement of the Imperial family in Japan's war effort remains enigmatic. An American author, David Bergamini, claims in *Japan's Imperial Conspiracy* (New York, Morrow, 1971) that Tennô Heika (Emperor Hirohito) and other family members were directly engaged in strategic planning. One of the Imperial princes, Konoye Fumiyoshi, was adamantly *opposed* to the war, believed that Japan would lose, and repeatedly voiced his opinions. This claim is amplified in Herbert, P. Bix, *Hirohito and the Making of Modern Japan* (New York, HarperCollins, 2000).
40 Associated Press, 'Physicist Tells of Japan Bomb', *IHT*, 20 July 1995, p. 5.
41 Laurie M. Brown and Yoichirô Nambu, 'Physicists in Wartime Japan', *Scientific American*, December 1998, pp. 96–103.
42 Two American journalists, reporting in early 1995 on Israel's refusal to sign the Nuclear Non-Proliferation Treaty, placed that country's level of armament at 'about 200 nuclear devices'. John Lancaster and Bart Gellmann, 'Nuclear "No" Sours Egypt–Israel Relations', *IHT*, 20 January 1995, p. 1.
43 Malik was interviewed by Tony Clifton, 'Report from the Battlefield', *Newsweek* (Atlantic edn), 9 August 1999, p. 29.
44 Gist of an article signed by Pierre Billaud (with Hervé Kempf), a *Polytechnicien* who in 1968 became director of military applications at the French Atomic Energy Commission. See 'Comment la France a fait sa bombe H' (How France Made Its H-Bomb), *La Recherche*, 293, December 1996, pp. 74–8. Billaud provides details of the professional frustrations of the time in *La véridique histoire de la bombe H française* (The True History of the French H-Bomb) (Paris, La Pensée Universelle, 1994).
45 Richard L. Garwin and Wolfgang K. H. Panovsky, 'Nuclear Secrets: Rush to Judgment against China', *IHT*, 3 August 1999, p. 8.
46 The views of Dollezhal were published by Znaniye in Moscow; cited in Holloway, *Stalin and the Bomb*, pp. 205–6.
47 Mohamed El Baradei, in an address before the Royal Institute of International Affairs, London, 15 January (2001).
48 Boniface directs the Institut des Relations Internationales et Stratégiques (IRIS) in Paris. IRIS sponsors an annual summer school, Conférences Stratégiques, co-organized with NATO and the Aérospatiale corporation.
49 In a panel discussion, Ecole Normale Supérieure, Paris, 19 November 1997.

6

Optimizing Human Resources: Procurement, Training, Management

'It is worth thinking about what you can do with an individual soldier or a very small military unit by making a very large investment in them, their training and equipment, make them mobile, able to communicate, with large fire-power, good target acquisition ability.'
Harold Brown, physicist, US Secretary of Defense (1963)[1]

BASIC SOCIAL SCIENCE

Selecting, using and holding on to human resources to fullest advantage is the classical optimum describing the management of a military force. That challenge is examined in this chapter.

One of the significant factors in Britain's build-up of a navy that ruled the waves for so long – after foreign forces invaded the island twice in the twelfth and thirteenth centuries and four times in the fifteenth – was the careful management of both technics and skills introduced in 1570 by Elizabeth I's naval minister, John Hawkins.[2] Personnel management has since become the basic social science applied among fighting men and, now, women.[3] The new terrorism seems to apply some of its methodologies.

Through the centuries, common sailors and soldiers came from the economic classes most in need. Like ammunition, troops were expendable. They were led by officers whose sole qualification often was family land, other wealth, or title. Even after the press gangs that were used to find crews for navies disappeared, discipline was long maintained largely by flogging and the harsh bawling of boatswain's mates. In 1842 an American naval officer, Uriah Phillips Levy, commanding the USS *Vandalia*, brought the beginning of an end to this barbarous method. When he made offending crewmen wear signs indicating drunkenness or thievery, the Navy Department court-martialed him for 'scandalous punishment'. Levy was suspended from service for a year, then reinstated and promoted to captain in 1844 at the instigation of President John Tyler,[4] and later served as commodore of the US flotilla in the Mediterranean.

Since then most military organizations have learned that sailors, air personnel and ground troops must be trained and treated humanely, and today in a manner that is also system-specific in order to handle the complexities of modern military equipment, instruments and weapon systems.

WOMEN AND MEN

Women now play roles contrasting sharply with the nurse, *cantinière*, sutler's wife, laundrywoman, or camp-following prostitute of not so many wars ago. The place of the woman in organized conflict was, until the modern era, one of exclusion from the fighting ranks. History records, it is true, cases of women or girls assuming the uniforms and gear of men or boys in fighting units throughout the wars. Anne Bonny and Hannah Snell masqueraded as males to go to sea with Britain's Royal Navy in the eighteenth century, and in revolutionary France numerous women posed as males in order to be in the thick of things – but these were isolated instances.

Women in China – and many of them – joined the Eighth Route Army in Yenan as early as 1934: a turnabout in Chinese history. During the Great Patriotic War fought between the Soviet Union and Nazi Germany women took up arms in great number. After 1948 and the creation of the new state of Israel, national conscription of females became near-universal. (Israel's mobilization, however, was of the Jewish populace. The Arab population not being integrated into national society, Jewish men have been the core of the nation's fighting strength, the Israel Defense Force, IDF.)

This national policy makes it possible for the Israeli military to exploit technical evolution as it occurs while benefiting from well-educated women and men – the Jewish population being better educated than its Arab counterpart. A core of 20,000 professional soldiers exercise command over five times this number of conscripts and reservists. When crisis demands, the IDF can grow to 600,000 within 72 hours. Officers are promoted from the enlisted grades and, to instill troop confidence, they are expected to lead 'anywhere but from the rear'. A sequel has been high casualties among company- and field-grade officers (lieutenants to colonels). But here women have been spared.

Personnel strategy of the military elsewhere (France, Germany, the Netherlands, Canada and the United States among them) permits women increasingly to do military work previously restricted to men. The line remains drawn on assignment to combat posts *during* hostilities. Other lines remain rather clearly drawn, at least in the spirit if not in the letter of legislation. In the last years of the twentieth century it was a woman, feminist Linda Bird Francke, who determined that traditions already millennia old continued to govern the attitude of both leaders and the led in regard to women among the troops: discrimination, harassment in various forms, demeaning evaluation of their occupations. The male motives, seldom pronounced publicly according to Francke, include 'institutional promotion' of the male's dominance, an 'aura of hypermasculinity', and a generalized imperative of the male 'to disparage ... women in the military'.[5]

Democracy and human rights reinforce a woman's option for a career in the military. One needs to imagine, however, the nature of the public's reaction – and this includes the reactions of women themselves – when one day battlefield reports begin to list female deaths, pregnant women among them, and the attribution of awards and decorations to women achieving the greatest number of 'kills' among enemy forces. Fifteen women died on the Coalition side during the Gulf War of 1990–91. Reports were not available of similar deaths among Iraqi forces, if any, but one can expect more female military casualties in similar future conflicts.

RECRUITMENT STANDARDS

We look at the health aspects of the military establishment in Chapter 11 and, throughout, the economic pressures of paying for a fighting force together with the research required to supply and reinforce it. Keeping competent staff until retirement is often a goal of military personnel policy, alternatively turning out personnel who fail to meet standards. The setting of proper norms is essential, therefore, for the modern military organization.

Educational, health and performance standards have been finely elaborated by a good many national military establishments. With multinational forces casting wide their presence since about 1960, screening and weeding out have become indispensable processes in force management: techniques often applied with more vigor and definition than in civil life, where labor laws often protect ineffective or redundant employees.

Many, if not most, military services today accept the challenge of human-resources management as equal in importance to two other sides of a triangle that we may draw as in Figure 1.

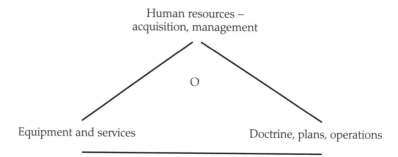

Human resources –
acquisition, management

O

Equipment and services   Doctrine, plans, operations

Figure 1:
Integrating Personnel with Doctrine and Equipment

Note: The three sides connecting the vertices may be interpreted as communication, the *formal* rather than the *informal* kind. The center of the triangle (**O**) represents centralized command or final objectives (or both). That the paramountcy of humans is today equal or superior to materiel and doctrine should be clear in the minds of most military executives. Fine materiel and clarity of doctrine are useless without competent human resources to exploit them.

Doctrine is based on a range of thought stretching from the military histories of Thucydides (fifth century BC) and Xenophon's *Anabasis* (a critical chronicle, experienced at first hand, in the fourth century BC), through the philosophical-military treatises of Sun Tzu in the third century BC to today's political testaments, legislation, executive stance (often *ad hoc*), and the myriad staff manuals accumulated in recent centuries. Such doctrine is complicated because, while it purports to mark off the ethico-philosophical framework of war, it must provide guidance for its implementation.

Training handbooks for the military, militia included of course, were slow in being developed. The Roman army had instructive treatises of a sort (including technical descriptions of how to proceed, in occupied lands, with crucifixion), but formal instructors took a long time to materialize. Sir George Carey, on the Isle of Wight, drafted directives as early as 1583, to be used by company captains within his area of command. The first vademecum for instructors in the English-speaking world was *Instructions for Musters and Armes, and the Use Thereof. By Order from His Majestie's Privy Counsayle*[Council], published in 1623.[6]

Colonel William Barriffe's *Militarie Discipline*, published in six editions from 1635 to 1661 during Oliver Cromwell's military leadership, was the first manual in which were 'discoursed and shewn the Postures of both Musket and Pike'. Still in the English-speaking world, Thomas Simes' *The Military Medley* (1768) carried the subtitle: 'Containing the Most Necessary Rules and Directions for Attaining A Competant Knowledge of the Art, to which is Added an Explanation of Military Terms, Alphabetically Digested'. This manual was used in North America by both the British and Continental States sides during the War of Independence of 1776–83.

A century and a half later, Hitler wrote *Mein Kampf*. He meant it to be followed as the new orthodoxy on a scale far grander than that of a battalion or a ship's company. Mao Zedong invoked the role of technical progress in the development of doctrine, with his insistence on the 'power that comes from the mouths of guns'. Mao emphasized that as the world advances, 'the future is radiant, no one can change this general current in history. We should constantly make the population aware of this progress and its luminous prospects, so that the people can have confidence in victory.'[7] And today's international terrorists have their own manuals.

In the cold light of translating military thought into action, doctrine that is developed for pedagogical purposes takes into account the differences between classroom theory and field reality. Order and system are meant to overcome disarray and improvisation. 'Every man for himself!' remains the command of last resort, when all sense of organization, *esprit de corps*, and command and control have failed.

THE ORDERED FORMATION

Five centuries ago Swiss phalanxes armed with pikes roundly defeated mounted Burgundians. A few years later a Spanish commander (Gonsalvo de Cordoba), fighting at Cerignola near Foggia in Italy, took another step forward when he committed a well-drilled combination of harquebusiers and cannon to smash an attack by massed pikemen, also supported by cannon, against the Duke of Nemours' French troops. The Spaniards were outnumbered but they carried the day, resulting in the eviction of occupying French forces from Italy.

Training, unit exercises and balanced deployment of troop formations are among the deciding factors implicitly at work for victors – regardless of the war, its era, where it takes place, or the military service engaged. These elements were applied with effect by Gustavus Adolphus when Swedes and Saxons clashed with Germans of the Holy Roman Empire near Leipzig in 1631 at Breitenfeld. The Swedish king ordered that pikes and muskets be shortened, and body armor lightened; he interspersed one pikeman with every two musketeers in companies formed of 126 soldiers. His disciplined forces maneuvered easily, kneeling or standing in four or five ranks, firing then reloading, alternating their controlled fire. All the while cavalry was present close by, spaced regularly among infantry units.

Cavalry was used as often, behind infantry, to prevent retreat ('stiffen resolve') of line soldiers as it was to charge the enemy. Once combined, foot and mounted troops developed through incessant drill volleys of sustained and rhythmically steady gunfire, fast reloading, and an assured supply of ammunition arriving rapidly from the rudimentary *étappes* (stores of supplies) not far behind.

Where to find recruits for military service and how best to prepare them for battle has been a problem since the beginning of social organization. Its tried but not always true modes have been volunteers, impressment, slaves, mercenaries, conscription and career professionalism. Ottoman leaders permitted military service, afterwards rewarded with land and exemption from taxes, only to faithful Muslim applicants. The Turkish volunteer usually participated in struggles associated with land acquisition or protection, but land itself was always the sultan's property. Elsewhere impressment usually fell on the lowest economic orders and, if the subjects survived battle, service was short-lived. Slavery is out of the question in the modern world – although some military slaves did become sultans, kings, even emperors. Mercenaries contract for a fixed period of paid service. Conscription – the young male serves, whether he likes it or not – made possible the huge European armies of the nineteenth and early twentieth centuries, and their high casualty rates. The draft could be evaded, theoretically, only by disease, deformity or mental limitations.

Fifteen decades before the massive conscription imposed in France (1790s), the Swedes had their *imdelningsverk* in operation during the Thirty Years' War. This was a semifeudal arrangement that exchanged land for service under arms, a step ahead of the chivalric tradition of 40 days' service per year by knights – and several steps ahead of the Chinese T'ang dynasty's method (during 618–907) of conscripting for extended service almost exclusively the peasantry. Swedish officers and soldiers received a plot of land, or else part of the revenue derived from it. Thus was created a matrix of yeoman militias capable of mobilizing for the crown, in record time, about 100,000 troops. What *indelningsverk* lacked, however, was a coherent system of supply, and this ultimately brought defeat to Sweden's King Charles XII in his long struggle with Tsar Peter I during the Great Northern War of 1700–21.[8]

Numbers have been used to carry a weight proportional to the operation mounted, as the battle of Fontenoy in today's Belgium demonstrated in the mid-eighteenth century. The paper cartridge then used was fitted into a musket's breech, and the ring bayonet had been developed to permit a trooper to fire *while* thrusting or lunging with his bayonet. Rates of fire increased as the bayonet offered a safeguard for the reloading musketeer. The pike was gradually abandoned. At Fontenoy 100,000 men were committed to battle, the tactics developed by Gustavus Adolphus were applied by the British against their French opponents. The sheer mass of numbers won this encounter in May 1745 for the French side, led by the German-born Marshal Count Maurice de Saxe.

LEADERSHIP

After France's revolutionary Terror (1791–94), officer ranks were depleted by a combination of political executions, exile and unexplained disappearances. The shortage was compensated in part, as the conscripts of the Directory grew and engaged the enemies of France, by massing infantry advances behind a few sharpshooters. These formations were intended to exploit natural cover or concealment as much as the terrain permitted. While this massed-infantry gambit may have saved a few lives of privates and junior noncommissioned officers, it was a stopgap to compensate for the lack of officered leadership.

The same problem, in different form but present on a much larger scale, affected the Soviet Union's army, air force and navy after the Stalinist purges of the late 1930s, as it did the German Wehrmacht diminished by the foot-dragging of some generals and the abortive plot of July 1944 against Hitler. In these cases new unit commanders and staffs had to be selected, broken in, and accepted by subordinate leaders and the rank-and-file. Political cleansing – even when charges of indiscipline, insubordination, disloyalty or treason prove to be unfounded – devastates military solidarity and efficacy.

Yet special training for leaders (or those intended to become so) has, despite its accepted need, a ragged history. When the Royal School of Engineers was created in eighteenth-century France – mainly to improve the management of fortifications, artillery and ammunition – candidates had to present, first and foremost, aristocratic credentials. Not only were officers in many of the world's regions selected on the basis of their socioeconomic origins, commissions were also easily bought, in either case without training. Other ranks were trained on home grounds or aboard small, local sea craft by noncommissioned personnel. Standards for enlisted promotions were often those of harshness of discipline, or else those of whim or favoritism.

Today, officer training is normally done in officially constituted military academies, although Germany calls its two campuses, in northern Hamburg and southern Munich, military universities. Continuing education for commissioned officers occurs in staff colleges or normal universities (civil institutions awarding masters' and doctors' degrees or their equivalents), or while the officer is detailed to industrial enterprises in support of procurement contracts with suppliers. The last condition leads, not infrequently, to resignation of the officer to join civil industry as, consultant: a loss to the service but a gain for the business concerned.

Enlisted personnel in many national services are trained in technical fields or as noncommissioned officers. Special criteria for the selection of technicians are required for aircraft maintenance, or the operation of submarines and tanks. The repair of computer and telecommunication systems requires testing by examination. Especially hazardous work, that of submariners or parachutists or air crews, requires stamina and usually earns special-duty pay.

Colonel Thierry Cambournac, a former commander of the French Army's 17th Parachute Engineer Regiment, is experienced in the training of bomb-disposal experts. 'The first thing we teach our applicants', he stresses, 'is that they can lose an arm or a leg. There's no point in bravura or trying to outshine your comrades when your life is in peril. We insist too that, once on a disposal job, these specialists be relieved every 20 minutes.'[9] When UN/NATO (United Nations/North Atlantic Treaty Organization) troops entered Yugoslavia's mine-strewn Kosovo province in 1999, the force's demining pathfinders were France's 1st Foreign Legion Cavalry Regiment, fully mechanized but also highly motivated and trained for the grisly work involved. They were hampered in part because Serbian miners had lost, or failed to map at all, many of the sites mined. And there were casualties.

CONCEPTS OF DISCIPLINE

Discipline is a complex process involving the individual and his or her relationship with the surrounding social structure (we scanned discipline aboard submarines in Chapter 5) and its obligations and customs. Most parents understand this rapport. Instructors have an equal appreciation of its importance in the schoolroom, training shop, laboratory, or on the drill field. Yet discipline is at times inconsistent in principle, form and application. The example given in the Box 5 demonstrates what can happen *in extremis*, when the rules are broken at the same time that they are respected, leaving those concerned circumspect, confused and in qualms well after the incident. The story is true.

Stefan's story is echoed on the other side of the world, only in fictional form, by Okuizumi Hikaru in his sensitive novel, *The Stones Cry Out.*[10] Holed up in a cave on Leyte in the Philippines, a band of Japanese soldiers is surviving, lost and demoralized. Manase, a conscript, listens to the philosophical ruminations of a lance-corporal who is at death's door. In the same group is a traumatized captain who makes every effort to have the dying put out of their shame (because they failed in face of the enemy) by those still alive. The reader, left to his imagination, wonders how far 'discipline' will be taken.

A former gunner, also drafted, and assigned to a Japanese mountain-artillery battery serving in Korea, told the author after the war that the savage beatings he received from his noncommissioned officers turned him against any wish to serve his superiors loyally. The fictional Manase and the real-life gunner *resisted*. The war came to its end, and both Manase and the gunner returned to a quiet life where they would not forget what happened in the turbulent months before their country's defeat.

HEROES AND FOOLS

At about the same time that the Japanese artilleryman was being slammed around in Korea, attacking German forces selected the weakness of a single US battle unit against which to launch the battle of the Bulge in the winter of 1944–45. A chronicler who was involved in the campaign, platoon leader Paul Fussell, relates:

> In the opinion of British military historian Max Hastings, [this force] was so bad (and actually so were most of the British)'that when Allied troops met Germans on something like equal terms, the Germans almost always prevailed.' Thank God the troops ... didn't know how bad we were. It's hard enough to be asked to die in the midst of heroes, but to die in the midst of stumblebums led by fools – intolerable. And I include myself,

proclaims Fussell, 'in this indictment'.[11] This is *net assessment* in subjective form, but surely at its most authentic.[12]

Loyalty downwards, generating in turn loyalty upwards, seems to be the secret of *Shackleton sensitivity*. Sir Ernest Henry Shackleton, explorer, naval reservist and army officer, led two (failed) South Polar expeditions, organized strictly along military lines, in 1907–9 and 1914–16. He succeeded in maintaining the highest fidelity and disciplinary response among his crews. This he achieved through concern

BOX 5 DISCIPLINE ON 20 JULY 1944 … FIFTY YEARS LATER

An officer from a Panzer division relates unorthodox events when news reached his temporary unit in Germany that Hitler had been assassinated.

You have asked what I was doing on that fateful day. In July 1944 I was a lieutenant of armored troops just released from hospital at Meiningen, Thuringia, after operations for wounds incurred the third time (of four) in Russia. On 6 July I was posted temporarily to a unit of the Home Army [*Ersatztruppe*] in Jena, whose commanding officer recognized me immediately because we had served together on the Russian front. I still remember this officer, a major so badly wounded that he no longer qualified for combat, as a decent and upright type.

During these weeks of transition while awaiting orders to send me back to the line, the major and I had long, personal conversations. He repeatedly expressed his concern about the military situation in Normandy subsequent to the Allied landings the previous month. He spoke, too, about the troublesome relationship between our army and the National Socialist Party (NDSAP), doubting seriously that Germany could win a two-front war.

And then came the 20th of July. I had my own room in the barracks, where a sergeant came running that day to fetch me to see the major, who told me that Hitler was dead. 'A Party clique wants to take over and confront the army with the help of the SS. Orders have come to us from above to arrest leaders of the SS. There are 600 soldiers here, but only a few Party people.' He ordered me to find and seize Jena's top man in the 'Black SS' (not to be confused with the Waffen SS). My surprise at these instructions was complete, especially when the major added, 'Your orders are unconditional, especially since we can expect danger.' Accompanied by two sergeants armed with machine-pistols, I left immediately in a staff car awaiting us.

I was used to carrying out 'unconditional' orders. We found the SS commander; his arrest went smoothly, and we brought him to the barracks, where I reported 'mission accomplished'. The major replied, 'I have done my duty. All we need do now is apprehend the two top leaders of the Party because the army must ensure, at all costs, calm and order.' At that very moment, the radio announced that Hitler was alive and the Wehrmacht's attempt to set up a new government had failed.

The major immediately issued me travel orders, backdating them to 19 July, orders that would return me to Russia. He then drove me personally to a railway station two towns away, as he thought that the Jena station was no longer secure. This immediate transfer was the major's effort to protect my life, since he knew that the SS, the police and even the Party had no legal right to grab soldiers in transit to frontline duty – especially on the eastern front.

I learned later that the major and several others were arrested and executed. The outcome of the 20 July attempt against Hitler's life depressed me terribly. As far as I was concerned, I was convinced that I had acted correctly and honorably. I was given an order, I carried it out, and that was that. The same applies to the major. I can never forget this episode.

Yours, [signed] Stefan

Communicated in conversation in July 1994 and transmitted to the author in writing on 21 July 1998.

for their safety and welfare, while everyone suffered stress and long periods of inactivity and isolation in the Antarctic environment.[13] In 1918, while serving with the British intervention force at Murmansk under Major-General Charles S. Maynard, Major Shackleton 'was in close attendance on his general, giving him the loyal and affectionate service to which he had been long accustomed from his own tried followers'.[14]

The same attitude pervades a fictional work published in 1968, *Once An Eagle*, now as much a behavioral guide for officers of the United States Army and Marine Corps as their required-reading staff manuals.[15] In *Once an Eagle*, author Anton Myrer pits the behavior and attitudes of soldier's soldier Sam Damon against the ambitious, favor-currying Courtney Massengale. Damon cares about his troops, and acts accordingly. Massengale, always on the alert to make the right 'career moves', damns ordinary soldiers and steams ahead full speed to satisfy his ego. Readers will recognize these types pervading human-resources management, whether military or civil.

Disobedience through action undertaken without the knowledge of superiors is not unknown among the modern military, especially at the small-unit, tactical level. Overbearing, cruel or cowardly junior officers were murdered by subordinates on the Third Reich's Soviet front and during the US war in Vietnam. At the strategic level, at least one source has cited the ordering by General Curtis LeMay of the

United States' Strategic Air Command of unauthorized – and perilous – missions. Author Paul Lashmar reveals that during the Cold War LeMay dispatched a number of aerial missions over the Soviet Union, intended both for reconnaissance and to incite the USSR to retaliate against the West. LeMay acted without presidential authority.[16] In 1956, on the other hand, a Marine sergeant in the United States was court-martialed for his responsibility for the deaths of six trainees, non-swimmers who were marched into the Carolina swamps as a punitive exercise. The defense used as argument that officers had left too much prerogative to NCOs, implying that the absent officers had a moral responsibility for the event.[17] Yet no officers were prosecuted.

Years later, an incident of *institutional disobedience* occurred in Kosovo during the NATO intervention of 1999, when British Lieutenant-General Sir Michael Jackson refused an order by multinational–NATO commander General Wesley Clark (of the United States) to occupy the airfield at Pristina in order to trump an unannounced Russian occupation of the air base after its evacuation by Serbian troops. The British officer explained to Clark that he did 'not want to be responsible for World War Three'. (No court-martial followed.) An inversion of this lack of hierarchical obedience occurred not only in Kosovo but several times during the Bosnian campaign of mid-1995 when at least one government, that of the United States, undercut the descending line of command in NATO to force the hand of local combatants and thereby set the scene for the Dayton Accords. Military analyst Tim Ripley has carefully reconstructed the Bosnian events in his book, *Operation Deliberate Force.*

While discipline is taught in military circles as an upwards fealty, vassal to lord, this is not consistently so. Discipline works laterally in a more compassionate sense, too, between grades of similar rank and experience – particularly in times of prolonged hardship. There exists even an inverse interpretation of the customary canon, as a retired British lieutenant-colonel, Ian Hywel-Jones, tells it. After 33 years spent in regiments of the line, Hywel-Jones devoted almost another 14 as a civilian in the Foreign and Commonwealth Office, coordinating his country's military attachés abroad. He perceives a marked contrast in how military and civil servants interpret their responsibilities within the professional pecking-order:

> There is a crucial difference in attitudes between officers of the armed forces, internationally, and members of the foreign or diplomatic services. In the British case, from the time the remarkable young men and women who join the diplomatic service leave their universities and start

their first jobs at the Foreign Office, they quickly learn that there are three most-important groups in their lives. These are the Foreign Office Ministers, the Prime Minister's Office, and Parliament. When they reach their first posting abroad, they add a fourth group: the hierarchy of the country in which they work. They regularly look upwards. We of the military, from the day we entered Dartmouth, Sandhurst or Cranwell, learnt that the most important people in *our* lives would be the people 'beneath' us – the people we were privileged to lead.[18]

ORIGINS OF MODERN TRAINING

There is little disagreement that an effective fighting force needs proper training for the management of matériel and technical services as well as for the maintenance of discipline – and the assurance of victory in time of hostilities. The Royal School of Engineers, already mentioned, was opened in 1750 at Mézières in northeastern France by Count Marc-Pierre d'Argenson in a sweeping reorganization of Louis XV's ground forces, occasioned by their poor performance during the War of Austrian Succession.

It was at Mézières that an eighteenth-century novelty emerged in military training: scientific system.[19] Vauban's seventeenth-century, threefold geographic network of fortifications along the Rhine, Escaut and Meuse rivers had spawned a corps of siege engineers. (These Vauban fortresses, incidentally, are the likely thematic origin of the US 'systems' of coastal artillery – first, the Atlantic; second, the Southern and Gulf; and third, the Pacific – created during the 1800s to defend the United States littoral against invasion. The advent of aircraft made coast-artillery defense superfluous by 1940.)

The double strength of these military technologies of the Enlightenment was the skill they required in making detailed architectural plans: using theory and accurate measurement to improve the crafts of mason and carpenter, while developing the principles of relief and defile to control fields of fire. All these techniques were applied to the methodical design and construction of ramparts – bastions with face, flank and gorge; escarps, glacis and counterscarps, and other defenses intended to update the parapet, moat, portcullis, keep and dungeon of the military architecture from the Middle Ages and Renaissance. Geological, hydrological and economic factors thus joined topography and geometry in the conception and building of strong points.

A professor of mathematics at Mézières was Gaspard Monge, inventor of stereotomy (cutting solids to specific form and dimension).

Monge and J.-B. Meusnier introduced shading hachures, elevation contours and sloping scales to portray relief in military cartography, later taken up in civil mapmaking. These techniques enabled Britain's Ordnance Survey to create excellent mapping of its home soil and of many parts of the British Empire in the nineteenth century, an example followed closely by other countries. Monge also began the first studies of the chemical composition of water while another instructor, Charles Bossut, invented static mechanics, mechanical dynamics, and basic hydrodynamics. Bossut added, besides his other initiatives, studies of friction and fluid flow.

Mézières being a military school, its treatises and other texts that dealt with this variety of disciplines were considered official secrets. None was published openly, although the publications became available after the Revolution. Instruction gradually combined theory, mainly mathematical, with practice in the field. This legacy was passed on to the new Ecole Polytechnique when France's post-revolutionary leaders decided in 1794 that the Royal establishment had fallen into irreparable disuse and that the new nation's munitions industry was in critical need of saltpeter – and thus of chemists.

The Mézières teaching staff also made exact draftsmanship a preliminary requirement for matriculation, instead of an end-product of all the student's previous instruction.[20] Mézières goes down in history as a formidable contribution by the military to the advancement of science and engineering – an indispensable stage in the growth of the dual-purpose concept. Besides the merging of practice with theory and the sophistication of its mathematical teaching, the royal school introduced experimental physics to its curriculum.

The mathematician Condorcet saw to it that the military precept of fusing theory with practice was adopted as a working principle by the French Academy of Sciences before the eighteenth century expired (and Condorcet himself beneath the guillotine during the Terror). Monge's disciple Meusnier developed differential geometry and joined the chemist Lavoisier to develop 'new chemistry'. Graduates P.-L.-G. Du Buat (1750) and J.-C. Borda (1758) became masters of hydraulics and hydrodynamics. C.-A. Coulomb (1760) went from soil mechanics and the resistance of materials to new theories in electrical flow. Lazare Carnot made the transition from geometry and mechanics to military and political leadership via his insistence on widespread civil participation in military actions (1771). And, not incidentally, Carnot fathered Sadi Carnot, the founder of thermodynamics.

EFFECTIVENESS OF ORDER AND DISCIPLINE

In sixteenth-century pike squares (complex box-formations favored by the Italians, among others), *picche secche* or unarmored pikemen were trained to press, during battle, 'the backs of *picche armate* in front and push forward into their places if they were killed'. The exercise was a veritable ballet involving several companies consisting of not only pikemen but halberdiers, musketeers and harquebusiers, all pivoting about a central 'ensign'. Their work implied real-time accounting for losses and replacements in the immediate vicinity, reckoning that required 'a good understanding of mathematics and systematic [mental] records. Knowledge of multiplication and division and square roots' was obligatory for the lesser grades commanding these real-life drills, 'skills far from widespread in early modern Europe'.[21]

Napoleon demolished the Prussian army at Jena in 1806, in part because young Germans had difficulty understanding orders. This blow conveyed how important mass troop-instruction became in the minds of Gneisenau, Scharnhorst and their colleagues of the Prussian general staff. Their recommendations concerning the military's responsibility to train young recruits in the basics of reading, writing and numeracy set the standards for civil instruction throughout the fast-evolving Germany of the nineteenth century. The military were thus better able to abet functional literacy and cope with limited skill in mathematics, but not yet deal with the overall quality of the young civilians to be made into soldiers.

How is such quality to be assessed? Officers, today identified with the white-collar class of executives presumably educated in part at university level, contrast with noncommissioned officers. The latter are the foremen and masters of the blue-collar category deriving from the age of guilds. The grades of corporal, sergeant and sergeant-major, and corresponding naval petty officers, have existed since at least the sixteenth century.[22] Yet the German NCO, even before the Second World War, was assigned functions often entrusted to commissioned officers in other national establishments.[23] How do such varying attributions affect the way a battle force functions?

In its collectivity of officers, noncombatants and private soldiers, according to a British appraisal, Germany's

> army of 1914 was the finest military machine of its day, perhaps of modern times. In its commanders, its arms and equipment, its training, its supply services and communications, its cadres of long-serving officers and NCOs, in the quality of its general staff and the planning they produced ... it was generally superior ... On top of this came its vast

superiority in self-confidence and morale … The German army had
known only victory for longer than anyone could remember. It regarded
war as the apotheosis of its existence, not as some baleful interruption
to the pleasures of peaceful garrison life.[24]

In terms of skill, steadfastness and effectiveness, the reliability and
performance of the German military during the Second World War
have been assessed repeatedly in studies prepared by both the British
and United States general-staff schools as individually the most cost-
effective (to use the terminology of contemporary business) of all
combatants in that conflict. This evaluation took into account the performance of riflemen in general and in particular the *Panzergrenadier*
(armored infantryman), the tank crewman, the parachutist and the
submariner, while it tended to praise considerably less the effectiveness of *Luftwaffe* crews – too often the products of hurried training.
The renowned 'Slam' Marshall – American Brigadier-General S. L. A.
Marshall – conducted ethological research on his own army's frontline troops in action. These behavioral studies showed that only 25 per
cent of individuals in contact with the German adversary actually fired
their weapons. Such appraisals are particularly significant in view of
the *Materialschlacht* (fight for supplies) facing the German military in
both world wars.[25]

Similar evaluation has been made, but for shorter periods, of
France's *Légion étrangère*; the Soviet drafted soldiery of the Great
Patriotic War; the Japanese fighting men of the 1941–45 conflict; of
Britain's Royal Air Force, Brigade of Guards, and Royal Marine commandos; Canadian and Polish units in general, the United States
Marine Corps and the US Army's Rangers and US Navy SEALS (naval
commando units), and – until the great civil disturbances of the two
intifada – the Israel Defense Force.[26] The capacity of a military establishment to use resources to best effect may be nothing more enigmatic, therefore, than a function or an adjunct of the prevailing
sociopolitical situation within or among countries: is a country's entire
society in the process of cohesion and rallying round the flag, or is the
social fabric fraying and its individuals caring less and less? The nature
of the questions parallels that of why election participation tends to
diminish in many democracies.

TESTING INTELLIGENCE

Progress in the sociological sense waited another century until the
advent of the French physiologist and experimental psychologist

Alfred Binet, and his collaborator, Théodore Simon. Between 1904 and 1911 they devised mental-aptitude tests for schoolchildren, assessments meant to identify elementary-school students needing help to learn. Their work on 'intelligence levels', despite heated contest until our day (seriously affecting educational reform, for example, in the Britain of the 1960s), was adapted by American psychologist Lewis M. Terman and German philosopher William Stern to become the even more challenged

$$\text{intelligence quotient} = \frac{\text{mental age}}{\text{age in years}},$$

modified again by the United States Army in 1917 into the Alpha test. The Alpha is the ancestor of many aptitude tests now used in employment agencies, industry and the service sector. It filtered out army recruits with an insufficient IQ (intelligence quotient), and was used by personnel administrators to screen almost 1,750,000 men.

The average IQ is considered to vary between 90 and 110 – 100 is thus the rounded average – on a scale ranging from roughly 40 ('feebleminded') to about 150 or more ('genius'). Recruits demonstrating an average IQ are considered, in those military establishments subscribing to this psychological formula, qualified to enter officers' training schools in wartime. The 'pivotal moment' for Binet and the other 'social engineers' was the testing of military personnel', according to historian Gary Wills. 'The techniques and aspirations of [those] who pioneered the tests … led to the founding of the *Journal of Applied Psychology*.'[27] When the military make use of intelligence testing, they rely on it more than does civil life for training and the work to which new personnel are exposed.

Early in the twentieth century, Charles Spearman in Great Britain showed that there is consistent correlation in the results of tests administered in different categories: grouping and classifying, reading, doing arithmetic or mechanics or electricity – a factor that he called G. Spearman and disciples such as John C. Raven were able to develop matrices showing surprisingly consistent relationships among the various test results. These, too, caught the eye of the military.

Since intelligence testing began with Binet, his school and its results[28] led military services to rely on test-filtering in order to determine general suitability, mechanical aptitude, strength in handling concepts and reasoning, or a bent for administrative and clerical work in their selection of personnel. Military testing gave rise to special applications in civil life, such as the Wechsler Intelligence Scale for Children (WISC): testing for acquired information, understanding, capacity in arithmetic, vocabulary, recognition of similitude, and assessing other performances, for example, bringing order to multiple images.

The validity of intelligence tests is still debated,[29] but the military's expansion of originally civil ideas has contributed immeasurably to the growth of psychometry and its methods.

TOO MANY FIGHTING FORCES

There is a recurring phenomenon in the good administration of forces *en masse* when, with the ending of hostilities or other tension, greatly expanded forces find that they must suddenly contract. In the states of the former Soviet Union, the military population diminished markedly as an aftermath of the Cold War. From more than 5 million men and women members of the armed forces in 1987, the military census of 1996 in Russia was less than a million and a half. There were, besides, in the inevitable tradition of Russian national security, several hundred thousand internal (that is, police) troops to be trained, fed, clothed, housed and paid. *Konvertsiya* (reconversion) of former military personnel thus became a major goal of the 1990s, one strikingly contrary to recruitment. Military establishments, as almost all social institutions, must replenish and maintain their human resources – motivated, selected, trained and prepared, fed and fit – even while ridding themselves of the superfluous.

While enlisted personnel and young officers tend to adjust quickly upon returning to civil life, because they either pursued their own vocations while in uniform or were trained specially, the problem with older officers is more serious. There are relatively few analogous calls in civil life for which experienced officers are suited, leaving as they do a privileged caste. 'Civilian life can be shocking … [it] is like a world of guerrillas', states former Lieutenant-Colonel Zbigniew Dolega of the Polish Army's Warsaw Regional Command.[30] (Poland had an army of 410,000 at the end of the Cold War, an unbelievable 200,000 of whom were officers.)

After a career of training to oppose NATO forces, Dolega abruptly found himself on the street, tried his hand at running a small firm, but abandoned this in order to take management courses and then join a venture capital company. He did this under the supervision of another lieutenant-colonel, Adam Sowa, responsible for the army's Reconversion Bureau, working with a training specialist, Colonel Marian Fiejdasz. The approach of Fiejdasz and Sowa to the outplacement problem was to emphasize each candidate's strong points and coach the individual to develop a specific action-plan for himself. They used a 'CD-ROM simulation game called "Career" or fill[ed] out a "professiogram" to find a suitable field of work – and many [candidates] have found one'.[31]

The idea is corroborated by former Colonel István Varga, who served as director of the Hungarian army's information, film and cultural-affairs unit. His view is that several decades of service provide officers with organizing skills and good contacts in government. 'Former officers', he adds, 'are being headhunted by private companies because of their precision, responsibility, loyalty and discipline ... We help reprogram their minds.'[32]

Reconversion is not a perennial function of the military, of course. In the United States, the Institute of Defense Analysis (IDA), a private contractor, serves the Department of Defense in the broad area of social applications known as research on military personnel and training. IDA is an R&D center funded from federal sources, performing analytical studies requested by the Office of the Secretary of Defense. The size of the US forces (regular, reserve and National Guard) diminished in total number from 2 million in 1990 to about 990,000 in 1998. In the latter year the Department of Defense had nearly 34,000 of its personnel working in 81 countries outside the United States. In Bosnia it supplied (besides combat troops) 200 civil-affairs officers, of whom 199 were drawn from non-regular components. In 2000, the same department found that many non-regulars were being held too long, seriously jeopardizing their value to the civil employers concurring in their military absence. In the case of combat in Afghanistan, such detention could prove long indeed.

The reduction of personnel ceilings is closely allied, too, to problems of reducing procurement of matériel and limiting the number of army posts, naval bases and airfields on which governments spend considerable sums and (almost everywhere) pay no taxes, locally or nationally. These processes are by and large manageable, although manageability proved not to be the case in post-Cold War Russia. There management failed, discipline collapsed, disorder reigned, and the image of the armed forces had to await the second war in Chechnya in 1999–2000, under Acting President Vladimir Putin, before it would rise again.

NEW IDEAS ON GOOD BEHAVIOR

New research during new conflicts means understanding shifts in the common values of those hired to fight. Peacekeeping, or peacemaking, may erode the professional warrior's attitudes of patriotism and loyalty to the nation and subordination to one's superiors. The overriding supervision of an intervention by the UN, for instance, has changed the juridical position of officer and enlisted man.

How far may a commander to go in ordering his subordinates to respond – not to a court-martial, but to a court of enquiry related to events that occurred in Somalia, Rwanda, Bosnia, Kosovo, Macedonia, East Timor or Afghanistan, incidents that may brand intervenors as terrorists or war criminals? Fighting personnel may thus discover an atmosphere rather different from that formerly associated with communities of sailors, airmen or soldiers. For this reason some combat forces now take 'judgment training'. This asks, among other things, if legal and moral calculation is a legitimate part of the ethical instruction being given (more and more) to troops.[33]

JUST BEHAVIOUR, DEATH AND REAL MOTIVATIONS

As we end this sequence on quality control of military man- and womanpower, there remains one important topic to be broached. Among the military is the ever-present, yet seldom voiced, apprehension of death that may be violent and sudden. 'Death is part of their duty' may be an old maxim for military personnel, but the mood is changing towards the growing fashion for *zero deaths* among warfighters. Today 'zero deaths' are publicly subscribed to in some countries because the end of conscription is a major change in the peopling of armed forces – *the major change* since the Marquis de Louvois persuaded Louis XIV to adopt professional-army standards for the nation-state. Yet many of us realize that the no-fatalities slogan is intrinsically inoperable.[34]

Death, or the fear of it, and efforts in applied behavioral science to help fighting forces cope with its prospects lie within the responsibilities of the corps of chaplains, the psychological counselors and psychiatrists in the medical service, and inevitably troop commanders themselves. In some fighting forces – especially those structured within a totalitarian system, a combatant's death is tantamount to the heroics of martyrdom or to eternal glory.

The terrorist seems to be in a category of his/her own. This individual simply sees life-and-death differently. Timothy Garton Ash, who has met irregulars in Kosovo, Macedonia and Afghanistan, stipulates four elements to observe 'in deciding whether someone is a terrorist, and... what kind: biography, goals, methods and context'. These elements 'may serve as a modest template, but the content in each case will be very different ... Only a combination of the four will yield an answer', says Garton Ash in a recent analysis of the bad and the good of the terrorist.[35] Christian Schmidt, director of the Laboratoire de l'Economie et de la Sociologie des Organizations de Défense, University of Paris-9, has used game theory to develop what appears in Figure 2,[36] to some extent reinforcing Garton Ash. To these analysts it is clear that the assailants of 11 September 2001 knew fully what they were doing, why and how.

While remaining inconspicuous, the terrorist learns how people live and work in the target country (in this case the United States), how the mail, media and other communication systems function, and the

Figure 2:
The Way Some Game Theorists View the Terrorist's Gamble

Decision process – the WHY

Actor : protagonist – **terrorist**	*Actor*: antagonist – **victim**
Has initiative ⇒ is determined ⇒ persistent ⇒ reckless	Is prudent ⇒ apprehensive ⇒ fearful ⇒ dreads loss
⇓	⇓
• Metaphor: dedicated game player; 'go for broke' gambler; bidder at auctions	• Metaphor : sporting player; charity 'gambler'; or non-gambler

Decision process – the HOW

• Protagonist knows rules of the game that he makes the rules: an asymmetry of knowledge *vs* information	Antagonist ignores rules of the game or disregards them as not binding: cedes to strategy of protagonist or organizer
⇓	⇓
Is rational: follows rigorously a strategy towards single goal; willing to take risks, • for self, • for others; believes others will *not believe protagonist will act* (i.e. such action is hard to imagine)	Does not know how to be rational; believes that others are not rational (irrational); tends towards non-hostile, even compassionate, attitude *vis-à-vis* his competitors
⇓	⇓
Wins all, even if only temporarily; when he loses, he loses *all*	Wins rarely, loses often, 'it's only a game'; may lose his life
⇓	⇓
WINS (conditional*)	⇐ RESULT ⇒ (the **WHAT**)	LOSES (perhaps even his life**)

But to arrive at WINS, the terrorist must (1) decide to act <u>or to accept the *status quo*</u>. If he still accepts the rules (2) he proceeds, <u>or he refuses and sets out to change the rules</u>. This leads the terrorist (3) to WINS, <u>or else to find and accept alternative rules</u>.

Notes:
*Actors external to the decision process may take vengeful or hostile measures against the protagonist, thus neutralizing or overcoming him.
**In postmodern fighting, the new terrorism holds that everyone must conform to the will of the self-appointed few.

detailed mechanisms of financial export–import for all their material needs: how an entire society, free and democratic, is vulnerable to the 'stealthy gambler' seeking his own ends. (The 'freedom fighter', working on home soil, fits some of the description.)

What might future analysis add to the terrorist's portrait, as the stealthy gambler readies bio-neurological attack and sustained psychological warfare? Only preparations *sub rosa* for a nuclear surprise seem at the present to be beyond the capacities in infrastructure – technical facilities – required. Certainly not lacking today are *decision, discipline* and *determination*. Added to these are *secrecy, stealth, surprise, targeting innocents*, and *knowing the target*. If only the same levels of energy were channeled into constructive and creative effort.

NOTES

1 Harold Brown, 'A Weapons Plateau?', interview with the editors of *International Science and Technology*, September 1963, p. 52.
2 See N. A. M. Rodger, *The Safeguard of the Sea: A Naval History of Britain, 600–1649* (New York, W. W. Norton, 1998).
3 One of the few sources on military sociology prepared for the non-military reader is Pascal Vennesson and Théodore Caplow, *Sociologie militaire* (Paris, Armand Colin, 2000).
4 According to an exhibit on display in 1998 at the National Museum of American Jewish Military History, in Washington, DC.
5 Linda Bird Francke, *Ground Zero: The Gender Wars in the Military* (New York, Simon & Schuster, 1997), *passim*.
6 David Eltis, *The Military Revolution in 16th Century Europe* (New York, Barnes & Noble, 1998), pp. 110, 129 n.120.
7 *Citations du Président Mao Tsé-toung* (Paris, Editions du Seuil, 1967), p. 46.
8 One portrait of the events is Brian M. Downing, *The Military Revolution and Political Change: Origins of Democracy and Autocracy in Early Modern Europe* (Princeton, NJ, Princeton University Press, 1992), pp. 203–7 and 245.
9 In discussions held in Paris, March 1998. Cambournac is now on the general staff of his army.
10 Okuizumi Hikaru, *The Stones Cry Out*, trans. James Westerhoven (New York, Harcourt Brace, 1999).
11 Paul Fussell, *Doing Battle: The Making of a Skeptic* (Boston, MA, Little, Brown, 1996), p. 173.
12 Net assessment is a coldly detached evaluation-of-the-enemy methodology developed at the Pentagon almost single-handedly by economist Andrew Marshall, who kindly received the author as the present book was researched.
13 Shackleton has not lacked biographers, most of whom have taken strongly pro or con positions. A balanced, well-illustrated account of the 1914 expedition is Caroline Alexander, *The Endurance: Shackleton's Legendary Antarctic Expedition* (New York, Alfred A. Knopf, 1999).
14 Hugh Robert Mill, *The Life of Sir Ernest Shackleton* (London, William Heinemann 1923), p. 260. An early biography, written by an 'old friend'.

15 Anton Myrer, *Once An Eagle* (New York, Holt, Reinhart & Winston, 1968; New York, HarperCollins repr, 2000).
16 Paul Lashmar, *Spy Flights of the Cold War* (Stroud, Alan Sutton, 1996), as cited in a review by Stephen Twigge, *Intelligence and National Security*, 14, 2 (1999), p. 213.
17 An American lawyer, judge and former Marine published a detailed account: John C. Stevens III, *Court-Martial at Parris Island: The Ribbon Creek Incident* (Annapolis, MD, Naval Institute Press, 1999).
18 Personal communications with the author from Lieutenant-Colonel R. I. Hywel-Jones (Retd.), once an officer in the South Wales Borderers and the Royal Regiment of Wales, 26 December 1998, 15 January 1999.
19 See the chapter 'L'Ecole Royale du génie de Mézières', in René Taton (ed.), *Enseignement et diffusion des sciences en France au XVIIIe sèicle* (Paris, Hermann, 1964).
20 Bruno Belhoste, 'L'Ecole de génie de Mézières: l'alliance entre théorie et pratique', *La Recherche*, 300 (1997), pp. 40–5.
21 Eltis, *The Military Revolution*, pp. 54, 61.
22 Ibid., p. 103.
23 Francis Fukuyama, *Trust: The Social Virtues and the Creation of Prosperity* (London, Hamish Hamilton, 1995), p. 221.
24 Gordon Brook-Shepherd, *The Austrians: A Thousand-Year Odyssey* (London, HarperCollins, 1996), p. 173, in a comparison by the author (a former British army officer) of the German and Austro-Hungarian forces during the First World War.
25 See Alan Milward, *The German Economy at War* (London, University of London/Athlone, 1965), and John Keegan's *The Battle for History* (London, Hutchinson, 1995), esp. ch. 5, 'The Brains and Sinews of War'.
26 'Coping with Intifada' is a chapter in Martin van Creveld, *The Sword and the Olive: A Critical History of the Israeli Defense Force* (New York, Public Affairs, 1998), pp. 335–52.
27 Gary Wills, 'A Reader's Guide to the Century' (review of Oliver Zunz, *Why the American Century?*), *New York Review of Books*, 15 July 1999, p. 27.
28 Stanford University contributed greatly to the expansion of Binet's work.
29 Jacques Lecomte, 'La mesure de l'intelligence', *Sciences humaines*, November 1998, pp. 44–6; cf. Robert Sternberg, *Beyond IQ: A Theory of Human Intelligence* (Cambridge, Cambridge University Press, 1985).
30 Daniel Michaels, 'Old Soldiers Can't Hope to Fade Away in Central Europe', *Wall Street Journal Europe*, 19 June 1998, pp. 1, 5.
31 Ibid.
32 Daniel Michaels, 'Col. Varga Is to Hungary What Col. Parker Was to Elvis, Sort of', *Wall Street Journal Europe*, 19 June 1998, p. 5.
33 See Mark J. Osiel, *Obeying Orders: Atrocity, Military Discipline and the Law of War* (New York, Transaction, 1998).
34 French General Philippe Morillon, an early commander of UN forces in Bosnia, asks, 'Who are these soldiers who are ready to kill [but] not ready to die?'
35 Timothy Garton Ash, 'Is There a Good Terrorist?', *New York Review of Books*, 29 November 2001, pp. 30–3.
36 See Christian Schmidt, *Les jeux de l'avenir* (Games of the Future) (Paris, Editions Odile Jacob, 2002), on game theory applied to military perspectives.

Part II:

Warfare and its Management

Armed struggle and its mechanics are what we now put under the microscope that science has bequeathed us. Battle, whether defensive or offensive, requires physical preparation well beyond the selection, training and improvement of the human material in its ranks and how adequately these ranks are equipped. Preparedness is conditioned, as in ordinary life, by factors both internal and external to the fighting force.

The internal element consists, among other critical items, of the organization of defense – or battle and supply – for those engaged in operations. The men and women of fighting establishments require uniforms, food and ammunition, weapons of course, reliable and secure means of communication and health care, appropriate transport, and the more abstract skills applicable to planning and organization, doctrine and teaching, practice exercises and evaluation, and finally, response to overall command and control.

Warriors win or lose, at least in part, as a result of the direct support received from the supply services and (behind these) a nation's economic capacity. Martin van Creveld estimates that a victorious force may depend as much as 90 per cent on its logistical back-up – the evidence for which has appeared time and again since the early conflicts involving Persians, Greeks and Romans. A group of terrorists, no matter how large, suffers from poor endologistics.

The external environment, including nature's foibles, is another matter, for the greater part beyond the control of human beings. Climate and the weather are paramount. Oceans and continents, river water and deserts, mountains and plains, forests and meadows, clay or peat or wetlands: physiography and topography play effective roles in facilitating life for, or dogging, a determined commander.

Staff planning and the direction of operations require forethought, integration, policy supervision, assessment and constant correction to ensure optimal conduct of a battle and the progress of the war of which it is part. While some fighting forces leave the prerogative of decision to commanders in the field (the 'theaters' of operations), others observe the more traditional pyramid of command, with all major decisions (on mass deployment, attack plans, supply systems) made at a centralized point such as the national capital or a regional command-level close to the action.

Secure communication is the domain in which the military have put science and technology to work, with sometimes spectacular results. Enciphering and deciphering, used also in diplomacy, trade and banking, and sometimes by the police, have been transformed from sheer pencil-and-eraser drudgery into slick and quick procedures by the computer (today's *digital encryption*): tasks assigned by the military to the information technologies more than 50 years ago. Communication can be 'bent', too, to deceive an adversary real or potential. Deception may even – alas – have an adverse impact on those clearly on 'our' side, even on those ultimately responsible for one's own nation's governance and the security of its citizens.

Security of communication takes another form: radar. This was born of entirely military inspiration, since it emerged from the grinding fear (well founded, as events proved) of defense planners in one country. They foresaw the effectiveness of the air arm of another nation, one that might win – by aerial-bombing its way to victory – for the first time in history. These countries were Great Britain and Germany, each spiraling its way upwards in the progress made on radar during the years before and during the Second World War. Today, we cannot imagine air traffic, civil as well as military, deprived of its radar support.

Because there are bound to be casualties in war, an efficient system of health protection and medical treatment demands still another kind of system: preventive care and effective 'repair' of the sick and wounded. The military depend partly on what the civil world can offer for adaptation to wartime needs, while the civil world has learned (probably much more) from the military's own ways and means of being the Good Samaritan – and doing it swiftly. While many of us find it hard to believe the military have been among the pioneers in the field of medicine and public health, Chapter 11 may come as a surprise. The military lead, however, in certain fields of both preventive and therapeutic medicine, a road that has improved from pot-holed country trails used for the evacuation of the battlefield's wounded two centuries ago to far smoother highways of medical attention and rehabilitative care today. This story has not been told, in this way, elsewhere.

Science and technology thus play increasingly important roles in the exercise of all the qualities in a fighting force: chemistry and biology in feeding and medical care; physics in aerial flight and the applied mechanics of weapons and communications; environmental science in regard to troop safety, transport, shelter in the field, and the efficacy of a great variety of vehicles; and the social sciences in the gaming and simulation realms called management, maneuvers and other massed rehearsals, as well as in functional appraisal: *critiques* of exercises, tactics, operations, entire campaigns and wars.

We look, therefore, at how the strategy for besting the opponent confronting us can be simulated before physical engagement occurs. We see, too, how extensively the various mathematical techniques of operations research have been developed by and for the military, then adopted for civil applications.

Irregular forces, such as insurgents, 'freedom fighters', guerrilla formations, even criminal terrorists, borrow and apply many of the approaches and methods described in this section. The latter, in turn, often feed back to the military.

7

Endologistics: Forts, Food, Feed, Fuel and Freight

'Logistics make up as much as nine-tenths of the business of war.'
Martin van Creveld[1]

'Hurry up, and wait! Why do we have to rise at 03:00 hours, grope in the dark for a half-warmed breakfast or none, stow our weapons and gear, march an hour to a rallying point, only to be on our way finally at 08:30 hours? And, besides, miss all that sleep!' And in the heat or cold, rain or snow, wind or dust or mud of the moment. How many of us who have done military service have not heard this lament?

While the answer is simple, it represents but a small part of the complexity lying behind military activity. Time, planning and patience are required to organize and coordinate, issue orders for, supervise, correct and control the movement of hundreds, thousands, sometimes hundreds of thousands of human beings, their war paraphernalia, means of sustenance and manner of dress, and ultimate replacement by other human beings. Baron Henri de Jomini, in his *Précis de l'art de la guerre* (1836), included even reconnaissance and staff work as well as the efforts of engineers in his definition of logistics. We seek here to understand the complications that the broad domain of logistics seeks to solve.

In Greek, *logistikos* meant 'calculating skill'. In French, *loger* signifies housing or billeting, and a *maréchal des logis* was originally a non-commissioned officer accountable in his unit for lodging and supplies. Within a few decades Jomini designated logistics as the *practical art of moving troops*. The term caught on in the 1880s, when an American naval officer construed logistics as the back-up of military forces with an entire nation's economy – including its manufacturing and service potential. The officer was Admiral Alfred T. Mahan, also his country's first geopolitical expert.

To this Jomini–Mahan contribution to the military lexicon, we add here the term *endologistics* to differentiate man-conceived supply from the external conditions that nature imposes on the sailor, airman and soldier in getting their work done. Those conditions we shall survey in the next chapter.

IT BEGAN WITH THE ROMANS

The Roman military engineer Vitruvius, author of *De architectura,* is one of the first recorded specialists who borrowed knotty civil processes for military application.[2] Marcus Vitruvius Pollio distinguished himself, under Caesar and then Augustus, by codifying the principles of Hellenistic architecture in the use of its orders and proportional systems. Order swiftly became the watchword of the Romans, showing up in urban design as the grid, a conventionalized pattern bearing a principal north–south axis called the *cardo* (whence the cardinal points of the compass), and an east–west artery known as the *decumannus.*

The axial community was really an old town-planning form, dating perhaps from Egypt's Twelfth Dynasty.'Fortress, camp, and city have a common base in military regimentation', Lewis Mumford has emphasized.[3] The 'Roman road', straight and level and many kilometers long, remains a Europe-wide vestige of Rome's military presence two millennia ago and the work of its army engineers. The history and design of Inca and Aztec communities in South and Central America, undocumented as they must probably remain yet assessable from their ruins, often reflect a similar regimentation of community layout and street plan.

Vitruvius construed design and function as expressions of beauty, durability and convenience, and the Roman military opted for the last two qualities as the ones paramount[4] to safeguarding the reaches of empire. Vitruvius also believed that the techniques of making mortar were such a vital contribution to military building that this tradition of quality persisted, in Iberia, for instance, all the way to the Peninsular War – when Wellington and the French generals learned that they needed twice as much ammunition to reduce cemented redoubts than was required in the brick fortifications of the Low Countries and northern France.[5]

Specialization was implicit in the supply and administration of Roman forces. Personnel of the *fabrica* in permanent posts made weapons as well as bricks under the supervision of an NCO called *magister.* The *custos armorum* was in charge of weapon maintenance, the *actuarius* maintained personnel rolls, and the *quaestor* was paymaster under the orders of the *officium rationum* (finance and accountancy section). The *lanius* was meat-cutter; the *dispensator* bought grain supplies, while the *molendarius* oversaw flour milling. (A single legion of 5,000 men consumed, in six months, the wheat harvested from a tract of 8 hectares or 20 acres.) The *librator* was surveyor attached to the engineer troops, and the *metator* selected camp or fortification emplacements. Message transmission was handled by specialists who relayed torch signals,[6] much as with the later Chappe telegraph described in Chapter 9.

Fixed fortifications throughout medieval Europe and in western Asia, China and Japan took on proportions monumental in size and durability, proving themselves useful to those engaged in the Crusades or to the Chinese Han repelling Mongol incursions against the Great Wall – just as the warlords of Honshu and Kyushu sought to protect their feudal fiefdoms from raiders internal or external. Forts assumed shapes peculiar to their locale's topography and natural resources. During the Hundred Years' War, farms and villages (together with their churches) in many parts of Germany and France were walled or re-inforced with towers of masonry, sometimes parapets and often *meurtrières*: vertical slits splayed outwards to expand the fields of fire of harquebuses inside.

NATION-STATES AND FORTRESSES

The Thirty Years' War produced, besides a virtual end to religious wars in Europe and the founding of the modern nation-state, a Swedish supply system for the military – developed under Gustavus Adolphus. The Swedish monarch dispatched his quartermasters to the four corners of Europe, taking stock of local economic resources and appropriating them to his needs. Money was disbursed locally for stocks and re-supply, so that the economic impact locally was an improvement on the earlier practice of pillage and theft.[7]

In the sixteenth century, the Christian knights ringed the new capital of Valetta Templar on the three rocky Mediterranean isles of Malta with a chain of fortresses intended to repel Ottoman marauders and invaders. Far up the Adriatic Sea in Italy's Friule region, the town of Palmanova (not far from where the Austrians and Italians savaged each other near Caporetto during the First World War[8]) was estab-lished in 1593 as a fortress town. Palmanova is circular, with a small command tower as its hub, connected by unobstructed radial streets leading directly to nine bastions equally spaced along its town wall.[9]

Passing mention of the Knights Templar should be a reminder of an essential item of logistics, combined with transport and at least the appearance of valor. Armor for knight and horse was the most expensive

> **BOX 6** A VICTORY NOT SO CLEAR
>
> When Austria-Hungary's fortunes reached their near-nadir in 1917, her German allies assigned General Konrad Krafft von Delmensingen – an expert just returned from mountain warfare in Romania – to the task of routing Italian forces from their hilly strongholds. Krafft and his staff organized nine Austrian and six German divisions into the synthesized Fourteenth Army. This formation demolished Italy's Second Army: 10,000 dead, 30,000 wounded, and nearly 300,000 taken prisoner, thus winning for the Austrian empire its sole victory over the Italians during the entire conflict.
>
> Gordon Brook-Shepherd, *The Austrians: A Thousand-Year Odyssey* (London, HarperCollins, 1961).

single item of the medieval fighting man. Its weight spiraled upwards as jousting and battle increased. As the weight rose, so did the cost of craftsmanship and maintenance. In Europe a suit of armor was worth the same as 40 head of cattle. A knight had two or three horses, and the entire expense was borne as part of his commitment to a noble-man (or -woman), well before the costs of warmaking would be paid by the state.

Peter the Great built the Peter and Paul Fortress within his newly founded St Petersburg, a bulwark to repel Swedish invaders in a region consisting then of little more than river delta and swamps. Decades later, Marshal Sébastien le Prestre de Vauban ringed Louis XIV's France with elegantly conceived and executed stonemasonry meant to thwart English and Austrian onslaughts. His structural layouts had math-ematically calculated ramparts, bastions and other components of military architecture intended to outsmart or rebuff the fast-spreading field artillery of gunpowder and iron shot.

In far-off America the French devised field fortifications to help their royal regiments survive harsh Canadian winters; Jacques Cartier built the first fortified encampment on the St Charles river estuary in 1535. As European–Amerindian relations deteriorated, the forts were redesigned to keep Iroquois and Huron warriors at bay. French engineers had a scientific understanding, relates John Keegan, of walling and entrenchment[10] unparalleled elsewhere. 'The purpose of high walls', adds James Burke, 'was to make them difficult to scale: the longer it took the enemy to climb, the greater the chance of killing him before he reached the top.'[11] It was as simple as that.

Towering walls were of little assurance to the besieged, however, even when safely ensconced behind impenetrable defenses. On the contrary, the state of mind of townspeople (and sometimes the armed defenders), locked behind thick masonry, responded alternatively 'with terror, resignation or fortitude'. In an age when a typical battle began and ended the same day or more often within a few hours, besieged troops were on constant alert, day after day for as long as two or three months.[12] The wear and tear on the psyche must have produced early versions of post-traumatic stress syndrome (see Chapter 11).

Management of the logistics of his campaigns during the 1620s by the Duke of Wallenstein, a Czech who became a principal German strategist and financier from a base near Prague, augured poorly. Yet this master of supply, who helped incarnate the post-medieval transition from static warfare to rapid-movement combat, carried his armies successfully from the northwestern reaches of the Ottoman empire to Brandenburg, Würzburg and Denmark during the first decade of Thirty Years' War.[13]

Vauban's innovations were not lost on the British in North America, who built not one but two defensive installations called Fort William Henry. (The lauded William Henry was the Duke of Cumberland, son of George II.) Major-General William Johnson built the wooden version at Lake George (New York) in 1755, complete with well laid-out bastions and glacis, while a three-storied, round structure of masonry at Booth Bay Harbor may be the first stone fort built in Maine.[14]

TIME'S INFLECTION POINTS

The great pivots of history are what Andrew Grove (founder of Intel, the electronic-chip maker) calls *strategic inflection points*: those moments in the evolution of our species when new circumstances change drastically how the world works. These turning points may mean victory or defeat for military forces. One inflection point in the duality of technical progress in military, as well as civil, life is found in the war between the Prussians and the French of 1870–71. Historian Martin van Creveld relates:

> If the industrial revolution may be said to have begun a hundred years before 1870, it was nevertheless the Franco-Prussian war that truly ushered in the age of coal and steel. As factory chimneys grew ever taller, so did the size of the military instruments maintained by the major [European] powers.[15]

Guns and ammunition were cheap to make and replace, and the fast-expanding railways depended on a good supply of iron and steel for tracks, locomotives, rolling stock, and signaling networks. Conversely, the experience of the northern forces during the Civil War in the United States encouraged a former military transport specialist, Grenville Dodge, 'to put the working end of the [Union Pacific line] on a military basis' in 1866, according to historian Stephen E. Ambrose. 'Without that military organization, it is doubtful that the UP could have been built at all ... The numbers [of workers] ... approached 10,000 ... They were like an army in so many ways.'[16]

In the nineteenth century, railways proved to be the essential vector of how major military forces were moved and supplied – on land, at least, because the navies of the world were still forced to factor-in the element of enormous distance while stocking supplies and ammunition in advance of movement. Napoleon's system of 'magazines' (storage depots) worked better than in the past, but less effectively than in the future because it still relied on traction by animals.

The Prussian evolution of the derivative *Etappen* system (from the French word for stage or phase, *étape*) prior to the war with France in 1870–71 improved on the magazine system, but the use of railways and animal trains proved unable to keep pace with advances by troop units often of army-corps size. (A corps classically comprises a minimum of two divisions, its own staff and special troops including heavy artillery and transport, and may number from 35,000 to as many as 100,000.) By the time of the swift German march across northeastern France one war later in 1914, troops raced ahead of supply capacity so that entire units lived off the land as they pushed back the French army.

Between 1870 and 1913, the production of coal and lignite (the energy sources for mechanical power) in Germany, France and Great Britain rose from less than 160 million tonnes/year to 612 million tonnes. Pig-iron production expanded in the same period, rising from 7.5 million to 29 million tonnes annually.[17] After 1868 industrialization came to Japan, too. Its land forces evolved along western European lines and grew, while Imperial Japan's navy modernized and multiplied its equipment, manpower and strategy to the point that it could destroy the Russian fleet in 1904, enabling Japan to rise politically to the status of world power.[18] Some economists call such 'inflectional' events *secular shifts*, as indeed were these German, French, British and Japanese models – and in which we again detect dual purpose because their national civil economies also grew.

Table 3:
Daily Supplies of all Types for an Army Division, Then and Now
(in tonnes)

Year	War	Daily supplies (tonnes)
1870	Franco-Prussian War: food, fodder	50
1916	First World War, including artillery	150
1942	North African campaigns, with petroleum	300
1944	Normandy campaign	650
1990s	Typical US armored division	+3,000
– or a growth factor of 60 in less than a century-and-a-half		

Sources: Martin van Creveld, *The Transformation of War* (New York, Free Press, 1991); James F. Dunnigan, *How to Make War: A Comprehensive Guide to Modern Warfare* (New York, William Morrow, 1982.

Operation *Barbarossa*, the Third Reich's plan to overwhelm the Soviet Union (1941), took a year to plan. More than two years were needed to mount the Allied push to the Continent via the Normandy campaign of 1944. The German military force that launched its expedition against the USSR in 1941, however, 'was a poor army with strictly limited resources'. Its success depended logistically 'above all on a correct balance between railways, wheels and tracks'.[19] Indeed, the lightning-like advances of the Wehrmacht across Ukraine, Belorussia and Russia *looked* as if the logistics were under full managerial control by *Oberkommando Heeres*, the Armed Forces High Command.

But supply for the Soviet adventure was no stronger than the weakest elements of Germany's war economy: raw-material supply, manufacturing labor and distribution within the military services. Economics was not a strong suit of Germany's *Führer*. The Western Allies caught up with their own logistical lag by (in part) applying operations research to the design of special clothing, equipment and vehicles for cold-weather and jungle operations, the architecture of aircraft and landing vessels for seaborne campaigns, the composition and size of transoceanic convoys, and the morphology of artillery projectiles. Production then rose in enormous quantity, and quality was an added feature in most instances (some called the latter over-engineering).

THE SCIENTISTS ARRIVE

With fortresses a defense of the past – even along coasts and estuaries – only a few months after the First World War burst upon Europe, sturdy constructions not principally intended to resist military attack, such as cathedrals and manor houses, nevertheless showed surprising invulnerability to massed artillery fire and aerial bombardment. Forts fell in Belgium and northern France, Verdun became a charnel ground, and the stately Gothic cathedral nearby at Rheims (since completely rebuilt) finished the war as a near-ruin.

The most heroic structure of the Second World War, by all accounts, remains the sixth-century Benedictine monastery atop Monte Cassino in Italy. This site served as a western hinge of Hitler's defensive Gustav Line, along which battle raged for the first four months of 1944. The German defense at Cassino and along the Gustav Line, a delaying action that reduced the abbey to rubble, meant that another 11 months would be required before Allied forces could reach the Po river valley 300 km to the north. Meanwhile the Soviet Union maintained its abrasion of German forces on the eastern fronts, as complex staff preparations took shape for the Allied campaign against the Third Reich via the Atlantic approaches.

John Desmond Bernal was already an accomplished crystallographer and, as a member of the British Communist Party, a socially committed scientist when the Second World War began. A few years previously Bernal demonstrated, in *The Social Function of Science*,[20] that the relationship between scientists and soldiers was not a novelty. Indeed, he devoted an entire chapter of this work to the quantification of contemporaneous costs of military research and their social consequences. He agonized, too, over the needless deaths in combat of great scientific minds, citing the example of experimental physicist H. J. G. Moseley at Gallipoli in 1915.

Although not called up in uniform, Bernal went into wartime civil service for his country, first in the department of research and experiments at the Ministry of Home Security. There, during the Battle of Britain, Bernal studied the physics of explosions and the resistance of buildings to different shocks. Simultaneously, his colleague, Solly Zuckerman, worked on the concussive effects of shock waves transmitted through the ground to persons seeking refuge in air-raid shelters. Bernal had already published, together with associates in the Cambridge Scientists Anti-War Group, a study called *The Protection of the Public from Aerial Attack* – criticized in *Nature* (10 April 1937) for destroying confidence in the government's defensive plans and tending to create public panic. The two scientists publicly denied any such intentions.

Two years after the outbreak of war, Bernal and Zuckerman were Britain's specialists on bombing effects. Their 'Quantitative Study of Total Effects of Air Raids (Hull and Birmingham Survey)', a Ministry of

Home Security report of 1942,[21] embraced not only human casualties and physical destruction but the effects of bombing raids on industrial production, personnel evacuation, absenteeism, and other implications for civilian morale. The main findings of their analysis were that

- the intensity of air raids does not affect morale overall;
- fire, rather than high explosive, causes most damage to physical plant;
- losses in production result mainly from damage to plant.

Bernal and Zuckerman joined, as a result of a proposal made by Sir Henry Tizard – another scientific civil servant engaged in defense matters – the combined-operations staff of Lord Louis Mountbatten in 1942. Their function as scientific advisors was to analyze techniques and matériel for application in the projected landings by the Western Allies on the European continent. Raised to life peerage in 1971, Lord Zuckerman became a champion of the rationalization of the increasing costs of nuclear arms for both NATO and the Warsaw Pact.[22]

With another colorful civilian, non-scientist Geoffrey Pike, Zuckerman and Bernal constituted Mountbatten's so-called 'Department of Wild Talents'. Plans moved ahead during this time for an invasion along the French coast, the exact site known secretly to the military as early as 1942. It was likely to be the Arromanches-Courseulles area of Normandy, instead of the closer and more obvious Pas de Calais several hundred kilometers to the northeast.

Mountbatten absorbed the two 'scientific liaison officers', Bernal and Zuckerman, directly within his planning staff. Bernal's communist affiliation made him suspect, however, to Vannevar Bush, President Franklin Roosevelt's chief scientific consultant. This tended, along with other factors, to complicate the American–British relationship in combined operations. Yet Bernal's job was to study ways and means of making the landings as practicable as possible through a clear understanding of the types of soil, subsoil and beach gradients the Allied forces could expect to cope with.

Throughout history amphibious approaches had concentrated on ports and harbors.[23] The massive landings of troops along the Black Sea's coasts by the British, French and Turks during the Crimean War had exposed the Allied strategists to the complex logistics – area knowledge included – implicit in such operations. Seventy years later, however, the Gallipoli disaster had demonstrated clearly to military and political leaders that governments ruled by law cannot afford such human losses. This constraint made the scientific analysis undertaken by Bernal not only obligatory but critical.

These analyses had another effect, this one in the dispute concerning area bombing as opposed to pinpoint bombing. The first, the strategy of bombing a zone in which military or military-industrial targets are known or suspected, was strongly favored by Air Marshal Arthur 'Bomber' Harris of the RAF and Winston Churchill's scientific advisor, Lord Cherwell. The second was seen as a strategy to spare civilian lives and strictly civil objects such as schools, hospitals, churches and cultural sites after careful selection of military targets.

The dispute was not resolved then, not by the end of the war, nor since; each side of the controversy continues to have its vocal proponents throughout much of the world – Afghanistan and its cities included.

PLANNING AHEAD

The Allies' Gallipoli campaign in 1915 was inauspicious from its start. Lord Kitchener (field marshal and Secretary of State for War) and Winston Churchill (then First Lord of the Admiralty) hit upon an effort in the Dardanelles against Turkey as a means to take pressure off the Russian ally. Kitchener appointed General Sir Ian Hamilton to command a force of five divisions that could be spared for the expedition.

Hamilton took his leave of London 'with no staff, no maps and no information about Turkish defenses' more recent than nine years old.[24] His transport vessels arrived on the scene with all priority equipment stowed deep in their holds. This necessitated a return of the ships to Alexandria for unloading and reloading, ineluctably putting Turkey on the alert, and incurring a month's delay in launching a doomed campaign. When British empire troops finally landed, they found six Turkish divisions awaiting them. Realities such as these are intimately linked with climatic and other factors to be explored in Chapter 8.

To return to the planning of the Normandy landings, Bernal dug up physiographic and geological data from sources such as Anglo-Norman poetry, studies by Vauban, and the archives of the Linnaean scientific societies of Caen and Cherbourg, *Guide bleu* travel books and privately collected tourist photography, aerial reconnaissance and data supplied by the French Resistance, to study the effects of currents, tides and winds, as well as the location of submerged defenses. Specially mounted commando raids on German-occupied France yielded soil, pebble and vegetation samples. The military-scientific staff ruled out being able to count on using extant port facilities in France for landing personnel and all their supplies, so the idea of building transportable docks to be sunk off the coast became the costly but reasonably successful Mulberry project: artificial, floating harbors for locations lacking mooring facilities.

Sandtables and other models were constructed, and analogous beaches in Norfolk on England's east coast were used to test resistance to the mass and movement of both tanks and wheeled vehicles as well as of men weighed down with arms and equipment. Bernal also had access to a world specialist on sand, R. A. Bagnold, by then a wartime brigadier (brigadier-general) in the British Army. Sand deployed naturally – since it responds to gravity, wind, heat or cold – daunted the military with special problems of resupply and vehicle upkeep. Once General Erwin Rommel had landed his first mechanized division in North Africa, he was faced with assuring that unit alone a minimum of 350 tonnes/day of all supplies, water included,[25] across hundreds of kilometers of sand. The exigencies of resupplying combat units led Rommel to adopt the following command philosophy:

> Quartermasters often tend to work by theory and base all their calculations on precedent, being satisfied if their performance comes up to the standard which this sets. This can lead to frightful disasters … [T]he commander must be ruthless in his demands for an all-out effort. If there is anyone in a key position who … has no natural sense for practical problems of organization, then that man must be ruthlessly removed.[26]

The logistical demands on the Afrika Korps and associated Italian forces were to be repeated, with many variations on the theme, before the defeat of the Axis forces in Africa.

THAT DEVIL IN THE DETAILS

Along northern Europe's shores, the computing of tidal effects raised peculiarly military problems because an error of 5 cm in tide level at a given spot could translate into a depth 200 times as much, or another 10 m of water, farther along the shore. Such data were taken into account, together with meteorological forecasting for early-to-mid June 1944, by General Eisenhower's staff preparatory to the decision to strike in Normandy on 6 June (recounted in Chapter 8). The full story is told critically by a Bernal biographer, Maurice Goldsmith, in *Sage: A Life of J .D. Bernal.*[27] (For a further-ranging appreciation of modeling by the military, see Chapter 12.)

We have mentioned the Mulberry harbors designed by British engineers. Two of these complex structures were built, with components scraped together despite the desperate shortage of raw and semi-finished materials, then towed across rough seas to the French coast. On the way, the Mulberry assembly managed by the Americans made it through the gales fairly successfully, yet was nearly destroyed by wind before it could begin operation. The Mulberry under British control fared less well, but the losses were made good by resorting to the scuttling of a few ships as protection for the unloading of personnel and cargo. The American infantry captain's cajolery in tactics to 'keep it simple, soldier' had not been heard, perhaps because of the complexity of the operation and the prevalent gales, but the technical effort deeply impressed Erwin Rommel and raised his esteem of the opponent.[28]

The 'Department of Wild Talents' team produced another plan, this one nearly falling into the realm of technology fiction. Project Habbakuk, conceived by non-scientist Pyke, was intended to overcome the extreme shortage of aircraft available in the right places at the right times during the war's early stages. It envisaged building a huge 'aircraft carrier', 600m long with a hull 9m thick, of reinforced ice, a natural or artificial substance possessing only 0.01 per cent the strength of steel. The fortified ice was baptized *pykrete* by its inventor. Extraordinary as the scheme sounded, the proposal was approved and awarded high priority by the British Prime Minister, who made available naval R&D funds of £1 million in December 1942. The properties of ice reinforced for military purposes began to be studied full-time, coincidentally in 1943 in Canada and the United States, by a young Austrian specialist in molecular structure named Max Perutz.

The Admiralty's deputy controller of R&D, a physical chemist by the name of Charles Goodeve, disliked ice ideas for reasons both scientific and logistical: frozen water is not normally accepted as a structural material, and by 1943 the first vessel – on paper – required 45m (150ft) of draft and was calculated at 1 million tonnes in displacement.[29] Pykrete took the form, in experiments conducted at the Brooklyn Polytechnic Institute by Bernal's friend, Isadore Fankuchen, of a combination of water and about 9 per cent wood pulp. By 1944, the project foresaw huge steel skeletons needed to reinforce the floating airbases. Solly Zuckerman considered the Habbakuk scheme nothing short of nonsense, and the technologically ambitious idea died on the drawing board.

Yet, despite the ability of the Western Allies to land in France with 'more motor transport than any other army' before, the skill of its planners and commanders should not be exaggerated. Historian van Creveld, admitting that the advance from the coast to the environs of Paris was 'successful and even spectacular strategically', claims that the expanding beachhead proved to be 'an exercise in logistic pusillanimity unparalleled in modern military history'.[30] In other words, with the Luftwaffe virtually immobilized, the Allied generals could and should have pushed east faster and farther to shorten the war and lessen both military and civil casualties.

During the Gulf War almost five decades later, the Coalition forces pressed ahead extremely hard and the logistics kept up, but the uppermost command stopped its victorious units short of Iraq's capital at Baghdad and capture of the country's leader.

MARCHING ON THE STOMACH

Food is a complicating factor for armies because of the problems of procurement, storage, transport, preparation and timely distribution to each waiting mouth. Historically armies lived off the land: they simply took (but occasionally paid for) what they needed, on the spot, as their units moved ahead. A field force inevitably was forced by the arithmetic of supplies found *in situ* to become a 'food-producing machine that milled grain, gathered wood, baked flour, and reaped fodder', all operations inevitably interfering with the fighting or 'regular functioning of an army'.[31]

In the eighteenth century, a European expeditionary force typically had 60,000 men, consuming about 600 tonnes of bread alone every ten days: 1 kg/day/man. To assure its supply of flour, the force foraged a large swath of ground measuring roughly 150km by 15km, so as not to wander beyond 8km – 5 statute miles – on either side of the road leading to the enemy. Vauban, seldom confining his computations to the needs of military engineering alone, was 'obsessive' about calculating the provisions required to sustain forces staging or resisting a siege. He estimated that a pound of tobacco, for example, although not needed to sustain human metabolism, equaled '112 pipefuls, and would permit twenty-eight soldiers to enjoy four smokes each' daily.[32]

Ever the thorough manager too, Vauban worried about another kind of consumption by the troops: alcohol. In his *Traité des Sièges* the great fortification specialist noted that, while sappers earned escalating cash premiums for extending their saps towards the fortress besieged, they ran the risk of never collecting their money because of overconsumption of spirits. He urged officers to beware lest these hardy pioneers 'throw every precaution to the winds and have themselves killed off like brute beasts'.[32]

The European wars drove the new country of Belgium (created in 1830–31) to make a colossal construction effort so that its territory would never again be crisscrossed by invaders from east or west. It commissioned a native-son engineer, Henri Alexis Brialmont, to design and build a string of impregnable fortresses from Antwerp to the Meuse River. In 1914, General Brialmont's defenses proved as power-less to stop fast-moving German infantry, cavalry and artillery as would the Maginot Line when France encountered the *Blitzkrieg* of May–June 1940.

Navies, more provident because of the nature of their mission and the distances they were forced to travel, stored fresh provisions (and occasionally alcohol) for as long as these could last aboard ship. When provisions ran out, misery raised its head. Biscuits and dried meat then became the daily ration, with fresh water doled out to make it last. Carbohydrates and proteins could thus be assured in most cases, but vitamins, minerals and essential trace elements were sorely lacking during long voyages.

The Hapsburg armies of Austria seem to have been the first to organize a supply arm (in 1783) because of their generals' evolving doctrine that precluded living off the land. This policy surmounted the very low 10 per cent of expendable supplies that field forces could carry, in an age when even the most strong-willed commanders knew that their units could advance no more than 15km daily on average.

WATER AND OTHER SUPPLIES

Armies have always had a water-supply problem, but with navies it was worse. When Zheng He, the court eunuch in China who first assembled a navy worthy of the name, had his ships designed and built early in the fifteenth century, he gave much thought to long-haul water supply. The Chinese fleet, exploring farther and farther west-wards until it reached the African coastline, tried to stop at ports 10 sailing days apart to top-off potable water holds and do business ashore. Zheng also had special water-carrying vessels built to accom-pany China's 'treasure fleet', so called because of its commercial mission,'the first such convenience for a large armada anywhere in the world'.[34] Today naval vessels both load fresh water and desalinate sea water aboard ship.

Pemmican, made from hot animal fat poured over lean meat, dried fruits and berries, was the invention of northern Amerindians. European expeditionary forces adopted pemmican in the mid-eighteenth century as sure nourishment during adverse weather. Water, derived from snow and ice in the northern latitudes, is essential to flush and help metabolize this compact foodstuff. Pemmican-type preserves have since been supplanted by canned or dehydrated goods, frozen foods and freeze-dried materials.

The invention of canning early in the nineteenth century helped alleviate the problem of food storage during the long expeditions of empire-building and scientific exploration that lasted until the First World War. Nicolas Appert in Paris boiled vegetables in jars for several hours, effectively eliminating most of the air and micro-organisms present (though he must have been ignorant of the latter's existence),[35] for the benefit of the French navy in the Caribbean. The British, in at least alimentary if not political alliance with the French, acquired Appert's patents and shifted the containers used from glass to 'tins', and *their* expeditionary forces in far-off India benefited from unspoiled, pre-prepared rations.

During the Peninsular campaign in Iberia against the armies of Napoleon, the Duke of Wellington (although attended by a French chef) breakfasted simply on tea and toast. Nutrition in terms of the adequate absorption of vitamins and proteins, combined with tasteful preparation and pleasant service – always far short of the epicurean – remained unresolved. This austerity critically diminished recuperative power among the sick and wounded, as Florence Nightingale realized during the Crimean War, despite a military system of regular food supply that came into being by the 1850s.

Napoleon instituted a system to improve the Austrian method. He combined the responsibilities of *commissionaires de guerre* (centralized service-corps directors) with those of staff officers, typically at division level, called *ordonnateurs* or unit quartermasters. They were in charge of delivering supplies and assuring transport directly to forward formations. Napoleon also directed that baked goods be prepared in advance, for example, the hundreds of thousands of field biscuits prepared and waiting at Ulm on the Rhine, prior to the arrival of the Emperor's columns. After Napoleon's forces took Ulm, they developed a system of ammunition resupply, based at Heilbronn – probably the world's first – that furnished line troops with as much as 100,000 rounds of fresh ammunition daily.[36]

Napoleon's march on Moscow several years later, utter calamity that it proved to be (10,000 men returned from an original force of more than 400,000), is paradoxically recognized today for its thorough planning by Bonaparte's staff. Van Creveld, for example, calls it an irony that the Russian campaign of 1812–13 was the action for which the French leader 'assembled means, human and material, out of all proportion to anything that went before'[37] in recorded military campaigns.

After Moscow but before Waterloo the Prussians invented a 'train apparatus' that combined columns of provisions for four days with mobile bakeries in the field, ambulance vehicles and remount depots. In 1831, with the advent of steam railways, this mechanism was converted into train companies, one per army corps, whose specially prepared officers had been detached from cavalry regiments. In 1859, the Prussian chief-of-staff, Field-Marshal Helmuth von Moltke ('the Elder'), formalized the railway units as *Eisenbahntruppe*, ordered to work in close conjunction with civil railway contractors.

NEW ATTITUDES ABOUT FEEDING

During the second Seminole War (1835–42) in the United States, as the value of mobility and supply was upgraded by the American army, Brigadier-General Thomas S. Jesup supervised the development of a light yet substantial daily ration of a little more than 300gm.[38] Hardtack, or tough biscuits, and pickled or tinned 'bully' beef also made their way at this time into the fighting man's field or sea diet. Thus it was that, during the Second World War and after, the Americans and Canadians, some allies, and even their enemies, could consume a canned or packaged diversity of food, drink, preserved fruit and confectionery in (sometimes) endless supply.

While food delivered to the frontline soldier took the form, decades later, of 'meals ready to eat' – the MRE of Gulf War fame – quality continued to plague the quartermasters as much as quantity, if not even more. The United States Army, long a leader in questioning the supply and quality of potable water available, ordered in the 1990s a study to determine if its troops might not suffer qualitative under-consumption of nourishment in field conditions. The outcome was an enlightening analysis, *Not Eating Enough* (1995), to which a special contribution was made by experts in military environmental medicine. Underlining a fear perhaps as old as armies, the Institute of Medicine in Washington emphasized in this study that 'the rapid deployment of troops may not give [them] the opportunity to regain weight lost between missions', otherwise a happy thought for many obese civilians.

As early as 1855, the British Secretary of War authorized the services of a professional restaurateur to ease the discomfort of the army bogged down in Crimea. Alexis Soyer, French chef at London's Reform Club, traveled to the war zone at his own expense to set up shop at the Barrack Hospital. Nurse Florence Nightingale commented that 'none but he [had studied food preparation] for the purpose of cooking large quantities of food in the most nutritive and economical manner for great quantities of people'. Cecil Woodham-Smith adds that Soyer ended the 'frightful system' of boiling ingredients – concocting, instead, recipes 'to make excellent soups and stews' from army rations. Soyer trained soldiers who were permanently assigned as cooks.

Soyer failed, however, to convince the authorities that meat rations should be based on *boned* meat in order to avoid weighed single portions consisting solely of bone. Service regulations had not yet foreseen this quantity/quality detail.[39] Nearly a century later the food-supply picture would have virtually metamorphosed, as Table 4 makes clear.

Table 4:

Food Consumed by 2,000 Men and Officers aboard US Battleship, 1941–45

(in pounds, unless stated otherwise, each half-month)

Flour	2–3 tons	Eggs (each)	37,000	Frozen beef	20,000
Tomatoes	1,800	Asparagus	1,800	Frozen veal	4,000
Potatoes	18,000	Sweet potatoes	1,800	Luncheon meat	500
Carrots	3,000	Lemons	2,400	Frozen fish	1,000
Celery	1,200	Oranges	3,800	Smoked ham	1,500
Lettuce	2,400	Rhubarb	1,000	Coffee	2–4 tons
Ice cream (not available on smaller vessels) 2–3 tons					

Source: James E. Dunnigan and Albert A. Nofi, *Dirty Little Secrets of World War II* (New York, William Morrow/Quill, 1994), p. 314.

THE RIGHT DECISION AT THE RIGHT TIME

One of the aims of military education is to train the young officer and noncommissioned officer, and many of the lesser ranks too, to be prepared for the unexpected. One still hears instructors explain that there exists no 'school solution' to such-and-such a tactical problem. The instructor patiently repeats that resolution of a particular problem 'will depend on circumstances and how the small-unit commander assesses the tactical situation'. Cynics call this, in both military and civil life, 'managing the mess', but there is often no other plausible response to certain questions on tactics: the leader on the spot makes the immediate decisions.

Timely decisions proved to be the case when General Erich von Falkenhayn launched the mega-battle of Verdun in 1916. Verdun is the historic site where Gaul was transformed into France, in 843, and of later French defeats by the Prussians in 1792 and 1871. Highly symbolic in the history of Gaul/France's relationship with her Rhenish neighbor, Verdun also witnessed the first effort to gain mastery of the airspace above a battle zone. For our purposes, a crudely dynamic equation of the Germano-French encounter at Verdun might be formulated as follows:

Germany: bleed France in Lorraine = *France*: hold the line at any cost

This dynamic proved to be the classic zero-sum game but, historically, a super-gambit whose stakes were colossal, as we shall see.

In 1897 the commanding generals of the French VI and XVIII Army Corps authorized the participation, for the first time, of motor vehicles in seasonal maneuvers within their respective areas. Although there would be no funds for the purchase of automotive equipment until a few years later, an engineer colonel named Fix lauded its performance in the field and endorsed the replacement of horses by the internal-combustion engine – but only for medical evacuation, mail and supply services. The year coincided with the first identification of radioactive elements, as we saw in Chapter 4. Two entirely new eras, the automotive and the nuclear, were thus about to unfold; we saw in Chapters 4 and 6, too, how the discovery of radioactivity would bring a paradigmatic change to military thinking and the pitting of offense against defense.

Part of the gigantic struggle at Verdun included a new exercise in complexity intended to mitigate at least a major challenge – ensuring enormous supplies – with

> massive road convoys along 67km of the two-lane road leading from Bar-le-Duc to Verdun … This was the brainchild of a young staff captain named Aimé Doumenc. Ten thousand territorial and home-guard soldiers spread 700,000 tonnes of crushed stone and gravel … to [surface] the 'Sacred Road' that would bear 3,500 Berliet CBA flat-bed trucks, 500 Renault EG tractors and 3,000 assorted Peugeot, Latil and Saurer ambulances, liaison vehicles, and utility models mounted with radios and pigeon lofts.[40]

Other numbers round off the description of this feat in logistics invented by a junior officer, a stupefying contrast with the support available a century earlier to the Napoleonic and British incursions in Iberia during the Peninsular War. The Sacred Road to Verdun required, in time, a huge team of 300 officers and 8,000 other ranks. They managed to transport daily an average of 13,000 fighting men, 7,900 tonnes of ammunition, supplies and equipment, while consuming 2 tonnes of grease, 20,000 liters of engine oil, and burning 200,000 liters of fuel. The movements were apportioned to 20-vehicle sections equipped to handle replacement personnel, health needs, fresh-meat transport, telegraphic communication, road maintenance and vehicle repairs.[41] The zone became an enormous network of resupply, breakdowns, repairs and replacement of everyone and every- thing.

On the other side of this demonic scene, where Doumenc was adjusting his desperate kind of game theory to fluid circumstances that were anything but play, Falkenhayn's supply system suffered from too many horse-drawn vehicles combined with too little rubber (tires were made of straw-filled leather) and a dearth of petroleum. The German rail network proved inflexible, and mud was the ground's unchanging texture under the passage of transport. The human toll taken by the eleven-month campaign, stretching from one winter to the next, was the cataclysmic loss by Germany and France of nearly 600,000 of their young male populations born between 1880 and 1899, many more hundreds of thousands wounded, a fortune in horses, ordnance and other matériel and victory of any kind.

EVOLVING MOBILITY

The horse had become vital to the military over the centuries for maneuvering, scouting and message-running, and moving supply trains and artillery – on all the continents. John Keegan points out that between about 1650 and 1890 the Indians of the North American plains, for example, acquired horse *and* gun, adapting them quickly and expertly ('terrifyingly effective') as warriors' tools. Keegan reckons that 'it is difficult to think of any other preliterate group which … made so rapid and complete a transition from primitive to sophisticated warriordom in so short a space of time'.[42]

Returning to the First World War, we need to add a word about feeding horses. During the early months of the 1914–18 conflict, General Alexander von Kluck led the German First Army (whose infantry would be stopped near Paris by the 'taxis of the Marne', hundreds of Peugeot G7 sedans, impressed into service). This German formation had 84,000 horses. The 'petroleum' of the day was dry fodder, required in prodigious quantities for such a herd of animals. The horses consumed nearly 1 million kg (1,000 tonnes) of feed per day and, if transported in a single train, the convoy would have consisted of almost 1,000 regulation fodder wagons. This was impossible, so the horses were turned loose on local harvests in northern France, feeding on green wheat and other cereals. Inevitably, this resulted in animals ill and weak from green feed, and there was no remedy. A second consequence was impaired mobility for artillery batteries. Sufficient veterinary services had, quite simply, not been foreseen.

The transport management devised by Captain Doumenc was destined, here again, to have major sequels. The motorized truck proved itself in adverse conditions along the Sacred Road. The horse, increasingly replaced by high-performance fleets of trucks, was doomed to disappear after hostilities as the prime mover in Western economies. In the Second World War, Doumenc's model served to create the 'Red Ball Express highway', the Allied supply chain stretching from Cherbourg almost 1,000 km east towards the Rhine.

The Red Ball Express rushed almost a half-million tonnes of ammunition, food, petroleum and other necessities to the field armies moving rapidly east. The Red Ball became, too, the model for today's worldwide, highly competitive – and environmentally hazardous – trucking industry. Other civil outgrowths of Doumenc's innovation are bodies such as the European Logistical Association and trade journals on distributive flow of all kinds (for example, the French *Logistiques Magazine*).

MASS MOVEMENT

Let's glance at other logistics prevailing in Europe before hostilities began in 1914. (Then retired) General Feldmarschall Count Alfred von Schlieffen's war planning included, in its fifth stage – mobilization – the 'military travel plan'. Before war broke out, the Imperial German mobilization exercise had been reduced and tested: it was one lasting only 13 days, 'involving 11,000 trains moving a million men, 600,000 horses and the necessary supplies'.[43] In the east, Imperial Russia was drafting the twentieth version of its own mobilization, effective in September 1914, 'which would have cut the time needed to put seventy-five infantry divisions into the field from thirty to eighteen days'.[44] The preparedness was excellent, but both empires lost the war.

After the First World War, the US Army field-tested, using its new transport, the condition of the United States' road system: an exercise in homeland defense. These trials in 1919 lasted 62 days, supervised by an unknown lieutenant-colonel named Dwight Eisenhower. Three hundred troops took a convoy of assorted utility vehicles (including a blacksmith's workshop) from Washington to San Francisco, only to learn how defective were the nation's highways. The findings instigated new construction programs throughout the country culminating in 1957, after another world conflict, when President Eisenhower signed into law the new Interstate scheme of freeways intended to minimize rising fatalities and injuries caused by traffic accidents at junctions and crossroads.

Competence in transport, even in the highly industrialized setting of the governmental G7 and European Union economies of the early twenty-first century, highlights some service deficiencies among the military that seem downright implausible. Echoing remarks by Henry Kissinger in his *Diplomacy* of 1994, for example, French strategist Philippe Delmas comments that it was unthinkable in 1996 that no European government could transport 'in an emergency 10,000 troops over a distance of 2,000 km'.[45] Yet this is so: in repeated peacekeeping interventions in Africa since the 1960s, the French and Belgian governments called on the US Air Force or that of Ukraine to supply transport craft and crews to transfer a few rifle companies or, at most, a battalion of commandos.

Air transport became a critical factor in the Kosovo campaign in spring 1999. After a month of combat, it was clear to NATO commanders that movement of Allied troops over long distances was straining the system. This proved to be the case in the long-distance deployment of troops and equipment, exceptionally so for tanker aircraft. The commercial airport at Frankfurt-am-Main was commandeered under NATO requirements to reserve for these refuelers all priorities for landing, refilling the airborne reservoirs, and take-off. One commercial airline, Lufthansa, lost $5 million a day because of flights it was obliged to cancel.

Curiously, an American special committee had published only weeks before its conclusion that

> revolutionary changes in battlefield mobility ... are unlikely to be attained before 2025 ... Air carriers capable of meeting operational lift requirements for a force of 15-tonne vehicles are also technically feasible, but these carriers may not be affordable and would add significantly to the overall fuel burden.[46]

Air support for the Afghanistan campaign was financed by extraordinary appropriations made instantly by the US Congress.

Mobility and surprise, combined with supporting logistics, Basil Liddell Hart wrote in both his biography of William T. Sherman (1929) and *Strategy: The Indirect Approach* (1964),[46] were restored to military doctrine by General Sherman during the American Civil War. This culminated in his capture of Atlanta in September 1864. Liddell Hart attributed to Sherman's views the creation, later, of Britain's mechanized land force in the 1920s and ultimately General Heinz Guderian's lightning-like movements of armor.

Logistical expenses are now, well after *Blitzkrieg,* a fair proportion of defense budgets. The dimensions of military logistics are exemplified by what it has cost to deploy US nuclear weapons. A private think-tank, the Brookings Institution, published in 1998 a comprehensive reckoning of the cost of being a nuclear power during the six decades between 1940 and the time of the 680-page report's appearance: $5.5 *trillion* in 1966.[48] Among the various costs attributable to R&D and construction, deployment, targeting, control, defense against analogous systems, dismantlement and clean-up maintenance, it is *deployment* that has been the single most costly item at $3.241 trillion. The report's principal author, Stephen Schwartz, added that nuclear weapons still cost $35 billion annually to protect and service.

RATIONALIZING PROCUREMENT

The Kosovo campaign in the Republic of Yugoslavia revealed organic defects of a potentially calamitous scale. British troops confronting the Serbian army in June 1999 suddenly discovered flaws in the operation of their portable radios and small arms. They were forced to borrow equipment from other NATO units. Months later the BBC revealed parts of post-action reports prepared by the commander of Britain's intervention force in the war zone and an aide, Lieutenant-Colonel Paul Gibson, commanding the 1st Parachute Battalion. These reporters were outspoken in their criticism of 'inappropriate' matériel[49] and in their recommendations for immediate rectification.

In his book, *Lifting the Fog of War* (2000), former vice-chairman of the US Joint Chiefs of Staff William Owens warns that the successful future of defense establishments will depend largely on rationalized procurement of equipment and services. Owens believes that 'joint requirement' committees are needed at national level. Otherwise, all the 'joint' operations and interservice communications of today will not equal the critical reforms needed in *intraservice* management and coordination.[50]

One consequence: British armed forces, under the stewardship of Major-General Tony Raper, and Defence Logistics, Communication and Information Services and Support, are exploiting the Internet, reviewing 'the way they buy and store supplies', in order to 'become the world's most wired up military'.[51]

And yet weapons, ammunition and other supplies, transport, and the miscellaneous essentials of combat management – not to speak of the adequacy of human numbers – cannot be maintained without a fundamental appreciation of the workings of nature. This is still almost wholly beyond the control of mere mortals; it is the interface between science and war (and, not infrequently, terrorism).

NOTES

1 Early in his chapter on 'Logistics in Perspective', in *Supplying War: Logistics from Wallenstein to Patton* (Cambridge Cambridge University Press, 1977), p. 231.
2 Noted by Daniel J. Boorstin in *The Creators* (New York, Random House, 1992), p. 101 ff.
3 In *The City in History: Its Origins, its Transformation, and its Prospects* (New York, Harcourt, Brace & World, 1961), pp. 207–8.
4 The interpretation is that of John Peter, designer and architectural historian. Private communication to the author, 18 September 1996.
5 Christopher Duffy, *Fire and Stone: The Science of Fortress Warfare, 1660–1860* (London, Greenhill, 1996), p. 44.
6 Yann Le Bohec, *L'armée romaine sous le Haut-empire* (The Roman Army under the Imperium) (Paris, Picard, 1989), pp. 53, 233, 24 and 161.
7 Brian M. Downing, *The Military Revolution and Political Change: Origins of Democracy and Autocracy in Early Modern Europe* (Princeton, NJ, Princeton University Press, 1992), p. 71.
8 The seesaw of 12 major battles between Austrian and Italian forces at Caporetto inspired Ernest Hemingway's *A Farewell to Arms*. Cf. Mario Morselli, *Caporetto 1917: Victory or Defeat?* (London, Frank Cass, 2001).
9 A bird's-eye view of the fortified town appears in James Burke, *The Day the Universe Changed* (Boston, MA, Back Bay/Little, Brown, 1995, 2nd edn), p. 83.
10 John Keegan, *Warpaths: Travels of A Military Historian in North America* (London, Random House/Pimlico, 1995), p. 99.
11 James Burke, *Connections* (Boston, MA, New York, Little, Brown/Back Bay, 1978/1995), p. 253.
12 Duffy, *Fire and Stone*, pp. 180–2.
13 The story of Albrecht Wenzel Eusebius von Wallenstein (1583–1634) is told in detail by Hellmut Ditwald, *Wallenstein: eine Biographie* (Munich-Esslingen, Bechtle Verlag, 1969).
14 Although the Lake George site is a reconstruction, both installations are open to the modern tourist.
15 Martin van Creveld, *The Transformation of War* (New York, Free Press, 1991), p. 109.
16 Stephen E. Ambrose, *Nothing Like It in the World: The Men Who Built the Transcontinental Railroad, 1863–1869* (New York, Simon & Schuster, 2000), pp. 172, 211, 213, 253.
17 Van Creveld, *The Transformation of War*, p. 109 ff.
18 Jean Esmein of France's Académie de Marine believes that Japan's defeat of Russia and the ensuing Treaty of Portsmouth led the Japanese to begin a century-long study to understand 'the West' that has no analogy among Western nations interested in Japan. He bases his view on the two-volume

Cent ans de pensée japonaise (A Hundred Years of Japanese Thought) by Y.-M. Allioux (Paris, Editions Picquier, 1996). Personal communication with the author, 23 April 1998.

19 Van Creveld, *The Transformation of War*, pp. 177–8.
20 J. D. Bernal, *The Social Function of Science* (London, Routledge, 1939), p. 165. This may be the seminal examination of science–society relationships published by a practicing scientist.
21 Report No. 2770, Ministry of Home Security, London, 8 April 1942.
22 See, e.g., Solly Zuckerman, *Nuclear Illusion and Reality* (New York, Viking, 1982).
23 Thucydides tells us that as early as the Peloponnesian War (431–404 BC) amphibious landings were a part of wars between states, with commando-style raids made by Athenian forces to harass the Spartan enemy.
24 David Saul, *Military Blunders: The How and Why of Military Failure* (New York, Carroll & Graf, 1998), p. 51.
25 Van Creveld, *The Transformation of War*, p. 185.
26 B. H. Liddell Hart (with Lucie-Maria Rommel, Manfred Rommel and Fritz Bayerlein), *The Rommel Papers* (New York, Harcourt Brace, 1953), p. 92.
27 Maurice Goldsmith, *Sage: A Life of J.D. Bernal* (London, Hutchinson, 1980), esp. chap. 7, 'Days of Fulfilment' (pp. 89–123); see also Sylvia Arditi, 'La préparation scientifique du débarquement de juin 1944', *La Recherche*, 266 (1994), pp. 690–3.
28 Liddell Hart, *The Rommel Papers*, p. 522, n. 2 by Fritz Bayerlein.
29 Draft is a ship's depth in water in relation to a given load.
30 Van Creveld, *The Transformation of War*, p. 215.
31 Ibid., p. 35.
32 Duffy, *Fire and Stone*, p. 99.
33 As cited in Duffy, *Fire and Stone*, p. 160.
34 Louise Levathes, *When China Ruled the Seas, The Treasure Fleet of the Dragon Throne, 1405–1433* (New York, Simon & Schuster, 1994), p. 83.
35 Until Louis Pasteur made his discoveries in microbiology a half-century later.
36 Van Creveld, *The Transformation of War*, p. 57.
37 Ibid., p. 36.
38 Herman Hattaway, *Shades of Blue and Gray: An Introductory Military History of the Civil War* (Columbia MO, and London, University of Missouri Press, 1997), pp. 10–11.
39 Cecil Woodham-Smith, *Florence Nightingale, 1820–1910* (New York, McGraw Hill, 1951), pp. 147, 150.
40 J. G. Richardson, 'The Historic Boundlessness of the Creative Spirit', in J. G. Richardson (ed.), *Windows on Creativity and Invention* (Mt Airy, MD, Lomond, 1988), p. 311.
41 Christian Benoit, 'La Voie sacrée et la naissance des insignes militaires', in Claude Carlier and Guy Pedroncini (eds), *L'émergence des armes nouvelles* (The Emergence of New Weapons) (Paris, Editions Economica, 1997), pp. 191–216.
42 Keegan, *Warpaths*, p. 270.
43 Niall Ferguson, *The Pity of War* (London, Allen Lane/Penguin, 1998), p. 95.
44 Ibid., p. 96.
45 In a presentation on 4 June 1996 during the 1st Annual Strategic Lectures of the Institut de Relations Internationales et Stratégiques, Paris.
46 National Research Council, Committee to Perform a Technology Assessment Focused on Logistics Support Requirements for Future Army Combat Systems,

Reducing the Logistics Burden for the Army After Next (Washington, DC, National Academy Press, 1999), p. 160.

47 B. H. Liddell Hart, *Sherman: Soldier, Realist, American* (New York, Dodd, Mead, 1929); repr., with intro. by Jay Luvaas (New York, Da Capo, 1993); and by the same author, *Sherman: The Genius of the Civil War* (London, Benn, 1930); *Strategy: The Indirect Approach,* (New York, Praeger, 1954).

48 Stephen I. Schwartz *et al.*, *Atomic Audit: The Costs and Consequences of US Nuclear Weapons Since 1940* (Washington, DC, Brookings Institution, 1998).

49 Reported by Jacques Duplouich in *Le Figaro*, 4 January 2000, p. 4.

50 William Owens (with Ed Offley), *Lifting the Fog of War* (New York, Farrar, Straus & Giroux, 2000).

51 Ben Rooney, 'Logistics, E Company', *Industry Standard Europe*, 15 November 2000, pp. 53–9.

8

Exologistics: How the Natural Environment Conditions Battle

'In war the enemy does not behave as expected, orders are misunderstood, friendly fire falls on one's own troops, equipment breaks down, the weather does not obey forecasts, the terrain is not what the maps say it should look like.'

John Keegan[1]

Even for an operation purely 'humanitarian in character', stresses serving French officer Jean Claude Gruaut, 'good weather data are essential for its success'. In the last chapter we saw that the ability to wage battle is a function of having the appropriate economic-technical resources combined with skill and intelligence in their use. Perhaps next in importance to the mix of humans, weapons, strategy, tactics, supply and communications, and surprise are soil, water, air and vegetal-cover factors that play vital – if not determining – roles in the outcome of action.

WIND AND WEATHER

The founder of the Mongol dynasty, Kublai Khan, was determined to extend Chinese sovereignty over Japan. His seaborne expedition to Hakata (today's Fukuoka) in 1274 was thwarted, however, as much by divine winds (*kamikaze*) as by Japanese resistance. The 'divine' wind was a typhoon or hurricane, of course, one that recurred in 1281 when Kublai Khan attempted a second amphibious expedition. Nature outwitted ambitious human strategy.

During the war between Pisa and Florence in the sixteenth century, the Florentine military council intended to use the Arno river as a weapon – engineered under the supervision of the rulers, the Gonfaloniere Signoria. The young Niccolò Machiavelli was secretary of the committee, whose idea was to deprive Pisa totally of the river's flow. The feat was to be accomplished by creating a diversion of the river, with hydraulics designed and supervised by Leonardo da Vinci, working under contract with the seigniory. In 1503, 2,000 Florentines, protected from Pisan raiders by a 1,000 soldiers, excavated a new course for the Arno but – upon testing the deviated bed – their work caused a dam to burst and valuable farmland to be flooded. The engineering work was canceled.[2]

Two and a half centuries later, a battle that was a prelude to France's loss of its North American colonies, thanks to its defeat on the Plains of Abraham near the city of Québec, was a temporary setback occurring to the British at Gibraltar-like Louisbourg in 1757. British forces were convinced that a run up the mighty St Lawrence River to Québec and eventually Montréal subsumed the elimination first of Louisbourg (today Louisburg) in Nova Scotia. London ordered a force under John Campbell Loudoun to neutralize Louisbourg, but poor weather delayed the invading force.

The British, together with their 60th Royal American Regiment, frittered away a year either idle or in alternative actions. Louisbourg was taken anyway, in 1758. Loudoun was succeeded by James Wolfe who would die, struck by a bullet the following year. Montréal fell next. Stormy weather may therefore have been the only cause delaying, by two years, the defeat of the French, and Britain's acquisition of Canada.

When French revolutionary forces took Belgium in 1794, they moved north during one of the coldest winters of the entire eighteenth century to 'liberate' the Dutch Republic from the British Duke of York's army. The cold worked to the advantage of the French, who crossed frozen streams that normally served as water ramparts, and mauled the British formation. Two years later, the weather overturned a French effort to land nearly 15,000 men in 46 ships in Ireland to foment an uprising against British rule.[3] The French revolutionary expedition, under the command of General Lazare Louis Hoche, saw a storm blow its flotilla's flagship so far out to sea that command lost control and the mission was aborted.

Lieutenant-General Sir Arthur Wellesley bided his time aboard HMS *Donegal* in the Cove at Cork for days on end in summer 1808. Storms from the Gulf Stream crashed down on Ireland. Wellesley waited longer. The weather eased, and his ships left on 12 July, reaching Portuguese territory three weeks later in the Mondego river estuary. There his expedition began the war against Napoleon in Portugal and Spain. Wellesley became Baron Wellesley, Viscount Wellington, a year later, finally driving the French from the peninsula in June 1813.

WEATHER, FOE AND FRIEND

Modern weapon designers know that familiarity with the atmosphere's properties can determine the efficiency of missiles. They try to understand atmospheric phenomena through two approaches.

- Direct measurement reveals the atmosphere's aerodynamic qualities: wind intensity and direction, temperatures close to or remote from the Earth's surface, humidity and precipitation, storm conditions, and the like.
- 'Optical signatures' reveal levels of electromagnetic activity such as atmospheric and ground emissions, solar and multiple scattering. Noise disturbances in the undersea environment, for example, are detected at an average acoustic level of about 70 decibels, usually transmitted at a mean frequency of around 300 hertz (cycles per second).[4]

Heavy electrical storms with drenching rains may produce traumatizing encounters. Napoleon and Wellington (once again) experienced one of these towards the end of a hot June day at Waterloo. Rain thoroughly dowsed troop units on both the French and Prussian-British sides (the latter joined by Hanoverians, Hollanders and Belgians), causing some to flee for dry shelter in rare farm buildings – further demoralizing already hungry, thirsty, fatigued or wounded troops on both sides.

Paul Nathaniel of Nottingham Trent University paints another feature into the picture of battle, something he calls military geology. 'Wellington set up his defenses', Nathaniel relates, on slightly higher ground than Napoleon's.

> The French were on a wet, clay area, it was drizzling [during the preceding night] and the French officers decided that it was far too wet for them to sleep on the ground, so they slept on their horses. Come the next day and the advance, the [French] horses were tired, the ground was wet and sticky, the cavalry didn't move as fast as it should have, Napoleon's guns got stuck in the mud. As a result, Wellington was able to outmaneuver and destroy the French army.

In other words, a 'geological victory for Britain'.[5]

During the US Civil War, the original strategy of the Northern states was to seize the Atlantic seaboard and the continental frontiers of the rebellious Southern states. This was the 'Anaconda' plan, brainchild of the victor of the American conflict with Mexico a few years earlier,

Winfield Scott. General Scott intended to close on the South through a series of concentric constrictions of the Confederacy's territory. John Keegan notes that President Abraham Lincoln and his military advisors considered Anaconda a relatively bloodless concept, one requiring few more than the meager 16,000 troops the United States Army fielded in 1861.[6] The navy remained largely loyal to Washington, so that a squeeze by the sea force was perceived as altogether feasible.

The North had not counted, however, on Southern determination to keep Union troops as clear of their soil as possible – a goal never realized – and to avoid a posture of wait-and-see. On the contrary, Southern strategy and operations exploited the large landmass involved, the many rivers and tributaries, and the scattering of Union strongholds along the sea coast to make hit-and-run raids, disrupt rail and other communications, harass supply lines, and pin down units as frequently and widely as possible.

The South used geography as a weapon against an adversary whose strategy sought, from the outset, to pre-empt these very advantages. A thwarted Washington saw itself dragged reluctantly into a national rupture lasting four years. Major-General Ambrose E. Burnside's defeat at Fredericksburg in 1862 was typical: Burnside lost sight of his objective, the dispersal of Robert E. Lee's forces, in his determination to capture the city of Richmond. The 'weather and, specifically, the poor condition of the roads',[7] however, were the real determinants.

POSTPONING 6 JUNE 1944?

After the Civil War, the United States Army spent the next 25 years putting the final touches to the massive ethnic thinning[8] of Amerindians from their native habitat. Naval forces were barely involved, as the army ranged over the new western states, based at small posts scattered over a wide expanse of plains, deserts and mountains. The soldiers fought 'in all manner of drastically variant climates' with 'much violent activity ranging from guerrilla actions, skirmishes, pursuits, massacres, raids, [to] campaigns and battles'. Yet the resolving factor was logistics because the Indians needed grass for their horses. The Americans had all the grain they needed. 'The Indians proved to be some of the world's best light cavalry, but the army's challenge was equally one of environment ... distances were immense, causing much difficulty with supply, movement, and communication.'[9]

Writing of western Europe, John Keegan contrasts two distinct forms of terrain within the same geographical region, different not only for the troops engaged but for the logisticians and supporting artillery: the Argonne near Verdun in France and the marshy Flanders region in Belgium.

> [T]he Argonne proved unsuited for offensives as, for different reasons, did the Flemish coastal zone. The former was too broken, stream-cut and tree-choked, the latter too waterlogged for the delivery of attacks that required firm, unobstructed avenues of advance ... Shelling into the Argonne threw the woodland into a jungle of broken vegetation; in the sea-level fens of Flanders, shelling quickly reduced the soil to a quag-mire.[10]

In the first of the endless combats constituting the Isonzo (or Caporetto) campaign between Austria and Italy (1915–17), 2,000 Italians died and 12,000 were wounded in June 1915. This was a high proportion of wounded to killed, attributable to the fact that explod-ing artillery shells fragmented the surrounding karst rock. Rock and pebble splinters became projectiles in themselves, causing much damage to eyes and skulls.[11] Artillery bursts on the stony terrain were the cause, too, of '70 per cent more casualties per rounds expended than on the soft ground in France and Belgium'.[12]

Desert operations in the 1940s proved to be a near-insurmountable challenge in the German–Italian and British battles in the Western Desert: northwestern Egypt and northern Libya. Opposing forces had to learn to survive moving sand and swirling hot air. These affected not only the nose, throat and lungs, but the air-intake mechanisms of internal-combustion engines, as well as the handling of petroleum products. Consequently supplies of every kind proved critical – all the time, at all levels of command, on both sides. 'Operating in the desert, neither the British nor their German opponents had the slightest hope of finding anything useful but camel dung.'[13] Much later, during the Gulf War, the British deputy commander commented on the technical problems attributable to sand:

> Helicopter engines were found to be suffering severe wear from sand ingestion. Even with sand filters fitted, the average life of a Lynx engine came down from its normal twelve-hundred hours to only one hundred (without a filter it lasted about ten).[14]

Battles have been won throughout history by seizing, on land or sea, perspectives of this sort, or else won in part by good weather, lost in part by bad weather. It was not until the Second World War, how-ever, that the weathermen could play a decisive role in the outcome of combat planned or battle engaged. Secret reports poured into French military centers early in 1940, during the 'phony war', indicating a

German assault in the offing. On 3 May, a week before the German invasion of the Netherlands, Belgium and France, Colonel Hans Oster, of the German Abwehr, reported surreptitiously to the Western side that attacks against the Netherlands and Belgium were set up for the next few days 'and, weather permitting, probably would begin on the 8th'.[15]

The weather permitted. The factor holding back the German onslaught for 48 hours was a final check by the Foreign Office in Berlin on, not nature's elements, but the legal instruments regulating the two Low Countries' neutrality. This hesitation could not last and, despite patches of fog in northern France, the assault began early on 10 May.

On the eve of the spectacular Allied landings in France four years later, the exact date and hour were determined almost solely on the basis of the weather expected and tidal schedules. May is normally a lovely month in northwestern Europe, with little precipitation and a fair number of sunny days. The weather charts for the years 1893–1943 confirmed this. The season seemed ideal until operations officers faced persistently low cloud cover, rain and wind in mid-spring 1944. All possibility of an expedition in May had to be delayed by a month. Dwight Eisenhower and Bernard Montgomery finally set the date of 5 June for the first wave of air-and-sea landings in occupied France.

Because of extremely poor conditions between 1 and 4 June (more 'January than June', according to Allied meteorologists) and their expected continuation the following day, the commanders were forced to cancel the action planned for the 5th. What to do? Postpone again for 24 hours? Or delay the entire debarkation until about 18 or 19 June, the earliest predicted time when a combination of favorable weather and exploitable tides would permit massive movements? If the operation proceeded regardless of weather, three airborne divisions aboard some of the 11,500 aircraft scheduled to participate would surely miss their drop zones by kilometers. And all the landing craft, crammed full with combat-ready infantrymen, engineers, artillerymen, signalmen, medical troops: where would they find shelter from inauspicious sea and sky?

Time, incidentally, had taken on new meaning in military staff planning and logistics with the introduction by the Americans of the railway back in the Civil War. The British solution to the complexity of standardizing the hours/minutes of arrival and departure was the single, national time possible in that geographically small nation. In North America, noon in New Orleans or Nashville was not the same as noon in New York, and the difference energized the Americans two decades later (1883) to invent time zones which, a year later produced the International Meridian Conference in Washington and ultimately (1911) Greenwich Mean Time – now called Universal time.[16]

AN UNFLAWED DECISION

The supreme commander of the Western powers about to land in Normandy, Eisenhower, realized that his decision was in the hands of his principal weather forecaster, Group Captain J. M. Stagg of the RAF (assisted by his deputy, American Colonel D. N. Yates). Stagg depended, in turn, on synoptic reports arriving in cipher from a number of military commands: sea, air and land. The weather-center commanders conferred every few hours via telephone scramblers. 'No one could have imagined weather charts less propitious for the greatest military operation in history than those we had before us'[17] on the evening of 4 June (see Figure 3). The dilemma of the strategists was poignant.[18]

In reply to a question put to him by the expedition's supreme commander on 4 June about postponing the attack by one day, Stagg the scientist was able to reply only that 'general conditions must continue to be regarded as disturbed … but there is good reason for expecting a trend to improvement'.[19] Stagg, in the words of another historian,

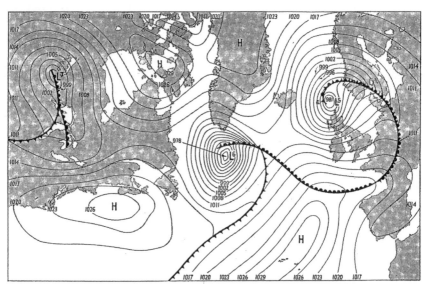

Figure 3:
Synoptic Weather Reporting, 5 June 1944.

Synoptic reporting accumulated by 1300 hours Greenwich Mean Time on 5 June 1944 shows a barometric low (L6) moving east from Newfoundland-Labrador and another (L5) moving south to the British Isles and towards the Channel. Generally bad weather, in other words, for the invasion force of over 1 million waiting to land on the European continent. (*Source: Forecast for Overlord*, London, Ian Allan, 1971, p. 117.)

'courageously backed a hunch and Eisenhower said, "Let's go"'.[20] Laconic, and far from uplifting perhaps, this was the pondered forecast of the best that meteorology could provide. The date of 6 June, with the first airborne pathfinders on target shortly after midnight, became the day that could not be postponed.

In virtual corollary on the opposing side, the commander of Germany's Army Group B charged with the defense of Normandy, Erwin Rommel, accepted the prediction of *his* meteorologists that Channel weather would be bad until mid-June. Only a few days before, Rommel had warned some of his officers that they should not count on the enemy appearing before them 'in fine weather and by day … If we cannot throw the enemy into the sea within 24 hours, then that will be the beginning of the end.'[21] Confident in the poor weather foreseen for the next fortnight, Rommel chose this period to leave for a holiday in Germany for his wife's birthday,[22] together with their 16-year-old son, Manfred.[23]

In the notoriously shifting miniclimate of the Channel, the longer-range forecasts made by the Allies for 18–19 June proved wrong. On those two days the worst local storm since 1904 made the seas and skies so turbulent, between England's southern counties and France's northern departments, that 800 of the 6,000 vessels used in Operation Overlord were destroyed, as well as the American segment of the Mulberry harbor floated from Britain two weeks before. Alistair Horne estimates that if the attacking Allies had waited until these meteorologically adverse days, the invading force would probably have met the same fate as the Spanish Armada –'scattered and sunk without a shot fired from shore'. The labors, through deception, to keep these and other data from the enemy have been told elegantly by the strategic planner involved, Roger Hesketh.[24]

The combat arenas of the Second World War, as they developed in Europe, thus provide *operational* insight into the effects – whether positive or negative – of nature's principal stage setting for armed conflict, the weather. Now we shall see how this natural force appeared to the German side of the second great war.

After the defeat of Poland in September 1939, Hitler wanted to invade France via the Low Countries in a new scenario of the one staged in 1914. Although he set the date of 12 November 1939 for this assault, the *Führer* was dissuaded from it by his first soldier, Field Marshal Wilhelm Brauchitsch, 'because of weather conditions and the still inadequate offensive capabilities' of the *Wehrmacht*. This we have from Siegfried Westphal, at the time Chief of Staff to the *Wehrmacht*'s Commander-in-Chief West.[25]

BOX 7 FROM TINY EDDIES MIGHTY STORMS GROW

We do not know, even in principle, what aspects of climate are predictable. Even the most elaborate climate models, running on the most powerful computers, cannot reproduce today's climate without introducing uncomfortable levels of artificiality. Chaos theory emerged from the insights of our Professor Edward N. Lorenz, who discovered that perturbations of a system so small as to be unobservable can lead to dramatically differing results over time. Scientists are now trying to learn what elements of climate are chaotic, as well as how interaction among the sub-systems of climate (such as the oceans, the polar icecaps and the clouds that help cool the Earth) will amplify or damp the human impact on climate.

Charles M. Vest, Massachusetts Institute of Technology,
President's Annual Report, 1995

In autumn 1940, Germany's anti-RAF phase of the Battle of Britain was coming to nought in part because of 'the deterioration of the weather' over north-western Europe, conditions that would affect the *Luftwaffe*'s capacity to destroy the RAF both in the air and on the ground.[26] During the same autumn 'the weather would not permit landings' in Britain of the massed German *Seelöwe* or Sealion invasion force, so Hitler was forced to postpone invasion of the British Isles until 1941.[27] The effort was never resumed. Doubtful weather proved to be a deterrent of belligerence at the historical moment when British forces in all likelihood would have had enormous difficulty in repelling an invasion or preventing occupation of their country.

A WINTER'S TALE

Operation *Barbarossa*, the invasion of the Soviet Union, originally planned for 15 May 1941 was deferred because (a) of a late thaw and (b) the River Bug still overflowed its banks in early June. The four-month summer in western Russia ends with the October mud or *rasputitza*, so that Hitler's strategy suffered more than five weeks' delay when the would-be *Blitzkrieg* was finally unleashed on 22 June. This left barely three months of summer for an invasion for which no 'winterizing' provisions had been made – in terms of clothing, transport, food supplies, or medical service.[28]

The invading forces finally bogged down some tens of kilometers southwest of Moscow, repeating Napoleon's fiasco of 130 years before. The Wehrmacht could not proceed further until the muddy period ended in mid-November 1941, after which the soil froze and hardened enough to support armor and other vehicles – but at temperatures rapidly falling to −30°C. The German armies included formations coming from vassal states such as Hungary, Romania and even occupied France. Four battalions of the volunteer French Legion, attached to the German Fourth Army, 'could not stand up to the fierceness of [Russian] attacks [or] to the cold and blizzards, so unlike anything they had ever known'.[29] As mass maneuver, *Blitzkrieg* lasted less than two years. The strategy vanished from military planning and operations almost as quickly as it had appeared.

Meanwhile, however, both the Germans and the British were intensifying their aerial wars – modified blitzes, to be sure – against one another. The British favored night bombing of German targets, mainly industrial cities, because darkness provided a welcome cover. The Germans, beginning to feel a growing shortage of air crews and fuel, based their squadrons chiefly in occupied France and the Low Countries, close to their targets, and struck Britain mostly by daylight. Air defenses, for both sides, were interceptor aircraft and anti-aircraft batteries (AA) on the ground.

How effective was defense? A visiting American scientist working on air defense, George Valley, spent a few nights in a hotel near London's Marble Arch in autumn 1942. His observations during a particularly heavy German raid led him to conclude that, first, AA fire was largely an exercise in futility, and secondly, if microwave radar could be made practical, an air force would be more efficiently equipped to penetrate the defenses both of nature (rain and cloud-covered winters in Europe) and of armies (AA cannon). On returning to his permanent base at the MIT Radiation Laboratory, Valley persuaded director Lee DuBridge to phase out AA detection research in favor of means for intensified bombing through improved navigation by radar.[30] Thus began a methodical transition to the equipping of bombers with microwave radar, that is, radar that generates electromagnetic waves of 1mm to 30cm in length, waves that 'see' through clouds. (Radar development is covered in Chapter 10.)

NOT ONLY THE COLD, BUT TIDAL SURPRISES, TOO

Not only did frozen soil deprive the USSR's German invaders of rudimentary field shelters (foxholes, trenches and earth revetments), but the cold quickly reached weapons and vehicles while Soviet artillery set fire – in classical scorched-earth style – to farms and villages abandoned by retreating civilians, to deny the enemy all shelter. Oil and grease in 'artillery pieces froze, the mechanism of the machine guns froze. It was frequently impossible to open the breech', according to one German account.

> There was no glycerin, nor fuel designed for use in the extreme cold. At night it was often necessary to keep small fires burning underneath our tanks, lest the engines freeze and burst. The tanks frequently slipped on the icy ground and slid over inclines.[31]

These conditions persisted during the Germans' first Soviet winter and would recur the following winter at Stalingrad.

On the Stalingrad front along the Volga, tactical, operational and ultimately strategic situations deteriorated. Hitler's orders to the Sixth Army commander, Friedrich Paulus, were that his units would not cede a millimeter – even to straighten lines of resistance severely dented by the Soviets. In Panzer Corps H (22nd Panzer Division and Romania's 1st Armored Division), while readying for battle in late November 1942, weather conditions became 'atrocious: there was ice everywhere and the snow fell incessantly and formed drifts. There were only a few hours of daylight'. Soviet tanks then poured through 'a huge gap' in the German front, and 'the true situation was [that] Panzer Corps H was doomed before ever it was committed'.[32] (A half-century later commercial pilots in North America knew from experience that weather is the cause of 40 per cent of aircraft accidents and of 65 per cent of air-traffic delays lasting longer than 15 minutes.[33] In wartime the arithmetic worsens.)

The meteorological extenuations affected replacement supplies flown in for the Germans besieged in Stalingrad, troops who were already eating their horses. Needed resupply was calculated by the Army General Staff in Berlin at a minimum of 300 tonnes/day. Allowing for the many days when flying was impossible, this figure was adjusted upwards to 500 tonnes/day, a quantity that the *Luftwaffe*'s chief, Reichsmarschall Hermann Goering, assured his *Führer* would be delivered.[34] This was never the case, and Hitler wrote off sacrifice of Marshal Paulus's Sixth Army 'in order that a new front might be built. Bad weather ... stopped the air force from keeping the army supplied ... Hitler never once admitted that he himself was to blame or that he might have made a faulty appreciation of the situation.'[35]

Bodo Zimmerman retired from the army in 1920, but was recalled to the General Staff in 1939. From 1942 until the war's end, Lieutenant-General Zimmerman was chief operations officer of Army Group D in France. He recalls that on 5 June 1944 Germany's ground and naval forces were preoccupied by

> tides, weather and wind ... The system was that if these looked likely to favor an [enemy] assault in the early hours at any particular point, the troops stationed there would be alerted. The total number of dawn alerts which therefore were ordered at one spot or another was well nigh astronomic. The strain on the men, who were already carrying out training exercises and building defenses at high pressure, was ... possibly even excessive.[36]

Weather conditions that night – despite a nearly full moon and low tide expected the following morning at about 5 o'clock – indicated, as we have seen, that Allied landings would not be possible in Normandy. Germany's Seventh Army commander canceled all alerts.[37] Tides played another role, forcing the orchestration of Allied landings to take into account tidal times at diverse points along the shore. High tide on the most westerly of the invasion beaches, UTAH, came 40 minutes before high water on the easternmost of the landing areas, SWORD.

Demolition squads targeting underwater obstacles had to be on site three hours before disembarkation and take into account natural, and ubiquitous, impediments such as outcropping rocks and deep pools. So H-hour for each beaching site had to be calculated separately, with the hope that the noise of wind might muffle some of the early blasting.[38] A few hours after the first Allied troops landed, German Naval Group West's headquarters in Paris, after ordering immediate readiness of all fleet units along the Channel, entered in its official log, 'Increased defensive patrols in the Bay of Seine are not being ordered on account of the unfavorable tide conditions and the weather. No further signs of an enemy landing.'[39]

LOGISTICAL OBSTABLES

The first conception of Operation Overlord called for an invasion date of 1 May 1944. May's weather is normally fair, as we have noted. General Eisenhower – together with the campaign's chief planner, British Lieutenant-General Frederick E. Morgan – wished to exploit all of May in the event that the beachhead operation should extend through the summer. Yet persistently low clouds, rain and some wind, together with shortages of amphibious equipment, delayed the landings for five weeks.

Truly amphibious bridgeheads were experiences born of the Second World War. The Japanese made many landings, it is true, in their takeover of Pacific Ocean islands. These were in most cases passive, simple disembarkations from troop transports, meeting little or no resistance. The Allied forces, in their sustained counteroffensive along the way to Tokyo, developed multi-service ('combined') operations and equipment to assure the success of their own landings (albeit at sometimes frightful cost in casualties, for instance the frontal assaults on Japanese-held Makin and Tarawa in the Gilbert Islands).

Tides inevitably played a role in the planning of such attacks, both in the Pacific and simultaneously along the southern shore of the Mediterranean, afterwards in Sicily and on the Italian peninsula. In Normandy, tides were anticipated as a major factor in establishing port logistics for unloading troops and equipment, and so they proved to be. As early as May 1942, Winston Churchill advised his chief of combined operations, Vice-Admiral Lord Louis Mountbatten,

> Piers for use on beaches: They must float up and down with the tide. The anchor problem must be mastered ... Let me have the best solution worked out. Don't argue the matter. The difficulties will argue for themselves ...[40] This must be quite unexpected by the enemy, and will enable the build-up to proceed with very great independence of weather conditions.[41]

East of the main landings near the city of Caen, tide differentials around the Bay of Mont St Michel are among the greatest in the world. The planners' solution to this natural impediment was to invent the necessary technology, the prefabricated floating harbors already mentioned, Mulberry A and B – built in Britain and towed across the Channel as the assault began. In *Overture to Overlord*, Frederick Morgan credits one of his senior naval planners, Commodore John Hughes-Hallett, with the Mulberry innovation.[42]

Conversely, of course, the cleverest of artifacts may fail because of contingencies: 'Equipment must be looked after. Enemy fire and Mother Nature conspire to keep everything dirty, damaged and generally on the verge of breakdown.'[43] Or, to invoke Murphy's famous first 'law', if anything can go wrong, it will – and, inevitably, at the worst possible moment,[44] as we shall see below.

During the Allied parachute-and-glider attack early on the morning of 6 June 1944, men of the US 82nd Airborne Division were carried by strong winds away from the parachutists' main target of Sainte-Mère-l'Eglise on the Cotentin Peninsula. Farther on, the British 6th Airborne Division had no such difficulty and was not even attacked by Rommel's mobile reserve, the battle-scarred yet reliable 21st Panzer Division. Moderately strong winds on land meant that there were the same at sea nearby, and indeed all along the invasion beaches. There, 15-knot winds caused many landing craft to leave troops near shore hundreds of meters east of their intended destinations.

On 19 June a furious gale destroyed Mulberry A before it could be maneuvered into final position, seriously hampering the Allied logistical flow towards France. The storm lasted until 21 June, stranding 800 craft on the beaches; this number included almost half the landing craft-tank (LCT) available. In three days the weather did five times as much material damage to the Allied invasion forces as that caused by the German adversary between 6 and 21 June. The unloading of supplies fell sharply, too: from more than 24,000 tonnes on 18 June to 4,500 tonnes on 20 June, leaving ammunition stocks very low.[45]

Later, when the United States' First Army was engaged in wresting the Cotentin Peninsula and Cherbourg port from the Germans, it faced an unusual dilemma. Its commander, General Omar Bradley, could rely on 14 divisions to oppose only six divisions of the Wehrmacht's Seventh Army. His front, however,

> was so constricted by natural obstacles that he could not bring his superiority to bear. The deep valley of the Vire River obtruded his left flank and the enemy-held town of Saint-Lô; his right was no more than a foothold on forested, steep slopes.

At his center, there were 25 km of 'treacherous alluvial swamps of the lower Vire and the Taute' rivers.[46]

While nature connived to assure daunting defenses, tactics – combined with firepower superior to that which the Germans could muster – finally made a breakthrough possible. The situation replicated somewhat the insects, reptiles and jungle vines, combined with defensible beaches and the many caves used by the Japanese in the Southwest Pacific, that slowed Allied movements towards the islands lying ever closer to Japan.

KNOWING THE TERRAIN

In Germany's final western push of the Second World War, Field Marshal Gerd von Runstedt's Ardennes offensive was spearheaded by a general officer experienced in piercing enemy lines in the region where Germany's frontier converges with those of Belgium, Luxembourg and France. Hasso-Eccard von Manteuffel and his colleagues

> knew the terrain in the Ardennes well. We had advanced across it in 1940 and retreated through it only a few months before. We knew its narrow, twisting roads and the difficulties ... they could cause an attacking force, particularly in winter and in the bad weather conditions

that the Germans deemed prerequisites to the launching of the Germans' final western effort[47] in the cold, snow, ice and fog of December 1944. *Herbstnebel*, Autumn Fog, was aptly the code for the operation.

The Western Allies were taken aback by the attack, enhanced on the German side by exemplary radio silence and night movements only. They experienced deep penetration of their lines, but recovered quickly and resumed their progress eastwards to join the Soviets in Berlin and Czechoslovakia – finally speeding the European phase of the Second World War in May 1945. 'General winter' proved, once more, a redoubtable strategist, just as significantly as the Sahara's aridity, hot winds and sand had first won, then lost, Libya and north-western Egypt for Rommel's Afrika Korps a few years earlier.

Anyone who has experienced aerial flight in an unpressurized aircraft at 12,000 feet or higher appreciates how much hard work is required simply to breathe. Indian and Pakistani troops suffer pain when hauling automatic weapons and lugging elements of field guns to altitudes of 5,400 meters (17,717ft) in the on-again, off-again combat occurring along Kashmir's Line of Control since Pashtun tribesmen first attacked the capital at Srinagar in 1947.

Pakistan's Chitral Scouts and Northern Light Infantry today maintain body tone by eating Energile, a protein-rich packaged ration supplemented occasionally by sugared snow, while India's White Devils – mountain commandos – continue to perfect their rock-climbing techniques.[48] Kashmir is now the longest-lived of the UN's peacekeeping surveillances, dating from 1949–50 and, by the time this book goes into print, may again be as active a theater as neighboring Afghanistan.

NEW WAYS TO TRICK NATURE

Nature's conditions have changed very little for fighting personnel since the climatic and meteorological vagaries of the twentieth century's major conflicts. What has changed, and remarkably so, is the state of the earth and environmental sciences. Group Captain Stagg, Eisenhower's resident meteorologist, wrote a quarter-century after the Second World War that none of the advances in these disciplines 'has disproved the inherent unpredictability of the behavior of the atmosphere.'[49]

Stagg's appraisal applies as well to our knowledge of the oceans, continental water, geology and geodesy, geochemistry and radiochemistry, and of biological influences and those of near-space physics: the environmental sciences of today and tomorrow – and to the truly impressive contributions made by the military. The quest to detect possible nuclear attack prompted much of the research involved, to be sure, and between 1950 and 1990 there was no hesitation by a number of governments to make the necessary financing available.

Preparing synoptic reports on the weather, especially in the Atlantic Ocean, was a continuing and often frustrating requirement of the German submarine fleet during the Second World War. Weather in the Atlantic, as observed in Chapter 3, forms and develops in its southwestern and northwestern quadrants before moving towards Europe. Denying access to this information was one of the multiple aims of the Allied naval and air forces seeking to contain the marauding *U*-boat. The Overlord experience, notably its final weather analysis, joined other studies of nature's forces to improve our knowledge of exologistics.

After the Second World War, research activated by the military of many nations helped widen and deepen our knowledge of the globe's natural structures. Gravity mapping, meant ostensibly to contribute to the refinement of plate tectonics in the new geosciences, played an incontrovertible role in the development of guidance systems for missiles. It was the military who funded most of these investigations. The Vietnam War produced, for instance, the Geophone: to detect the infantryman's unseen opponents' footfalls, otherwise even unheard. Available since 2001 for as little as $40, this high technology is being applied by scientists in seismic signaling – it emulates the elephant's use of its feet as sensors – to sense not only imminent earthquakes but also the direction and distance of approaching thunderstorms.

ENVIRONMENT SENSED FROM ON HIGH

With orbiting surveillance of the Earth's surface made possible by satellites, an American peace dividend took what should prove to be an extraordinarily beneficent form. Since 1995, initially under the aegis of then Vice-President Al Gore, the American Congress has required that all 'spy' satellites launched after the Cold War take on another task. Project MEDEA (*m*easurements of *e*arth *d*ata for *e*nvironmental *a*nalysis) has some hundred monitors circumnavigating the planet with a single-minded aim. It is to obtain evidence whether there exists long-term global change in the climate, a condition implying other threats to the environment. There will ultimately be 500 satellites assigned this task.

Dual-use advantages of the MEDEA type, instead of scrutinizing targets primarily of a military nature, mean that the imagery detectors aboard 'spy' satellites are used to monitor cloud formation, rainforests, deserts, glaciers and sea ice. This concerted scientific effort should confirm (or not) that climatic shifts are truly under way. To this end the US government announced that its National Imagery and Mapping Agency had begun (1999) the ambitious, three-dimensional mapping of 80 per cent of the globe's surface.

This stereographic *Weltanschauung* – viewing the heights, flatlands and depressions of our world as seen from high overhead – will consolidate by computer all imagery gathered by satellites, space shuttles and observation aircraft, and even missiles. A civil market is sure to follow. The estimated cost (barring any commercial returns at first) until 2008 will be $10 billion, one-tenth of what the United States alone has spent since the end of the Second World War to keep tabs on nature's shifts in appearance.[50]

Environment-conscious Al Gore encouraged development of the reconversion of military equipment and turnover of its product, and the Congress supported him in directing the selection first of two dozen observational sites, a figure rising gradually to the 500 mentioned. The dean of the School of Environmental Science at the University of California's Santa Barbara campus appraised MEDEA as follows: 'In terms of turning swords into plowshares, this is about as good an example as I can think of.'[51] MEDEA is managed under the auspices of the National Reconnaissance Office in Washington, in coordination with the Central Intelligence Agency. It is an effort in civil–military partnership whose success should augment enormously our store of knowledge in the geosciences and suggest new guidelines as to how to make the best use of natural resources. This is, besides, a most practical translation of the United Nations' goal of *sustainable development*.

There is little reason why such collaborative studies should not continue indefinitely in spite of increasingly diversified demands made on wealthy countries' defense budgets. One can expect that, as transient conflicts and years pass, governments will collaborate along

MEDEA lines much as they do in other cooperative science originated by the military.

In this chapter we have seen how external conditions determine the effectiveness of strategy through their influence on military operations and even tactics. Both exologistics and endologistics contribute to – and often help resolve – the fog of war first pinpointed by Clausewitz. How effectively the new terrorism might exploit these remains to be seen.

NOTES

1 In a review of Rick Atkinson's *Crusade: The Untold Story of the Persian Gulf War* (Boston, MA, Houghton Mifflin, 1993), *IHT*, 21 October 1993, p. 9.
2 This interpretation, contested by some historians, appears in Roger Masters, *Macchiavelli, Leonardo and the Science of Power* (Notre Dame, IN, University of Notre Dame Press, 1996).
3 William Doyle, *The Oxford History of the French Revolution* (Oxford, Clarendon, 1989), pp. 209, 216.
4 Communicated by Lyonel Gouedard of the Délégation Générale pour l'Armement, French Ministry of Defense, before the Entretiens Science et Défense symposium, 11 May 1993.
5 Paul Nathaniel interviewed by Anna Grayson, *Science Now*, BBC Radio 4, 20 April 1996.
6 John Keegan, *Warpaths: Travels of a Military Historian in North America* (London, Random House/Pimlico, 1995), pp. 198–202, 207 ff.
7 Herman Hattaway, *Shades of Blue and Gray: An Introductory Military History of the Civil War* (Columbia, MO, and London, University of Missouri Press, 1997), p. 111.
8 The countryside pogroms during the 1980s of the Romanian dictator Nicolae Ceaucescu to establish 'racial purity' and the subsequent Bosnian conflict of 1992–95 contributed 'ethnic cleansing' to the language.
9 Keegan, *Warpaths*, pp. 247–8.
10 John Keegan, *The First World War* (London, Hutchinson, 1998), p. 202.
11 Keegan, *Warpaths*, pp. 247–8.
12 Ibid., p. 371.
13 Martin van Creveld, *Supplying War: Logistics from Wallenstein to Patton* (Cambridge, Cambridge University Press, 1977), p. 182.
14 Peter de la Billière, *Storm Command: A Personal Account of the Gulf War* (London, HarperCollins, 1992), p. 122. For statistical degradation of artillery, tanks and armored personnel carriers in January–March 1991, see Lawrence Freedman and Efraim Karsh, *The Gulf Conflict 1990–1991: Diplomacy and War in the New World Order* (Princeton, NJ, Princeton University Press, 1993), table 12, p. 373.
15 William L. Shirer, *The Collapse of the Third Republic: An Inquiry into the Fall of France in 1940* (New York, Simon & Schuster, 1969), p. 601.
16 Derek Howse, *Greenwich Time and the Discovery of the Longitude* (Oxford, Oxford University Press, 1980), ch 4, 5 and 6; Dava Sobel, *Longitude: The True Story of a Lone Genius who Solved the Greatest Scientific Problem of his Time* (New York, Walker, 1995), pp. 165–8.

17 J. M. Stagg, *Forecast for Overlord June 6, 1944* (London, Ian Allan, 1971, and New York, W.W. Norton, 1971), p. 111.

18 Alistair Horne (then a member of the Guards Armoured Division), 'June 6, 1944: Disaster Could So Easily Have Struck', *IHT*, 6 June 1994, p. 9. See also Horne, with David Montgomery, *The Lonely Leader: Monty 1944–45* (London, HarperCollins, 1994), *passim*, and Norman Gelb, *Ike and Monty: Generals at War* (New York, William Morrow, 1994) for another view of Montgomery.

19 As cited in Chester Wilmot, *The Struggle for Europe* (London, Collins, 1952), p. 224.

20 Ibid., p. 322. Stagg's account confirms this.

21 Hans von Luck, former German army major commanding the 125th Panzer Grenadier Regiment, 21st Panzer Division, cited by Rick Atkinson, 'Major von Luck's Longest Day', *IHT*, 2 June 1994, p. 9.

22 Popular historian Henri Lamouroux, broadcasting on Paris radio station France Inter at 8:40 a.m., 27 May 1994, was among the chroniclers to recall, 50 years after the event, the Channel's unsure weather conditions.

23 By a strange irony, a half-century later, Manfred Rommel would be the German Foreign Ministry's coordinator of Franco-German Affairs. Manfred Rommel and the author were participants in a seminar on possible warfare of the future, held at the Peace Memorial, Caen (France), November 1997.

24 Roger Hesketh, *Fortitude: The D-Day Deception Campaign*, with intro. by Nigel West (London, Overlook, 2000).

25 This and the passages that follow are based on eyewitness accounts of the sources cited in *The Fatal Decisions* with intro. by Cyril Falls and commentary by former Lieutenant-General Siegfried Westphal (London, Michael Joseph, 1956), p. 4 ff.

26 Werner Kreipe in *The Fatal Decisions*, p. 17. In 1940 Kreipe was chief operations officer, 3rd Air Fleet, Luftwaffe.

27 Westphal in *The Fatal Decisions*, p. 24.

28 Günther Blumentritt, chief of staff of the Fourth Army, in *The Fatal Decisions*, p. 36.

29 Blumentritt, in ibid., p. 61.

30 Robert Buderi, *The Invention that Changed the World* (New York, Simon & Schuster, 1996), pp. 182–3 ff.

31 Blumentritt, in *The Fatal Decisions*, p. 63.

32 Kurt Zeitzler, chief of staff, Army Group D, in 1942 and (as colonel-general) chief of the Army General Staff by the time of Stalingrad, *The Fatal Decisions*, p. 135.

33 Inspector-General of the Department of Transportation, Washington, DC, cited in the cover story of *Time* (Europe edn), 31 March 1997.

34 Zeitzler in *The Fatal Decisions*, p. 144.

35 Zeitzler, in ibid., p. 165.

36 Zimmerman, in ibid., p. 185.

37 Ibid.

38 Wilmot, in ibid., p. 220.

39 Ibid., p. 246.

40 Winston Churchill, *The Second World War*, vol. II (London, Cassell, 1948–51), p. 215: cited in Wilmot, *The Fatal Decisions*, p. 183.

41 Gitta Sereny, *Albert Speer: His Battle with Truth* (London, Macmillan/Picador, 1996), p. 433, attributes this sentence to Churchill in *The Second World War: Triumph and Tragedy* (Boston, MA, Houghton Mifflin, 1953), p. 8.

42 Frederick E. Morgan, *Overture to Overlord* (London, Hodder & Stoughton, 1950), pp. 261–2. Wilmot, *The Fatal Decisions*, tends to credit the idea to Churchill and Mountbatten, p. 183, n. 2.

43 James E. Dunnigan, *How to Make War: A Comprehensive Guide to Modern Warfare* (New York, William Morrow, 1982), p. 26.

44 The author of these 'laws' was Captain Edward Murphy, an air-force development engineer, working in 1949 on USAF Project MX981 with civilian George E. Nichols of the Jet Propulsion Laboratory. See Paul Dickson, *The Official Rules* (New York, Delacorte, 1978), pp. 122–8.

45 Wilmot, *The Fatal Decisions*, p. 322.

46 Ibid., p. 349.

47 Von Manteuffel in *The Fatal Decisions*, pp. 225–6, 237. The bad weather immobilized the respective air forces from 16 to 22 December 1944, after which the Allied air arms were turned loose on German ground forces to help reverse their movement westwards (p. 249).

48 Michael Fathers, 'Fighting in the Heavens', and Ghulan Hasnain, 'Under Cover of Night', *Time* (Europe edn), 12 July 1999, pp. 34 and 36–7.

49 Stagg, *Forecast for Overlord*, p. 127.

50 See Walter Pincus, 'US to Improve Its Eyes in the Sky', *IHT*, 22 January 1998, p. 10; Robert Matthews, 'Science Keeps a Weather Eye on Spy Data', *Sunday Telegraph*, 25 January 1998, p. 16.

51 William J. Broad, 'Spy Satellites Turn to Natural Targets', *IHT*, 28 November 1995, p. 3.

9

Communicating, Commanding, Controlling … and a Little Deception

'[T]he march … and of thousands must inevitably produce a strange confusion of dissonant clamours, which [reach] the ears of the watch-men of the towers.'

Edward Gibbon, on the fall of Constantinople in 1453

The nervous system of a military establishment is its communication processes, operating on an increasingly instant and accurate basis. Communication, in all its forms, enables military leaders to command and control units at a distance, even halfway round the world. The military communicate *among* themselves – vertically between command levels, laterally between comparable units – and *about* themselves, as well as to the highest authority and to the public, and sometimes with the enemy. Here we review these different forms of rapport but say almost nothing of message forms, letters, telegrams or 'cabled' exchanges. Our beacons in this chapter are *control of resources, command of the situation*.

OVERCOMING DISTANCE

A centuries-old tradition among the peoples of the Italian, Austrian, Slovenian, Swiss and French Alps is the setting of controlled fires to signal trouble, whether of natural or human origin. (And occasionally for pure jubilation, as on midsummer's night.) Gunpowder's first use was as a signaling medium, and now it is still used by infantry as flares or smoke grenades, air-rescue units and navies for self-identification or location, to warn of an adversary's tactical threat, or to mark the local state of belligerency.[1] We shall cover the broad organizational strategy the Americans call C^{4}I: command, control, communications, computers and intelligence[2] – with the strongest emphasis on communication because this ties together the other four elements.

For millennia couriers, whether human or animal runners, supplementing the transmission of messages by flame or smoke, were the most reliable communicators among the military. Animals were replaced in some cases by bicycles during the nineteenth century, elsewhere by the visual, then the electrical telegraph. But before the telegraph of Wheatstone, Gauss, Morse and their peers became a reality in the 1840s, there was also the Chappe – or Edelcrantz, or Gamble – semaphore telegraph and the heliograph. Later, motorcycles and telephones came into field communication.

The semaphore system, or optical telegraph, appeared during the early 1790s; it resembled ship-to-shore flagging. One of its developers was a French clergyman, Claude Chappe, who lost his clerical status with the revolution of 1789. He published five papers in physics, by which he attempted to come to grips with the transmission of electrical impulses over wire. Probably thwarted in part by the scant knowledge of electrical principles at that time, he conceived visual alternatives and in 1791 demonstrated his first efforts near Le Mans in western France. Simultaneous inventors were Niclas Abraham Edelcrantz, a Swedish nobleman, and a British military chaplain, John Gamble. The latter proceeded to improve the Chappe method.[3]

These processes were similar, using geometric shapes as coded signals visible on the far horizon. The initial system comprised several stations stretching over 16km, each station containing a pendulum clock and two large panels on either side. One panel was black, the other white. Each clockface had ten different sections, and each of these had different number values. A single hand swept around the clockface in 30 seconds; its message codes were based on numbered entries in a special glossary of phrases, words and individual characters. By 1799 Chappe's 'dictionary' had more than 25,000 entries. As transmission began,

> the sender turned the panel to indicate when the hand of his clock reached the zenith; that allowed the receiver, watching through a telescope, to set the clock on [his] end. Subsequent numbers were sent by flipping the panel from white to black each time the pointer of the sender's clock passed over the appropriate position. By looking at the position of the local clock, the receiver could determine what number the sender intended.[4]

The Chappe system was approved by French authorities because of its military application, an argument persuasive at a time when France was in conflict with several adversaries, Austria and Britain in particular. The British could send a message at that time, using a similar method, between Portsmouth and London in 20 minutes. The Swedish variant of the Chappe system used shutters in the place of articulating semaphore arms. By 1850, the French system extended to Spain, Italy, Germany, Belgium and the Netherlands. The Swedish circuits, following an experimental line serving Stockholm and built in 1795, ultimately stretched about 400km on Sweden's east coast and nearby islands. Within 50 years, however, the electrical telegraph was supreme.

Wireless telegraphy's advent in the 1890s (a multilateral effort of the Germans Hermann Helmholtz and Ferdinand Braun, the Briton Oliver Lodge, the Frenchman Edouard Branly, the Russian Aleksandr Orlov and the Italian Guglielmo Marconi) quickly found a role in military signals. Radiotelegraphy was fully operative on the military front, on land and at sea, by the war of 1914–18, and was adopted at the same time by the air arm.

In 1915, Swiss physicist Paul Scherrer was engaged in studies at the University of Göttingen with the German mathematician, Richard Courant. Courant realized that telegraph wires could not long survive artillery aimed at trench systems; searching for an alternative solution to impeded communications, he enlisted Scherrer. Together they developed a method, funded by the German military, that they called earth telegraphy: a technique of long-distance communication exploiting the ground as a conduit. In 1915, Courant and Scherrer completed such an apparatus, with a range of 2km, which Courant installed in one of the western front's sectors.[5] (Scherrer would prove most useful to the Western Allies during the next war by making contact with the nuclear physicist, Werner Heisenberg, in Germany.) Much later, towards the end of the twentieth century, an effort by naval authorities to make the entire continental territory of the United States a huge, low-frequency antenna for communication with submarines at sea was defeated in Congress because of high cost and concern about the creation of an environmental eyesore.

Incidentally, the commonplace and universal taximeter in its pre-electronic configuration may derive from the invention of a clock-maker and noted conjurer, Jean-Eugène Robert-Houdin. Before his death in 1871, Robert-Houdin invented a linear-distance gauge for use by the army, but the instrument soon found another and more profitable dual purpose. A certain Wilhelm Bruhn installed the first taximeter (1891), combining odometer and clockwork, but *not* on military vehicles.

THE COMING OF PHOTOGRAPHY

There is no record of who was first inspired to use animals other than horses as message couriers. For a long time, however, pigeons were used for exactly this purpose by military, diplomatic and commercial services, bearing messages in either plain language or coded text.

The period of anti-German hysteria in France subsequent to her defeat in the Franco-Prussian War would last, in one form or another, until after the Second World War. In early 1894, a legislative bill was introduced in Paris to prohibit foreign governments ('that some day may be hostile') from using carrier pigeons on French territory. A local newspaper reported that the draft law decreed 'imprisonment from three months to three years [for] persons convicted of organizing a secret pigeon service, or having aided and abetted any pigeon in communicating with a foreign point'.[6]

Reconnaissance of topography and terrain from the air using photography came about after the industrial revolution. Balloons, we have already noted, whether stationary or mobile, emerged from the last years of the Enlightenment and the French Revolution. Inspired by innovator Nicolas-Jacques Conté, the French attached an 'aerostatic' corps to artillery, one meant to fly and observe enemy movements. But Napoleon disbanded this service in 1802,[7] upon his return from the Egyptian campaign. The first photographer to operate from a balloon was Félix Nadar, although not until 1858. Balloons were used as observation posts for eye and camera during the American Civil and Franco-Prussian Wars; in 1914–18, the camera flew in airplanes.

Britain's Royal Flying Corps took its first aerial photographs, using amateur equipment, in September 1914 while the battle of the Aisne raged below. The results showed details of the German approach towards Paris and enabled the Allied armies to stop the German advance at the Marne river. Had this not happened, the German crush westward might have met its objectives before the end of autumn, foreshortening what was ultimately a long war of abrasion.

Photo-observation gradually became a tool in the planning of combat at all levels. In the late 1930s the highest useful altitude for aerial photography was about 2,300m, a limit determined by cloud cover or haze or fog, although both infrared photography and radar quickly pierced these natural barriers. Image detail was lost at high altitudes, and the condensation of water vapor on optical components could leave photographic negatives unreadable. Condensation, a natural phenomenon occurring in gases as they cool, indicates the instability of a gas or aerosol such as water vapor. In aerial cameras, the liquid phase of water vapor tends to form on lens-system surfaces with rising altitude and diminishing temperature. Drops of water form, furthermore, around any nuclei such as ions or dust particles adhering to optical surfaces.

In 1939 specialists in the British and French air forces, using oxygen-equipped American Lockheed-14 aircraft mounted with Leica cameras, pushed their working ceiling to almost 6,100m (nearly 20,000ft) – and produced startlingly clear negatives. They discovered that 'with the engines running, warm air was coming out of the heated cabin and flowing beneath the camera lenses' mounted within the underside of the fuselage,[8] thus counteracting reduced temperatures and rarefied air. This serendipity enabled both air forces, shortly afterwards, to reconnoiter the Mediterranean coast of northern Africa from Algiers to Tobruk and then the Italian naval bases on the Mediterranean's shores and promontories. 'Dockyards, harbors, aerodromes – everything was photographed in detail.'[9]

Aerial photography found many uses of a non-military nature and became another dual-use technology, this one founded on science-based development stimulated largely by military needs. Kenneth St Joseph, a geologist who was dean of Selwyn College at Cambridge University (1939–62), was instrumental in the development of aerial photography for the detection and investigation of forts and other vestiges of masonry dating from the Roman occupation of Great Britain. St Joseph did this work during the years following the Second World War, and his methods were later adapted by the French to investigate prehistoric human settlements.

OPTICS EVOLVE

This dual nature of photography, and later of electronic imagery mounted aboard satellites, is well illustrated by the radar mission undertaken by the *Endeavor* space-shuttle mission of April 1994. Six astronauts were charged with testing a new type of radar, the $366 million Space Radar Laboratory. The radar's targets were ocean currents, wetlands and ice floes; farmland, forests and desert regions; and mountain ranges in South America and Europe. The radar's piercing 'eyes' also recorded geological fault lines and ancient human settlements buried for centuries beneath sand.

Geologist Diane L. Evans, the project's chief scientist at NASA's Jet Propulsion Laboratory, explained that the novel system was expected to provide a 'look at the planet in a way that's never before been possible'.[10] In a series of nearly 500 discrete maneuvers, the astronauts pointed the radar at seascapes and landscapes in order to determine how the new technology could 'map different terrains and distinguish between natural and human-induced environmental changes'. The thousands of images of the Sahara Desert that the astronauts 'photographed' three-dimensionally have obvious environmental value for hydrologists and geologists, as do those of such large masses as Mount Everest and the North Sea. Yet the double value of this imagery to identify missile emplacements or monitor the building of new research facilities and their ongoing use does not escape notice.

From observation of the terrestrial surface to watching the universe by using new technology is a leap permitted almost solely by financial investment. Frederick Seitz of Rockefeller University in New York stresses the financial element in a discussion of a technology called adaptive optics, used on telescopes operating within the visible spectrum. In a letter to *Science,* Seitz recalled that adaptive optics were first proposed in 1953 by Horace Babcock but made possible (40 years later) only because of a 'huge Department of Defense investment' in these advanced methods. This was a system, conceived for military applications by MIT's Lincoln Laboratory, installed in 1992 on the 60-inch optical telescope at Mount Wilson. 'To my knowledge,' writes Seitz, 'the Mount Wilson images are the closest to the diffraction limit ever achieved at visible wavelengths for a large telescope on the Earth's surface.'[11]

A PARADIGM SHIFT

The dual-purpose phenomenon reappeared, beginning in 1947, with the advent of the transistor and the microchip. The American defense establishment, with its readily available hundreds of millions of dollars for R&D, is now accepted as having been the prime mover in using the invention of transistors to stimulate development of the computer industry and its systemic applications of particular value to communication – and thus, to command and control.

The urgency to develop fast information-handling technology was pushed in the 1950s by the need for early warning of a Soviet nuclear attack, the strategic requirement in the 1960s to develop the roaming nuclear-armed submarine, and the pressure to verify in the 1970s and 1980s the USSR's nuclear readiness. These broad shifts in technological prowess made possible the intensive, yet brief, Coalition conflict against Iraq in the Gulf War.

Thomas Kuhn, historian and philosopher of research trends, called major events such as the appearance of the transistor *paradigm shifts*[12] in the evolution of scientific understanding and technological potential.

In the next chapter we shall look at radar but here we concentrate on other sophistications of the use of nature's most abundant of all elements, silicon.

Clementine is the name given to a compact space-observation vehicle designed by the American military; its original mission was to have been testing optical instruments developed for the Star Wars strategy of the 1980s. When launched in 1994, the vehicle was sent instead on a voyage to the Moon, the asteroid belt, then Jupiter and beyond. *Clementine*, a small package (226kg, 1.2m long), was not expensive; it cost $80 million until launching time.

Clementine's program manager was Lieutenant-Colonel Pedro Rustan of the United States Air Force – the Department of Defense, rather than NASA, being the vessel's builder. The project functioned well and remained on budget. Almost grazing the Moon's surface at only 400km in May 1994, *Clementine's* miniaturized cameras recorded and transmitted 5,000 images during several circumlunar orbits of five hours each. According to the project's chief scientist, Eugene M. Shoemaker, the efficient craft exploited different wavelengths to reveal sedimentary layers in the walls of our natural satellite's craters – while also seeking the presence of ice at the Moon's poles.

The venture showed that the Moon's crust 'is not nearly as vertically homogeneous as had been thought'. *Clementine's* lunar passes were planned to map all of the Moon's surface, using a technology known as the LIDAR method (see Chapter 1) 'that could be used to direct missile interceptors to their targets'.[13] After its electronic moongazing, *Clementine* went on to observe, in July, cometary fragments colliding with Jupiter's mass, and proceeded to record about a thousand images, in August, of a small asteroid called 1620 Geographos. With these missions accomplished, *Clementine* headed for outer space, true to her oblivion in American folk music – 'lost and gone for ever'.[14]

LENGTHENING THE WORKING DISTANCE

Lost for ever, very likely, but the *Clementine*, inspired and managed by the military, promised to make contributions, too, to longer-term lunar expeditions. These were discussed during the mid-1990s by ESA, the European Space Agency, and NASA, later joined by the space agencies of Russia, Japan and China. At a workshop held in Switzerland in June 1994, the space planners proposed a program of 'expeditions to explore, exploit and colonize the Moon'.

Planned to begin around 2005–6, the program's first phase is designed to send to the Moon several orbiting observatories equipped with multipurpose sensing technology. The second phase should include robotic telescopes and other instruments placed on the lunar surface. A third cycle would involve direct use of such lunar resources as soil and minerals, low gravity and available light. The plan's concluding phase would be the establishment of an artificial ecosystem to support permanent, human presence[15] on the Moon. The timing for the last phase remains uncertain.

The anticipated product of this fascinating adventure should be 'a vastly improved understanding of the distribution of rock types and, by extension, of the geologic evolution'[16] of our solitary satellite. Meanwhile, review of the 5,000 images that *Clementine* sent from the Moon revealed that there could be water on our satellite. This water, *not* present since the little globe's formation, is most likely to be found in a crater called the Aitkin Basin at the Moon's South Pole. This crater's floor area of more than 15,000 square km is the bottom of a bowl about 13,000m deep and fully shielded from the sun's light. Scientists believe that ice from impacting comets may be sheltered here, for ever congealed – a supposition confirmed by *Lunar Explorer* as it orbited the Moon in 1998 only 100 km above its surface.

An extended *Clementine*, however, may not materialize. *Time* magazine's science editor, Leon Jaroff, criticized the White House when President Bill Clinton vetoed the *Clementine II* program in 1997. This brought a rebuttal from the president's assistant for science and technology, physicist John H. Gibbons. Gibbons stressed in a letter to the journal's editors that the presidential veto was made primarily because of 'the fundamental weaknesses of the program', a 'disguised version' of the Brilliant Pebbles missile-defense program abandoned in the 1980s. The science advisor noted that NASA was planning, nevertheless, an asteroid-research mission.[17]

The discovery of frozen water on the Moon may not facilitate humankind's intentions to establish colonies there. (The unexpected crash of *Lunar Prospector* on the Moon in July 1999, meant specifically to detect water, advanced our knowledge in no way.) Water would still have to be brought from Earth or somehow created electrochemically on the spot, at the lunar bases eventually built. We now understand from this – originally military – quest that, in order for such bases to offer optimal utility, the lunar encampments

> would best be sited at the Moon's equator, where the maximum amount of sunlight is available to power them. Dragging snow balls from the [South] pole to feed them would not be much easier than making water

from the local rocks, or even bringing it from Earth. It is one of nature's many little jokes that the only place on the Moon where there could possible be any water is the one place where it is of almost no use at all.[18]

COMMUNICATION HAS OTHER PURPOSES

'*Lying*: Deliberate falsification of the truth in order to confuse or mis-lead. This is an essential weapon for self-protection; and for societies, especially in war, to put an enemy off his stroke. Although condemned by moralists, lying can have high survival value.'

Richard L. Gregory[19]

Despite the straightforward nature of most signals and other messages, there are alternative purposes to be served by the activity that we call communication.

In the centuries before the Christian era, the Chinese made con-stant use of subterfuge in military operations. Much later, the famous Southern strategist of the Civil War in the United States, 'Stonewall' Jackson, considered deception canonical: 'Always mystify and mislead the enemy.'[20] In combat his own troops misidentified their own general, who died from 'friendly' fire.

In wars of the twenty-first century, cautions the director of strategy of the French Atomic Energy Commission, 'massive use of the infor-mation technologies [will] open the way to ruse, imposture and dis-information of virtually infinite possibilities'.[21] Furthermore, explains Ronald Lewin,

> tactical deception consists of misleading the enemy about one's inten-tions within a specific battle area. A successful example is the dummy vehicles and tanks, the false water-pipeline and other devices used to persuade Rommel at Alamein that Montgomery would attack his line in the south and not in the north. In strategic deception the object is to persuade one's opponent that the real battle will occur [elsewhere] – even in a different country. The aim is to create an imaginary threat [making] the enemy divert large forces from the area where something is about to happen to a region where nothing is going to happen at all. The range of such deception in a world war can obviously embrace whole continents and even become global.[22]

As the Weimar Republic became the Third Reich under Hitler's National Socialists, a deceptive device was required in order to hide forbidden military research. Education and research in Germany had been under the tutelage of the Preussischer Ministerium für Wissenschaft, Erziehung und Volksbildung, that is, the executive department concerned with Learning, Education and Training of the People. While this ministry made the transition to the new government's *Reichserziehungsministerium*, or REM, the German leadership saw fit to retain it as a major organizational unit within the new administration.

There were in fact, from 1934 to 1937, *two* ministries of 'learning' in Germany. These were called W I (which continued as the erstwhile Prussian department) and W II, in reality the army's research office. The latter was headed 'nominally by the chief of the research section in the army weapons department, Erich Schumann, but actually run by the chemist Rudolf Mentzel. Mentzel [profited from] the support of both the army and the SS.'[23] By 1937 Hitler was no longer pretending to observe the military restrictions imposed by the Treaty of Versailles, and the subterfuge was abandoned. Military research in Germany once again became, for both external and domestic consumption, an overt function of the defense establishment – as we saw in Chapter 4.

For the Russians military deception, or *maskirovka*, is a fine art practiced at least since the time of Catherine the Great and her soldier-minister, Marshal Grigori A. Potemkin. Beginning with the reforms in staff structure and military doctrine made during the early Soviet era by another marshal, Mikhail N. Tukhachevsky, *maskirovka* assumed complexity and subordinate terminology. Military analyst Shimon Naveh describes maskirovka's variants as, first, '*siurpriz*, representing the abstract idea of surprise, in the universal or civilian sense. Secondly, there is … *neozhidannost* (tactical surprise).., an unexpected tactical act, like an attack from an unpredicted direction'. Thirdly, the term *vnezapnost* (operational surprise) implies 'the materialization of some occurrence lying beyond the mental threshold of the rival command'.[24]

The techniques, skills and success of camouflage are probably as old as the doctrinal 'cover and concealment' practiced by military forces. The term comes, through the French, from the Italian *camuffare*, to disguise. The military did not call upon skilled artists to join technicians in this enterprise until the First World War. French forces summoned Cubist painter Guirand de Scévola to give a hand in making things seem what they were not. Scévola accepted, and soon Marcel Duchamp, Georges Braque and Fernand Léger were assisting him by using natural greenery added to painted tarpaulin and fabricated decoys to dissimulate. Their unit's insignia was the image of a chameleon.

Scientists were not involved with these French artists whereas, on the other side of the Channel, John Graham Kerr, a trained entomologist who had studied rare biota in their Paraguayan habitats, helped induce Britain's Royal Navy to accept the surf-colored 'dazzle' patterns painted on warships. The training of artists and craftsmen in visual perception and deception, the so-called optical illusions and related cognitive processes, made their wartime work as essential as the combat effort itself.

The tables of deception were turned against the Third Reich during the Second World War, at least partially, when the British Army engaged the services of a professional prestidigitator, Jasper Maskelyne. Beginning with the assumption that an audience's *perception* – a form of communication that may deform reality – of what the conjurer does can be manipulated by a skilled performer, Maskelyne and his Magic Gang trained at a special camp in Ontario. Afterwards, they spent much of the war applying their talents from a base at Abassia near Cairo. There the small unit of unusual specialists was known officially as the Camouflage Experimental Section, Royal Engineers. Using various non-strategic materials in a war theater often lacking much vitally needed equipment, Maskelyne and his art-clever handymen devised parks of dummy tanks and other vehicles, bogus arrays of artillery weapons, landing fields with phantom aircraft parked nearly wingtip to wingtip, all carefully crafted to delude the *Luftwaffe* by fooling its infrared aerial cameras.

Major Maskelyne, master illusionist, even brought a disabled warship back to life and helped to 'hide' a good bit of the Mediterranean island-fortress of Malta. This he did by focusing his 'whole imagination and knowledge on the problem of how best to mobilize the world of magic against Hitler'.[25] This practitioner of large-scale, directed misperception – macro-illusionism if the word existed – created substitutes for non-existent fire support and logistics by stretching his own imagination to confuse that of others. 'Some people are bright at figures, others pick up languages,' he later explained. 'I just see things differently than other people.'[26]

This precept was applied successfully a half-century later by the Serbian army in Kosovo, where inflatable 'tanks' were equipped with space heaters to produce thermal waves and fumes to deceive NATO attackers. The frequent use of this ploy led USAF Lieutenant-General Joseph Ralston, deputy chairman of the Joint Chiefs of Staff in Washington, to lament that,

> The tank, an irrelevant item in the context of 'ethnic cleansing', became the symbol [in the NATO mind] for Serb ground forces. How many

tanks did you kill today? All of a sudden this ['tank plinking'] became the measure of merit that had nothing to do with reality.[27]

For discussion of camouflage in the context of environmental modification, see Chapter 12.

TAMPERING WITH THE PSYCHE

A different purpose of communication is embodied in psychological warfare (PW). On his way to Egypt in 1798, Napoleon arranged to 'borrow' from the papal seat in the Vatican the only Arabic-language printing press available in the Western world. He anticipated that communication with a public in a language that was not French might pose difficulties for his expeditionary force. He was right, and the press, borrowed from Catholic authorities, served to print what may have been the first mural newspapers published by a military occupant. This was intentional propagandizing, however, not the fabrication of lies. (Records fail to show, incidentally, that the press was ever returned to its owners.)

During the 'Indian Wars' in the United States, the new Americans engaged in pushing the frontier ever west relied on alcohol and bribes to win over recalcitrant tribes of Amerindians, as had French and British invaders before. Depriving the native Americans of grasslands hurt them economically, making them more nomadic, refugees from alien encroachment on their soil. The building of strong points to house the military and store their goods was confirmed by the Board of Indian Commissioners to the Sioux chieftain, Red Cloud; it was the policy of 'the Great Father [in Washington] to put war-houses all through the Indian Country'. One general officer, Edward Ord, claimed that building military posts on the territory of the Indians 'demoralizes them more than anything else except money and whiskey'.[28] The strong points proved as effective psychologically as they were providential to the cavalry regiments.

During the First World War leaflets distributed to the enemy by each side met with some success. During the Second World War the leaflet became aggressive propaganda of both the 'white' (whose source is clear) and 'black' (the source is masked) varieties. PW was concerned with civil populations as much as with the enemy's military activity. John Peter, a professional artist and graphic communicator, designed for the PW unit of the Allied Expeditionary Forces' headquarters a poster intended to calm the citizens of Paris in August 1944. It depicted a blue rooster, the symbolic *coq gaulois*, surmounting the message *Le*

Figure 4:
Illustrations of Psychological Warfare, First World War, reproduced by kind permission
of the German magazine, *Damals*, August 1998, and Rudolf Jaworski.

jour se lève (Day is Dawning), all under the flags of the combined Allied powers. *Le jour* had been a popular film on the eve of the war, starring Jean Gabin and Michelle Morgan.

Towards the end of hostilities, the Allies' 12th Army Group issued leaflets to its combat and support troops, in which the author explained the reasons why Allied troops should not fraternize in any way with German civilians or former military personnel, male or female. The purpose was to sustain the wartime, hate-the-enemy mentality as the peace-to-come was being worked out. The effect was not long lived.

Print warfare was reinforced by aggressive radio operations by both sides, represented by Germany-based Lord Haw-Haw and Berlin Sally in Europe, and Tokyo Rose in the Pacific-Asian theater. A fairly thorough account of the radio effort in psychological warfare originated by the US Office of Strategic Services and, during the Cold War the derivative Central Intelligence Agency, is found in Lawrence Soley's *Radio Warfare*.[29] Although radio and even television played roles during the events in ex-Yugoslavia of the 1990s and by the Taliban in Afghanistan, PW via radio, film and television remains poorly documented.

In the mid-1990s the press in the United States reported with amusement the case of the psychics on the payroll of the Defense Intelligence Agency (DIA). Ten or more seers were employed by DIA to concentrate intensely and then visualize where American hostages might be held, or to describe the uses of certain unidentifiable buildings on an adversary's territory, invoking a parapsychological phenomenon known as *remote viewing*. A DIA summary of these activities, obtained by the mass media, listed among the psychics' accomplishments the unmasking of a submarine construction program in the USSR in 1979. The Department of Defense spent at least $11 million on its diviners and a related research effort using their techniques. The American Institutes of Research, private contractors engaged at the instructions of Congress, concluded in 1995 that continuing support for the the psychics was not justified, although several prominent legislators pleaded for maintenance of the activity.

Deception is not always intended for the peacetime adversary or wartime enemy. When the 'Star Wars' initiative (SDI), was ten years old in 1993 – by that time renamed the Ballistic Missile Defense Organization, BMDO – reports appearing in the media indicated that SDI was to be, essentially, a defensive system based in space against nuclear attack of the North American continent. But the public and some members of Congress bridled at the costs and estimated level of effectiveness. Development of SDI limped along despite its high price and the stratagem of deceiving the taxpayer as to the program's real worth.[30] Today, the program is operational.

A parallel strategy used by its proponents, early in the SDI gambit, was one of calculated misrepresentation to a possible adversary. This took the form of deciding during the design process on how best to dispose of mobile MX missiles (intercontinental weapons with ten warheads), once these were in place during the 1980s. The solution found was a plan for the surreptitious displacement, back and forth, of some intercontinental projectiles among a total of 4,600 possible silo sites. The silos were real; but the missiles, although real, would fill few underground receptacles. A gamesman would calculate the 'rate of deception' thus developed as approaching nearly 100 per cent.

Part of SDI's strategy was to mislead the USSR about the program's true capacity and future potential: deception, or at least misinformation, in the classical sense. One of the American inspirations for this aspect of the project was, according to four unnamed officials in the 'former Reagan administration', to induce the Soviets to 'spend themselves to economic extinction'.[31] This part of the effort succeeded admirably, according to William E. Odom, because there developed in the USSR a veritable 'paranoia over the American SDI program'.[32]

FALSIFICATION, WHATEVER THE AIM

False, or at least exaggerated, information designed to mislead found its way deep in the halls of the United States Congress. '[I]n the process of fooling our adversaries,' said one military officer, other people are 'fooled as well.' When the *New York Times* asked verification from the then defense secretary, Caspar W. Weinberger replied, 'You're always trying to practice deception. You are obviously trying to mislead your opponents and to make sure that they don't know the … facts.'[33]

A scientist associated with early testing in the program added, in connection with the launching from Kwajalein Atoll in the Pacific Ocean of an intercontinental ballistic missile serving as target,

> We rigged the test. We put a beacon with a certain frequency on the target vehicle. On the interceptor, we had a receiver … The hit looked beautiful, so Congress didn't ask questions … We would lose hundreds of millions of dollars in Congress if we didn't perform it successfully. It would be a catastrophe.[34]

The rigged test was later confirmed when a former army major-general, Eugene Fox, admitted that the target vehicle had been heated, making the missile ten times more visible 'to a sensor on the interceptor than an actual Soviet warhead would have been'. The General Accounting Office of the US Congress 'audited seven SDI tests conducted between 1990 and 1992. The auditors found that three of the tests had been accurately described to Congress. Those three tests were complete or partial failures. SDI officials told Congress that the other four tests had been successes. That was untrue, the auditors said.[35]

The revelations and finding of excuses, as concluded by the official enquiry, was that 'a deception had been planned but not implemented. The target was heated to match Soviet warheads, and its beacon could be received only by [American] ground stations.'[36] In 1994, the United States government admitted publicly that an essential component of SDI was the deception of its main adversary during the Cold War, the Soviet Union.

Later, as if to confirm this strategy but from the other side, Andrei A. Kokoshkin, deputy director of the Institute of the USA and Canada at the Academy of Sciences in Moscow, declared in the *Mediterranean Quarterly* that the doctrine of Soviet and Warsaw Pact leadership had shifted as of 1987:

> One of the first steps in this direction was formulation of the concept and then program of countermeasures involving asymmetrical response to [SDI], countermeasures that were cheaper than SDI itself. Principal provisions of this asymmetrical response program were developed with active participation of civilian scientists, and their research results were published in a number of open publications in the USSR.[37]

The estimated total cost of Star Wars between 1983 and 1999 was about $75 billion.[38] The hoodwinking of the public was portrayed in a television production aired by the BBC's *Pandora's Box* series in 1992. *On the Brink of Eternity*, a one-hour program, recapitulated how science and scientists as well as officials in the United States were exploited from the time of the war in Vietnam until the fall of the 'Evil Empire' in 1991 in order to further new, superweapon projects.[39]

A decade after the launching of SDI, the undertaking had consumed $30 billion. We have seen that it was renamed the BMDO and given, among its missions, the task of exploring the use of a space-borne telescope because 'channeling the light from an extremely powerful laser might be used as a space-based anti-missile defense. The two-way telescope would track a rising missile and then, when the laser beam was turned on, destroy it.'[40] It is not surprising that the head of

BMDO's technology unit was an astronomer, the Colonel Worden mentioned in Chapter 1.

Edward Teller, the Hungarian-born physicist turned champion of science-based military preparedness, urged (during a meeting held in 1994 by the Heritage Foundation in Washington) restoration of cuts in military funds imposed by President Bill Clinton's administration in 1993–94. As reported by an observer of the American Physical Society, Teller applauded the inauguration of SDI by President Ronald Reagan, although he 'acknowledged publicly ... that it was not practical to defend against thousands of missiles'. Teller added that it was now feasible to defend against smaller arsenals of superweapons by the use of the aforementioned 'Brilliant Pebbles', a metal chaff spread in the atmosphere to deceive detection apparatus.[41]

SAFEGUARDING THE MESSAGE

Interference with communications has been a commander's bugbear since the first ambush of a runner carrying oral messages between military units. Midway through the Cold War the American military sought an answer to their puzzlement about how orders could be passed in the event of total disruption of electronic communications by nuclear attack. Not only could a breakdown be envisaged of the normal channels: radio, telephone and teletype, telex (where used), telefax and even television; a nuclear blast's radiation effect on electronic transmission, called the electromagnetic pulse, would also make all efforts to circumvent the disabled channels temporarily futile.

In 1964, the RAND Corporation developed a communication network based on computers having no 'neural' center, 'no central switching station, no governing authority', one assuming that the links tying one site to another were unreliable. Its inventor, Paul Baran, devised a counterpart to an ordered, efficient network. In electronic terms, Baran cut a message into small 'strips' enclosed in 'envelopes' or packets consisting of parts of the message, each unit carrying the name and address of both sender and receiver. 'The packets were then released like so much confetti into the web of interconnected computers, where they were tossed back and forth over high-speed wires in the general direction of their destination and re-assembled when they finally got there.'[42,43]

The first such 'web' was subsidized with $1 million by the US Department of Defense's Advanced Research Projects Agency (ARPA) and baptized ARPANET in 1969, an entity not decommissioned until 1990. The system, soon known as Internet, was an application of the mathematical subdisciplines of network analysis, queuing theory and other operational research. Two of the net's main creators (who included J. C. R. Licklider and Lawrence Roberts) remain associated with it today, Vinton G. Cerf and Robert E. Kahn. They were responsible for conceiving and mounting a remarkable example of a dual-purpose system.

For Cerf, then a graduate student at the University of California, Los Angeles, and already involved in testing F-1 rocket engines and the orbiters' thrusters that made possible the first landing on the Moon,

> No such thrill marked the ARPANET project he was working on ... Though technically fascinating, it seemed narrowly military and academic. No one saw in it the launch of a movement that would make global knowledge accessible from desktops. In fact ARPA even had trouble getting computer centers to open this precious resource to outsiders.[44]

The nascent network – four university nodal points along the United States' west coast – managed to cope with the lack of a standardized operating system for computers, individual units being incapable of intercommunication. And although the focus on nuclear survival was well known to ARPA's computer specialists, 'their primary goal remained research for research's sake',[45] a mutually supportive technology between military scientists and the scientific community as a whole. Would there be a next step?

During the 1980s the US National Science Foundation built the long-distance data links (NSFNET) that became the Internet's spinal cord. Concurrently, Tim Berners-Lee, a British physicist working at CERN in Geneva, developed a system called ENQUIRE to master the maze-like information system at the European particle-research center. This was the genesis of what is now the World Wide Web, a notion first conceived – in theory only – by the United States' wartime director of scientific mobilization, Vannevar Bush.[46]

Things moved ahead quickly, making the Internet a burgeoning universal communications tool used increasingly by academic and industrial researchers, businesses, governments and the United Nations, national libraries, weather services, technical documentation repositories, medical instructors and operating surgeons, the mass and specialized media, publishers, and millions, then more and more millions of home users.

Operating costs were soon assumed by the principal users: high-technology firms, universities, national laboratories and governments calling upon Internet's facilities. By 1993, a decision in Washington made Internet the basis of a more complex web called the National Information Infrastructure, facilitating access to industrial documentation, meteorological imagery derived from satellite observation, electronic newsletters, teleconferencing and universities and libraries. This is how the diminutive electron took on a multidisciplinary, civil task in the mid-1990s, almost planetary in coverage, thanks to an original military requirement in one country. The military initiators of the Internet scheme, for their part, remained inapparent and thus securely isolated within the interstices of millions of connections thanks to their cryptological shields.

In the mid-1990s, the Internet found a political mode, too, when it was used to link candidates with voters during the mid-term elections in 1994 for both houses of the United States Congress and some state governorships. A gubernatorial candidate in Minnesota, Will Shetterly, interpreted this use of Internet as a novel and 'crucial platform for political debate'. The *New York Times* observed that Internet was indeed worldwide, linking about 2 million users at the time, enabling them to 'leap from one computer database to another at a click of a mouse, following ideas, color photographs, interactive diagrams, sound and video clips – all linked through a technology known as hypertext'.[47]

So far as can be determined, the Internet has not been a principal means of communication for the international criminal element responsible for the September 2001 attacks on the United States. Akin to radio silence, 'Internet silence' may have prevailed – a sign of premeditation, rigorous discipline and shock effect on the part of the al-Qaeda network.

HOW SECURE WILL 'SECURE' BE

Creation of the Web stemmed, then, from an initiative taken in 1989 by one physicist, Berners-Lee, as a means to distribute and rapidly examine document-based data among the world's high-energy researchers. Both Internet and its reincarnated Web remained insecure however, in the integrity of their data and for financial transactions. In spite of these constraints, the network has doubled in size with the passing of each year.[48]

By the mid-1990s, serious thought was given to the potential of Internet and Internet-like communication webs for use 'live' to (a) review progress on a given experiment in scientific research, and (b) supplant, outright, the printed scientific journal. The arguments in support of (a) were clear: real-time sequences in an experiment could be critiqued in real time as well, a factor especially important in biological laboratories. In the case of (b) the cost of journals had more than doubled within a decade, besides continuing to be slow to referee and print. So an inspiration originally military in origin was rapidly becoming a highly visible implement in the processes of civil research.[49] (The scientific journal has not yet disappeared.)

Public acceptance of these new information superhighways probably became fact when researchers within the American military-industrial complex were accused of exploiting the system for obscene purposes. The weekly magazine *Science* noted that computers at the Livermore National Laboratory were found to store 90,000 'sexually explicit' images requiring an enormous number of megabytes of memory among (at least some of) Livermore's 30,000 computers. The laboratory, officially under the management of the federal Department of Energy, was ordered to investigate – at a cost of about $1 million – the hard disks of at least 10 per cent of Livermore's computers to find the culprits.[50]

An option to assure the control of command in case of sustained nuclear attack on Washington was the Pentagon's Doomsday project. Projections for survival in the event of a Third World War were first discussed during Harry Truman's presidency (1945–52), a result of which was the construction in the 1950s of underground command centers in the Maryland mountains northwest of the US capital. All the crucial points were linked by secure telephone and radio.

By the 1980s – after decades of 'mutual assured destruction' brandished by the two superpowers of the time – the American strategy for fighting a nuclear war required infallible command connections between the president, his secretary of defense and the uniformed chiefs, together with the key agencies of governance wherever they might be scattered by fast-moving events. Control of the firing of nuclear weapons, for example, had to be assured from any point on the national territory as well as from sea and airborne platforms widely dispersed across the globe.

In January 1983, President Ronald Reagan signed National Security Decision Directive 55, an executive decree intended to ensure governmental continuity during and after a nuclear assault for a duration of six months. The plan included a web of command communications known as the Presidential Survivability Support System.

Once the destruction of the capital city could be verified, this plan envisaged the linking of members of the leadership (by now secure in a series of subterranean bunkers) by way of satellite communications and a small fleet of lead-lined trucks racing along the highways of the continental United States while evading nuclear warheads arriving from the Soviet Union. The plan remained extant until its cancellation in 1994 (and an investment of $8 billion), in part because of the end of the Cold War but in part because the program's secrecy had raised a 'bureaucratic nightmare to the nth power'.[51]

THE NEW INTERDISCIPLINARY COMMUNICATION

'Those whose minds are on aggression are in the nature of things less concerned with intelligence of any kind than are those who inopportunely find themselves with their backs to the wall.'

Peter Calvocoressi, in *Top Secret Ultra*.[52]

Calvocoressi, historian and political scientist, was a member of the interservice team at Bletchley Park in Britain who brought communication engineering, mathematics and linguistics to bear on enemy ciphers. He and his colleagues, as well as the Americans reading the Japanese ciphers, made a contribution to the shortening of the war that remains immeasurable.

Protecting the communication of sensitive information is the domain combining logic, applied mathematics and language known generically as cryptology (also cryptanalysis) or, in information technology, digital encryption. Science is not involved, strictly speaking, nor is technology. It is, rather, mathematics. Its communication engineering is the transmittal of data and images along electrical (wired) or electronic (atmospheric-spatial) pathways. With the advent of the computer, the United States is the first country with stringent laws on exporting digital-encryption technology. There are more and more specialists engaged in this field, through peace and war.

In this book mention is rarely made of mathematics as an independent discipline. Most of us studied mathematics as the discrete subjects of arithmetic, algebra, geometry, trigonometry, and (rather fewer) calculus and mathematical theory. What most of us learned in school (linear mathematics) is the orderly presence of numbers and proportions in predictable presentations and solutions. While mathematics is thus neither a natural science nor a social science, its numerical values and utility apply to all the sciences – and sometimes to philosophy, to which it properly belongs.

Nonlinearity, on the other hand, is a late twentieth-century form of mathematics finding new applications all the time. Civil uses include investigations of neural networks in animal species, financial economics, magneto-hydrodynamics, chaos theory (especially in meteorology-climatology), and the formation of stars and galaxies – to name a few. Military applications are growing, too. Nonlinear mathematics is increasingly pertinent to the study of trajectories, the mathematics of logistics, queuing theory applicable to resupply and transport problems, the different functions of cryptology (enciphering, deciphering, the random processes inherent in the building of the one-time pads used in espionage)[53] and many other problem areas.

NOVELTY COMES TO CIPHERS

From the Renaissance to the present, military and diplomatic agencies devised methods for coding (the substitution of a word or phrase for another) and cryptography (a complex system of substitution of individual letters and numerals combined with coding). Indeed the military, whether in the early Arab world, western or eastern Europe, North America or Japan, have been and remain at the forefront of developing cryptanalytical technology.

When Peter the Great returned from his 17-month embassy to western Europe in 1699, he brought with him knowledge of the so-called black chambers (deciphering centers) at work in the post offices of Austria, France and England. Coding and ciphering in Russia improved under the tsars of the eighteenth and nineteenth centuries, and the tradition was continued and expanded after Lenin's creation of the Cheka in 1917. The Americans, who organized their own cryptological arm to service wartime needs in the conflict of 1914–18, abandoned a cipher service during the 1920s and did not renew their energies in this field until a decade later. Today governments

> are always on the lookout for better cloaks to go with their daggers. The ultimate cryptographic feat would therefore be a mathematical proof that all choices of a particular problem useful in code-making are forever intractable ... A cryptographer who invented such a system might well be tempted to keep it secret, because he would quickly put fellow-inventors out of work.[54]

Fast elliptic encryption (FEE), a method employing the algebra of elliptic curves, is one of the many techniques used to protect plain language and change it into something else for secure transmission between two points.

Using … the newfound Armengaud-Woltman prime [number] $2^{1,398,269} - 1$ as a basis, the FEE system could readily encrypt [an] issue of *Scientific American* into seeming gibberish. Under current number-theoretical beliefs about the difficulty of cracking FEE codes, it would require, without knowing the secret key, all the computing power on Earth more than $10^{10,000}$ years to decrypt the gibberish back into a meaningful magazine.[55]

Civil spin-off from codes and ciphers takes many forms, especially the protection of data concerning medical records, banking and other finance, currency circulation, databanks storing personal credit and other commercial data, and repositories of judicial and criminal matters.

Early on during the Second World War a number of mathematicians, physicists and champions of bridge and chess were called to the United States Navy's cipher school in Washington in order to 'read' enemy submarine-force and other naval ciphers. Their painstaking, manual methods developed into machine analysis by 1944, when they were able to compress hundreds of hours of calculation into a few minutes of mechanically aided work. The British, meanwhile, built prototype partial computers (for example, the Colossus) to simulate the wheel settings of Germany's Enigma machines. This work was done by a Post Office civil servant, Thomas Flowers, whose machines replaced laborious manual efforts.

Some of the American naval specialists decided, once demobilized, to form a company called Engineering Research Associates (ERA) in St Paul, Minnesota. In 1951 a young engineer-mathematician named Seymour Cray joined ERA and soon demonstrated extraordinary talent in assembling arrays of computing power that led to the creation of supercomputers. These processors found use in cryptanalysis, missile applications, meteorology and demographic tabulation for the census. Supercomputers, first installed in two military-research centers (Los Alamos and Livermore), generated more design concepts, spawning several generations of 'hyper' machines that finally drove the Cray interests out of business.

SCIENCE FICTION NO LONGER

Let us return to the individual military man or woman. In the context of developing the United States Army's '21st Century Land-Warrior System',[56] helmet-mounted displays are proposed for battlefield soldiers. The purpose is to transmit data directly to individuals in the field. The electro-optic technology involved, put to work by special forces roaming through Afghanistan, promises to raise the amount and accuracy of information received by individual combatants. Experience already shows that individuals receiving *more* information, *directly*, have a better chance of accomplishing the mission and surviving than otherwise.

A civilian panel of the National Research Council in Washington is concerned with a soldier's ability to perform 'normally' even when equipped with special detectors. The Panel on Human Factors in the Design of Tactical Display Systems for the Individual Soldier foresees that data displays could lead to blockage of view, poor visual perception, eyestrain, loss of equilibrium and fatigue.[57] So the first of these instruments is likely to concentrate on the source of hostile fire taking direct aim at him or her.[58]

Communication circuits have covered long geographic and scientific distances since the first relaying of signals. The Morse code and then the semiconductor brought the greatest changes in speed and volume handled. Current research, backed in part by naval funds,[59] is helping researchers at Cornell University to explore the possibility of a universal substrate or base upon which individual and pure crystals of virtually any semiconducting substance might be grown. Once such a common substrate is found, new kinds of semiconductors – in addition to the well-known microprocessing chip – should become applicable to sensors, lasers, switches and devices for storing and communicating data ultra-rapidly.[60]

At the Lawrence Livermore National Laboratory, IBM's computer known as 'accelerated strategic supercomputing initiative White' (ASCI White, worth $10 million), performs 12.3 million calculations each second. It can track at once, via three-dimensional models, how a billion atoms react and age. This may prove to be a key role in maintaining nuclear stockpiles and thus assuring deterrence.

NOTES

1 James F. Dunnigan and Albert A. Nofi, *Dirty Little Secrets of World War II* (New York, William Morrow/Quill, 1994), pp. 112–13.
2 The significance of 'information dominance' and the security of communications are the keynotes of a report, 1999, by a committee of the National Research Council in Washington, *Realizing the Potential of C4I: Fundamental Challenges*.
3 James Burke, 'Connections', *Scientific American*, May 1998, pp. 86–7.
4 Gerard J. Holzmann and Björn Pehrson, 'The First Data Networks', *Scientific American*, January 1994, p. 112.
5 Thomas Powers recounts the story in *Heisenberg's War: The Secret History of the German Bomb* (New York, Alfred A. Knopf, 1993), pp. 272–3.

6 *New York Herald-Tribune* (Paris edn), 22 January 1894, as reproduced in the *IHT*, 22 January 1994, p. 6.

7 James Burke, *The Knowledge Web: From Electronic Agents to Stonehenge and Back – and Other Journeys through Knowledge* (New York, Simon & Schuster, 1999), p. 164.

8 F. W. Winterbotham, *The Nazi Connection* (New York, Harper & Row, 1978), p.194.

9 Constance Babington-Smith, *Air Spy: The Story of Photo Intelligence in World War II* (New York, Harper, 1957), pp. 8–10, 196. This real reconnaissance is treated semifictitiously as an undertaking of Britain's Royal Geographic Society in the film *The English Patient*, based on the book by Michael Ondaatje (produced by Saul Zaentz, directed by Anthony Minghella, 1996).

10 'Earth View: Shuttle Tests New Radar', *IHT*, 11 April 1994, p. 3.

11 Frederick Seitz, 'Adaptive Optics in Astronomy' (letter), *Science*, 264, 8 April 1994, pp. 185–6.

12 Thomas S. Kuhn, *The Structure of Scientific Revolutions* (Chicago, IL, University of Chicago Press, 1970).

13 Linda Rothstein, 'Star Wars Redux', *Bulletin of Atomic Scientists*, May/June 1994, p. 9; Georges Charpak and Richard Garwin, *Feux follets et champignons nucléaires* (Will-o-the-Wisps and Mushroom Clouds), (Paris, Editions Odile Jacob, 1997), p. 238.

14 John Noble Wilford, *IHT*, 29 April 1994, p. 8.

15 'Programme for Moon Exploration', *Outlook on Science Policy*, June 1994, p. 69.

16 Corey S. Powell, 'Darling *Clementine*?', *Scientific American*, August 1994, p. 8.

17 Letter to editor, *Time* (Europe edn), 8 December 1997, p. 6. The Brilliant Pebbles project was proposed to President Reagan's administration by the physicist, Edward Teller (inventor of the X-ray laser); both Congress and the scientific community considered the scheme unreliable and costly. See William J. Broad, *Teller's War: The Top-Secret Story behind the Star Wars Deception* (New York, Simon & Schuster/Touchstone, 1992).

18 'In A Cavern, In A Canyon', *The Economist*, 7 December 1996, pp. 96–7.

19 Richard L. Gregory (ed. with O. L. Zangwill), *The Oxford Companion to the Mind* (Oxford, Oxford University Press, 1987), p. 442.

20 Recalled by John Keegan, *Warpaths: Travels of A Military Historian in North America* (London, Random House/Pimlico, 1995), p. 214.

21 Thérèse Delpech, *La guerre parfaite* (The Perfect War) (Paris, Flammarion, 1998), p. 137.

22 Ronald Lewin, *Ultra Goes to War: The Secret Story* (London, Book Club Associates-Hutchinson, 1978), p. 299.

23 Alan D. Beyerchen, *Scientists under Hitler: Politics and the Physics Community in the Third Reich* (New Haven, CT, and London, Yale University Press, 1977), p. 57.

24 Shimon Naveh, *In Pursuit of Military Excellence: The Evolution of Operational Theory* (London, Frank Cass, 1997), p. 27, n. 67.

25 David Fisher, *The War Magician* (New York, Coward-McCann, 1983), p. 5. An earlier Maskelyne was Nevil, fifth Astronomer Royal who, with Isaac Newton and Edmond Halley, sat on a special committee created by the British Parliament with the Longitude Act of 1714. The Board of Longitude was intended to select the most valid proposal to find a reliable means to detect longitude to the nearest half-degree of arc in order to assure the safety of the country's military and merchant fleets. A self-educated carpenter named John Harrison contended for the prize with his invention of the chronometer.

Maskelyne consistently opposed Harrison's nomination, but Harrison finally won recognition 40 years after applying for the award. All of todays's time-pieces are derived from the response to the original naval/commercial require-ment. See Dava Sobel, *Longitude* (New York, Walker, 1995), pp. 8–9 and *passim*.

26 Fisher, *The War Magician*, p. 25.

27 Dana Priest, 'Strikes Divided NATO Chiefs', *IHT*, 22 September 1999, pp. 1, 3.

28 Both quotations are from Keegan, *Warpaths*, p. 263.

29 Lawrence C. Soley, *Radio Warfare: OSS and CIA Subversive Propaganda* (New York, Praeger, 1989). Chapter 6 deals with Soviet 'psywar'.

30 See Note 21, above.

31 As reported by Tim Weiner, *IHT*, 19 August 1993, p. 1.

32 In a review of a book by a former communications officer of the KGB, Victor Sheymov, *Tower of Secrets* (Annapolis, MD, Naval Institute Press, 1993) in *IHT*, 14 October 1993, p. 5. Odom once directed the National Security Agency of the United States.

33 Ibid., p. 3.

34 Ibid.

35 Tim Weiner, 'SDI Official Admits Making Missile in Test Easier to Hit', *IHT*, 28 August 1993, p. 3.

36 Dave Dooling, 'Technology 1994 – Aerospace and Military', *IEEE Spectrum*, January 1994, p. 66.

37 Andrei A. Kokoshkin, 'The New Soviet Military Doctrine: Political, Strategic, and Economic Dimensions', *Mediterranean Quarterly*, 1 (1990), p. 41, n. 1.

38 Bruce van Voorst and Jay Peterzell, 'The Ploy that Fell to Earth', *Time* (Europe edn), 30 August 1993, pp. 32–3.

39 Adam Clapham, director, *On the Brink of Eternity*, BBC 2, *Pandora's Box* series, first aired on 22 June 1992; James Burge, mathematician and independent television producer, personal communication with the author, 3 October 1993.

40 'Space Telescopes: Second Sight', *The Economist*, 17 July 1993, p. 81.

41 Robert L. Park, *What's New* (American Physical Society), 25 November 1994, item 2; ibid., 9 December 1994, item 3. 'Brilliant Pebbles' is reminiscent of the 'Window' operation, the dropping of airborne aluminum strips by the Royal Air Force to jam German electronic defenses early in the Second World War; the method worked.

42 Philip Elmer-Dewitt, 'First Nation in Cyberspace', *Time* (Europe edn), 6 December 1993, p. 34; Gordon Powers, 'How to Get Caught Up in the Internet', *Globe and Mail*, 21 September 1994, p. A12.

43 A remarkable preview of the communications revolution, published before creation of the Internet, is an entire issue of *International Science and Technology*, April 1968, pp. 6–130. A concise chronicle of the genesis of the Internet itself is Charles du Granrut, 'Futurs d'antan: Une brève histoire d'Internet' (Yesteryear's Futures: A Brief History of Internet), *Futuribles*, November 1996, pp. 73–80.

44 John Adam, 'Architects of the Net of Nets', *IEEE Spectrum*, September 1996, p. 58.

45 Albert L. Shapiro, 'The Internet', *Foreign Policy*, Summer 1999, pp. 14–27; Jean-Claude Guédon, 'La force de l'intelligence distribuée', *La Recherche*, February 2000, pp. 16–22.

46 Robert Wright, 'The Man Who Invented the Web', *Time* (Europe edn), 19 May 1997, pp. 42–5.

47   A *New York Times* feature, '1994, the Year of On-Line Democracy', *IHT*, 7 November 1994, p. 3.
48   Published as 'A Home in Internetville, A "Network Within" Smooths Access', *IHT*, 3 November 1994, pp. 11, 15; see also Bradford Spurgeon, 'Navigating the Internet: Directions Are Required', and 'For Information on the Internet', *IHT* (Telecommunications/A Special Report), 29 November 1994, p. 16.
49   Gary Stix, 'Trends in Scientific Communication: The Speed of Write', *Scientific American*, December 1994, pp. 72–7.
50   Anon., cited in 'Le savant était pornographe' (The Scientist was a Pornographer), *Courrier international*, 3–9 November 1994, p. 42.
51   Tim Weiner, '$8 Billion Survival Kit is Scrapped by the Pentagon', *IHT*, 19 April 1994, pp. 1, 8.
52   Peter Calvocoressi, *Top Secret Ultra* (London, Cassell, and New York, Random/Pantheon, 1980), p. 106 of the American edition.
53   Daniel Kunth, French astrophysicist, speaking before the Association Science Technologie et Société, Paris, 5 February 1994.
54   'Cryptography, Puzzling Secrets', *The Economist*, 7 September (1996), p. 91.
55   Richard E. Crandall, 'The Challenge of Large Numbers', *Scientific American*, February (1997), p. 61.
56   The '21st Century Land-Warrior System' is a complex of armaments, protective clothing, and information-processing tools designed to give the soldier immediate data on targets, enemy movements and other reconnaissance elements. The study cited was funded by the US Army's Natick Research, Development and Engineering Center.
57   Reported in National Research Council media release, 'Advanced Technology for Soldiers Requires Extensive Research before Being Used on the Battlefield', Washington, DC, 13 November 1996.
58   Gary Stix, 'Sounding Out Snipers', *Scientific American*, July 2001, p. 22.
59   Support comes from the Electronics Division of the US Office of Naval Research.
60   New York Times Service, 'A New Twist in Making Computer Chips', *IHT*, 29 March 1997, p. 11.

10

From Military Aviation's Radar to Computer Notebooks

'Complete automation, or something very near it [is] both practicable and necessary in air warfare where the environment is very simple and speeds very great.'

Martin van Creveld[1]

Many of us learned as schoolchildren of the exploits of Marconi and other researchers who were instrumental in bringing radiotelegraphy to reality. Radiotelegraphy using hertzian waves soon grew into radio-phony as transmitters, receivers and antenna concepts were perfected. The companion medium of television materialized several decades later, although it was not to be found in homes or workplaces until after the Second World War's electronic warfare gave video transmissions their civil impetus in the late 1940s and 1950s. Here, briefly, is what happened and what seem to be the promises for the future.

WHAT MAKES RADAR DIFFERENT

*Ra*dio *d*irection *a*nd *r*anging – radar – is perhaps as important a communication medium as radio transmissions and broadcasts.[2] Experts on the war of 1939–45 attribute without hesitation how the conflict was fought, and concluded, to three major developments. These were

- the enormous advantage to the Allied side of being able to read many of the opponents' secret messages,
- the war-terminating nature of the atomic bomb, and
- radar's capacity to neutralize most aerial offensive potential and, in the last two years of combat, the potential of submarines of the tripartite Axis powers.

What is doubly noteworthy of these factors is that they were all based on scientific knowledge, much of which was transformed into high-performance technology within the timespan of the war years themselves.[3]

ORIGINS

How scientists and the military collaborated to develop and exploit one application of radar had its beginnings in the challenge posed by the air raids staged during the First World War between German and Allied heavier-than-air and lighter-than-air craft. This was the imperative to *detect* incoming intruders, whether airplanes or airships. No mechanical solution came forth during this period, however, to supplement human ears and eyes – and not a soul suspected that electrons would perform better.

Fully within the duties of governance, British Prime Minister Stanley Baldwin warned the House of Commons in 1932 that 'there is no power on Earth' to protect against air raids in the event of a new conflict – much as would seem the case in 2001 to find a defense against anthrax and other bioterrorism.[4] Baldwin's position was shared wholeheartedly by an Oxford University physicist named Frederick Lindemann (later Viscount Cherwell) and an Air Ministry functionary in London, A. P. Rowe. During the First World War, Lindemann had worked on the problem of overcoming uncontrolled spinning by descending aircraft. Both he and Rowe saw the United Kingdom's salvation, in case of war again after the debilitating conflict of 1914–18, only in scientific research.

In 1934, the Air Ministry created the Committee for the Survey of Air Defense, with Rowe as recording secretary. The Committee's first action was an offer of £1,000 sterling to anyone developing a 'death ray' capable of killing a sheep at a distance of 100 yards. There were no takers, but the Committee itself began serious work in January 1935 on calculations meant to detect aircraft five to six miles away by using a radio transmitter emitting on one kilowatt of power. This was the specification set by Robert A. Watson-Watt, then radio superintendent of Britain's National Physical Laboratory. 'Radio detection' thus superseded the dead-end 'radio destruction' directed against unsuspecting farm animals as targets to be 'rayed' to death.

Detection by reflected radio waves was now on its way to toilsome elaboration. In 1935, a small team of British civil experts succeeded in distinguishing, albeit primitively, the signal on a cathode-ray display left by an RAF Heyford bomber piloted overhead at 10,000 feet. The Britons labeled the technique 'radio direction-finding', and RDF would remain both the official identifying abbreviation of the technique *and* a military secret until well into the war years to follow. The Americans preferred the term *radar*, adopted it in November 1940, and the British followed suit in July 1943.

Expressed in terms of the electromagnetic spectrum, radar uses the spectral portion occupied by Hertzian waves, more specifically waves ranging in length from $3 \cdot 10^7$ cm or 'meter' waves, down through medium waves, the S-band and X-band microwaves, to the K-band 'centimeter' waves measuring $3 \cdot 10^{10}$ cm in length. By applying emission and reception techniques that improved progressively each year before the Second World War burst upon the world, British scientists and engineers working for the military managed to establish a defensive network of RDF points known as Chain Home stations along England's eastern and southeastern shorelines. When Germany's *Luftwaffe* began concerted attacks on the British homeland a month after France's capitulation in June 1940, the British were ready with Chain Home and a system to filter sightings that was based at Bentley Priory, north London.

Between 1940 and December 1944, there was a spiraling of progress in electronic measures and countermeasures used for warfare. At the former date the British were using 'identification, friend or foe' (IFF) and the Germans were exploiting their Knickebein airborne apparatus to receive signals from transmitters on the ground for improved accuracy in bombing at night. In Germany, Telefunken had already developed equipment operating on a wavelength of some 50cm, and were experimenting with simple chemical compounds (such as lead sulfide and silicon carbide) to improve noise measurement.[5]

By March 1942 the Allies had in operation the Gee system, airborne navigation operating on ground signals. This helped air crews as distant as 600km from transmitters to fix their own location within a 10-km radius. By the end of 1944 and the battle of the Bulge, the Allies had developed the Perfectos technique to home in on (by then) German acquisition of IFF as targets in themselves. In 1944, too, almost the entire American electronics industry was engaged in the production of a single 'secret weapon', radar. Of this industry's total sales of $2.7 billion (mainly radio sets) that year, radar accounted for $1.2 billion.[6]

THE MAGICAL MAGNETRON

Specific high-technology that British scientists developed during the 1930s was the resonant cavity magnetron, a flat disk some 10 cm in diameter and made mostly of copper. This was radar's transmitter.

The invaluable little device emitted radio energy in the microwave range, signals that bounced back from their targets quickly enough to allow operators to detect the echo returned faintly from the metal cladding of airframes as far distant as 200km. But the magnetron more than equalized the advance the Germans had taken over the British in the race to perfect RDF science and technology during the 1930s. Today, as we turn on our magnetron-energized microwave ovens in the family kitchen, most of us are unaware of its militarily dictated origins.

Microwave-radar development during the Second World War refined the capacity of loran (*lo*ng-*ra*nge *n*avigation) and led almost directly to the invention of the transistor, via wartime work with solid-state semiconductor crystals inherited by the Americans from Britain's Telecommunications Research Establishment. These efforts were also the genesis of the maser (*m*icrowave *a*mplification by *s*timulated *e*mission of *r*adiation, a first cousin of the laser) and of nuclear magnetic resonance, the latter known today as MRI and a near-indispensable aid in clinical diagnosis.

The potential of radar early in the Second World War was, nevertheless, most elementary. To take one illustration, gunlaying in anti-aircraft defense, the determination of an aircraft's altitude by radar observation from the ground was not possible. Only range and bearing were determinable. Robert C. Winton, an engineer who served with British forces at Alexandria (Egypt) in 1941, realized the importance of his detachment's work in order to safeguard the British fleet's primary base in the Mediterranean. He describes how three radar units ringing the harbor sent range-and-bearing messages to a central control, where a map of the harbor bore three holes to represent the three radar installations. Each hole was fitted with weighted strings.

Then, Winton explains, a 'length of string corresponding to the range given … would be pulled out of the hole representing the radar's position, and held to correspond with the relevant bearing'. The point where the three strings met above the map would be the position of the target at the moment of the taking of measurements: a do-it-yourself triangulation, and indeed rudimentary. The procedure was obviously too long for downing an intruding bomber, but gunners were able at least to fire barrages – lines of bursting shells slightly ahead of the anticipated straight-and-level runs of enemy bombers. As a result of this primitive reaction, the attackers altered course and had to aim their bombs elsewhere.[7]

SETTING NEW STANDARDS

Two rather different theaters of war showed contrasting performances in research applied to the military. To compare what took place simultaneously in the European and Pacific theaters of war, a survey of the Japanese electronics industry made after the conflict by American specialists produced an assessment that today raises eyebrows. The contrast, stated this report,

> between the technical abilities of the Japanese scientists and engineers and their lack of effectiveness in applying these powers to the war efforts was very striking ... [t]he production radars of the Imperial Army and Navy were four to five years behind ours in design and engineering.[8]

Yet unsurprisingly, note analysts James Dunnigan and Albert Nofi – because the Japanese navy, ground and air forces all at least doubled during the 1930s – the growth of all Japanese industry between 1935 and 1945 was a direct result of the expansion of these armed forces.[9]

With the war not yet ended, the *New York Herald-Tribune* of 1 February 1945 hazarded the opinion that radar, which it described as radio-location apparatus permitting the detection of objects that the eye cannot see, was 'the most distinct scientific achievement of this war ... It was the instrument which probably won the Battle of Britain in the summer and fall of 1940.'[10] Even in later retrospect, many still agree with this assessment. An early account of what was accomplished by Robert Watson-Watt, the individual commonly considered the direct father of radar (and, as one consequence, later knighted), appeared in the issue of *Nature* magazine dated 15 September 1945.[11] Radar proved, indeed, to be the science-based technique that won the Second World War for the side best equipped with it.[12] Other narratives include Vannevar Bush's *Modern Arms and Free Men* (1968) and Robert Buderi's detailed *The Invention that Changed the World* (1996).[13]

The subtitle of Buderi's volume is *How a Small Group of Radar Pioneers Won the Second World War and Launched a Technological Revolution*. Buderi says of Vannevar Bush, President Roosevelt's top scientific counselor, 'His tremendous success in directing civilian military science ... heavily influenced the way the United States funds research, both for the military and otherwise, in the postwar age.'[14] Hyperbole, some may think, but Buderi's appraisal is not far off the mark.

AN INNOVATION BREEDS OTHERS

Radar astronomy and radioastronomy, the latter once considered a professional dead-end even after its feasibility was proved after the Second World War, could not have developed without radar.[15] They have become essential adjuncts to the panoply of astronomers' techniques and tools. Radar helped astronomers refine, through electrical engineering, the value of the astronomical unit (the mean Earth–Sun distance), detect the retrograde sense of the rotation of Venus and the exact rotation rate of Mercury.[16] The electrical engineers working at MIT's Lincoln Laboratory and in the Mojave Desert, in conjunction with the design of the distant early-warning system (DEW) during the 1950s and the subsequent ballistic-missile early-warning system (BMEWS), devised the measurement methods needed for these computations. In the process, the same research engineers created for astronomers the entirely new field of planetary radioastronomy.[17] Today an engineer who once designed radar capable of missile tracking, Steven Gulick, is using his talents at Cornell University to monitor herds of unseen elephants via microphone arrays deployed in the forests of Ghana. His aim is to begin to understand elephant 'language'.

The point-contact transistor made possible truly portable radio receivers not dependent upon heavy battery-packs, reduced the bulk and weight of television sets, improved the computer to the point that desktop models (so-called microcomputers) became a reality in the 1980s, followed by miniaturized electronic 'notebooks' in the 1990s. All of these resulted from the adoption by the Americans of crystals to detect radio activity and intensive investigations in several countries of the potential of silicon, germanium and other solid substances. The advent of the mobile telephone is attributable, furthermore, to the ingredients making up the technological package that we call sonar.

The military entirely funded the transistor's development for the first dozen years after its invention in 1947, and Japan's Sony Corporation first exploited the civil market. The aim was to replace vacuum tubes – reliable, but heavy and excessively heat-generating – by miniaturizing circuit boards with the, at first, less reliable but minuscule transistors. Japan's war-wrecked industrial infrastructure proved more amenable than that of the United States in making the leap directly to transistors without trying to resuscitate vacuum-tube technology. A cornucopia of consumer products followed.

Synthetic-aperture radar, developed at the University of Michigan during the 1950s and kept a military secret because of its all-weather advantages, was used by the NASA Jet Propulsion Laboratory's Seasat satellite of 1978 and in the Magellan project's mapping of Venus. Then came over-the-horizon radar and the 'stealth' technology for making military aircraft resistant to detection by radar.

ONWARDS TO SPACE-BASED LASERS

From radar emerged, too, both X-ray astronomy and infrared astronomy. These had their origins in military efforts, respectively, to detect nuclear explosions and to explore the possibilities of seeing in the dark.[18] Such applications may seem to have little to do with the workaday concerns of life, but they are important to ever-expanding science, improved understanding of our planet's climate, constantly improving weather reports on television, new prostheses for those who are visually impaired, and the night work of guards and watchmen.

As far as radar's original aim is concerned, to detect from afar invading objects in the sky, the advent of stealth aircraft capable of thwarting radar detection raises new technical problems. Gérard Garnier, of France's Office National d'Etudes et de Recherches Aéronautique (ONERA) summarizes the future effectiveness of radar as follows.

> The use of ultra-high and very-high frequencies seems henceforth indispensable to overcome stealth. The real problem is the cluttering of the spectrum in the metric wave-lengths, for which radar was never designed. The technology for this [will] not be expensive to develop … Airborne solutions can even be foreseen of early-warning surveillance ensuring the detection of low-altitude stealth targets.[19]

Television today is the defining mass medium throughout the industrialized world and in major cities of developing countries. It is also used extensively in distance learning. For general communication, however, radio still carries the day in regions outside the political or economic centers of the industrializing world. The Internet and World Wide Web are following rapidly behind, so fast that their exponential growth rate is phenomenal – although they have yet to become pervasive in many industrialized countries. What lag there is can be attributed to the much smaller number of personal computers available in the great majority of the world's 189 countries, their relatively high cost, and the limited availability of lines to service them on national telephone networks.

A major challenge in radar R&D today is to improve finely focused X-band detection in missile defense so as to distinguish decoys from warheads and to confirm destruction of the real thing. A related effort is the space-based laser (SBL), being designed for testing in 2012, operating with a laser beam. When aimed at another body, SBL's powerful beam would not be absorbed into the high, thin-air atmosphere while on its way to target.

NOTES

1 Martin van Creveld, *Technology and War: From 2000 BC to the Present* (New York, Free Press, 1989), p. 241.
2 A transmission is acknowledged by its intended receiver. A broadcast is a message emitted widely, with no provision for acknowledgment of its receipt.
3 Standard reckoning in civil R&D allows two to five years to develop and market a new product or service; in the pharmaceutical industry, however, this time may extend to ten years.
4 Although Austrian and Danish researchers reported in November 2001 the development of spray repellents.
5 H. F. Mataré of Malibu CA, in a personal memoir published in *IEEE Members Newsletter*, 2nd–3nd quarters 2000, pp. 4–5.
6 Robert Buderi, *The Invention that Changed the World* (New York, Simon & Schuster, 1996), p. 223.
7 Robert C. Winton, 'Stringing Up a Better Way', *IEEE Life Members Newsletter*, 2nd–3nd quarters 1997, p. 5.
8 As quoted in Buderi, *The Invention that Changed the World*, p. 241.
9 James F. Dunnigan and Albert A. Nofi, *Dirty Little Secrets of World War II* (New York, Simon & Schuster, 1996), pp. 307, 36, 209.
10 Cited in *IHT*, 2 February 1995, p. 6. Chester Wilmot, in *The Struggle for Europe* (London, Collins, 1952), *passim*; he mentions repeatedly the important 'scientific' contribution of radar to the Allied victory.
11 R.A. Watson-Watt, 'Radar in War and Peace', *Nature*, 15 September 1945, pp. 319–24.
12 Recalled by, among others, William Aspray in his review of Robert Buderi, *The Invention that Changed the World*, in *Science*, 274 (1996), p. 199, n. 5.
13 Vannevar Bush, *Modern Arms and Free Men* (Cambridge, MA, MIT Press, 1968).
14 Buderi, *The Invention that Changed the World*, p. 469.
15 Ibid., pp. 16, 273–307, 342–3, 417–50.
16 Ibid., p. 431.
17 Andrew J. Butrica, 'In Conjunction with Venus', *IEEE Spectrum*, December 1997, pp. 31–8.
18 The author is grateful to Raymond Spier, editor of the journal *Science and Engineering Ethics*, for having emphasized both of these accomplishments, personal communication, January 2001.
19 Gérard Garnier, 'The Future of Radar', *Science & Défense*, 47, February 1996, pp. 11, 12.

11

Military Medicine Saves Fighting Strength

Faccia che al campo giunga   May heaven protect them
Con fortunati auspici!   On the field of battle!
from Dorabella's recitative in Mozart, *Così fan tutte*, I, 6

HOW MANY LIVES?

A member of the United States Strategic Bombing Survey recalled well after the Second World War how bleakly the American leadership in Washington had foreseen the human cost of an invasion of Japan. In June 1945 President Harry S. Truman (in office less than ten weeks) asked his advisors how many American casualties could be expected of Operation Olympic, the landings on Kyushu scheduled for 1 November 1945. Varying estimates, some of them sheer guesses, were the replies to the president's question; an anonymous economist advised the secretary of war, Henry L. Stimson, that the cost would be high, indeed: between 500,000 and 1 million killed, wounded and missing.[1]

Stimson admitted later in his autobiographical *On Active Service* that the decision to use atomic bombs resulted in death for over a hundred thousand Japanese (who were mostly civilians). He maintained that the historical fact could not be changed: the destruction was premeditated and deliberate, but the bombing of Hiroshima and Nagasaki brought an end to the conflict. More than a half-century after the event, the total accepted by all parties of the numbers who died directly and indirectly from the nuclear bombing of the two Japanese cities is 170,000. At Hiroshima, 90 per cent of the *medical* personnel working there on 6 August 1945 'were killed or disabled'[2] – contributing significantly to the total who lost their lives or were injured.

Gilbert W. Beebe, who once directed the statistical and epidemiological unit of the National Academy of Sciences in Washington, studied the history of atomic-raid survivors in Japan for most of his professional life. He has observed that, in the atom-bombed cities, 'the majority of people in the combined populations of Hiroshima and Nagasaki escaped physically unscathed'. He estimates that, of the 300,000 people who survived the bombings, some 1,500 died of cancers of nine different types caused by radiation over the 50-year period, 1945 to 1995.'The original fears of other long-term effects like acceler- ated aging and genetic damage among the survivors and their children', Beebe adds, have been mostly unfounded.[3] Age samplings taken in 1996–97 showed, with astonishing perversity, that nuclear-bomb sur- vivors were relatively more numerous than contemporaries of the region who had little or no exposure to radiation and died of other causes.

The basis for forecasting large numbers of casualties was the experience gained during the war in the Pacific, from the tumultuous combat on Guadalcanal and New Britain in 1942,[4] through the Philippine campaign in 1944 and the hard-fought seizure of the Japanese redoubts of Iwo Jima and Okinawa in 1945. Okinawa, an island about 150 km long, was Japanese since it had been taken from the old Ryukyuan kingdom in 1879 to serve against a possible southern attack upon Japan. In 1945, the Japanese military swore to defend Okinawa to the last Nipponese – and Okinawan – corpse. The three- month conflict turned out to be the Pacific war's bloodiest. Military deaths numbered 60,000 Japanese and 12,000 American, but another 133,000 civilian deaths included Okinawans as well as Koreans and Taiwanese impressed into wartime labor for Japan.[5]

To these bases for calculation were factored-in the tolls of the 'firestorm' aerial raids on Hamburg, Dresden and Tokyo. The incendiary destruction of the Yoyogi and contiguous districts of Tokyo in March 1945, for example, took 50,000 lives and possibly more overnight. Virtually all these fatalities resulted from asphyxiation because the available oxygen at ground level fed the flames from incendiary bombs rather than letting humans breathe.

The Olympic landings were to be followed no later than spring 1946, after the creation of a logistical base on Kyushu, by Operation Coronet: a 25-division strike force targeting the Tokyo–Yokohama area. This maneuver was intended, according to the wording of an official document prepared in Washington, to be 'a knockout blow to the enemy's heart'. Last-ditch resistance by the Japanese, both military and civil, who would be deprived by then of their war production, was expected to be desperate – and grim – for both defenders and invaders.

In comparison with the estimates of probable American casualties in the taking of Japan, an eyewitness to the management of concen- tration camps in Java, J. C. Ramaer, recalls that between 1936 and 1945 'some 900,000 Asian forced laborers died, including 300,000

Indonesians. About 122,000 Allied prisoners of war died. Roughly one in four [Netherlanders] living in Indonesia' perished. 'Given this record', Ramaer adds, 'hundreds of thousands surely would have died if the war had continued for only a few months. Instead, savage killings of civilians were stopped by a savage weapon.'[6] All the prisoners concerned suffered from inadequate sanitation, medical care, safety at work, and nutrition.

Shocking though these figures seem, it should be recalled that the battle of Stalingrad of August 1942–February 1943 destroyed so many human beings – 800,000 German and other Axis troops, 1,100,000 Soviets – that the precise numbers of dead or still unaccounted for may never be known. In a month's-long defense of the heights of Mamayev *kurgan* (hill) overlooking greater Stalingrad, the Soviets alone lost 47,000 soldiers. The Germans destroyed represented two entire field armies, the Sixth and the Fourth Panzer, and their support units. Identification tags disappeared with the fallen, many of whom were covered for months by drifting snow and frozen mud.

Losses on the battlefield that discounted prisoner neglect or abuse could, indeed, be atrociously high. The Soviet Union's ground forces suffered such decimation of many of their units that they were simply abandoned as such, and their meager remnants reassigned. This also occurred in the order of battle of British Commonwealth forces. In Germany's Wehrmacht, the 26th Infantry Division from the Rhineland emerged from near-annihilation in combat a total of nine times, with replacements coming from the same region along the River Rhine. Nine was also the number of times that any single battlefield-officer slot had to be refilled throughout the German army. The United States' 3rd Infantry Division was renewed several times over, between 1942 and 1944, in North Africa and France. Merely serving on the battlefield in an infantry regiment can be equated to a 100 per cent chance – in game theory, 'no-win' odds – that an individual will become a casualty: killed, wounded, prisoner or missing, perhaps for ever.

REDUCING LOSSES FROM UNEXPECTED CAUSES

The Joint Chiefs of Staff in Washington found the projected military casualties for the invasion of Japan in 1945–46 too high. American forces had, only a few months previously, suffered 31,000 casualties during the first four weeks of the liberation of the Philippines from Japanese occupation. Similarly heavy losses during the Normandy landings the same year, reckoned together with the losses on Okinawa, made the president's advisors wary of what an assault on

Japan's main islands might cost the United States, and this without taking into account American allies' losses. A figure of 268,000 was finally settled upon as the likely number of Allied soldiers, sailors and airmen who would be killed, wounded or unaccounted for during the planned invasion of Japan's home islands in 1945–46.

This arithmetic gives some idea of the pains taken by the military to estimate casualties and develop the means, both institutional and technical, to minimize losses.[7] A soldier saved is, in many cases, a fighting person returned to combat often more than once. This proved to be true with the Soviet, British Commonwealth, German and Japanese armed forces during the large-scale fighting of the Second World War; it applied, too, in later conflicts in Korea, Vietnam and on the Coalition side during the war in Kuwait and Iraq in 1990–91. The truism did not apply, however, to later wars fought in western and southern Asia, for example, between Iran and Iraq, between Afghanistan and the former USSR, in Armenia and Chechnya, and around Africa's Great Lakes and the two Congos – where casualties were high.

The Iraq–Kuwait hostilities produced an unanticipated ailment of its own. Depleted uranium (DU) is a by-product of the enrichment technology used to produce reactor-quality uranium, the kind used to fuel nuclear-power stations. While the main component of the fission reaction involved is, indeed, the uranium-235 isotope, the balance of the fuel used is uranium-238 which the enrichment process is intended to eliminate. By the 1990s, worldwide DU stocks exceeded 1 million tonnes, a quantity rising annually by 50,000 tonnes.

A high-density material heavier than lead, strongly resistant and cheap to produce, DU alloys easily with titanium to make artillery projectiles having superior aerodynamic characteristics. These projectiles travel at supersonic speeds surpassing Mach 5, easily adding another kilometer to the range of normal artillery and thereby reaching rear-area support. DU shells have good armor-piercing potential, and the high temperatures generated by the penetration of steel turn what is left of the projectile into a high-performing incendiary agent.

While DU has low radioactive toxicity (about 1 curie per tonne), its chemical toxicity is characteristic of heavy metals. A penetrating DU projectile produces in the immediate environment vapor and smoke, based on an aerosol; this can enter the human organism through the breathing of the ambient dust. Weapons using DU ammunition, and many of them, mounted aboard American Abrams tanks, were fired in combat for the first time in Iraq's deserts in January 1991.

Lungs, kidneys and liver can be affected by such contamination. The DU phenomenon may be a cause of the complaints made by hundreds of American and British soldiers and veterans – months, even years after the hostilities in Iraq. Civil victims of this form of poisoning include Iraqi youngsters who found undetonated projectiles (duds), adopted them as toys, and developed a form of leukemia. A German physician, Siegwart-Horst Günther, found a growing number of children in southern Iraq losing hair, suffering from unexplained hemorrhages, or with abdomens distended by renal and hepatic irregularities. In January 1995 Iraq's delegate to the UN sent a note to the International Committee of the Red Cross protesting against the use of DU devices.

Besides the USA, DU projectiles are manufactured by France, Germany, Britain and Russia. A number of non-producing nations, too, are clients for this ammunition. Two commentators on the DU issue, Naïma Lefkir-Laffitte and Roland Laffitte, called its use 'a monstrous military imbecility'.[8] Weapons originating in the West and used during the war in Bosnia (1992–95) numbered 11,000, while another 31,000 were used in the Kosovo campaign of 1999.

Cases of leukemia among veterans of Bosnia and Kosovo in France, Belgium, Italy, Britain and North America – not to speak of parts of ex-Yugoslavia itself – turned up in 2000–1, most of them denied by these governments to be of military origin. The scientific director of the International Epidemiology Institute in Maryland, John Boice, stated that uranium-238 has a half-life of 4.5 billion years, meaning that it takes the age of the universe for one-half the element's radioactive life to decay. Dr Boice pointed out that radiation must penetrate to bone marrow to cause leukemia, and it does not do so. Radiation biologists elsewhere supported this view. While legal action proliferates, DU remains available.

EARLY LIFE-SAVING LORE

In the morning of recorded history, about the year 3300 BC, humankind already had a rudimentary knowledge of medical care, especially in China. The victims of animals of prey or of battle died not only from the bleeding or trauma of wounds incurred but also from sepsis. Infection arose from micro-organisms that culture quickly in unsteril-ized lacerations, gashes from cutting weapons or gunshot, or in skin broken by shattering bone, and sometimes from amputation. While it is doubtful that early military formations had health attendants of much skill and in adequate numbers, whatever specialists were available to care for the sick and wounded knew at least what *Oetzi*, the Tyrolean 'ice man' discovered in the Schnals valley on the Austro-Italian border in 1991, knew.

The kit of this mountain inhabitant of 5,000 years ago included a copper ax and a dagger of flint – normally thought of as the material for arrowheads, and a new bow not yet strung. Oetzi carried fungus as tinder to light campfires, as well as a birch fungus with antibiotic properties. Italian anthropologist Luigi Capasso, in a letter published in December 1998 in *The Lancet,* stated that the antibiotic was *Piptoporus betulinus* whose toxic oils combat intestinal worms.[9] Oetzi was thus his own first-aid attendant and physician as well as hunter.[10]

Self-reliance of this kind very likely applied to communities such as the military. People of Oetzi's time knew how to apply primitive splints to limbs in order to immobilize and set bone fractures. They and their 'medicine men' could not cure disease, of course, a procedure that became effective only when physicians could neutralize bacteria nearly five millennia later. Paul Valéry's 'completed world' (*un monde fini*) of the 1930s was, in fact, still far from perfection in the context of public health. This came in the 1940s, when military medicine made leaps in effective treatment of patients analogous to the advances made by radar and jet engines.

DISEASE AND INJURY VERSUS WOUNDS

The Greeks and the Romans worshipped Ares and Mars as the gods of war and agriculture, a merging of the forces of dark and of light – a Manichean combination found again in military rescue and healing. The list of those seeking to alleviate misery and suffering among persons wounded or injured on the battlefield must be endless and, mostly, anonymous. In writing of the struggle between Turks and Greeks at Constantinople (AD 1453), Edward Gibbon states

> The single combats of the heroes of history or fable amuse our fancy and engage our affections: the skillful evolutions of war may inform the mind, and improve a necessary, though pernicious, science. But in the uniform and odious pictures of a general assault, all is blood, and horror, and confusion.[11]

And in Gibbon's time little was possible to overcome the results of armed violence. Yet things would soon begin to change, as we shall see.

Another of the traditional discomforts of the warrior, the skin disease provoked by such non-essentials to his kit as the flour-and-water stiffening of eighteenth-century wigs (described in the novel, *Barry Lindon,* by Henry Fielding) began to demand attention. Unnecessary discomfort began to assume importance at about the same time as the industrial revolution began.

Mosquito-borne yellow fever ('yellow jack') may have journeyed from western Africa to the New World. In his *Plagues and Peoples* (1976) the historian William H. McNeill ascribes the epidemiology of the disease's vector, *Aedes aegypti*, as a movement to the Caribbean from Africa in 1648. More than a century later, in 1782, the majority of a British force besieging Havana fell victim to the malady and in 1793 at Santo Domingo another 6,000 troops from Britain died of the same illness against 100 who perished in battle,[12] a ratio of 60:1.

The French Revolution generated new medicine and public health. Pre-1789 social attitudes, bolstered by few university courses, gave the physician status and privilege. The latter allowed him to hold personal theories about disease and cure. Mumbo-jumbo about privately concocted potions helped or 'saved', in fact, few patients. Surgeons, although poorly trained in theory, based their skills on good knowledge of anatomy and physiology and hands-on treatment of broken or amputated bones, lacerated tissue, burns or fevers. Pharmacists and barber-surgeons completed the quadrumvirate of health practitioners.

The sudden need in France for emergency treatment and care of many tens of thousands of casualties created by her wars with Austria, Prussia and Britain during and after the Terror gave supremacy to the surgeons, placed a premium on training and practice, and led to the achievement of new levels in health management through the French revolutionary forces. Mobile hospitals assured better care on the battlefield (although aid stations were not to be closer than a league or 4km from the fighting front), and fixed hospitals served as training centers. Entirely new views governed the treatment of open wounds, simple and compound fractures, amputations (there were many), burns, the itch, venereal ailments, fevers and epidemic disease. Proper bandaging, fresh air and convalescent diets became obligatory, and the autopsies demanded by military surgeons guided the reform and spread of new doctrines in civil medicine.[13]

POLITICAL AND MEDICAL REVOLUTIONS

Despite the bellicose tensions between France and England, in 1793 British Surgeon-General John Hunter democratized considerably the appointment of medical staff in emulation of the French model. In France François Chaussier, a physician from Dijon, blazed the trail in legal medicine: accidents, negligence, liability, claims for damage – studies of these and like topics found their way into medical curricula in 1794.

Pierre Joseph Desault, who died in 1795 at the age of 41 and was part of the military-inspired medical revolution, founded the first modern surgical clinic. He left at least two disciples who revolutionized care and treatment of patients in the public charge. One of the students, M. F.-X. Bichat, was an anatomist who concentrated on the contractibility and sensitivity of human tissue. As an anatomical pathologist, he contributed to advances in embryology; as a physiologist, he defined life itself as 'the collection of functions that resist death'. Bichat died at the age of only 31, and one of the major Parisian hospitals is named after him.

The second of Desault's heirs was Baron Jean Corvisart, a specialist in internal medicine. Corvisart's strength lay in his insistence on finding a scientific basis for clinical (patient) medicine by linking it as closely as possible with what was known of pathological anatomy at the turn of the nineteenth century. France's nascent republican army, from the time of the Bastille to the advent of Napoleon, was also instrumental in the dissemination of medical lore and technology among the civil populace. '[W]ar and the thinking of military medical men ... forced widespread acceptance of the hospital as the key medical institution of the future.'[14]

Corvisart's work soon came to the attention of Napoleon, who appointed him surgeon-general. The chief surgeon's work as physician to both government and throne led him to the compilation of his *Essai sur les maladies et lésions organiques du coeur* (Essay on Organic Diseases and Lesions of the Heart), published between 1806 and 1811. Much of Corvisart's efforts stemmed directly from Napoleon's revulsion at how the wounded and ill of his Grande Armée were treated – largely caring for one another. Napoleon was particularly horrified on the Sunday morning of the indecisive battle of Eylau (7–8 February 1807), combat that took 40,000 French, Russian and Prussian lives. Among the 'cordwood' of stacked cadavers were 10,000 of his best troops.[15]

Twelve hundred French were wounded at the battle of Wagram in July 1809 and hospitalized along the Rennweg in Vienna, nearby. According to historian Henry Lachouque,

> 600 had been returned in a few days to their corps where the medical staff looked after them; 254, including 38 amputees, were evacuated to France; 145 died of their wounds (from tetanus, gangrene, fever ...); 80 amputees 'completely recovered'; 150 seriously wounded were retired as 'unfit for duty' and pensioned.

In a footnote the same chronicler commented, 'If one consults the medical records of the Crimean, [US] Civil and Spanish-American Wars, one will find this recovery record unsurpassed in the annals of military medicine' before the First World War.[16]

Not far from Wagram and on the same eastern bank of the Danube, the town of Essling had witnessed a truly grand massacre several weeks earlier. The victor, Archduke Karl of Austria was one of few opponents who could score over Napoleon, and this he did at Essling. There, 30 hours of combat during 20–22 May resulted in 42,000 casualties under all flags; one soldier died every three seconds. French historical novelist Patrick Rambaud tells us that Essling was the site of 12,000 amputations of arms and legs;[17] this was no exaggeration. One has difficulty imagining the individual and collective trauma suffered.

Baron Dominique Jean Larrey, chief surgeon of the Grande Armée, accompanied Napoleon in all the general's campaigns until Waterloo. He was present in Würzburg in April 1812 with the four field hospitals assigned to the Imperial Guard. 'If [this] great practitioner's art was considerable, his administrative talent was even greater', according to the praise of historian Lachouque. 'Speaking in a commanding voice with an imposing assurance, he could teach [others] chemistry and mathematics. "An honest man withal – in fact the greatest man I have known", the Emperor said of him later.'[18]

Larrey's ambulance kits for Napoleon's 'New Guard' contained typically 72kg of rolled bandages, 22kg of sheets, 12kg each of gauze and towels; 30 surgical splints, 12 litters (stretchers) and 6 pallets, a roll of tape, 1,000 pins, 50 needles and two skeins of thread; 60 gm of beeswax, 250gm of string and 80gm of sponges. After fractures had been set and wounds sutured, medical attendants could also call upon miscellaneous supplies. A medical'chest'contained 250gm of lead sub-acetate (Goulard's extract), 100gm of lead cerate, 600gm of camphor, 125gm of laudanum (the morphiate of the day), 180gm of compound spirits of ether, 90gm of ammonia, 125gm of sticking plaster and 500 individual dressings, 15 packages of emetic – and two liters of brandy.[19] The medical specialists of the time were indeed resourceful in palliating pain, but unable to cope with pathology.

ADVENT OF RATIONALIZATION AND ORDER

In June 1815, Waterloo took such a toll of men and officers on both sides in 11 hours of combat that military medicine again took a turn for the better. The encounter occurred before the advent of antiseptics and anesthesia, still four decades away. News of the engagement and its casualties inspired young physicians from several hospitals in London to join a 'flying ambulance' to the battleground in rolling countryside near Brussels. On farms and in the fields the British doctors succored many wounded, from both the Anglo-Prussian and the French sides – casualties who had waited days to be tended, but otherwise would have died. The Scottish anatomist, Charles Bell, a medical veteran of the Peninsular War, served in a civil capacity as army surgeon with field hospitals at Waterloo. Bell sketched many studies of wounds, enabling him to publish in 1830 modern neurology's first text, *Nervous System of the Human Body*.[20]

Guillaume Dupuytren, an autopsist at the age of 18 and then a highly performing army surgeon, founded the subdiscipline of anatomo-pathology. After the Napoleonic period, Baron Larrey served as professor at the Val-de-Grâce military hospital in Paris, publishing numerous works on the state of the art of military diagnostic medicine and surgery. Jumps forward applied from military to civil medicine and back to military pathology qualify for what Renato Mazzolini of the University of Trento terms the great advances made in biomedicine between the sixteenth and nineteenth centuries.[21]

The British borrowed the expression 'flying ambulance' from the French army's *ambulance volante*, introduced 20 years earlier, a light cart with two wheels, equipped with litters for rapid evacuation of the wounded. Each French infantry division of about 18,000 men had 12 of these rescue vehicles, together with four wagons of supplies and 130 mounted medical staff. The British, by comparison, had almost no sanitary train, although their surgeons were amply supplied with instruments for incision, non-antiseptic cleansing and ligature, and amputation.

Amputation, as we saw, was commonplace. The farther the damage to a leg bone shattered by ball or shot was from the hip, the better the chances of successful amputation and the attachment afterwards of a prosthesis.[22] One of the Duke of Wellington's staff, Major-General Colin Campbell, had a shattered arm amputated while he distracted himself from the agony by resolutely poring over maps spread on a field table before him.

Napoleon was convinced that the weight of numbers won battles and wars: more men, more horses, better supplies in quantity, accelerated movement, missions accomplished. The better his casualties were tended on the field of combat, the more reliably and resiliently his forces would perform in encounters to come. With the hospitalization of casualties far from the fronts providing real convalescence, French hospitals of the early nineteenth century were much in advance of those elsewhere.

British doctors crossed the Channel 'to take notes'[23] – surely the acme of cultural encomium between traditional political enemies. Sick-ward rounds and diagnosis with the new stethoscope inspired the evaluation of pathological data on a growing scale, the keeping of records, and the compilation of medical statistics. This progress gave new authority to physicians and institutional staff, transforming healers from mere barber-surgeons to curative specialists.

LOSSES: DOWN, THEN UP

Napoleon's trust in numerical force arose in an age when the statistical toll in military casualties was dropping, despite improved equipment and craftsmanship in the arts of killing or maiming human beings.

As the state grew in coherence between the seventeenth and nineteenth centuries, warfare too became increasingly regulated. Fighting at night or in severely inclement weather remained rare and by 1815 battlefield losses in absolute numbers, according to French analyst Pierre Chaunu,[24] diminished. Combat deaths varied from 10 to as low as 1 per cent of the forces engaged, compared with an estimated 11 per cent in Europe as a whole in 1710, when the War of Spanish Succession with Austria had brought France to the brink of financial and political ruin.

The century between Waterloo and 1914 is often singled out as a pacific period despite Europe's continued colonialist expansion. Statistically speaking, the ten decades of comparative peace in Europe reflect the 'lowest level of losses ever attained on the global scale, closer than ever to zero level'. But this period was followed by what Chaunu calls the 'real Thirty Years War', lasting between 1914 and 1945, and tallying enormous destruction of human life[25] and property.

Isambard Kingdom Brunel, the Franco-British engineering genius renowned for his bridges, tunnels and ships, designed during the Crimean War of 1853–56 a 1,500-bed military hospital in kit form. Crimea, in which the French and British were involved in 1854–55 with the Turks and Sardinians against Russia, became disastrous for the forces involved: non-combat disease accounted for a disproportionate number of the quarter-million casualties suffered by either side. (Much later, during the Second World War, the prevalent ailments would remain non-battle typhus, malaria and epidemic hepatitis.[26])

Prefabricated in Britain, Brunel's demountable hospital had no component that was too heavy for two men to handle. The installation was designed, built and shipped, then erected (February–August 1855) in Renkioi, Turkey, by 20 men. The facility was an innovation in several ways; it was designed so as to be fully equipped, once assembled, with plumbing and ventilation systems. It pumped 25 cubic feet of air, cooled and humidified, per minute to each bed. External kitchen modules were created to function in conjunction with the Brunel hospital.[27]

Brunel's ideas were adopted by the American Union (Northern) forces a decade later during the Civil War, expanded upon by the Americans during the two world wars into an evacuation chain of aid stations, collecting and clearing points, field-surgical, general and base hospitals, and then reconceived as semi-autonomous modular medical units during the conflict in Vietnam. Alexis Soyer, French retired chef and food critic (see Chapter 7), redesigned field kitchens for British units in Crimea, and the basic design using bottled gas in the place of wood or coal was still in use a century and a half later during the Gulf War.[28]

What nursing director Florence Nightingale and Russian Surgeon-General Nikolai Pirogov perceived, simultaneously and more quickly than military administrators, was the lack of both *organization* and *system* in how the wounded, diseased and otherwise ill should be cared for. Nightingale's background as a nursing manager in London and Pirogov's extensive experience in St Petersburg dealing with surgical recoveries won the essential backing of, respectively, Sidney Herbert, secretary of war in London, and Grand Duchess Yelena Pavlovna in Russia. Field medical care benefited from innumerable innovations introduced during the Crimean struggle, not the least of which was *triage*, a contribution made by Pirogov: handling immediately the least complex cases as well as those wounded who might otherwise die quickly as a result of inattention. Triage remains the sorting basis of evacuation doctrine to this day, among both military and civil-defense organizations; it is poorly handled, or not at all, by terrorists and insurgents.

The British military establishment was further goaded into action by the reporting of William Howard Russell, special correspondent for *The Times* of London, who described the maltreatment of sick or wounded combatants. Russell, a penetrating observer who held a doctorate in law, summarized his views in *The British Expedition to the Crimea*, a book published in London by Routledge in 1858. The perceptive Russell concluded paradoxically, 'If war is a great destroyer, it is also a great creator.'

The mortality rate in British hospitals serving the Crimean campaign, once the statistics were compiled, was nearly 50 per cent of the patients admitted. It was Nightingale and Pirogov, with their direct influence on the destiny of the wounded and the diseased, who changed again – as had the French revolutionaries a half-century earlier – 'the course of military medicine forever'.[29] Yet Nightingale realized only after her Crimean service that lack of elementary sanitation among troops and their amenities was as much (or more) of a cause of disease as the hidden germs of pathology itself.[30] This enabled her to contribute enormously, during the 1860s, to the improvement of health-delivery systems in India.

THE HUMANITARIAN DIMENSION

Henri Beyle, the novelist whose pen name was Stendhal, was born before the French Revolution. A veteran of Napoleon's armies – Beyle took part in Waterloo – he was later so affected by the ravages of the Austrian Army during its occupation of Italy that emotion enabled him to dictate, in two brief months, *The Charterhouse of Parma* (1839). Then, after the Crimean War, the campaigns of Napoleon III in Italy became the genesis – catalyzed by the battlefield observations of a young Swiss philanthropist named Henri Dunant at the battle of Solferino in 1859 – of the Geneva-based International Committee of the Red Cross (ICRC).

Thanks to Dunant and the ICRC, the first international humanitarian agreement governing the treatment of war-wounded was signed in 1864. There are now 600 such convention articles, revitalized in August 1949 and expanded by the Additional Protocols of 1977; they constitute international humanitarian law. This ethical code is intended to protect and ensure the humane treatment of non-combatants as well as the sick and wounded, together with prisoners of war. The conventions, ratified by 188 states, continue in force despite their repeated abrogation in various conflicts. The ICRC is the prototype, too, for hundreds of other benevolent groups created throughout the world since the 1860s.

The American Civil War was the first to make theater-wide use of rail and telegraph. It quickly became a conflict exploiting the movement of large troop units over long distances. Enlistment was massive in both North and South, but medical examinations intended to flesh out, literally, the 1,000-men regiments hastily recruited by both sides were superficial. After a year, the typical regiment often had less than half its original complement because of illness, the toll of battle and desertions. Summary training and the inexperience of young urbanites and farmers only increased the often unnecessary casualties.

Emergency care was available in the field, at medical posts, or arranged at any suitable house, barn or shed. Evacuation and further treatment, especially by the Northern side, was to general hospitals:

multidepartment facilities capable of treating numerous casualties and convalescents. A regimental chaplain of the 35th Mississippi Infantry, William L. Foster, described typical conditions in a letter to his wife:

> The weather is excessively hot and the flies swarm around the wounded – more numerous where the wound is severest. In a few days the wounds begin to be offensive and horrid … Nor can this be avoided unless a nurse were detailed for every man – but there is only one allowed for every eight men … Never before did I have such an idea of the cruelty and barbarism of war.[31]

On the Southern side, the Chimborazo General Hospital near Richmond became the world's largest installation of its kind: it had 250 pavilions each housing roughly 50 patients, together with 100 tents that accommodated ten patients each. This made an in-patient population of about 13,500 within a single facility, huge even by the standards of the years 1940–2000.

American women tending the sick and wounded, especially women in the South, frequently modeled their efforts on Nightingale's work. Sally Louise Tompkins, one of these Nightingale emulators, became an army captain running an efficient hospital in Richmond.[32] Most nurses remained, however, active (male) soldiers – some of whom could not distinguish 'castor oil from a gun rod nor laudanum from a hole in the ground'[33] – or else convalescent troops. Otherwise, the attendants were slaves or former slaves impressed on the spot.

In the North the energy of the first woman in the country to obtain a doctorate in medicine, Elizabeth Blackwell, helped form the Women's Central Association for Relief. The WCAR created the country's first organized training program for nursing staff and became the nucleus of the new United States Sanitary Commission. 'The Sanitary', basically a benevolent group, helped indoctrinate soldiers in field hygiene; it had legislation passed in 1862 to move promising young men high up in the Army's Medical Bureau, thereby immobilizing 'all the venerable do-nothings and senile obstructives that now vex the health and embarrass the safety of our troops'.[34]

The American reformer of shelters for the insane, Dorothea Dix, oversaw the wartime recruitment and training of mainly female nurses; she transformed nursing into a non-menial career. Mary Ann 'Mother' Bickerdyke won the profound respect of professional soldiers such as Generals Grant and Sherman. Clara Barton harassed military surgeons in the field; after the Civil War she agitated for American affiliation with the ICRC in Switzerland, leading to the formation of the American Red Cross. A generation later, Amy Wingreen was an American army nurse who learned to care for yellow-fever victims during the Spanish-American War in Cuba – patients until then left to die.[35] Nursing became both general care and specialist attention, each requiring longer training. It was the military who were directly responsible for most of this evolution.

Poet Walt Whitman visited the Virginia battlefields and did volunteer work in Washington hospitals treating wounded or ill soldiers from both sides. He was impressed by the presence of women among the nurses, and concluded that mature women, mothers of children, were best for the soldiers because of their 'soothing' presence.

NEW PROFESSIONALISM

Important progress in care and evacuation became the inheritance of today's military medical infrastructure. This includes paid professional nurses, medical and laboratory technicians, ambulance crews – an idea adopted immediately by French and German forces during the Franco-Prussian war, concurrently with the advances in microbiology and antisepsis by Louis Pasteur and Joseph Lister – and hospital trains and ships, as well as the expansion of fixed-base and general hospitals.

Sheer numbers of enforcers were available to the military when 'medical policing' was expedient, as when bubonic plague overcame Hong Kong about the time that the New Territories were negotiated in the 1890s. Troops from the Royal Navy, Royal Engineers and Shropshire Light Infantry were pressed into public-health service to evacuate civil victims from the most insalubrious of the Crown Colony's dwellings.

When South African General Jan Smuts arrived in German East Africa to take command of a force of combined nationalities against the local German commander, Colonel Paul von Lettow-Vorbeck, he set out in 1916 with two British columns from Nyasaland and Kenya, a Belgian one from the Congo and a Portuguese force from Mozambique. Lettow had about 16,000 men, mostly African *askari*, who were resistant to the parasitic ailments that felled Europeans. Smuts had a force of almost 40,000, many of whom were European and Indian. The toll taken among the latter by disease was such that Smuts had 31 non-combat victims for every battle casualty.[36] The anti-German forces failed to run Lettow and his men to ground. Later in the same war another German strategist, General Erich Ludendorff, blamed the global pandemic of influenza for the failure in July 1918 of his last great campaign of the world conflict.[37]

Troops still use the Lister bag, or any expediently cobbled equivalent, in the field or in garrison. This is a rubberized canvas container, filled with even polluted water when no other is available and then chlorinated or iodized with simple, disinfecting chemicals – making the water potable. (The cleansed water is often unpleasant in taste, odor and appearance.) More representative of water processing in the field today, however, is the French military forces' Aquamobil, which first distills water *in vacuo*, permitting the lowering of the boiling point from 100° to 60°C. Physical filters then complete purification, after which mineral salts are added to give the water a nutritional balance, all at the rate of 1,000 liters/hour.[38] Devices of this kind found ready civil application in emergency operations mounted in 1998 in Honduras, Guatemala and Nicaragua following the devastation of Hurricane Mitch.

Brunel's concept of a hospital in kit form emerged – following the experiences of American forces during the Second World, Korean and Vietnamese Wars – as the modular hospitals already mentioned. These expansible and contractable surgical and other units were later adapted by the Defense and Civil Systems unit of Dornier GmbH into the TransHospital of 1997–98. The German TransHospital is designed to respond to the specific needs of rapid-reaction forces,[39] an exigency typical of the evolving missions of NATO.

STRESS MAKES DISTRESS

Widening casualties in Europe among Russian, German, Austrian, Italian, British and French troops during the First World War reinforced the need for ever better medical attention. The spiral of wounds, deaths, more men recruited (and women for essential wartime work) grew and spread, demanding more and more resources: human, material, and inevitably financial. The costs of the long war in effect bankrupted the German and British national economies and grievously depressed others. Morale suffered, correspondingly, among both troops and those who remained on the home front to 'stand and wait'.

For many years after the war of the trenches and dugouts fought in France, psychologists and other social scientists examined, too, the ironic phenomenon of mutual non-aggressiveness that was born in the wetness, cold or heat, slime and pestilence, boredom and stupefying terror of trench warfare. A major reason for this episodic pacifism among soldiers of both sides was found (by both troop commanders and inspecting staff) to be based on 'the informal social relations which emerge among soldiers on the battlefield', including the altered performance of troops 'through informal networks of antagonists'.[40]

There grew among the line troops of each adversary an unspoken collusion to disregard orders from higher up to attack or sustain an assault, to maim or kill, to soldier with the discipline and aggression traditional of the battlefield. Malingering found its own forms of camouflage and, in many cases, there was little or nothing to be done about it – threats of courts-martial and even execution notwithstanding. The so-called mutinies in the French Army in 1917, subsequent to Verdun, were in fact protests by lower ranks against the unflagging strategy of attack, attack, attack – no matter what the cost and lack of advance.

This expedient psychology of the battlefield gave birth, as a direct reaction to the public trauma caused by a hard and costly war, to an antiwar culture, beginning with the founding of the Salzburg music festival in Vienna in 1917 by Hugo von Hoffmannsthal and Max Reinhardt 'as a sign of a first work of peace'.[41] The impetus extended into the postwar era with, for example, Erich-Maria Remarque's *Im Westen Nichts Neues* (All Quiet on the Western Front); it reappeared after the Second World War – notably with the founding in November 1945 of the European Forum Alpbach as an early meeting ground between former enemies (and later between East and West), and Norman Mailer's novel *The Naked and the Dead.* It was taken up during the Indochina wars of 1945–75 and the 'killing fields' of Cambodia, and among the mothers of Soviet/Russian soldiers in the conflict with Afghanistan in the 1980s and, later, in Chechnya.

The psychological phenomenon of 'shell shock' was taken into medical account in 1914–18. This pathology undoubtedly existed since the days of the first pitched battle between human beings. The anomaly would be called 'combat fatigue' during the Second World War, and shortly afterwards 'operational exhaustion'. It finally became understood as a psychosomatic disturbance – experienced again and again among both fighting forces and civil populations.

The condition is known now as post-traumatic stress syndrome (PTS). It is considered a consequence, as well, of vicious crimes and hostage-taking, as a result of serious automobile and industrial accidents, or because of severe psychological abuse. The trauma may be epitomized by the cases of the British poets Wilfred Owen and Siegfried Sassoon who, evacuated from the front during the First World War (Owen for total breakdown, Sassoon for rebellious insubordination), were treated by William Rivers, a Freudian psychologist, at Scotland's Craiglockhart Hospital. Owen recovered, was posted back to the lines, and then killed in action. Sassoon also returned to the troops, but survived the conflict.

PTS emerged as a principal after-battle disturbance among 'ethnically cleansed' population elements in the former Yugoslavia. The chief psychiatric officer of the Croatian army, Vlado Jukic, explained that his army was faced with fewer psychiatric problems than might be expected 'because our soldiers are defending their own soil and fighting for their own freedom'. Yet the only known psychiatric center to operate in former Yugoslavia was situated at Rijeka in Croatia, where the patients had 'committed or witnessed ghastly acts'.[42] The program director of this clinic and supervisor of group therapy, Ljiljana Moro, noted that in her culture 'there is a stigma of weakness attached to people who seek help'. With hostilities still in progress, 'society doesn't want to confront the problem because of the effect that could have on morale'. Yet treatment continued – taking a toll on therapists also, as they sought to help the victims of PTS. For children in the besieged Bosnian capital of Sarajevo, the treatment showing the most promise included drawing, painting and other applied arts.[43]

PTS took particular forms during the war between NATO and Serbia in 1999. Historian Aleksa Djilas took walks through the Serbian capital during the 11 weeks of air raids, in order to visualize what kinds of NATO targets to avoid. And 'everyone lost weight', he related, 'no matter how much they ate'. A psychologist at the Belgrade Institute of Mental Health, Vladimir Jovic, remarked, 'You must understand how the sounds of [air-raid] sirens are terrifying ... People were not used to such things.'

Victor Sassoon's line 'The hell where youth and laughter go', embraces death, of course. Just as there is not life without death, there is rarely combat without fatalities. Even in death, however, science may come to the succor of the bereaved – since nothing can be done for those who have perished. A correspondent of the respected Warsaw daily newspaper, *Gazeta Wyborcza*, Waclaw Radziwinowicz, spent some days during the second Chechen conflict (1999–2000) at the Russian military hospital in Rostov-on-Don. It is there that the Russians sent some of the their casualties from the combat raging 600km to the southeast.

The hospital had attached to it pathologists charged with identifying the remains of bodies shipped in anonymously. Besides disfigured corpses, there were many armored personnel whose bodies had been virtually carbonized while still seatbelted in their crippled tanks. Nearly 300 such unknown remains had accumulated by November 1999, stored in railway refrigerator cars suffering regularly from power shortages. As the cars heated and cooled again repeatedly, the human remains mummified and their stench reached housing nearby.

Attending personnel lacked the proper equipment to reduce bone fragments to the powder required for DNA (deoxyribonucleic acid) analysis and possible identification. They used instead meat and coffee grinders as field expedients, so the work of the pathologists was painfully slow. Mothers of the dead traveled to Rostov, taking it on themselves to force the military's hand to do more, faster. A few identifications were made by comparing the DNA prints of the dead with those of one parent.[44] Matching with the DNA of both parents is a more reliable procedure, if both parents can be located. Most of these Russian remains are thus likely to remain 'Unknown'.

THE TREATMENT CATALOGUE EXPANDS

Paul M. Zoll served as a surgeon with the US Army during the Second World War. He noticed that a soldier wounded by shrapnel lodged near the heart could have his heart stimulated – once the thorax had been opened to expose the organ – by the slightest prod of the back of a scalpel. He decided, on the spot, to make resuscitation of failed hearts his life's work. After hostilities, Zoll began experiments in Boston, and his first stimulator (outside the body and not portable) was designed to send an electrical charge to the heart muscle. He was able, by 1952, to reactivate stopped hearts. Semiconductors helped miniaturize stimulators (patented as Pacemakers®), implanted beneath the skin and equipped with light, long-lasting lithium batteries. Battlefield observations were thus the genesis of a device, one now applied a million times annually throughout the world, to prolong life.

A newly labeled affliction identified during the First and Second World Wars – undoubtedly suffered, too, since time immemorial by troops operating in the cold and damp – is trench foot. If Hannibal's troops did not react to this during their crossing of the Alps nearly two millennia ago, the painful and unsightly ailment certainly became known around 1700 by the troops of Peter the Great and Sweden's Charles XII during the Northern War, later by those of George Washington at Valley Forge in the late eighteenth century, and then by the British Royal Navy's Commander Robert F. Scott on his trek towards the South Pole and his death returning from his team's goal.

Finnish and Soviet troops, unable to find shelter from the cold, reacted to the necrosis-producing affliction while in combat in 1939–40 in Karelia. The discomfort was later suffered, especially by poorly clad German and Axis troops at embattled Stalingrad; during von Runstedt's final western campaign in the Ardennes forests in 1944–45; at the Choshin reservoir in northern Korea, where temperatures sank to −20°C. in the winter of 1950–51; and in the frigid bogs of the Falkland or Malvinas Islands in the early 1980s. Trench foot exacerbates sensitivity to low temperatures, produces a deterioration of joints, sometimes cancer of the skin, and occasionally necessitates amputation. It was not until 1994, rather incredibly, that the Department of Veterans Affairs in the United States finally accepted trench foot as a legitimate disability.[45]

DIAGNOSTIC MYSTERIES FROM THE GULF

A diagnostic enigma arose in the years following the Gulf War when Coalition veterans by the thousands claimed rashes, aching joints, breathing difficulties, persistent diarrhea, general fatigue, headaches, and inability to walk without canes. Some plaintiffs had served in a naval construction unit based in Saudi Arabia, more than 150km from the fighting front. On 20 January 1991, one of the naval engineers reported that he had been awakened by an exploding SCUD surface-to-surface missile. He soon smelled ammonia, and a 'whitish gray cloud' found its way over the American camp.[46]

The naval veteran in question, a reservist who was a fireman in civil life, was convinced that he and his friends had been exposed to pathogenic chemicals. Czech army technicians using specialized equipment were able to identify, during hostilities, detectable quantities of the nerve poison, sarin and mustard gas. It was not possible to establish the origins of these contaminants. Military physicians were less convinced, however. To reach accurate diagnosis regarding the curious syndrome, the American secretary of defense named in 1995 a board of enquiry, one of whose research directors was Nobel prize winner Joshua Lederberg of Rockefeller University.

Later in the year first reports indicated that there was no pathological basis to the complaints. In May 1996, the *Journal of Toxicology and Environmental Health* pinned down a cause: binary intakes of otherwise harmless chemicals. Implicated in this diagnosis were the drugs known as cholinesterase inhibitors, found in synthesized pesticides. By short-circuiting customary nerve signals, these agents – if two or more were present simultaneously, even in small doses – confuse the organism's defense system and ultimately damage slightly both brain and nerves. The phenomenon, recognized for some years as a nerve-damaging syndrome, is called OPIDN: organophosphate-induced delayed neural toxicity.

In 1996 the Pentagon declared that American troops had been exposed in 1991 to chemical weapons near Hafr al Batin, between

Saudi Arabia and southern Iraq.[47] Positive indications were recorded early in the conflict by Czech and French specialists: low levels of mustard gas or nerve agents. The toxin traces may have been left by the destruction of special-weapon stores by the US Army's 37th Engineer Combat Battalion, many of whose soldiers reported ill.

The findings were inconclusive. The *New York Times* then published details from Prague indicating that two special gas-detection units of the Czech army had encountered chemical weapons on the Iraqi battlefields. The Czechs, commanded by Lieutenant-Colonel Lubomir Smehlik and whose sole purpose was the detection of toxic agents, reported post-battle sickness in their own unit.[48]

Workers engaged in the preparation of a variety of chemical weapons (not to speak of ordinary chemical substances) suffer headaches, lassitude, disorders in the digestive and cardiovascular systems, general aches and pains, even the outward appearance of aging prematurely. The cholinesterase inhibitors are known to cause such signs and symptoms. Nerve gases tend to cause immediate reactions, but the survivors of such exposure usually suffer no lasting damage.

But doubters persist. An investigator, toxicologist John Thomas of the University of Texas in San Antonio, commented, 'Based on what we know about low-level exposure to this type of chemical, one would be very hardpressed to make [this] connection between veterans' illnesses and gas exposure.'[49] It was still thought that psychological as well as physical strains of battle lay behind the complaints.

The same panel virtually exonerated two *vaccines* – for anthrax and botulinum toxoid – and a chemical antidote called pyridostigmine, stating that there was 'no evidence that vaccines in general cause the nonspecific complaints associated with Operation Desert Storm'. Kurt Kleiner of *New Scientist* reported that, on the basis of tests made on chickens and rats, the Gulf-War syndrome 'may have been caused by the combined effect of a pill given to protect against nerve gas and an insect repellent'.[50]

The Institute of Medicine in Washington published an assessment of official programs meant to diagnose the health problems of Gulf War veterans: a comprehensive appraisal via data collection and compilation, clinical protocol, program implementation, 'out-reach' to former military personnel, and the training of those charged with their health care.[51]

The investigation continues, focusing on lingering indecision surrounding PTS pathology. We saw that PTS was not accepted as a scientifically sound anomaly until 'shell-shocked' soldiers in the First World War became a visible public-health problem. To discredit some medical claims arising from the Gulf conflict, it was believed at first that neurological agents required a certain mass before they could take effect.

The persistent signs and symptoms of the Gulf War's victims suggested, on the contrary, that only a few molecules of the deadly substances – perhaps in combination with prewar vaccinations and ambient smoke from petroleum fires – could be the guilty pathogens. The Pentagon conducted a medical census of as many as 24,000 people, engineers and infantry included, but the enigma became no clearer.

A physician at the Naval Medical Research Center in Bethesda, Captain Kenneth Hyams, published in *Epidemiologic Review* (1999) the results of his historical research to trace analogous consequences of wars past. To Hyams the Gulf War phenomenon is directly related to neurasthenia – a term dating from the 1850s but not in technical use today, a nervous exhaustion not attributable to specific lesions or psychological causes. Physician Simon Wessely, a chronic-fatigue specialist at King's College in London, agrees with Hyams' analysis. The victims are neither hypochondriacs nor fakers, nor are they guilty of what the British military call 'swinging the lead', that is, being a shirker (a *goldbrick*, in American terminology). The best treatment, according to Wessely: 12 weeks of exposure to cognitive behavioral therapy. This rebuilds a patient's self-confidence.[52]

The enigma may have a parallel origin because, in 1999, a report prepared by physician Beatrice A. Golomb for the RAND Corporation and the Department of Defense pointed an accusing finger at the vaccine/antidote pyridostigmine bromide. This was administered during the Gulf War to some 275,000 of 700,000 United States personnel, and to Canadian and British service people, as a precaution against biological and chemical agents (especially the nerve agent, soman) that might have been used by Iraqi forces.[53] The RAND findings conflict with the earlier, official analyses. The anthrax attacks against civil targets in the United States in 2001, clearly acts of bioterrorism, lend credulity to the reports of a decade earlier.

HAZARDS OF OTHER TYPES

The episode of the Gulf-War syndrome is reminiscent of another that occurred in January 1968, when an American B-52 bomber was patrolling the northwestern frontiers of the USSR during an alert mission. The aircraft, armed with nuclear warheads, crashed off the coast of Greenland near Thule, rupturing three of the warheads it carried and contaminating a mass of snow and ice.

Members of an emergency clean-up force, some 1,300 workers sent to clear the wreckage, ultimately reported cancer or various kinds of dermatitis that they attributed to radioactivity. During a public session held in Copenhagen (1995), specialists from Greenland and Denmark – physicians, psychologists, physicists, legislators, and some of the workers involved – reached other conclusions. They found that the incidence of cancer matched national averages, and that 'insecurity combined with the debate and doubts may have contributed to the symptoms' reported by the workers. 'The tests conducted so far have not established any health damages due to radioactive exposure', concluded the hearings.'[54] Apprehension and stress, rather than overexposure to radioactivity, may thus have taken their toll, both in Greenland and on the sands of Iraq.

The Institute of Medicine, in Washington, concluded that the various reactions associated with the Gulf War were based on 'insufficient evidence' after its detailed analysis of depleted uranium, sarin, various vaccines and a pretreatment used against harmful effects by nerve agents.[55]

PATIENT PATIENTS

The Russian minister of defense in winter 1996–97, former General Igor Rodionov, told *Trud* newspaper that a grave medical problem arose among the military after the collapse of the USSR five years earlier. According to Rodionov, underfed officers in St Petersburg no longer had the strength to work. Medical officers excused them from chores that were physically strenuous. The minister said that, in some air wings (battalions), officers voluntarily deprived themselves of rations in order to take food home to their families. Wives on the Kamchatka Peninsula in Asiatic Russia took to blocking with their bodies, as a sign of protest, the takeoff of aircraft from runways. One result was that 50 per cent of majors and colonels were not renewing their contracts, while the toll among junior officers was 70 per cent.

Rodionov stressed that an active military force in such condition can no longer safeguard a nation, cannot repel possible aggression from abroad, train and prepare reservists, maintain the capacity for full mobilization – cannot help the country as a whole to go on, or sustain, a war footing. 'For me', added the former soldier, 'the most horrible thing is to simply watch … the process of destruction under way in the military without being able to do a thing about it.'[56]

Another way to watch destruction is when emergency medical treatment available to the military cannot be applied to an ailing civil population because beds and supplies are too limited, it is not 'part of the mission', or it is 'against regulations'. The peacekeeping forces know the problem – in Cambodia, Bosnia, Rwanda and elsewhere. Yet 'peacekeeping' is a flexible term, as French forces (to take but a single illustration) with missions in their country's former colonies can testify. They have run, for example, a fully equipped emergency unit, the Centre Médico-Chirurgical 'L'Epervier' in Chad (north-central Africa), where local people come for consultations, treatment and medication free of charge. There, 25 medical professionals from France – men and women, all in uniform – handle everything from insect bites to surgery on ailing joints and more.

MEDICINE GOES POSTMODERN

Robotics came to medicine relatively late after its introduction to the advanced industrial processes of manufacture. It was only in 1987, for example, that IBM began designing Robodoc, an apparatus developed in the 1990s by Integrated Surgical Systems of California, to assist notably in the replacement of hips. The promise of an automated system of this kind is that physicians, not always available in the specialism suddenly needed away from large urban centers, could be replaced by technicians in what is known as 'telepresence' surgery. How does this work?

A physician could first simulate the operation in Vienna, for example, where facilities and reference sources are easily available. The doctor would check out the patient's individual pathology and medical particularities. A second specialist, in Tokyo, might perform the 'operation', using Robodoc. A consultant would be standing by via satellite in Sydney or Paris, while a physician or technician actually supervised the remote-controlled broaching and trimming of the patient's hip in the remoteness of a Brazilian town. Enthusiastic among the sponsors of telepresence surgery are the Technical University of Karlsruhe (Germany) and the United States' Advance Research Projects Agency (ARPA), source of the Internet (Chapter 9). At ARPA, Colonel Richard Satava dreamed of combining 'mechanically driven doctoring' with information technology and networking by satellite in order to 'see, feel and interact at a remote site from the patient. Surgeons will be able to operate in dangerous and inaccessible areas, from war zones to Third-world countries, without the expense and time of traveling there.'[57] The colonel's dream was more than a reverie, for in 1993 medical officers of the American army staged a field exercise of this kind at Fort Gordon, Georgia, a methodology foreseen as wholly practicable with the arrival of the twenty-first century.

Tim Beardsley of *Scientific American* reported an unusual sort of dual-purpose method emerging from the combined efforts of the United States Air Force's Materiel Command, the Cleveland Clinic Foundation, and medical-supply manufacturer Picker International. In clinical step 1: imaging by magnetic nuclear resonance, X-ray tomography via computer, and digital-subtraction angiography are first used in combination with a supercomputer to produce a view of the patient's brain. Step 2: with surgery under way, the computer follows the movements of surgeons'implements via ultrasonic pulses between these instruments and microphones nearby. Step 3: 'The computer "knows" the shapes of the instruments so that it can superimpose moving images of the tools onto its stored representation of the brain.'[58] In a final step, specialists working on the invention would add ultrasound scanning that will make possible a real-time view of the surgical site reflecting the activity of the tissues involved. The ultrasonic scan can then be 'bent' over the image in computer storage to conform with the tissue's configuration, with surgeons watching the entire procedure through a helmet-mounted display device comparable with those currently used by fighter pilots.

The synthetic environment of the operating room is developed within the computer – a 'virtual design' tool, from which real-life improvements in operating diagnosis and surgery should become as effective as they will be frequent. Real-time data derived from a nuclear-magnetic resonator, for example, already locate a tumor exactly, ultrasound destroys the growth, and the patient's body is left with no other signs of intervention.[59]

This is the theory, and the medical industry has proved slow in adopting information technology. Most physicians still write prescriptions, bill and keep their records without the aid of computers, and 'telemedicine' could have remained a phenomenon of fantasy[60] in Colonel Satava's imagination until events in Kosovo made *telemedicine* a functional word in the year 2000.

A British Army surgeon, Lieutenant-Colonel David Vassallo and a few determined physicians from civil life applied in their own way the steps listed above to rebuild the grossly disfigured head of Bessim Kadriu, a young Albanian Kosovar student of economics left for dead months earlier during shelling and shooting in Mitrovica. Dr Vassallo combined a digital camera with e-mail enquiries (and imagery attached) submitted from his laptop computer to specialists in facial and ocular surgery around the world.[61] Military specialists interfaced with their civil counterparts, and Kadriu began cheerfully what will be a long series of operations.

SUBSTITUTING FOR NATURE

Blood supplies on the battlefield still present problems for units separated from their main supply sources or isolated – in the field or
aboard ship – from progress in surgical techniques. The United States
Navy supported a scheme to use biotechnology to help make the right
type of blood (O, A, B or AB) available where and when needed. A
sugar molecule known as galactose is the sole structural distinction
between types O and B of human blood, and under normal conditions
blood is not transfused except when the match is known to be exact.
As the world's supply of safe blood contracts, there are intensified
efforts to derive supplies of compatible blood from animals. In 1999
highly purified bovine blood, used for the first time on an emergency
basis in a small military hospital in Tacoma (Washington), a first,
reversed a patient's depletion of red blood cells and saved her life. In
2001 professor of macromolecular chemistry Tsuchida Eishun and his
colleagues at Waseda and Keio Universities (Japan) were the first to
synthesize red globules.

Naval funds helped Jack Goldstein of the New York Blood Center
to develop a technique for 'snipping' galactose from the ends of proteins and fats found in the membranes of red blood cells. Dr Goldstein
uses alpha-galactosidase, available in the raw beans of coffee, to do
the snipping. Once transfused, the tailored cells carry oxygen properly
and do not seem to cause immunity problems.[62] Research is continuing
to make it possible to use all blood types interchangeably and, with
strong military backing, to discover an effective blood substitute.
Blood-plasma transfusions became standard procedure with some
military services during the Second World War, adopted immediately
after by ambulance and police services in civil life. On-the-spot treatment of the wounded needing immediate uncontaminated blood
replacement will remain a continuing requirement of the armed forces.

Another research area in which military medical services are active
is the quest in the biotechnologies for a substitute for human skin. At
present both military and civil services are dependent largely on a
single supplier of skin-substitute (in the United States), although
pigskin is often used as a stopgap. A world of opportunity, therefore,
awaits successful investigators and inventors of epidermal cell-and-
tissue substitutes.

The United States Army's researchers, working with those of the
American Red Cross, are developing a blood-stanching notion dating
from efforts abandoned during the Second World War because of
infection problems. The idea is to use clotting agents such as fibrinogen
and thrombin, in the form of pretreated bandages or instant spray-foam,

to stop hemorrhaging almost as soon as it begins.[63] Approval of these innovations by the Food and Drug Administration is expected in 2002–3, eliminating much of the anguish involved (by both patient and 'medic' or 'corpsman') in emergency interventions.

The Lawrence Livermore National Laboratory in California has done exploratory work on the 'welding' of animal tissue by laser. This is a technique already well known in the re-attachment of a retina separated from its normal position on the inner, dorsal surface of the eye. In the case of fusing tissue (basically its collagen fibers), surgeons cope with problems such as protein deformation or coagulation, the water content of the tissue in question and its temperature, the normal temperature of blood as a coolant for laser-heated tissue, and whether individual patients accept or reject treatment by laser.

Livermore's Inertial-Confinement Fusion project seeks to accomplish tissue repair by bringing about fusion at the atomic level, using plasma: highly ionized and dense gas. Scientists have already developed a computer program modeling what happens when a laser beam is directed on human tissue – and exactly how the beam's photons are scattered or absorbed. This was announced to the American Physical Society in November 1997, with adequate caution given that the research was to be lengthy and complicated.[64] The 'scar wars' between laser and human tissue promise to be complex and long.

The rejection by the military forces of industrialized countries and some developing nations of the concept – introduced by the advent of machine weapons – that high levels of firepower entail high casualty rates, is a sign of our times. It is a rejection of the ertswhile notion that 'determination to accept heavy casualties [will] bring victory'.[65] In rule-of-law societies, with the weight of public opinion on the ascendant, generals and admirals can no longer do as they once pleased.

One of the factors behind advanced research is not difficult to fathom: weapon systems acquired enormous killing power in the large and small wars of the twentieth century. They now combine with the growing menace of bioterrorism and threats of unconventional chemical and nuclear attack. This explains, in part, the detail of the present chapter; another part of the explanation is that war (and even terrorism) knows only one clear victor so far – medicine.

NOTES

1 Chalmers M. Roberts, 'A President "Very Much Perturbed" Over the Losses in Okinawa', *IHT*, 19 October 1994, p. 6.

2　Richard Rhodes, 'The New Morning of the World', *American Journal of Physics*, 12 December 1995, p. 1071.
3　Ken Ringle, '50 Years Later, Scope of A-Bombs' Horror Is Unclear', *IHT*, 7 August 1995, pp. 1, 7.
4　John Keegan, *The Second World War* (New York, Penguin, 1989), pp. 291–3.
5　Unsigned article, 'Sacrificial Okinawa', in *Asahi Shimbun*, reproduced in *Courrier International*, 6 July 1995, p. 25.
6　'Most Vulnerable in the Camps' (letter to editor), *IHT*, 15 February 1995, p. 9.
7　In preparation for the Franco-German engagement known as the Chemin des Dames (April–May 1917), General Robert Nivelle's staff realized that the army was short of medical personnel. It estimated casualties of 10,000, but the toll exceeded 100,000 and caused 'mutinies' by troops (mainly family men) demanding changes in strategy and operations. Courts-martial and 49 executions followed. Although he was relieved of command, an investigating committee found Nivelle free of blame. Eighty-one years later the French prime minister, Lionel Jospin, paid tribute to those executed after determination that many of the 'mutineers' suffered PTS syndrome.
8　Naïma Lefkir-Laffitte and Roland Laffitte, 'Armes radioactives contre "l'ennemi irakien"' (Radioactive Weapons against the 'Iraqi Enemy'), *Le monde diplomatique*, April 1995, p. 22. The subject has also been treated in *Chemical & Engineering News* (4 February 1991), *Bulletin of the Atomic Scientists* (May 1993), *Operation Desert Storm: Army not Adequately Prepared to Deal with Depleted Uranium Contamination* (Washington, DC, report of the General Accounting Office, January 1993), the *Dateline* program of NBC television, 22 February 1994. The Laffitte couple are the authors of *L'Irak sous le déluge* (Iraq Under the Deluge) (Paris, Editions Hermé, 1992). For a general commentary, see Pierre-M. Gallois (a retired brigadier-general), *Livre noir sur la défense* (Black Book on Defense) (Paris, Payot, 1994). France's Canal+ television channel ran a one-hour documentary, 'La guerre radioactive' (Radioactive War), 24 February 2000 at 10:10 p.m., concentrating on radioactive dust retained in the atmosphere after the use of DU weapons.
9　Reuters, 'Did "Ice Man" Use Natural Cures?', *IHT*, 7 December 1998, p. 11.
10　Konrad Spindler, *The Man in the Ice* (London, Weidenfeld & Nicolson, 1993), *passim*.
11　Edward Gibbon, *The Decline and Fall of the Roman Empire* (London, Dent-Everyman, vol. 6 (1910), p. 445.
12　David Spurgeon, *Southern Lights* (Ottawa, International Development Research Centre, 1995), p. 48.
13　The record is impressive because the notorious Committee of Public Safety put every decree, order and personnel assignment on paper, all archived by France's national governments that followed and military medical establishments such as the Val-de-Grâce military hospital in Paris. See also David M. Vess, *Medical Revolution in France, 1789–1796* (Gainesville, FL, University Presses of Florida, 1975).
14　Vess, *Medical Revolution in France*, pp. 190, 3, 21 and *passim*.
15　Max Gallo, *Napoléon, l'empereur des rois* (Napoleon, Emperor of Kings), vol. 3, (Robert Laffont/Pocket, 1997), pp. 108–19.
16　Henry Lachouque with Anne S. K. Brown (ed.), *The Anatomy of Glory: Napoleon and His Guard* (Providence RI and London, Brown University Press and Lund Humphries, 1961), p. 225.
17　Patrick Rambaud, *La bataille* (The Battle) (Paris, Grasset, 1997). The Essling

battle, although little written about, is better known to historians as Aspern-Essling.

18 Lachouque, *The Anatomy of Glory*, p. 167.

19 Ibid., pp. 285–6.

20 Paul Johnson, *The Birth of the Modern: World Society 1815–1830* (London, Weidenfeld & Nicolson, 1991), p. 84 (also pp. 585–6); Jacques G. Richardson, 'The Contract, Past and Future, between the Scientist and the Soldier', *International Social Science Journal*, 135 (1993), pp. 15–16.

21 Addressing a symposium, 'History of Science and Technology for A Better Understanding of Our Time', at the Cité des Sciences et de l'Industrie, Paris, 18 November 1994.

22 David Howarth, *A Near Run Thing: The Day of Waterloo* (London, Collins, 1968), pp. 149 ff.

23 James Burke, 'Connections – Highbrow Stuff', *Scientific American*, May 1996, p. 94.

24 Pierre Chaunu, 'Violence, guerre et paix' (Violence, War and Peace), *Politique étrangère*, 4 (1996), pp. 887–98.

25 Ibid., p. 894.

26 James E. Dunnigan and Albert A. Nofi, *Dirty Little Secrets of World War II* (New York, William Morrow/Quill, 1994), pp. 115–16.

27 James Dugan, *The Great Iron Ship* (New York, Harper, 1953), p. 23; Paul Kerr, Georgina Pye, Teresa Cherfas, Milk Gold and Margaret Mulvihill, *The Crimean War* (London, Macmillan/Boxtree-Channel Four, 1997), p. 92.

28 Paul Kerr, *et al.*, *The Crimean War*, pp. 92–3.

29 Ibid., p. 80.

30 Hugh Small, *Florence Nightingale: Avenging Angel* (New York, St Martin's Press, 2001), *passim*.

31 Cited in Herman Hattaway, *Shades of Blue and Gray: An Introductory Military History of the Civil War* (Columbia, MO, and London, University of Missouri Press, 1997), p. 134.

32 James M. McPherson, *Battle Cry of Freedom: The Civil War Era* (New York and Oxford, Oxford University Press, 1988), pp. 326, 474, 478.

33 Horace H. Cunningham, *Doctors in Gray: The Confederate Medical Service* (Baton Rouge, LA, Louisiana State University Press, 1958), p. 73, as cited in McPherson, *Battle Cry of Freedom*, p. 479.

34 Letter from Frederick Law Olmsted to John Murray Forbes dated 15 December 1861, cited in McPherson, *Battle Cry of Freedom*, p. 482.

35 For this and similar individual accounts, see Speer Morgan and Greg Michalson (eds), *For Our Beloved Country: American War Diaries from the Revolution to the Persian Gulf* (Boston, MA, Atlantic Monthly Press, 1994).

36 John Keegan, *The First World War* (London, Hutchinson, 1998), p. 322.

37 So writes Gina Kolata in *Flu: The Story of the Great Influenza Pandemic of 1918 and the Search for the Virus that Caused it* (New York, Farrar, Straus & Giroux, 1999), pp. 11, 50.

38 See *Sciences et Avenir*, May 1997, p. 36.

39 'TransHospital – Un hôpital mobile opérationnel', *AeroSpace* (French edn, published by Daimler-Benz Aerospace), 2 1997, p. 47.

40 Tony Ashworth, *Trench Warfare, 1914–1918: The Live and Let Live System* (London, Macmillan, 1980), p. 206 and *passim*: a study in human dynamics turned static.

41 Ulrike Kalchmair, *In Front and Behind the Scenes* (in English), and *Salzburg*

Festival Programme 1999 (Salzburg, Salzburg Festspiele, 1998); Edda Fuhric and Gisela Prossnitz (eds), *Max Reinhardt: The Magician's Dreams*, trans. from an original German text of 1987 (Salzburg, Residenz Verlag, 1993), pp. 105, 108–9; personal communications between Dr Lachmair, Dr Prossnitz and the author, 27, 31 August, 15 October 1999.

42 Stephen Kinzer, 'Aftershocks of Fighting in Ex-Yugoslavia', *IHT*, 10 January 1995, pp. 1, 4.

43 As reported on the 8 p.m. news, television channel TF1, Paris, 11 January 1995.

44 In an article translated from Polish to French, 'Le train fantôme des soldats inconnus' (The Phantom Train of Unknown Solders), *Courrier international*, 2 December 1999, p. 49.

45 'Korean War's Legacy of Frostbite', *IHT*, 29 April 1996, p. 3.

46 This account is based on Christine Gorman, 'The Gulf Gas Mystery', *Time* (US edn), 22 November 1993, p. 43.

47 Philip Shenon, 'Traces of Poison Gas Detected Near GIs during Gulf War, Pentagon Says', *IHT*, 23 August 1996, p. 8; 'Washington Kept Lid on 1991 Report of Nerve-Gas Risk to Troops in Gulf', *IHT*, 29 August 1996, p. 10.

48 Philip Shenon, 'Czechs Told US They Detected Nerve Gas during Gulf War', *New York Times*, 19 October 1996, pp. 1, 10.

49 David Brown, 'Scientists Dispute Nerve Gas as Cause of Gulf War Syndrome', *IHT*, 3 January 1997, p. 3.

50 Kurt Kleiner, 'Did Toxic Mix Cause Gulf Sickness?', *New Scientist*, 22 April 1995, p. 5.

51 Institute of Medicine, *Adequacy of the V[eterans] A[dministration] Persian Gulf Registry and Uniform Case Assessment Protocol* (report), Washington, March 1998.

52 Recounted by medical journalist Jane E. Brody, 'Syndromes Without a Cause', *IHT*, 22 March 1999, p. 7.

53 AlphaGalileo e-mail advisory of 20 October 1999; Steven Lee Myers, 'Study Suggests Drug Led to Gulf Illness', *IHT*, 20 October 1999, pp. 1, 10.

54 Associated Press, 'Illnesses Studied from '68 Crash in Greenland', *IHT*, 9 October 1995, p. 8.

55 Carolyn E. Fulco *et al.*, *Gulf War and Health*, vol. 1 (Washington, DC, National Academies/Institute of Medicine, 2000).

56 As cited in *Courrier international*, 20 February 1997, p. 10.

57 'A Trip to the Theatre' in 'The Future of Medicine' (special survey), *The Economist*, 19 March 1994, pp. 4–13.

58 Tim Beardsley, 'A New View for Surgeons', *Scientific American*, November 1994, p. 82.

59 'The Virtual Heart of the Medico-Industrial Complex', *The Economist*, 22 October 1994, p. 99.

60 'IT and Viruses: Bugs and Viruses', *The Economist*, 28 February 1998, pp. 70–2.

61 Cover story, *Time*, 6 March 2000, by Jonathan Margolis and Bob Collier.

62 'Blood Groups, O to Go, No Mayo', *The Economist*, 15 April (1995), p. 77.

63 Warren E. Leary, 'Bandage Therapy: A New Technique to Save Lives', *IHT*, 15 March 1999, p. 7. *Scientific American* treated the promises of tissue engineering more extensively in a special section on new organs, stem cells, encapsulated cells, 'engineered' skin, and obstacles to developing all of these; see pp. 60–89, April 1999.

64 See 'Beam Me Together, Bones', *The Economist*, 15 November 1997, pp. 95–6.

65 Keegan, *The First World War*, p. 175.

12

Simulating Strategy, Operations, Tactics

'The main field of application of game theory [is] national defense … Its principal results [are] zero-sum games, situations wherein one side wins exactly what the adversary loses.'

Christian Schmidt[1]

This book is about how we apply, for better and for worse, science and technology to the waging of war and, more recently, terrorism. In armed conflict, Martin van Creveld maintains that 'no success is possible – or even conceivable – which is not grounded in an ability to tolerate uncertainty, cope with it, and make use of it'.[2] While our main concerns are neither philosophies and doctrines nor the details of how best to succeed in armed conflict, this chapter will illustrate the *modeling* of battle contemplated, avoided, or fought as *preparatory surrogate* for the real thing. For this purpose we need a few definitions.

Strategy, operations and tactics, three terms dear to military instructors and analysts, are distinct conceptions; each one makes good managerial sense. The aims of a war and objectives of a campaign imply *strategy*. An *operation* is often a multi-arm action supporting the strategy selected, requiring fastidious planning and unfailing logistical support. Inherent in *tactics* are the mechanics of reaching an immediate goal quickly: usually one close by, such as taking a port or village or airfield.

The more encumbered becomes the specific combat entity engaged – whether an air division, a missile regiment, an aircraft-carrier battle group, or a dedicated guerrilla unit – the closer its planning, management and effect are enmeshed in strategy. Conversely, the greater the immediacy of an impact and its potential for quick reversal (artillery fire and counterfire), the closer we are to tactics than to strategy. Again, if the effect of a decision to undertake a certain action is inherently one for the medium or long term, the more it approaches operations or strategy and less the short-term tactical gain.

Strategy tends thus to be linear and stable, operations linear but often of unpredictable stability, tactics highly adaptive and disruptible but much less linear and of widespread effect.[3] Examples of each category are (i) strategy: the mounting of a full-scale, two-front war against the Third Reich (1940–45); (ii) operation: aerial strikes against the Taliban in Afghanistan (2001); (iii) tactics: threatening insurrections in Indonesia and the Philippines (1998–2002). Given the deadliness of the three, let us look at the kinds of non-deadly games warfighters play – not for fun, but 'for real'.[4]

ARE THERE DISTORTIONS OF ORDER?

Does order preclude disorder? During the Second World War, when George C. Marshall was Chief of Staff of the United States Army, he instructed his wartime planners to identify the basic endeavors of the combined Allied forces, that is, the 'essential undertakings without which the war would not likely be won'.[5] General Marshall's idea was that his staff specialists, while deciding *what to do*, should decide thereby *what not to do*. We may thus invert the first sentence: 'Does disorder warrant order?' In Osama bin Laden's perpetration of disorder among his targets, he first assured order among his own cohorts.

Order can be difficult to perceive, identify clearly, and transform into action meant to *apply* order as originally conceived (that is, sense, system). After the event, new analysis of the action undertaken may provide perception of what happened that contrasts perhaps vividly with the impressions of surviving actors. So we shall survey some of the different techniques devised through a variety of simulated approaches to the real thing, specifically when the military move from the ideational to the functional worlds, applying modeling theory to reality.

An unusual game played by three civilians and two soldiers took place in the winter of 1918–19 at the Hôtel de France et Angleterre, near Fontainebleau in France. A terrible war had finished a few months earlier, and negotiations to establish peace-treaty terms with a vanquished Germany were under way in Paris between the leaders of victorious France, Great Britain, Italy and the United States. Progress was slow in solving the peace: 'What do we do next?' (as opposed to resolving the hostilities, already terminated). The victors were bogged down in part by serious differences in outlook on a future Germany, in part by the growing movement to create a League of Nations – an initiative originally set forth as the final of the Fourteen Points advocated by US President Woodrow Wilson in January 1918.

The leader of the British delegation to the pre-treaty talks in Paris was the Prime Minister, David Lloyd George. One weekend in March 1919, Lloyd George convened his principal military advisor (also chief of the Imperial General Staff), the erudite Field Marshal Sir Henry Wilson, and three other aides to the Fontainebleau meeting. The aides were E. S. Montagu, later governor of the Bank of England; Colonel Sir Maurice Hankey, perpetual government servant and chronicler; and Philip Kerr, a young aristocrat. None was a specialist in international relations nor the proponent of a predetermined line to be pursued in concluding a treaty with defeated Germany. They were about to indulge in a rehearsal of what would later be called 'new diplomacy', a strategy which would not prevent a replay (some say resumption) of the Great War only 20 years later.

Lloyd George's instructions for the weekend exercise were that his colleagues should play roles in an improvised drama, assessing the draft treaty that was taking shape in Paris and Versailles amid dispute and even acrimony. Wilson was to assume the parts, in turn, of a German man and a French woman. Hankey was to convey the views of a typical Briton, while Montagu was to assume a kind of *Candide* role, that of a 'man from Mars' watching the earthlings. Kerr served as recording secretary, and the Prime Minister simply observed.

Playing the average German male, soldier Henry Wilson could see nothing but 'crushing terms' that would be forced on Germany by the Allies in order 'to kill me outright', and no need at all for Germany to join a 'crazy' League of Nations. Wilson's French woman, on the other hand, was physically and spiritually ailing from the war, totally unable to 'look into the mirror of the future from a dread of what she might see'.

Hankey, loyal servant of empire (who in another two decades became the goat in another kind of 'game', that of Soviet espionage), sought reparations of £500 million *annually* from Germany – a sum to be shared by all the victors;[6] demilitarization of the Rhineland; and colonial mandates for Britain over Palestine and Mesopotamia, East and South-West Africa, and the German islands in the Pacific Ocean. But Hankey cautioned, at the same time, against driving a desperate Germany into the arms of nascent bolshevism.

The result of this mini-*commedia dell'arte* as 'peace game', if not a treacherously perilous gambit in the evolution of international relations in Europe, was a text of strategy drafted by Kerr. The 'Fontainebleau memorandum' became an argument for a relatively soft peace for Germany, precluding any combination of

- shifts of large blocs of population anywhere on the German nation's periphery;

- a humiliating peace for the defeated Germans, and;
- reparations that could not be paid by the generation that had generated the war (whereas compensation would be paid to France for the loss of its coal resources).

The memorandum helped Lloyd George deal with the demands and hesitations of his French and American colleagues,[7] and a treaty with Germany was finally signed on 28 June 1919 – five years after the Croatian Serb, Gavro Princip, had fired lethal bullets into Archduke Franz Ferdinand, pretender to the Austro-Hungarian throne, and his wife, Duchess Sophie. The game played at Fontainebleau had its limitations: it was confined to strict parameters. But the outcome of the simulation, despite the good intentions of Lloyd George and his play-actors, did not avert the harsh settlement finally imposed on the former Austrian and German Empires.

MODELS TO SCALE

'Military qualities don't show themselves in an exercise on a sand model', Adolf Hitler harangued his generals towards the end of the Second World War. 'People who have brainwaves, ideas', the supreme commander of all German forces added, 'will get nowhere in the end unless they also possess strength of character, perseverance and determination.'[8] Hitler was saying that strategy, deployment and the tactics of movement cannot be portrayed in all their fine details on a mere tabletop – complementing, in effect, Tolstoy's adage in *War and Peace* that indomitable spirit will win against mighty regiments.

Nor can modeling with scaled-down simulacra of warriors, vehicles, guns, ships, aircraft and missiles necessarily reflect what might pass through the minds of the men and women directly involved – or guarantee that the details of experience will be remembered and used rationally. H. E. Hurst was a civil engineer building dams throughout the British Empire. In his studies Hurst wanted to learn if a time series of certain types of information might give evidence of possessing a memory, much as biologists have since shown that individual molecules and cells tend to develop a memory after encountering specific sets of circumstances (obstacles to their movement, in particular). Hurst originated a technique that he called *rescaled range analysis*: detecting if such tendencies to 'memorize' might last longer than one would expect.[9]

Thus far the mathematical analysis implicit in Hurst's technique has been seized upon largely by financial economists because its application to interest yields, dividend payments, inflationary rates and the like makes it especially beguiling[10] as a description of trends. A system's unseen properties and the fact of observing it can influence its effects, as we know from Werner Heisenberg's uncertainty principle.[11] There are also uses for this technique other than in subatomic physics: in turbulence studies, antiseismic engineering and population genetics, for example.

Prediction and *postdiction* (defining the causes, given the known outcome) thus may be inevitably different. In specifying results, one must beware of falling victim to the single-outcome paradox. Multiple finalities exist, after all, so that a result rather different from that envisaged by the strategist is conceivable. One's point of view matters, too, as much in warfare as in politics or even physics.[12] This means that a specific action's needs, especially in the calculation of troop logistics required as support, spare parts to be ordered in advance, and ammunition to be amassed and safeguarded (as we saw in Chapter 7), have to be defined before commitment to action. To do this, key questions need responses. What 'chaos' could be – worse, *will* be – found in the supposed orderliness (that is, linear progression or regression) of resupply and deployment, for instance, or how much order might one count on emerging from the same chaos?

OPERATIONAL ANALYSIS OR 'OR'

The mathematical fractal theories of the 1970s and the subsequent catastrophe and chaos theories at first held some promise that applied mathematics would help resolve quandaries such as these, all familiar to airmen, soldiers and sailors. The operational analysis devised by Britain's air and naval forces early in the Second World War was meant to help meet new military challenges in the sky and between continents. A striking example of this approach is explained in detail by the physicist, Freeman Dyson, in his autobiographical *Disturbing the Universe.*

In Chapter 3, which he mockingly titles 'The Children's Crusade', Dyson tells of his work as a very young civil mathematician with the Pathfinder Force of RAF's Bomber Command. (Dyson explains that he borrowed the chapter's heading from the subtitle of the account of the Allied air raid on Dresden in 1945 by eyewitness Kurt Vonnegut, *Slaughterhouse-Five.*[13]) Dyson was 20 years old in 1944 when the RAF assigned him 'a statistical study to find out whether there was any correlation between the experience of a crew and their chance of being shot down'.[14]

BOX 8 WHEN ACTION FAILS TO CORRESPOND TO STRATEGY

The game plan of Imperial Germany for the invasion of France while overcoming Russia in the east, devised by Field Marshal Count Alfred von Schlieffen, chief of the army's general staff, required eight years (1897–1905) of gestation. Although Schlieffen retired from the active list in the final year of this effort, his successor, Helmuth von Moltke the younger, maintained the scheme's overall form, one foreseeing a huge wheeling-to-the-left by five field-armies racing from the Rhine through Belgium and north-eastern France towards Paris in a genuine *Blitzkrieg.**

The German emperor ordered the assault in August 1914 but by the end of the month, he siphoned off seven badly needed divisions to check the Russian invasion near historic Tannenberg in East Prussia.† The westernmost First, Second and Third Armies, too, lost much of their resupply and their energy: the French stopped the invaders at the Marne river near Paris in early September and, after a desperate conflict, the Germans retired northwards beyond the Aisne river over which they had come only days before.

In France the German reversal was attributed to a combination of

- insufficient reserves to back up a very large, albeit fast-moving force experiencing considerable casualties from both military and guerrilla resistance;
- too wide gaps between, and exposed flanks among, three of the five armies involved, combined with inadequate electrical communications, and ;
- unthought-out solutions to recognized problems of troop transport and resupply.

Of these causal factors, historians believe that logistics was the most significant reason for the reversal of Germany's opening thrust in the First World War: probably a major explanation of why the conflict dragged on more than four additional years. No less an authority than Basil Liddell Hart reckons that although the design conceived by Schlieffen 'was bungled by his successor, it came dangerously close to winning the war within a month'.‡

*Blitzkrieg had its antecedents in the 'lightning campaigns' mounted by the Prussians against Denmark (1864), Austria (1866) and France (1870–71). See Donald Kagan, *On the Origins of War and the Preservation of Peace* (New York, Doubleday, 1995), p. 84. Angus Calder, *The Myth of the Blitz* (London, Pimlico,

1991), p. 2, attributes the term to non-German journalists describing the rapid German victory over Poland in 1939.

†The Russian rout near the Mazurian lakes resulted in part from hostility between the two rival Russian field commanders, Generals Aleksandr V. Samsonov and Pavel K. Rennenkampf. After losing 125,000 men near Tannenberg, Samsonov committed suicide while Rennenkampf made no move to aid his surrounded colleague. This animosity appears in novel form in Aleksandr I. Solzhenitsyn's *August 1914.*

‡B. H. Liddell Hart, *The German Generals Talk* (New York, William Morrow/Quill, 1979, republication of 1948), p. 10. Cf. Martin van Creveld, *Supplying War: Logistics from Wallenstein to Patton* (Cambridge, Cambridge University Press, 1977), esp. the conclusion to the chapter 'The Wheel that Broke', pp. 138–41.

The experience of the RAF until late 1943 was that there appeared, indeed, to be a correlation. This conclusion was used to good effect both in the training of air crews and in public relations, two vital morale-building components of air operations in wartime. It stands to reason that a battle-experienced crew had a better chance than a green team of returning a damaged aircraft to its base. Yet 'the total effect of all the skill and dedication of the experienced crews was statistically undetectable'. The correlation could not, in other words, be substantiated. Harsher facts, however, emerged.

When the latest RAF casualty data were incorporated in a new study conducted by Dyson and Bomber Command's Operational Research Section, the conclusions were scarcely reassuring. The section learned that No. 83 Squadron alone, a unit of 20 Lancaster heavy bombers, had been making a 'maximum effort' raid on Berlin nightly for two months. Each time, 83 Squadron lost an average of one aircraft with seven crew members. The bimonthly figures of 60 aircraft and 420 crew, multiplied by the number of active units, made the overall losses impressive and created stressful demands on training and equipment resupply. Air operations thenceforth would need rescheduling to take into account human resupply as well as aircraft availability.

Bombardment proved to be a random process, as experienced by the German side and as the British themselves came to perceive. The effort used more incendiary than explosive devices, dropped with the intention of making factory and town morale suffer simply from the destruction visible. But German air-raid defense proved to be more effective than the bombing incursions. Factories that had been hit were revealed by aerial photography, made only a few days after a raid, to be once again in virtually normal operation. German official statistics revealed at the war's end that, despite the growing shortages of raw materials and rail transport, more aircraft were produced in 1944 than in any single year between 1939 and 1943. The critical problem of Germany's air-force management would remain shortages of aviation fuel, lubricants and rubber.

The British operational researchers uncovered another factor, one that aircraft designers and operational commanders had not taken into account. Four of the seven crew-members aboard a Lancaster – the pilot, the bombardier and the two gunners manning the mid-upper and tail turrets – were the ones on the lookout for enemy fighters. But German fighters had evolved since the beginning of the war, and their pilots were now capable of firing upwards from a horizontal flight path, and the Lancaster was without a gun turret on the underside of its fuselage.

Consequently, Dyson's section recommended that elimination of the existing gun turrets would (a) improve the aerodynamics of the airframe and increase the speed of the bomber by almost 40 knots (80km/h) and make it more elusive to interception, (b) permit an even further increase in already heavy bomb loads, and (c) save two lives of seven in the event of a fatal hit on a Lancaster. The recommended changes did not materialize:'The gun turrets remained in the bombers, and the gunners continued to die uselessly until the end of the war',[15] mainly because of delays in preparing, forwarding and implementing the paperwork required for redesign, retooling and production processing. Today, system analysis would typify the phenomenon as an *externality* (unintended outcome), an element in system failure.

Dyson and his colleagues discovered something else. When a Lancaster had been crippled in flight and the commander gave the order to abandon aircraft, the crew members had to make their way to and through an escape hatch only 53cm wide – an unexplained narrowness not found on other British bombers. This proved to be a harrowing obstacle to escaping crewmen 'because they were inadequately prepared for the job of squeezing through a small hole with a bulky flying suit and parachute harness, in the dark, in a hurry, in an airplane rapidly going out of control'. An enlarged escape hatch, recommended doggedly by one of Dyson's team-mates,'became standard only when the war was almost over and the crews who might have been saved by it were mostly dead'.[16] Today the narrow escape-hatch would be termed a'technological lock-in'. Despite the better performance of an alternative, wider hatch, resistance to change carried the day.

How should, how could such misperceptions of reality be accounted for? Dyson explains that the 'root of the evil' lay in the adoption as early as 1936 of the doctrine known as strategic bombing. This concept, incidentally first formulated by United States airmen in the years before the Second World War as a 'school solution' to the problem of how to totally disable an enemy, and by which losses in air crew and major hardware were considered secondary to the main strategy, held that

> the only way to win wars or prevent wars was to rain down death and destruction … This doctrine was attractive to political and military leaders … First, it promised them escape from their worst nightmare, a repetition of the frightful trench warfare of the First World War through which they had all lived. Second, it offered them a hope that war could be avoided altogether by the operation of the principle that later came to be known as 'deterrence'.[17]

Dyson's work proved, according to fellow physicist Hans Bethe, 'traumatic, especially when he found that the bombing of German cities hardly affected the outcome of the war … It was a harsh encounter with death, entrenched bureaucracy, and the futility of much military action.'[18] The phenomenon would repeat itself in Kosovo in 1999 and, in part, in Afghanistan in 2001–2.

COMBINING SIMULATION WITH REALITY

The rain-of-death doctrine eventually found a home in the mind of the RAF's main bombing strategist, Air Chief Marshal Arthur 'Bomber' Harris, who made it reality by the massive destruction of cities such as Hamburg, Mannheim and Dresden. Later, the doctrine became dogma for the Strategic Command (SAC) of the US Air Force during the worst years of the Cold War, under the leadership of the second SAC commander, General Curtis LeMay. LeMay was a command veteran of the British-based Allied air strikes on Germany. Later, in the Pacific, as head of 21st Bomber Command, he devised night fire-strikes against Japanese cities and industrial concentrations. On the morning of 10 March 1944 Tokyo awoke to find 80,000 dead, deprived of oxygen, from a nocturnal strike and a million people homeless. Five months later LeMay oversaw the nuclear devastation of Hiroshima and Nagasaki.

Reality assumes other forms, too. The American Link trainer, invented in time for the war of 1939–45, was one of the first devices to help train flying crew by simulation exercises without leaving the hangar: simple and not expensive, clever. Decades later, training by simulation is widespread, used even within the little-known military program of the otherwise peaceful European Union. This activity is known as EUCLID, European Cooperation for the Long Term in Defense. EUCLID seeks to lower the cost of new military research by sharing expenses among the Union's member states – research and early development coordinated by the Western European Armaments Group (WEAG) and its Research Cell.

A typical WEAG project is a research and technological under-taking known as RTP 11.7, training that combines real and simulated elements. The air combat 'space' thus developed takes form, except for the real aircraft involved (two or three per exercise), as a scenario in virtuality made possible by computers. This is technology, of course, but of an imaginative technical quality that only science can make possible.

The object of RTP 11.7 is to develop, integrate and demonstrate the simulated use of a weapon system in aerial flight, using real aircraft to carry on board the system's 'sensor suite'. Reduced defense budgets in the 1990s meant a diminished availability of aircraft for full-scale exercises, pitted against the improved capability and complexity of weapon systems. So RTP 11.7 was designed to provide daily training for air crews in air-to-air 'combat', using a simulation scenario and weapons on board against virtual targets and other threats, all of which network with other aircraft similarly equipped. Firms from several countries are involved, including Germany's Daimler-Benz Aerospace, Fokker Space of the Netherlands, and the Tubitak Marmara Research Center in Turkey.[19] RTP 11.7 is a good illustration of com-plexity theory at work: the understanding of adaptive systems, whether large or small, operating at the boundary between order and chaos.

SOME TENETS OF WARFARE

'... the three military graces [are] strategic deception, tactical surprise and technical ingenuity.'

Chester Wilmot[20]

Misperceptions of reality or, perhaps more accurately the perceptions of unreality, have long been both solace and succor in the minds of military commanders. In May 1941, when Archibald Wavell launched Operation Brevity against Erwin Rommel's Afrika Korps west of Cairo, deterrence took another form – a form most unusual: a mixture of cement, flour, Worcestershire sauce and ... camel dung.

Major-General Wavell had, only days before, received from Great Britain a consignment of 238 armored vehicles, all painted a boreal green common to the forests of northern Europe. Wavell realized that, as a war color in Egypt's western desert, green was lethally inappropriate to the needs of his tank commanders trying to push Rommel back into the sand fields of Libya and Tunisia.

We saw in Chapter 9 how that unusual unit of Britain's Royal Engineers, the Camouflage Experimental Section commanded by Major Maskelyne, used sleight-of-hand against its enemy. Maskelyne undertook, through illusionism, to supply the other side with negative or false information. The simulations developed by this resourceful crew were full scaled, not reduced, using non-strategic materials such as crate wood, steel wire, burlap, flour and other simple foodstuffs, paint and non-critical (in wartime terms) dyes. They made tanks and armored personnel carriers over as prosaic transport vehicles. Their mock-ups, evolving deceptively enough to fool infrared photography from the air, also included trucks, tanks, gun emplacements, parked aircraft, and even vessels moored pierside. This massive force, all optical illusion, paid off in the form of tactical and even strategic decoys converted into highly effective military deterrents to the adversary.[21]

The RAND ('R and D') Corporation was set up along the boulevards of Santa Monica, California, by the US Air Force shortly after the Second World War. RAND was intended to be a think-tank contemplating the air wars of the future, nuclear conflict in particular, with a strong call on science, technology and economics.[22] Its mission was to 'think about the unthinkable', as it was described at the time. In 1970, the institution established a graduate school that, during the next 25 years, conferred more doctoral degrees in policy-analysis studies than Harvard University's John F. Kennedy School of Government.

The 'products' of the RAND Graduate School emerge from five research units, three of which are military (and seemed to justify the 60 per cent received in 1995, for example, from the military in RAND's total budget of $110 million). The two civil divisions at the RAND school are concerned with non-military research in the United States, and with critical technologies for the future. Two of the 15 graduates in 1995 entered the field of national security, whereas seven accepted positions in health-care delivery.

This fact is probably best explained by the parlous state of health delivery in a modern, industrialized economy such as that of the United States. Medical-care managers are concerned about cutting costs and tilting at macroeconomic windmills, whereas problems of a more pathological or even ethical nature remain secondary: how to gain access to health care, especially for the marginalized and the handicapped in civil life, and how to monitor and maintain its quality. It is in such areas of policy studies that specialists, schooled in approaches first devised by or for the military, can prove to be a boon in civil life. Governance today and tomorrow, in other words, may become overwhelmed by problems of quantity as much as by those of quality.

The same quality/quantity factors are inherent in the modern view of nine principles of warfare. These basic tenets are commonly accepted, more or less, as constituting overall aim: (i) offensive; (ii) mass maneuver; (iii) economy of force, or efficacy; (iv) unity of command, because too many cooks spoil the broth; (v) security; (vi) simplicity; and (vii) surprise. Military operations today subsume, of course, initiative; so to the first seven are added (viii) agility, depth and synchrony of movement; and (ix) versatility or adaptability. Note how these apply, with the exceptions of (ii) and (iv), to terrorism.

In ordinary civil life – quite removed from both terrorists and the military, the Microsoft Corporation is a good example of element (ix), versatility. All the others, with the exception of surprise, are applicable as well to both governance and the rights and responsibilities of the citizen. Once again, we note here dual purpose in this ethology of war.

In terms of doctrine, the four pillars of sound combat management are *leadership, maneuver, firepower* and *protection.* The navy, air force or army not prepared to apply any of these to the fullest extent is headed for serious trouble in the execution of its mission. Good game builders and game players will keep in mind, in other words, all four pillars. For the terrorist, firepower can mean nothing more than a coordinated mailing of envelopes bearing spores of anthrax bacteria or worse.

The value of these principles to applications in ordinary life, furthermore, are clear. When engineer Alfred P. Sloan, Jr, took over the management of General Motors (GM) in the 1920s, he applied planning, organization and strategy to his methods for streamlining a large and disparate firm. He left market development to the company's division heads – much as ministers of defense leave deployment decisions, in the manner of the strategist Helmuth von Moltke the elder,[23] to major field commanders. Sloan backed each GM division with tight, centralized administrative services: finance, personnel administration and other corporate support. And like the military, Sloan as chief executive officer did not abide labor strikes.

As early as 1914, the British engineering mathematician F. W. Lanchester developed equations to model pre-gun and post-gun warfare. The former is linear, claimed Lanchester: 1 fighting person on 'our' side = 1 fighting person on the other side. In post-gun combat the linear function is at least doubled, as much as squared: a force of 2,000 rifles opposing 1,000 is free to release half its number to concentrate fire on only a portion of the enemy's mass, allowing attrition gradually to annihilate the adversary.[24] This is a rudimentary model of firepower, probably more applicable at sea and in the air, but it exemplifies point (iii) above, economy of force. Leadership, maneuver and protection can be simulated mathematically, too, although the variables in their equations are manifold and complex.

FROM THEORY TO PRACTICE

Triangulation is an ancient surveyor's technique used to calculate the height of a tall tree, mountain, or almost any third point not readily attainable yet determinable geometrically on the basis of two other sure measurements. Its application to modeling of the 'laying' of a gun on an invisible, or otherwise elusive, target was well developed by artillerymen and naval gunners before the First World War. It took on a new form in the struggle against submarines during the twentieth century's second major conflict.

The Royal Navy's Captain Gilbert Roberts (a gunner, too), went to work with tiny ship models on a plastic 'sea' during the early efforts to defeat the wolfpack tactics developed by Admiral Karl Dönitz's roving submarines during the Second World War. The imaginative Roberts developed rudimentary variants on the technique – to be supplemented at sea by the judicious use of starshells and ASDIC – nicknamed Raspberry and Pineapple, Beta-Search, and Step-Aside.[25] In the Pacific, the war against Japan witnessed the emergence on the American side of the magnetic anomaly (or airborne) detector, MAD, and the nearly simultaneously developed Japanese *jikitanchiki*. Simulation, first in the form of scale models, quickly found its way into full-fledged, effective weapon systems.

MAD-*jikitanchiki* was based on the experience in earth physics that the presence of a metallic mass tends to skew the measurement of a magnetic field. The airborne detector aboard an aircraft reacted to the presence of a submarine as far below the surface as 120 m (67 fathoms), whereupon the device automatically released a colored slick of aluminum. The pilot kept his heading, dropped a second slick on the same bearing, then maneuvered to drop two more slicks, of a different color, along a bearing at right angles to the first. The center of the triangle formed by the first, second and fourth slicks was the location – simulated, of course – of the submarine. This was so, at least theoretically, until wind, sea currents and elapsed time falsified the geometry.

This tactic was developed to the point of detecting subs as deep as 240m beneath the surface, whereupon pursuing aircraft would drop a depth charge, alert nearby surface ships to join the chase, and hope that air-to-ship or ship-to-ship communications would be effective in closing on the target.[26] Mathematical theory and its symbols were transformed, once again, into practice; they helped to defeat an adversary and win a war.

On land the miniature battlefield may be put to work to facilitate the resolution of complex offense–defense confrontations. When the battle of the Anzio-Nettuno beachhead ended its fourth month in virtual checkmate between the invading 15th Army Group of the Western Allies and *Luftwaffe* Field Marshal Albert Kesselring's Army Group C, tens of thousands had died almost needlessly on both sides. Major-General Ernest Harmon of the US 1st Armored Division describes in his book, *Combat Commander*, some of the attentive preparations involved as the Allies planned the 'Buffalo' strategy of Operation Diadem in May 1944 in order to break through the German defenses of their Gustav Line. (Today, a concentration of PhDs working in the Bios Group of the consulting firm, Cap Gemini Ernst & Young, uses complexity-analysis software to model difficult battlefield problems for its military clients.)

Harmon ordered built a terrain model 16 m long, showing every natural and manmade feature his soldiers would need to recognize and, if necessary, overcome in the days ahead. A catwalk above and around the model permitted his soldiers to survey intensively the entire plan of the ground that they and their vehicles would traverse.[27] Company commanders and platoon leaders were given reconnaissance trips, furthermore, aboard liaison aircraft 'to enable them to study the route of advance from the air ... Every man in every unit had been thoroughly briefed'[28] as to exactly what to expect. Shortly afterwards the breakthrough succeeded.

A scaled-up version of this kind of modeling is found in the training exercises devised for a battalion of the British 3rd Parachute Brigade, scheduled to crash-land three gliders on the casemates of a German battery near Merville, about 6km east of Caen in Normandy, on 6 June 1944. While preparing for the invasion, the battalion's commander, Lieutenant-Colonel T. H. B. Otway, had a replica of the artillery emplacement built near Newbury, England. 'After five rehearsals by day and four by night, all with live ammunition, Otway was confident of success, but he could not anticipate what the weather would do to his plan.'[29] The weather was compliant, and this operation also proved a success, too.

MODELS ON THE LARGE SCALE

On a theater-wide scale, a steady-supply pattern of human beings and their supporting equipment and expendables were modeled, beginning 18 months ahead, by the strategic planners of the *Overlord* or Normandy campaign. This model's purpose was to provide a synthesis of all factors that might affect the *rate* of supply. A large simulation, it represented thousands of the elements involved, data both real and hypothetical. In time, *Overlord* as model demonstrated that the main factors comprised (i) the maximum of sea-going vessels that would be available, (ii) beach descriptions in all their detail and the access they would provide inland, (iii) proximity of the beaches to deepwater harbors and the capacity of the latter to receive and unload ships, and (iv) the feasibility of different kinds of air support.[30]

Peacekeeping assignments as military missions ('operations other than combat', or OOC) may be, on the other hand, the hardest of all the games. They are, in effect, contrived appeasement – undertaken by the military as servants of intergovernmental organizations. The experience of UN inspectors in Iraq during the late 1990s to enforce UN Resolution 487 (eliminating weapons of mass destruction) through on-site visits and inventories demonstrated the difficulties that resistance presents,[31] given the wiles of a dictatorial leader and the agility of his security apparatus. The NATO units still assigned to supervise ceasefires and truce arrangements in the former Yugoslavia know that their own game's end might be a fateful reversion to total war by the parties between whom peace is kept – in Bosnia and Kosovo – as the conflict extended into neighboring Macedonia.

PINNING THINGS DOWN: 'LAYERED ANALYSIS'

The battle of Anzio, mentioned earlier, offers an opportunity to plot *ex post facto* a critique along the lines that objective analysis has followed since its fundamentals were established by German and French military strategists during the nineteenth century.

John Gooch and Eliot A. Cohen proffer a fascinating post-conflict model of how things went wrong in five significant military debacles of the twentieth century.[32] Their examples cover the British–Turkish struggle at Gallipoli (1915), the catastrophe befalling the French army and air force during the German onslaught in 1940, the US naval failure in antisubmarine warfare to counter U-boats (1942), the rout of the US Eighth Army in Korea (1950), and the failure of anticipation by Israeli forces along the Suez Canal and on the Golan Heights (1973).

The pattern of analysis offered by Cohen and Gooch can be depicted schematically as in Figure 5.

If we translate the generic reasoning of the first three of the main points (•) in Figure 5 to the degraded situation confronting the Western Allies at Anzio between January and June 1944, we may establish *degrees of failure* and *at what levels* at least when this can be done with fair certainty.

Figure 5:
Reasoned Analysis of some Historical-Event Processes

- What is the event (success, stalemate, failure, retrogression)?
    ⇒ *Apply contrafactual analysis*: What would be needed to transform what happens into
    ⇒ *Something else?*
- Which critical tasks are successfully accomplished?
    ⇒ *List key elements contributing to success or failure.*
- Now do a 'layered' analysis, remembering that strategy requires an institutional dimension.
    ⇒ *Proceed to examine behavior at different levels of the organization (its hierarchy).* Relate these levels' inputs to the outcome of the process.
- Now draw up an *analytical matrix*, a simple chart of the steps in the overall process. This is a schema of the key moves involved. Finally,
- Trace the *pathways* to success (or failure). These become the broad-brush causes of success/failure.

Source: See especially Eliot A. Cohen and John Gooch, *Military Misfortunes: The Anatomy of Failure in War* (New York, Random House/Vintage, 1991), p. 55; also pp. 83, 147, 191, 209 and Ch. 9, 'What Can be Done', pp. 231–46.

Then, as a check on the validity of the analysis, we transpose the situation and examine the strategy as seen from the adversary's side: in this case, the German and Italian military forces opposing those of the Western Allies. A less dissective, more narrative, version of post-battle autopsy is the *after-action report*, a narrative written by the participants and long used by United States ground forces as the first record of an operation. The *histories*, assembled by professional historians, are compiled later when all-source material is available, data that could not have been known to all the participants or immediate observers.

The analysis in Table 5 demonstrates a combination of pathways, or thrusts of effect, in failure or semi-failure, indicated by the terms set in bold in the table. These had a combination of sequels:

- *Success*: the Fifth Army finally broke through after a third of a year, causing the immediate withdrawal northwards of Field Marshal Albert Kesselring's Army Group C;

Table 5:
Command layers of Inadequate Performance within Landing Operation 'Shingle',
Anzio-Cassino Area of Operations, 1944 (degrees of dysfunction are categorized as
marginal, partial or *critical failure*)

	Managerial phase		
Command level	Identification of military goal	Providing the means to reach the goal	Command, control, coordination
President, Prime Minister*	Denial of Cassino supply; capture of Rome; destruction of German Army Group C†	Western front (Normandy) would remain priority of Western Allies	Churchill, especially, tended to usurp authority of field commanders
C-in-C, Mediterranean Area	Deferred to CG, 15th Army Group	Deferred to lower command levels	**Marginal failure:** deferred to lower levels of command ⇓
CG 15th Army Group	**Failure:** acceded to next lower command ⇓	**Partial failure:** deference to next lower command ⇓	**Critical failure:** 'suggested' instead of ordered ⇓
CG Fifth Army	**Failure** because of personal goal of relieving Rome ⇓	**Partial failure** in that logistical priority unclear ⇓	**Failure:** usurped own objective when 'suggestions' were made ⇓
CG VI Corps‡	**Partial failure** in not securing inland strongpoints beyond beach-head	CG did (almost) the best with manpower and supplies provided	**Marginal failure:** ⇑ CG guilty of 'bunker complex'

Notes:
C-in-C = commander-in-chief; CG = commanding general; ⇓ = thrust of effect
*Missing in the left-hand column are the names of the incumbents: Franklin Roosevelt and Winston Churchill; Mediterranean (British), General Sir Henry Maitland Wilson; 15th Army Group (British), General Sir Harold Alexander; Fifth Army (American), General Mark Clark; VI Corps (American), Major-General John P. Lucas. Security clearance for Ultra intelligence was available to officers no lower than corps commanders, and at Anzio the cleared general officers received Ultra. The Germans, however, had no information of such significance on the enemy.
†The objective, in other words, was not maintained. This is a major cause of strategic, operational or tactical dysfunction in military movements.
‡This corps' assault units were the British 1st Infantry Division, the US 3rd Infantry Division, a US Ranger force of three battalions, independent US parachute units, the US–Canadian 1st Special Service Force (SSF), and the US 36th Engineer Combat Regiment. The Rangers and SSF were commandos.

- *Forcing* Hitler (who alone made the decisions on his side) to *call on reserves* from Poland, the eastern Soviet Union, and northern Italy;
- Heavy *loss of life*: about 15,000 on the Allied side, perhaps more than 40,000 among the Germans (statistics remain incomplete to this day);
- Intentional *bombardment* by the Germans *of the enemy's medical facilities*: the 95th Evacuation Hospital, other processing installations at Anzio;
- Purposeful *destruction* by the Allied forces of the 1,400-year old Benedictine *abbey* on Monte Cassino;
- *Stalemate*; probable *loss of time* in the strategic preparations under way to mount Operation *Overlord* – the Normandy landings of 6 June 1944 (the same day that units of the Fifth Army penetrated Rome after having neutralized Cassino).

The results of this analytical treading through command levels is confirmed in the findings of what was right, and what was not, about the Shingle (landing) and Diadem (breakthrough) actions around Anzio.[33] Can such assessment be tested, with both the benefit of hindsight and a detailed knowledge of the conditions in the possession of the battlefield managers at the time of the campaign? Yes, if we take the trouble to reverse the scheme of analysis by crossing the main line of resistance, as it were, and viewing from the adversary's side: a layered matrix of the situation, seen through German eyes, would appear as Table 5 inverted. Degrees of positive performance by opposing forces may then be labeled *marginal achievement, partial achievement, success,* or *overwhelming accomplishment.* Historically, there was no 'overwhelming accomplishment' on the German–Italian side. Kesselring fought a first-rate holding action in 1943–44, but not one that changed the course of the war or saved his side from ultimate defeat.

VARIETIES OF CRITIQUE

Critique by remote viewing may remind readers of an operational-research method devised late in the 1950s and used in the 1960s to rationalize and streamline the R&D and then production of the Polaris-equipped submarine force of the United States Navy, long-range submersibles equipped with nuclear-tipped missiles. The secretary of defense at the time was Robert McNamara who, whatever his shortcomings, was serious about applying mathematical methods to defense problems and their possible solutions.

One method was called *program-evaluation review technique* (PERT) – in some respects a competitor or complement to another technique made popular at the time in both military and non-military manufacturing called value analysis (VA). PERT was so highly regarded in industry that, within a few years, one-fourth of *Fortune* magazine's 500 top firms had adopted the system.[34] PERT and VA, although no longer much in vogue, are but two of the many forms existing for the application of social science and mathematics to military or dual-use needs.

In PERT, 'a series of spider-web networks [showed] when each part and component of the system came together with all the others'.[35] PERT's purported value was in the economies of scale achieved in programming the research, design and construction of both the *Polaris* undersea vessel and its nuclear ordnance. The method assuredly had value, especially since the main managerial standards it called for were manufacturing rigor and budgetary integrity. Some critics considered PERT, nonetheless specious and of most value in terms of positive public relations with Congress, the mass media and the public at large.[36]

PERT may have been less than perfect in design and production channels, but the *assessment of comparative worth of military units on both sides* of the battle line has grown in favor since the Second World War (when it was used consistently by the Germans and only later by the Russians, British and Americans).[37] Briefly, comparing one air force's fighter squadron with one of the opponent's of similar designation has little value if various factors are not included and given their proper weights. These factors include number of personnel involved by occupational specialty, number of aircraft and of what types and their age, numbers and kinds of weapons and ammunition, length of training and of combat experience of crews, access to resupply and maintenance (and of what quality), access to special equipment, and bad-weather performance – an *order of battle quality*.

In comparing ground-force battalions or regiments, for example, key questions to be formulated should include

- *Are the troops* mainly regulars, territorials (national guard), reservists, or conscripted?
- *How mobile* is the battalion (regiment)?
- *What damage* will the battalion (regiment) do to its opposite number?
- *How resilient to damage* will the unit be?

This analysis of offense–defense can also be ramified into what historian Trevor N. Dupuy, a former US Army colonel, calls the *quantified judgment method* (QJM). QJM seeks to assign a numerical value, usually in percentage form, of how 'superior' one force is to another: the 11 nations pitted against Japan during the Second World War, or the Iraqi forces over the Kuwaiti defenses during the Gulf War.[38] Dupuy's approach derives from the simpler *order of battle*: a simulation listing the opponent's (or opponents') units by identification number, size, names of commander and immediate subordinates, together with an appraisal of the commander's character, personality and reputed efficiency. An appendix to the English version of Helmuth von Moltke's *The Franco-Prussian War of 1870* did exactly this, while a Second World War personality profile of Adolf Hitler – classified at the time – was published years later as a remarkably accurate psychological analysis of this major figure of the twentieth century.[39]

Simulating the future, as strategy and operations undertake to do, has many variants. One, used by French military and civil planners, is the Micmac method by which a new side-arm for infantrymen was devised, a weapon to be in the hands of infantrymen by the year 2010. Michel Godet, a professor at the Conservatoire National des Arts et Métiers, relates that his team prioritized 57 types of variables (kind of projectile, aiming angle, cost, competitiveness, antipersonnel effects, configuration, and so on), permutating a total of 15,542 technical solutions possible. By applying a choice of multiple criteria and emphasizing realistic constraints, the analysts reduced the large number to 50 and then 20. Ten years after beginning their work in 1989, they had their new design, called PAPOP, a multipurpose gun adapted to different projectiles and aimed at an angle permitting the handler literally to 'fire around corners'.[40]

Another approach is that of the United States, by which a wholly new doctrinal idea is emerging. This concept, called the *command and information infrastructure* system, rests firmly on the new significance of information and communication – in all their forms – that was covered in Chapter 9. It seeks to streamline and synergize 'state-of-the-art information and networking technology to integrate widely dispersed human decision makers, situational and targeting sensors, and forces and weapons into a highly adaptive, comprehensive system to achieve unprecedented mission effectiveness'.[41] Within the combination of C^{4}I (command, control, communication, computing, intelligence), the approach integrates surveillance and reconnaissance: in other words, direct monitoring of the enemy. The salient feature of this doctrinal outlook is that it is almost entirely civilian-designed, within a unit of the National Academy of Sciences, the National Research Council.[42]

VERIFYING, DECIDING, COMMUNICATING

What did the UN set out to do with the ceasefire arrangement in Iraq, what were the aims of the then 185-nation body? If the adversary were overcome, what leadership and what form of government would take its place? What was the basic goal – as one is often forced to recall – to be reached? The most challenging aspect of human enterprise, especially of complex undertakings, may be remembering clearly what one has proposed to achieve – and to act upon it. In January 1991, the Coalition forces brought a halt to the armed conflict with Iraq, which had arisen because of the latter's invasion and annexation of neighboring Kuwait in the previous year. And was there a basis for reconciliation and agreement between the two sides?

Iraq agreed, in negotiations with the United Nations Security Council, to accept unobstructed inspections by the UN of its warmaking potential. Within four months of the ceasefire, Iraq was to have destroyed its existing weapons of mass destruction together with the arsenals producing them. Iraq's government was to hand over all instructions and other data related to the design, manufacture and deployment of nuclear, biological and chemical arms together with all long-range missiles. The UN also required Iraq to furnish lists, by name, of all non-Iraqi suppliers purveying to such systems.

These requirements and constraints were unprecedented moves, voted as Resolutions, in the half-century history of the UN's existence. Yet they tended to be forgotten each time that the Iraqi leader moved to thwart inspections or gain easement from the sanctions voted by the UN against Iraq, a process repeated several times in the decade following the brief war.

Reverting to Dupuy's QJM, we find that it has has a *qualitative* half-brother. When the Americans were ruminating the Desert Terror strike against Iraq's Saddam Hussein, war planning seemed to go beyond the selection of targets falling within the category prohibited by the UN, namely sites for the development, manufacture, storage and deployment of weapons of mass destruction. The Americans contemplated, from both Washington and their forward air headquarters in the town of Eskan, Saudi Arabia, striking 'thousands of aim points' in Iraq sheltering the apparatus that maintained Saddam in power.

This targeted structure included the leader's immediate entourage, key sites occupied by his Republican Guards throughout the country, Ba'ath Party units, the secret police – the elimination of whoever and whatever might preclude the acceleration of a change in government.[43] Strategic objectives and the expectations attached to them often posed a dilemma, but a quick undermining of Iraq's power mechanisms had as high a priority as the weapon installations.

The situation concerning Afghanistan, as worked out near Bonn (Germany) at the end of 2001, was quite different. Here a UN-sponsored meeting of various in-country factions *only* – in contrast to the Fontainebleau emulation described earlier in this chapter – sought to develop a five-tiered model for the renovation of a country ravaged by a terrorism-originated war. Time will tell how the model becomes reality.

Pondering specific civil actions and taking decisions about them are subsidiary to the military's preoccupations, especially since so many operational or tactical decisions of purely military concern must be made quickly, even in real time. Decision theory today is divided between two schools. One is the prescriptive/normative or standard-setting approach, that guiding the UN system (for instance) in the preparation of its plans, programs and budget. The other is the descriptive school, representing behavioral guidance based more on empirical, trial-and-error method.

A recent and perhaps unexpected simulation exercise by the military involved the United States Marine Corps and … the stock market. In the mid-1990s the Marines, because of a concern that they still had much to learn about real-time decision-making and ultra-rapid communication, arranged with the New York Mercantile Exchange to trade experiences and methods of work. Action sessions took place at the Marines' school for officers and a training site, the Warfighting Laboratory, both at Quantico, Virginia, and reciprocally in Manhattan aboard a museum ship nearby.

It is difficult to establish which group might learn the most from such exchanges of working environments, but both the Marines and the civilians managed to develop a fine appreciation for the knowledge and the rapidity of decision-making each group was able to demonstrate to the visiting team. Traders are accustomed to shouting at each other all day, 'wielding vast sums to make more sums; military leaders adopt battle plans, wielding lives to save more lives'. The traders in futures stocks (agricultural products, unleaded gasoline, natural gas, precious metals) had to learn quickly about a bevy of weapons that Marines deploy and use against adversaries, while the sea soldiers (including women officers and admirals) 'could see how the traders process information and do trading in chaotic situations'.[44]

Such a process is far from institutionalized between civilians and the military, in the United States and elsewhere, but it promises a degree of effective training for the mutual benefit of disparate participants. Some superior officers outside North America, such as

Brigadier-General Loup Francart of the French Army's Doctrine and Advanced Studies Command,[45] would like to see Europeans undertake this sort of brainstorming applied to the strategic picture.

NONLINEAR THINKING

Fiction – all games and other simulations are fictional constructions – that relates to planning or fighting a war often capitalizes on the games that governments are capable of playing in the use of their armed forces.

Two British journalists imagined (1997) in *Dragonstrike: The Millennium War,* on the eve of the twenty-first century, a feint-and-strike scenario involving the People's Republic of China, Taiwan, Japan, the United States, Great Britain, France, Germany, Vietnam and a few other countries.[46] This was to be a war, lasting from February until May in the year 2001, with a difference: an armed struggle for market shares in various economic sectors including aircraft and natural gas, with the manufacturing and service enterprises of the Chinese People's Liberation Army gaining fantastic profits in currency speculations.

In May 1997, Hong Kong's *South China Morning Post* published, curiously enough, two related news items. One reported Chinese maneuvers, citing the mainland daily newspaper *Wen Wei Po*, linked in reality with 'tensions over disputed territory in the South and East China Sea[s]'.[47] The second story recounted a recent war game played in the United States in which (the year is 2020) the People's Republic of China attacks Taiwan while the Americans are engaged in war with Russia over Ukraine. This report quoted a Professor Chen Yu-chun, who remarked that the US scenario was credible 'if Taiwan went ahead and declared its independence'.[48] In 2000, the Taiwanese population did vote out of office 50 years of Kuomintang rule and, in its place, voted in the country's major pro-independence party.

Is truth or fiction the stranger in the real world? We have reviewed a variety of simulations in this chapter, and it may be superfluous to comment that they have followed the more or less linear thinking that most of us use. Yet we know that linear thinking in the military arena, as in other quotidian life, does not necessarily lead to linear solutions. A superlative example is the wave of criminal terrorism commanded by Osama bin Laden. Simulation, therefore, regardless of how well thought-out it may be, cannot be an infallible guide to the true value and timing of the strategic impulses that might make all the difference between success and failure – victory or defeat for one or another party.

Speculation and hypothesis, both of which have a place as methodologies in the rapport between fighting elements and the applications of science, are variants of the *What if?* school of historical thought. An unusual book by France's premier futurist, engineer Jacques Lesourne, translated as *Those Futures that Never Happened*,[49] speculates what could have taken place in the twentieth century if the German military had not sent Lenin to Petrograd in 1917 and if Hitler had won the Second World War. Lenin did go; Hitler did not win.

Understanding the roots of armed dispute can remain a puzzle. Bosnia, Somalia, Rwanda, Kosovo, the al-Qaeda: we strive to understand the transition from no armed conflict to hostilities. The social sciences remain far from clear on causes and motivations, yet these 'transitions' continue to occur.

NOTES

1 Professor of economics at the University of Paris-9, Schmidt specializes in military behavior. His remarks identify the main interpreters of the game theory developed by Oskar Morgenstern and John von Neumann (1944); this comment appeared in the economic supplement of *Le Monde*, 15 March 1994, p. ix.

2 In *Technology and War: From 2000 BC to the Present* (New York, Free Press, 1989), p. 316.

3 Strategy, infinitely complex, is treated extensively in many languages. Hervé Couteau-Bégarie of the Ecole Pratique des Hautes Etudes has described its meanings, applications and 'disruptions': *Introduction à la stratégie* (Paris, Collège Interarmées de Défense and Editions Economica, 1996–97).

4 The layperson will find two titles especially useful: Thomas B. Allen, *War Games: The Secret World of the Creators, Players and Policy Makers Rehearsing World War III Today* (New York, McGraw-Hill, 1987); and Peter B. Perla, *The Art of Wargaming: A Guide for Professionals and Hobbyists* (Annapolis, MD, Naval Institute Press, 1990).

5 Recalled in The Commission on America's National Interests, *America's National Interests* (Cambridge, MA, Center for Science and International Affairs, Harvard University, July 1996), pp. 13–14.

6 Until 1945 the pound sterling had the purchasing power of almost US$5 (in 1945 values).

7 An amusing account of the weekend at Fontainebleau appears in Charles L. Mee, Jr, *The End of Order: Versailles 1919* (New York, E. P. Dutton, 1980), pp. 149–52.

8 Words addressed by the German chancellor to his inspector-general of armored forces, Major-General Wolfgang Thomale, the night of 29–30 December 1944 during Operation *Nebelmist* (battle of the Bulge). Walter Warlimont, *Inside Hitler's Headquarters, 1939–45*, trans. R. H. Barry (London, Weidenfeld & Nicolson, 1964), p. 495.

9 A schoolfriend of the author rose to general-officer grade; during the war in Vietnam, he made the error of sending the same unit five times, using

identical tactics each time, to take a sole objective. The effort was a failure, his unit decimated, and the general's career found an ignominious end.

10 See, for example, Edgar Peters, *Fractal Market Analysis* (New York, John Wiley, 1993), *passim*.

11 Heisenberg (see Chapter 4) postulated (1927) the uncertainty or indeterminacy principle: in microsystems the accurate measurement of an observable quantity necessitates uncertainties in our knowledge of the values of other observable quantities.

12 Roger D. Masters, *Beyond Relativism, Science and Human Values* (Hanover, NH, Dartmouth College and University Press of New England, 1993), p. 34.

13 Vonnegut and his fellow prisoners of war were housed in a former abattoir, No. 5, of the city of Dresden.

14 Freeman Dyson, *Disturbing the Universe* (New York, Harper & Row, 1979), p. 21. Strategic bombing of a 'target-rich environment' was developed in a course called 'Air Operations against National Structures' held at the Air Corps Tactical School, Maxwell Field (Alabama) in 1939. This section of the school's syllabus was based on studies made in 1932 and 1936 of the vulnerability of economic production and of cities. See John Keegan, *Warpaths: Travels of A Military Historian in North America* (London, Random House/Pimlico, 1995), p. 325 ff.

15 Dyson, *Disturbing the Universe*, p. 30.

16 Ibid., pp. 27–8.

17 Ibid., p. 30.

18 Hans A. Bethe, *The Road from Los Alamos* (New York, Simon & Schuster/Touchstone, 1991), p. 232.

19 See 'Successful Projects', *WEAG Research News*, 6 March 1997, p. 18.

20 Chester Wilmot, *The Struggle for Europe* (London, Collins, 1952), p. 294.

21 See David Fischer, *The War Magician* (New York, Coward-McCann), 1983, *passim*.

22 An early history of the RAND Corporation is Bruce L.R. Smith, *The RAND Corporation: Case Study of A Nonprofit Advisory Corporation* (Cambridge MA, Harvard University Press, 1966).

23 John Keegan, *The First World War* (London, Hutchinson, 1998), p. 119, quoting the historian P. Contamine.

24 George and Meredith Friedman, *The Future of War: Power, Technology and American World Dominance in the Twenty-First Century* (New York, St Martin's/Griffin, 1998), p. 246, p. 438, note 19; Van Creveld, *Technology and War*, p. 244.

25 Peter Padfield, *War beneath the Sea: Submarine Conflict 1939–1945* (London, John Murray, 1995), pp. 288–90, 325 and *passim*.

26 Ibid., pp. 400–2; see pp. 447–8 for the results inside a submarine made the target of such attacks.

27 Ernest N. Harmon, *Combat Commander* (Englewood, Cliffs NJ, Prentice-Hall, 1970), pp, 184–5.

28 Carlo d'Este, *Fatal Decision: Anzio and the Battle for Rome* (London and New York, HarperCollins, 1991), p. 356.

29 Wilmot, *The Struggle for Europe*, pp. 240–1.

30 Van Creveld, *Technology and War*, pp. 206–7.

31 See Peter M. Boyer, 'Scott Ritter's Private War', *New Yorker*, 9 November 1998, pp. 56–73.

32 See Eliot A. Cohen and John Gooch, *Military Misfortunes: The Anatomy of Failure in War* (New York, Random House/Vintage, 1991), chs 4–8.

33 These analyses include Ralph Bennett, *Ultra and Mediterranean Strategy* (1989); Martin Blumenson, *Anzio: The Gamble that Failed* (1986), and *Mark Clark* (1985); John Cunningham, *A Sailor's Odyssey* (1951); Carlo d'Este, *Fatal Decision*; Dominick Graham and Shelford Bidwell, *Tug of War: The Battle for Italy* (1986); Albert Kesselring, *The Memoirs of Field-Marshal Kesselring* (1953); Dan Kurzman, *The Race for Rome* (1975); Samuel Eliot Morison, *Sicily-Salerno-Anzio* (1954); Fridolin von Senger u. Etterlin, *Neither Fear nor Hope* (1954); Eric Sevareid, *Not So Wild A Dream* (1968); Siegfried Westphal, *The German Army in the West* (1951). Almost alone in his relatively optimistic view of the Anzio campaign is Chester Wilmot, *The Struggle for Europe* (1952), in an excellent early reconstruction of the European campaigns of 1941–45.

34 Claude Serfati, 'L'emprise coûteuse des technologies militaires sur l'économie' (The Costly Grip of Military Industry on the Economy), *Mondes en développement*, 83 (1993), p. 72.

35 Norman Polmar and Thomas B. Allen, *Rickover: Controversy and Genius, a Biography* (New York, Simon & Schuster, 1982), p. 551.

36 See esp. H. M. Sapolsky, *The Polaris System Development – Bureaucratic and Programmatic Success* (Cambridge, MA, Harvard University Press, 1972).

37 Known at the Pentagon as 'net assessment', in contradistinction to 'intelligence' and 'critique'. Its high priest is economist Andrew Marshall, a civilian prominent in the reorienting of overall US military make-up (structure, armament and deployment) in 2001–02.

38 DuPuy explains his mathematical model in *Numbers, Predictions, and War* (Indianapolis, IN, Bobbs-Merrill, 1979) and applies this reasoning to conflicts to come in *Future Wars: The World's Foremost Flashpoints* (London, Sidgwick & Jackson, 1992, and New York, Warner, 1993). See also the discussion by James F. Dunnigan and Albert A. Nofi, *Dirty Little Secrets of World War II* (New York, William Morrow/Quill, 1994), pp. 78, 82–3.

39 Field Marshal von Moltke's memoir, with revised translation and order of battle by Archibald Forbes, was published in London by Harper & Brothers, 1914; Walter C. Langer, intro. William L. Langer; *The Mind of Adolf Hitler, The Secret Wartime Report* (New York, Basic, 1972).

40 Michel Godet, 'La prospective en quête de rigueur: Portée et limites des méthodes formalisées' (Future Strategy in Search of Rigor, Scope and Limitations of Formalized Methods), *Futuribles*, January 2000, pp. 57–64.

41 Naval Studies Board, National Research Council, *Network-Centric Naval Forces: A Transition Strategy for Enhancing Operational Capabilities* (Washington, DC, National Academy Press, 2000), p. 1.

42 Related, new military doctrine: Headquarters, US Marine Corps, 'Operational Maneuver from the Sea', a conceptual description (Washington, DC, Government Printing Office, 1996); Department of the Navy, 'Forward … from the Sea', a conceptual description (Washington, DC, GPO, 1997); John M. Shalikashvili, *Joint Vision 2010* (Washington, DC, Joint Chiefs of Staff, The Pentagon, 1997). See also Naval Studies Board, National Research Council, *Technology for the United States Navy and Marine Corps, 2000–2035*, 9 vols (Washington, DC, National Academy Press, 1997); Joseph A. Sestak, Jr, 'A Maritime Concept for the Information Age', a brief (Washington DC, Office of the Chief of Naval Operations-N51, 18 November 1999).

43 As cited by Barton Gellman, *IHT*, 18 February 1998, p. 11, after a visit by several defense journalists to the US Central Command's base in Saudi Arabia

– an act that may have been political and psychological warfare mounted by American military and diplomatic planners.

44 Seth Schiesel, 'Marines and Traders Swap Lessons', *IHT*, 17 December 1996, pp. 11, 15.

45 See his perception of non-combat operations to come in the twenty-first century, with Jean-Jacques Patry, *Maîtriser la violence, une option stratégique* (Overcoming Violence, A Strategic Option) (Paris, Editions Economica, 1999). Franquart is now retired.

46 Humphrey Hawksley and Simon Holberton, *Dragonstrike: The Millennium War* (London, Sidgwick & Jackson, 1997).

47 Cary Huang, 'Military Exercises Clash with Real Disputes', *South China Morning Post*, 24 May 1997, p. 6.

48 Fong Tak-ho, 'Beijing "the Enemy" in US Scenario', *South China Morning Post*, 24 May 1997, p. 6.

49 Jacques Lesourne, *Ces avenirs qui n'ont pas eu lieu* (Paris. Editions Odile Jacob, 2001).

Part III:

Behind the Action, and Wars to Come

In the previous section the focus was on individual scientists, allowing us to see who they are, how these men and women entered on the scene, the relationships they maintain with their military employers or contractors, the careers they lead, and the compensations they receive or the opprobrium they encounter.

Employment is assured for life for many of these specialists, but sometimes careers are abruptly ended. This happened to Japanese, German and Italian scientists and technologists at the end of the Second World War, and it happened more recently to those of Russian or Eastern European nationalities working in the defunct Soviet Union. When political fortune or the economy turns sour, it may then be attractive and life-saving for these specialists to accept employment abroad – by authorities or institutions that not only pay but pay well. (Russian scientists have been notoriously underpaid, or not paid at all, since 1992.) A rogue market may be created, therefore, for otherwise desperate physicists, chemists, biologists and design engineers.

Paying and accounting for military R&D are concerns, too, for lawmakers and taxpayers. An American president, Dwight Eisenhower, warned decades ago that this sector could become a dominant element even in a democratic society, and experience has since shown that the admonition was not hollow.

We examine the reasons *why* military research is costly (sometimes astronomically so), and how what we spend on the design and building of novel weapon systems either fits into or competes with other public costs. The peace dividends expected after the demise of the Soviet Union may have been sincerely anticipated: we now examine the reality a decade later.

In the final section we tackle the difficult question of how available, and how willing, scientists might be in the future to help prepare the ground for new conflicts and even participate actively in them.

Scientists in the great majority are dependent, as we have demonstrated, on the largess of states – financial support in the form of contracts, fellowships and other bursaries, grants, salaries and bonuses. There have been, it is true, sporadic refusals of such support. But scientists, as almost everyone else, are forced to earn a living, so the material support afforded by the state to the research community has tended to solidify itself over time.

The book concludes with an uncompromising answer to our original question concerning war as an extension of science by other means. An Afterword follows.

13

Who Are the Scientists Working with the Military?

'The usual way is for the military man to use the scientist as an aid and auxiliary. It is essential that … the matter go further than that … approaching problems which … are always military and scientific.'
Vannevar Bush, testifying before a US Congressional committee during the Second World War

'if you pay people well and the work's exciting, they'll work on anything'
Mark Oliphant, Australian member of first British nuclear-arms project

The big wheels in the machinery of 'big science'/military research are known to the public, Andrei Sakharov and Vannevar Bush being among the prominent. In this chapter we look into who are the lesser, yet essential, lights in this specialized vocation, and take note of the scale of the economics required to pay such talent and their costly undertakings.

ORGANIZING MODERN TRAINING

The idea of persuading young people with scientific talent to direct themselves, early in life, to military applications of their knowledge, present and future, may be an ideal of an ideally functioning state. The tenet is not universal (nor even characterized in George Orwell's novel, *1984*), but France's Ecole Polytechnique made a good historical start in this direction.

In the France of 1794, the parliament was known as the *Convention Nationale*. On 11 March the Convention decided to found four new institutions dedicated to specialized learning and preparing the nation better for war. One of these was the Ecole Polytechnique – at first called the *Ecole Centrale des Travaux Publics*, the Central School of Public Works. The institution was voted into existence by the Convention in order to teach the building arts. The other schools were intended to train workers in the technical trades (Conservatoire National des Arts et Métiers, today a major engineering school); to teach advanced learning (Ecole Normale Supérieure); and to teach languages of the East for political and commercial careers (today's Institut National des Langues et Civilisations Orientales, or 'Langues O'.).[1]

The Ecole Polytechnique, as much a civil institution as were the other three, was militarized by Napoleon in 1804 upon his return from Italy. He assigned to the Polytechnique the motto of *Pour la patrie, les sciences et la gloire* (Science and Glory for the Nation), an expression whose meaning has changed and now connotes Nation, Science and Morality.[2] The school remains under the sponsorship of the defense ministry, which provides the institution's budget and its dean, a brigadier-general of engineers. Its students earn a monthly salary.

Among the most famous graduates of the Ecole Polytechnique are names intimately associated with the development of science and technology: Henri Poincaré, mathematics; Ferdinand Foch, general; André Citroën, automobiles; Alfred Sauvy, demography; Louis Armand, railways; Joseph Joffre, general; August Comte, sociology; François Arago, geodesy and astronomy; L. J. Gay-Lussac, physics and chemistry; Augustin Cauchy, mathematics; and M. F. Sadi Carnot, physics.

In its first two centuries, the specialized school produced 50,000 scientist-engineers for the military and civil services, for industry and education. Today the institution is coeducational and takes in annually a few non-French students. In the 1990s reforms were instituted whereby graduates are now equipped for employment in industry (50 per cent), research (25 per cent), and the engineering disciplines involved in service to the nation (25 per cent). 'Research' here signifies almost entirely applied research, especially basic technological research, including investigations pursued in behalf of the arms industry.

WHENCE THE TALENT?

Military-research talent is drawn from various sources. In the nineteenth century Canadian-born Simon Newcomb, astronomer and philosopher of science, was assimilated as a rear-admiral in the United States Navy through his work as a 'positional astronomer' and by his career-long, critical stance against the lack of methodical approach to social problems. Curiously enough, Newcomb was also a political economist who even attempted to bring the paranormal sciences within the ken of scientific knowledge[3] (ultimately, he stopped trying). Along with specialists such as Charles Darwin in Britain, Ernest Renan in France and Gregor Mendel in Austria-Hungary, Newcomb helped the public acquire a new faith in the scientific method and, thus, in science itself.

In Berlin during the First World War, well before pronouncing himself publicly opposed to armed conflict, Albert Einstein helped redesign aircraft wings and collaborated with Hermann Anschütz Kaempfe in the development of the first gyrocompass – of which Einstein became a patentholder. The gyrocompass was immediately installed in German submarines, yet in 1917 Einstein communicated to a friend, H. Zangger, 'Our entire much-praised technological progress, and civilization generally, could be compared to an axe in the hand of a pathological criminal.'[4]

One of several co-inventors of the submarine-related ASDIC-sonar was physicist Paul Langevin. The socially conscious Langevin studied under physical chemist J.-B. Perrin and physicist J. J. Thomson; he created the modern view of magnetism. In the early 1920s he took political sides with the destitute in a vanquished Germany. After the Third Reich defeated France in 1940, Langevin (by then almost 60 years old) was outspokenly anti-Nazi and placed under house arrest. His daughter perished at Auschwitz, his son-in-law was executed, while the physicist himself sought refuge in neutral Switzerland.

Between the two world conflicts, a Hungarian engineering physicist trained in Budapest and Göttingen helped confirm Einstein's views concerning the kinetic conception of heat (1912) regarding the specific heats of certain solids. He was Theodor von Kármán, who also uncovered the vortices in the wake produced by fluid flow around a cylinder. These vortices, now bearing his name, are capable of creating destructive forces such as those that destroyed the Tacoma Narrows bridge in 1940. He left Germany in 1928 to build wind tunnels in the Soviet Union. Then, passing through another kind of turbulence – China of the 1930s – von Kármán made his way to Japan for more wind-tunnel work. There he collaborated in designing the Mitsubishi Rei-rei pursuit aircraft, better known to the Allies as the Zero fighter[5] before establishing himself in the United States. His American contribution enabled the United States 'to become a world leader in the aerospace industry'.[6] The ex-Hungarian's laboratory at the California Institute of Technology became NASA's Jet Propulsion Laboratory. Von Kármán also became a leading light, together with his Czech-American engineering disciple and artist, Frank Malina, in the International Astronautical Federation.

During the Second World War, the major belligerents developed strategies for ensuring at least a limited supply of new students in the physical and engineering sciences, in mathematics, chemistry, medicine, and communications and cryptography – as well as in selected foreign languages. The Japanese, for example, enabled promising students to stay on at university, provided that they also took courses in military subjects. Aeronautical and mechanical engineering were strongly favored disciplines for both students and their military adminstrators; advanced physics, chemistry and biology were not. Two young technical graduates already serving in the Imperial Japanese Navy as engineers, Morita Akio and Ibuka Masaru, met during a wartime symposium.[7] Their association led them to found, after hostilities, a small firm making communication equipment, Tsûshin Kôgyô, today's Sony Corporation.

Biologist John Kendrew served as scientific advisor to Britain's RAF, wearing the uniform of a wing commander. Later (in the 1970s) Kendrew chaired the Defense Scientific Advisory Council – work for which he was knighted. He and his teacher, Max Perutz, created what is now the Laboratory of Molecular Biology at Cambridge University, where they worked on the structure of human muscle protein. Their achievements on the structure of its molecules earned them the Nobel Prize for Chemistry (1962). A strong believer in European cohesion and global unity, Kendrew became the first director-general of the European Molecular Biology Laboratory in Heidelberg, and ultimately served for six years as president of the International Council of Scientific Unions.

Great Britain, with Canada and the other British dominions of the time, strove to maintain a wartime population of university undergraduates. The Soviet Union and, later, the United States observed the same policy. General Charles de Gaulle, the Free French leader in exile, insisted on having scientific advisors among his closest aides; it was his physicists who expanded France's postwar activities in nuclear energy. And Australian-born physicist and Nobelist William Lawrence Bragg put his own experience in the previous conflict – locating artillery – to the plotting of incoming V2 missiles from the German side.[8]

MILITARY RESEARCHERS AS TARGETS

When the Allies of the Second World war 'got wind of the threat of attack by German rocket-propelled missions, their suspicions were dismissed with incredulity [*sic*] by scientists who declined to believe the Germans capable of making such weapons.'[9]

Germany, far more hard-pressed for young military recruits (and forced to draw heavily from young male populations in the occupied countries), was less successful in keeping its scientific pipeline filled. The German experience among the wartime scientific communities was also unique in another fashion. The night raid mounted by Britain's Royal Air Force in the early morning hours of 18 August 1943 on the R&D base for V2 and some V1 missiles, at Peenemünde on Germany's Baltic coast, may be the only foray during hostilities whose mission order specifically targeted research personnel. Bomber Command's Operation Order No. 176 of 9 July 1943, signed by the Command's senior air-staff officer,[10] stated in its introduction,

> The destruction of this experimental station, the large factory work-shops and the *killing of the scientific and technical experts* would retard the production of this new equipment and contribute largely to increasing the effectiveness of the bomber offensive [emphasis added].[11]

Reinforcing this mission order were the intelligence and target briefings given to air crews immediately before the sortie.

Peenemünde was responsible for R&D on the V2 weapon (in German parlance, the A4, as we saw in Chapter 1) and subsidiary development and testing related to the V1 and other weapons, but the British wanted to limit knowledge *among their own personnel* of enemy activities so as not to demoralize the military or cause panic in the civil population if the existence of advanced weapons in Germany became public knowledge. Bomber crews learned only that their target was a technical center developing sophisticated radio direction-finding equipment. There was

> some surprise among the men who were told that the housing estate [in Peenemünde] was to be their target; it was obvious that women and children would be hit. [The] crews were told that this was unfortunate, but that it was essential that the top scientists were killed: it was no good destroying the laboratories and workshops if the scientists survived and were left free to start all over again.[12]

One of the German research scientists working at Peenemünde, Siegfried Winter, later recalled what he perceived during the British raid. 'I began to realize that here I was, possibly sitting on the end of an English bomb, yet during the day I was working at preparing exactly the same thing, in rocket form, to send to the English.'[13] Thousands of the technicians working at Peenemünde and subsidiary stations were forced laborers who came from Russia, Poland, the Low Countries and France. Many of these were victims, together with their German co-workers, of the RAF raid on this research community on the Baltic coast.

How damaging, in fact, was the British aerial expedition of nearly 600 bombers that left from 38 airfields in Britain to drop 2,000 tonnes of bombs on Peenemünde? Chief scientist Wernher von Braun and the base commander, Walter Dornberger (an artilleryman by now holding the rank of major-general), emerged from the raid unscathed. The specialist responsible for the V2's propulsion department, Walter Thiel, and the chief production-maintenance engineer, Erich Walther, were the only major personnel casualties. 'The catalogue of destruction', according to British researcher Martin Middlebrook, 'does not contain a single item of scientific importance.'[14] The demolition of the Peenemünde facility, as was confirmed in an assessment conducted after hostilities, delayed the ability of the Germans to resist Allied military pressure by no more than two to three months. Yet the British raids *were* a retarding action: the delay equaled the period between the June 1944 landings of the Allied expeditionary force in France and the commencement of the V2 raids in September of the same year.[15] The missiles could have been used to repel the landing force, but the weapons were not ready.

Farther east, early in the German–Soviet war, promising students in the USSR were evacuated far from the front. We have seen that 18-year-old Yuri Novozhilov, from a family of physicians in Leningrad, found himself studying basic and theoretical physics far from home (Chapter 5). He was spared from military service, surviving the war to become a well-known theoretician in particle physics. Another young Leningrader of strong mathematical bent, Aleksandr N. Kholodilin, was drafted into the anti-aircraft artillery early in the war where he made a direct contribution to the defense of his native city. He also froze his hands while working calculating tables during attacks by enemy aircraft along the city's much-harassed perimeter, and had great difficulty thereafter in writing symbols, equations, or even ordinary notes. Kholodilin survived the war and became a specialist in naval hydrodynamics.[16]

FROM FIRST THOUGHTS TO FIRM DESIGN

How does transition occur from conception and design to military invention? Fifteenth-century Leonardo da Vinci was an unsurpassed craftsman and pragmatist, yet he is often still referred to as a 'scientist'. He developed, indeed, his own experiments in physics, mechanics, anatomy and mathematics. A 'lifelong distrust of bookish knowledge and training'[17] attracted him in the 1480s, however, to employment by the Duke of Milan, Ludovico Sforza. Leonardo executed for the

Milanese nobleman, besides numerous paintings, plans for hydraulic works, military architecture and weapons (and intricate weddings and other festivities). Later, in 1499, he developed a defensive system against the Turkish forces besieging Venice.

The artist later spent six years in the service of Cesare Borgia, serving in the papal troops reconquering Romagna and the Marches. Then, after a stint as military engineer during the Florentine war against Pisa (during which he came up with a remarkable plan to deny Pisa access to resupply made via the Tyrrhenian Sea), Leonardo did some scientific illustrating, sculpture and engineering back in Milan between 1506 and 1513. For the three remaining years of his life, Leonardo was in the service of the French king, François I, as consultant-in-residence (but little more) at Amboise in the Loire valley.

Biographers have had some difficulty in ascribing clear motives to Leonardo for his impressively original work for clients high in political-military standing. Clues may lie in the nearly 14,000 pages of note-book records, renowned for their disorderliness (although only about 3,500 of these have survived). 'Unlike Giotto, Dante, or Brunelleschi, he seemed to have no civic loyalty ... He willingly accepted commissions from the Medici, the Sforzas, the Borgias, or French kings – from the popes or their enemies.'[18]

We have as concrete vestiges few of Leonardo's finished works, and his military projects are conspicuous by their existence on paper only. Working models of these designs were made by others, posthumous to Leonardo's own lifetime of 67 years. Da Vinci realized, however, that 'technical advances depend on scientific knowledge' and that the latter relies, in turn, on mathematical proof; he was thus able to imagine 'aircraft, submarines, and many other inventions' that materialized only centuries later.[19]

Richard W. Hamming, a computer mathematician who at the age of 80 still taught at the US Naval Postgraduate School in Monterey, California, entered his chosen field via the Manhattan Engineer District project. Hamming often asked himself, during the mid-1940s, why the task of designing the bomb,'an engineering job if he ever saw one', was being pursued by a group of young research scientists instead of by engineers. Hamming concluded, most unorthodoxly, that 'engineering schools do not prepare students to work at the frontier of knowledge. Rather ... they prepare them to do run-of-the-mill work.'[20]

This view overlooks the pioneering work done by many engineers in both military and civil applications of scientific knowledge. The Montgolfier brothers, lacking engineering degrees (there were none yet), were inveterate tinkerers and defiant problem-solvers. The

Wright brothers were bicycle technicians who lacked university-level training. Yet they learned aerodynamics studiously, observing the maneuverings of birds in flight. It is true that the great test pilots of the new age of aviation – the twentieth century – were for the most part aeronautical engineers, as have been the pioneering pilots and co-commanders of manned space vehicles. While these technologists did not design, they proved the designed product true and fit for flight by others.

MULTI- TO INTERDISCIPLINARY

Then astronomers and chemists entered military research. Edwin P. Hubble was to become the scientist responsible for the cosmological theory of an expanding universe, developed between the 1920s and 1950s and strengthened by the work of numerous others. He was at the point of receiving his doctorate in 1917 and accepting a post at the Mount Wilson Observatory in Pasadena when war broke out between Germany and his native United States. Hubble had previously been a Rhodes scholar at Oxford University, an experience that left him with a strong affective relationship with Great Britain. So the young scientist joined the armed forces immediately after receiving his PhD in May 1917. He

> thrived in the military setting ... Soon after the Japanese attack on Pearl Harbor [in 1941], Hubble joined the staff of the US Army's Ballistic Missile Research Laboratory ... where he applied his early astronomical training to directing calculations of artillery-shell trajectories.[21]

During the Second World War, while at the Aberdeen Proving Ground the eminent astronomer and former major 'spent an afternoon test-firing bazookas, at great personal risk, to pinpoint a design flaw'.[22] A small trend among cosmic scientists became a permanent pattern until, towards the end of the twentieth century, one estimate stated that 'half of US astrophysicists are engaged in weapons research'.[23]

TWO NOTABLE CHEMISTS

How did the scientifically based 'Haber's constant' – the product of the concentration of a substance as parts per million in a fixed volume multiplied by time in minutes – become, during the First World War, the measure of effectiveness of chemical agents as weapons?[24] Visitors to the National Gallery in Ottawa are vividly reminded of the human sequel to the work of the German chemist, Fritz Haber, against Canadian and other infantry in Belgium (April 1915) by William Roberts's painting, *The First German Gas Attack at Ypres*. A comparable work by John Singer Sargent, *Gassed* (1918), is on display at the Imperial War Museum in London.

The Canadians found themselves adjacent to the troops hardest hit by the gas, a French territorial division and a division of Algerian infantry, all of them deployed north of the small Belgian rural community of Ypres. At 1700 hours on 22 April came a German bombardment, 'as sudden as it was severe'. The attack proved to be 'a dramatic forewarning of the enemy's power to upset preconceived ideas'.[25]

Fritz Haber, a German chemist, was among the many scientists and engineers working for his country during the First World War. He had achieved his place in the pantheon of research, before the conflict, by co-developing the Haber-Bosch process for the synthesis of ammonia from its elements – for which he would win the Nobel Prize for Chemistry awarded in 1919. Haber had obtained his doctorate at the Technical University of Karlsruhe, where he became professor of physical chemistry in 1908. A colleague described Haber as of lively spirit, impulsive, even capricious, a good lecturer who could discuss amicably almost any subject. His second wife, Clara Immerwahr, was the first woman to obtain a doctorate of science from the University of Breslau.

With the aid of his young British assistant Robert Le Rossignol, Haber was able to synthesize ammonia from hydrogen and nitrogen by resorting to new laboratory conditions: a temperature of 200°C and pressure exceeding 200 atmospheres, using as catalyst osmium (a rare metal – later supplanted by cheaper iron combined with aluminum, calcium and potassium oxides). In July 1909 Haber and Le Rossignol produced some 70 drops/minute of synthetic ammonia in the presence of directors of the world's largest chemical producer, Badische Anilin und Soda Fabriken (today's BASF). Four years later, on the eve of the Great War, Badische Anilin was producing commercially about 4 tonnes of synthetic ammonia daily.

In 1914 the blockade of German ports by the Royal Navy cut off Chile as Germany's source of nitrates for both fertilizer and munitions. The Germans were able to confiscate 20,000 tonnes of Chilean saltpeter found in Antwerp. (In all probability Germany's shortage of industrial nitrates might, otherwise, have caused it to negotiate a peace during the first year of the conflict.[26]) With war declared, Haber was appointed a reserve captain and worked to the point of exhaustion to develop toxic gases that could be used in the field: chlorine delivered not by projectile (the Hague Conventions of 1899 and 1907 outlawed this) but released from thousands of 100-kg containers deployed near the enemy's trench system.

Haber appears to have seen himself as a technical superstar, explaining to scientific colleagues such as Otto Hahn that Imperial Germany's use of gas was justified by the first use of (tear) gas by the French against German troops in December 1914. First use by the French was not true, however, according to his principal biographers, Dietrich Stolzenberg and son Ludwig F. Haber. A few weeks later Russian troops on the Rawka river west of Warsaw were attacked by a non-lethal lachrymatory gas, xylyl bromide, known to German military engineers as *T-stoff*. Ambient temperature caused this T-substance to solidify,[27] which invalidated its effectiveness.

Haber's tactical aim on the Western Front was to pierce the front lines with gas, over a distance of 25km, allowing German infantry to break through the British–French trenches. All German troop commanders refused to take part in this assault with the exception of Prince Albrecht of Württemberg, who faced the Allies in fierce combat at Ypres. German observers of the initial gas attack included, besides Hahn, James Franck and Gustav Hertz – on whom Nobel prizes (not related to the war, of course) would also later be conferred. Max Born, another future Nobelist, refused to be present.

After delays in launching the first attack by German *Pionierkommando* troops, the fifth alert occurred on the afternoon of 22 April, when 150 tonnes of chlorine were released from 6,000 pressurized cylinders in ten minutes over a sector 7,000 m wide, near Langemarck outside Ypres. The Franco-Algerian units were routed, but the Germans themselves (who were still without promised masks) were impeded by pockets of gas. Nightfall came, saving the day for the Allies, despite 5,000 killed and around three times as many injured by the toxic clouds.[28]

French and British forces retaliated in kind. Surviving soldiers were invalided out, many of whom finally coughed themselves to death. The professional activity of chemist Haber, who was back in Berlin by 1 May 1915 to receive friends at dinner, was the direct cause later the same night of his wife's suicide, using Haber's service pistol. Fourteen-year old Ludwig Haber (whose mother was Haber's first wife), awakened by a gunshot, found his stepmother in a pool of blood in the family's garden. 'Haber was, without a doubt, the originator of chemical warfare', the Nobel-winning biologist Max Perutz maintains.[29]

James B. Conant, the chemist mentioned previously, served during the First World War as a research scientist in the United States Army's chemical warfare service. He participated in the development of the toxic gas, lewisite, intended to replace the less-effective mustard gas stocked until then by a number of governments. Conant was known to make little distinction between using rifle cartridges or poison gas to kill an enemy. For him, lewisite was to be the grand American toxic agent that would win the First World War.

During the 1920s, Conant became prominent in the study and teaching of chemistry, married the daughter of the first American laureate of the Nobel Prize for Chemistry (Theodore W. Richards), became a member of the National Academy of Sciences, and at the age of 40 was named president of Harvard University. In 1940, before his country was directly involved in war, Conant took an active role in Washington to muster scientists committed to serve national defense. He was a proponent of intervention in the conflict then under way in Europe and very much a believer in the idea that, in the twentieth century, an armed United States would assure a *Pax Americana* to supplant the British hegemony of the previous century.[30]

Conant advocated that the atom bomb be used against Japan, without warning. The shock thus produced would not only persuade the Japanese to surrender, reasoned Conant, it would also convince both Americans and Soviets that international supervision over nuclear energy was essential. Once thermonuclear weapons had entered the geostrategic scene, Conant believed, the USSR could be induced to enter into a pact intended specifically to rid the world of nuclear arms.

There were doubts, nevertheless, in Conant's mind. He feared that the adoption of nuclear energy for the production of electricity could be used to mask the intentions of a state bent on the production of weapon-grade radioactive fuel. He was probably the first informed scientist willing to abandon the tight secrecy then surrounding most aspects of nuclear policy in exchange for obtaining Soviet willingness to permit inspections of their own nuclear facilities.

Conant's faith in his wish for international control over nuclear arms shifted somewhat as a result of the Korean War that began in 1950. In the same year the chemist and university head helped form the Committee on the Present Danger. The Committee's membership was one of mainly conservative, well-connected citizens from many walks of life who believed that their consciousness of the nuclear peril should be communicated to governmental insiders – much in the spirit of the Pugwash Conferences (founded in 1957, also in some desperation, under the auspices of Albert Einstein and Bertrand Russell).

In 1953, President Eisenhower named Conant the American high commissioner to occupied West Germany, where he helped establish a policy of keeping a large American military force in Europe while resisting rearmament of the Germans. With the emergence in 1955 of the Federal Republic of Germany, Conant was named ambassador, a post he occupied for two years before returning to Boston, to analyze there the deterioration of secondary education in American cities. He was not to realize 'his early ambition to join a president's cabinet'.[31]

Conant's attitudes on keeping Germany unarmed, and aspiring himself to a major role in government, were replaced by his championship of a policy of nuclear deterrence, which led, ultimately, to President Eisenhower's proposals during the late 1950s to negotiate test bans on nuclear weapons.

THE WORKING ATMOSPHERE

In what conditions do scientists and development engineers usually work on military objectives? As might be expected, their research is conducted in conditions of physical security well conceived and usually well policed – yet there have been major leaks such as the American H-bomb secrets to the USSR and, possibly, later to China between 1995 and 1999.

Perhaps of as much concern to military-research managers is how security considerations govern an essential part of the life of a 'normal' researcher: subjecting his or her work to peer review before release for publication. Competitiveness, in the intellectual sense of the term, tends to erode as the military (or even civil) scientist discovers isolation pervading the everyday goals of thorough scientific investigation in an otherwise democratic environment. The National Academy of Sciences and the United States Army, for example, as a result of an admirable exercise in self-examination of professional performance, in 1983 issued the following as a policy recommendation under the heading Opportunities for Professional Growth and Recognition:

> The Army and its laboratory managers should continue to encourage graduate training for its professionals, publication of their significant research and development results, their participation in technical conferences, *their communication with peers at other institutions*, and their job mobility within and among laboratories [emphasis added].[32]

The Soviets took their security precautions to extremes, not permitting R&D scientists and engineers to acquire exit visas in order to travel abroad to technical meetings, or to meet foreigners whose disciplines brought them to international conferences being held within the former USSR or its satellite states.[33] The working sphere of professional contacts was thus extremely limited in the Soviet Union. This was a world apart, compensated for by the specialist's remunerations: normally twice what his or her counterpart was paid in universities and in the research institutes of the Academies of Sciences, housing of better quality than outside the elite communities, often access to special shopping services and food supply, as well as special recreational facilities. These specialists worked in laboratories using equipment and research materials, such as fine chemicals, that were in short supply or lacking in civil laboratories. Little effort was spared to prevent the overall economy's shortages from affecting the specialist's R&D effort for the military.

For reasons not easily fathomed (given the strong mathematical tradition in Russia), the equivalent in the former Soviet Union of Silicon Valley was centered in the Caucasian 'republic' of Armenia rather than in the principal Russian Federation. The Yerevan Computer Research Institute, employing some 5,000 people, was involved in work 'so secret that ordinary Armenians did not know what went on' within its buildings downtown. Forty per cent of the mainframe computers intended for the military forces were, in fact, designed there. With the demise of the Soviet Union, the four brothers Martirossian – Armen, Karen, Babken and Gurgen – splintered away from the research center and formed a private firm of their own called Aragast B. As a commercial undertaking, this company soon specialized in software applications, compiling computerized dictionaries in Arabic, Armenian and Russian for use in schools as far distant as California.[34]

The military workplace itself, whether in Yerevan or elsewhere, has consistently posed the special problems of security mentioned above even in a republican, non-totalitarian setting. In the United States, France, Great Britain, Germany and Japan, barbed wire and guards enclose the research establishment, access to which is often authorized only via a recognition system based on identity badges, or magnetized 'smart' cards, or an electronic key code used at points of entry and exit, or even combinations of these systems – methods that may soon be replaced by an electronic sweep of the entrant's retinal characteristics.

Closer to the work locale, secret ('classified') work often takes place within special precincts of a larger research, design or manufacturing center. Robert Burgelman and Modesto Maidique, teachers of research management, point out in *Strategic Management of Technology and Innovation* the existence in some firms and other institutions of *skunk works*.[35] Skunk works are 'an unusual organizational technique to expedite new product design and introduction' using a specialized task force composed of personnel drawn from a variety of units within the same firm. This task force 'is assigned separate facilities, sometimes with extra security against industrial espionage', with the aim of recapturing 'the advantage of the small company: high motivation, focused purpose … and intensive and informal communication with a minimum of organizational barriers'. There are disadvantages to this *ad hoc* arrangement, however, since its effects can be disruptive elsewhere in the organization. Overuse of the skunk-works mode 'reduces opportunities for specialization, economies of scale (experience-curve economics), and routinizing of procedures'.

The public is familiar with some of the more sensational military output of the skunk works. Two examples are:

- the Lockheed U-71 reconnaissance aircraft – an outstandingly high-performance platform for high-resolution aerial photography[36] – shot down by the Soviets in 1960 and the cause of a major political altercation between Moscow and Washington; and
- the development by the Americans of the Stealth fighter-bomber capable of evading location by radar.

A variant of the skunk works is the situation found in countries such as Iraq, Libya and North Korea. In the last, UN inspectors found some of the critical installations half-hidden by earthen camouflage or else built in tunnels, and at least one other installation completely underground. There is also question of the real purposes of the Great Man-Made River project in Libya. This is a system of tunnels 4 m wide declared by the government in Tripoli to be for the transport of water from distant aquifers in the country's southern desert to the urban coast of the Mediterranean Sea. The route passes through Mount Tarhuna, site of a suspected plant assembling biological and chemical arms. A paradoxical feature of this huge civil-engineering project is that foreign firms have the main contracts, with peak employment of 12,000 workers from *outside* Libya[37] (whose population is only 3 million and not technically proficient). In Afghanistan, the Taliban took refuge from aerial bombs and missiles, in withdrawing from engagements with the Northern Alliance, in grottoes and caverns (although they had little science or technology to conceal).

In Iraq the production director of toxic weapons, Rihab Rashida Taha, is a biologist who after the Gulf War played cat-and-mouse with UN inspectors seeking data on the true production statistics of Iraq's overkill inventory. Taha ('Dr Germ'), British-trained, took the job in the late 1980s as her 'patriotic duty' and made it her mission to keep the UN's Special Commission on Iraq guessing as to how much aflatoxin (perhaps 2,200 liters), anthrax (8,500 liters?), botulinum (19,000 liters?), *Clostridium perfringens* (340 liters?), ricin (10 liters?), VX and other pernicious agents have been produced or destroyed.[38] Taha worked under the supervision of the designer of Baghdad's germ-warfare program, Nassir Hindawi (a microbiologist holding an American doctorate), whom the Iraqi leadership did all it could to prevent from being interviewed by UN inspectors. The Iraqis went to some pains to explain that Hindawi had been imprisoned because of his plans to defect abroad.[39]

REMUNERATION AND EQUIPMENT

Organization and money are almost as critical in military as in civil research, although there may be more of both in the case of the armed forces. Governments may sometimes unconsciously make the military key providers of the means whereby universities are able to pioneer in selected fields of scientific research. There are occasional efforts, too, to encourage military research to pay for itself.

In the United States, for example, once the Second World War had ended, the newly created Office of Naval Research (ONR) suddenly found itself in a position of both authority and financial power over research conducted beyond its own precincts. ONR came officially into existence only in August 1946, when the navy still had wartime funds to spend on R&D. In that month, a full year after the end of hostilities, the navy handed over $24 million in contracts to 81 universities and non-academic (mainly industrial) laboratories.[40] Such influence had an effect, inevitably, on the style as well as the substance of the research ordered.[41]

A major designer of optical systems, inventor Edwin M. Land, lent his talents to the military during the Second World War, thereby advancing photographic progress enormously. Second only to Thomas Edison in the number of patents held by an individual, Land had developed during the 1930s both polarizing elements for light transmission and lenses made of plastics. A costly component of polarizers at the time was quinine – already used as a malaria remedy. By seeking a replacement for quinine, no longer available because of the Japanese occupation of Southeast Asia, Land plunged into medical research too. He knew that his experience could help solve problems of a military nature: among them color filtering for reconnaissance photos, controlling glare and reflection, and using lenses in other than spherical form. After the war Land perfected instant photography via the Polaroid camera as well as image-reconnaissance by satellite, and collaterally contributed to the creation of NASA.[42]

The management of research destined to be used by the military (for example, technical planning and supervision of the transformation of science into needed technology) presents a structural problem in the market economies. In these countries ministers of defense are virtually never military personnel, a tradition in keeping with the tenets of rule by law and civil leadership. These ministers are almost as infrequently scientists or engineers, since technical specialists are seldom active within the leadership of political parties.

In the mid-1990s the Americans departed from this tenet, and named a mathematician and engineer as their secretary of defense. William J. Perry joined President Clinton's administration, after the election of November 1992, as deputy secretary of defense. He was promoted secretary (minister) a year later. Perry had previously served as the Department of Defense's director of research and engineering in Jimmy Carter's presidency, 1977–80. He fostered the development of cruise missiles, laser-guided aerial bombs, the F-117 Stealth fighter-bomber and the B-2 bomber. But he also concentrated on reform of the purchasing system used by the American military, and helping to save certain industrial sectors considered crucial in case of war.

Problematic in military procurement (every nation experiences the difficulty) is the usually unique nature of specifications for complex, high-performing or hard-use technical products used by the military services:

- the technology is often over-engineered by civil standards, purposely, to meet the rigors of use in battle or extreme environments (air, sea or land);
- the contracting methods applying to this procurement are similarly specific to precise operational needs; and
- the resulting cost of armaments, accessories and spare parts is high.

The B-2 bomber, for instance, rose in estimated cost 11 times during the 15 years elapsing between design-board conception and first manufacture in series: from $200 million per aircraft in the late 1970s to $2.2 billion each when production began in 1994.

POOLING RESEARCH TASKS

Scientists work for the military, too, through defense pacts and regional defense arrangements. An ambitious undertaking of NATO before, during and after the collapse of the Soviet Union is its Science Program. Consisting of short (four-day) workshops and longer (two-week) 'institutes' – most of which are oriented strictly to the demands of civil science – the Science Program admits participants from outside as well as from within NATO, and did so even during the most glacial years of the Cold War. Since then, NATO's Science Program has concentrated even more on civil themes but has added to its curriculum topics related to disarmament.

Characteristic of the civil subjects offered by NATO in 1995, a typical transition year between Cold War and times of lessened (or of other forms of) stress, were the following:

Advanced Research Workshops	*Advanced Study Institutes*
Analytical use of fluorescent probes in oncology (in macromolecules)	Biological magnetic resonance
	Fluctuations, self-assembly and evolution of biomaterials
Analysis of heterogeneous surfaces on nanometer scale	Quantum optics of confined systems
New methods in quantum theory	Solvents, self-organization of polymers
Crystals: supramolecular materials	Mathematical models in climatology and environment
Using long-term datasets to evaluate soil matter	
Modeling soil erosion by water	
Spatial and evolutionary responses of terrestrial biota	

Besides these topics, which may be construed as dual-purpose objectives of research, the workshops and institutes also offered, then and later, themes more directly germane to the atmosphere of arms reduction and environmental security, considered a matter of priority:

- scientific advances in alternative demilitarization technologies;
- pulsed metal-vapor lasers: physics and emerging applications in industry, medicine, science;
- recent advances in ground-water pollution control and rmediation;
- environmental and non-environmental determinants of the East–West gap in life expectancy;
- disturbance and recovery of Arctic terrestrial ecosystems;
- magnetism: a supramolecular function;
- mathematics of long-range aperiodic order.

The institutes and workshops take place in countries signatory to the Treaty and at selected sites beyond the Treaty states. Attendance at the workshops is mainly by invitation, although others qualified by education and experience may be admitted. Participation in the institutes is, according to a NATO circular, 'open to all suitably qualified applicants irrespective of nationality, upon application to [the Institute's] contact person'.[43] In 1998, NATO announced creation of a Mediterranean Dialogue, extending its area of research and discourse to Morocco, Mauritania, Tunisia, Egypt, Jordan and Israel.[44]

Ten years after the fall of the Berlin Wall, NATO's Science Programme was restructured to permit exchanges with most of the new countries formerly in the Soviet Union, and its assistant secretary-general for scientific and environmental affairs (France's Yves Sillard) paid official visits to Armenia, Georgia and Moldova as well as to Bulgaria.[45] By 2001, NATO was offering short courses in river and estuarine management (Idaho), geographical information systems in health-risk reduction (Croatia), hydrogeological problems in urban areas (Azerbaijan), and assessment and remediation of contaminated sites (Czech Republic), among other civil topics.

OTHER PATHS OF INNOVATION

In dreaming up new weapons there are sometimes ideas for the taking, sometimes talent for sale. James Marshall-Cornwall, who after the fall of France in June 1940 commanded the British Army's III Corps, was a guest of his prime minister for dinner at the official country residence, Chequers. General Marshall-Cornwall's table neighbor was Frederick Lindemann (Lord Cherwell), Winston Churchill's scientific advisor. The Prime Minister made the round of the table, asking each military and civil specialist present how his part of the war was progressing. At Lindemann's turn, he took from his pocket the standard rifleman's hand grenade, of First World War vintage.

> This, Prime Minister, is the inefficient Mills bomb, issued to the British infantry. It is made of twelve different components which have to be machined in separate processes. Now *I* have designed an improved grenade, which has fewer machined parts and contains a 50 per cent greater bursting charge.

Upon hearing this, Churchill ordered another table companion, Field Marshal Sir John Dill, chief of the Imperial General Staff, to have the Mills grenade 'scrapped at once and replaced by the Lindemann grenade'. The Prime Minister's wish was to prove far easier said than done, however, because orders for millions of the Mills device had already been placed with manufacturers in Britain and the United

States.[46] The anecdote may be another illustration, at the same time, of the wisdom of the engineer's 'if it ain't broke, don't fix it' philosophy.

Research fields may seem greener on the other side of the nationalist fence, given this (very human) quest of the scientist or engineer. The researcher disgruntled by conditions at home may thus be a candidate for recruitment by a foreign power to work there on new armaments. During the twentieth century's last two decades a typical case, among others, was that of the physical chemist Bruno Stemmler. This scientist worked in the then Federal Republic of Germany on the design and testing of gas centrifuges at MAN Technologie, in Munich. When Stemmler turned 50 in the early 1980s, he took stock of his situation and concluded that his creativity was not adequately appreciated and that he was insufficiently remunerated: a midlife crisis at the test-bench, as it were.

The centrifuges that the German scientist designed and tested were intended to produce enriched uranium as fuel for nuclear reactors, MAN having a vital role in the European Urenco consortium providing enriched uranium for civil reactors. Officials in Iraq learned, through a German firm regularly making purchases for Iraq in Germany and Switzerland, that Stemmler might be available to work abroad. The German researcher made two visits to Iraq, discreetly, in 1988–89. German security agencies learned of this, visited his home and, armed with a search warrant, interrogated him. The charge lodged against him was revealing secret information concerning the centrifuges.

Der Spiegel got wind of the story and told all. MAN, fearful of the impact of the revelation on its contracts at home and in the United States, suspended Stemmler. In 1991, the *Sunday Times* printed its version of the Stemmler story, and a year later a cerebral stroke incapacitated the scientist. The Iraqis had wished, by employing Stemmler and others like him, to foreshorten the long and costly R&D phase required to assemble and perfect centrifuges usable in the development of nuclear weapons. Stemmler claimed that he had not thought out the consequences of his acts, assuming that export controls – such as the restraints imposed by COCOM – would preclude strategic items falling into the wrong hands.[47]

Entirely different conditions from those Stemmler knew may prevail too, as governed (for example) by the military-budget reductions of the 1990s. In Western Europe these put pressure on governments to consolidate their largely nationalized armament firms, and any redundancies planned were bitterly opposed by trade unions. Privatization, as another solution, also led and continues to lead to reductions in force in reorganized R&D and production centers.

In job markets where unemployment rates already surpassed 10 per cent (the European Union average during the 1990s was almost 11 per cent), the restructuring of arms companies and their research laboratories meant downsizing, further aggravating the situation. Moreover, emphasizes Dominique Pestre of the Ecole des Hautes Etudes en Sciences Sociales in Paris, 'military R&D officers [today] are often no longer what they were; they have become contract managers and accountants'.[48]

With the same phenomenon occurring in California's aerospace industry, embracing telecommunications and computers as well, there was a marked lessening of employment in the decade between 1988 and 1998 (from almost 300,000 to fewer than 150,000 jobs). But during the same period employment in the motion picture and television sectors grew from 100,000 positions to 250,000. In a real turnabout, many of these posts in the entertainment world were filled by specialists migrating from highly trained, teamwork functions in aerospace firms and research centers, such as NASA's Jet Propulsion Laboratory. This continuing transfer, recorded in detail in the business pages of the mass media, prompted the *New York Times* to call this talent merger the creation of a 'military-entertainment complex'.[49]

SOME UNUSUAL REWARDS

There is often outstanding R&D being done by the civil servants and private-sector scientists and engineers working on military projects. Salaries and other compensation remain usually better than in non-military research, and prizes and awards – seldom announced publicly, but just as coveted as in the outside world – are found everywhere in this closed establishment.

To give one example of such awards: after the UN General Assembly adopted the Comprehensive Test-Ban Treaty, a team of French investigators began developing a detection system to look for certain physical indicators of nuclear explosions, whether underground, underseas or in the atmosphere. In 1999, researchers on this project from the military-applications unit of the French Atomic Energy Commission won the Commission's Nuclear Applied Research Prize. The winners were Bernard Massinon, Jean-Louis Plantet, Elisabeth Blanc and Yves Cansi,[50] named publicly.

Jean-Jacques Salomon, of the Conservatoire National des Arts et Métiers (CNAM) engineering school, has evoked the revolutionary but disputed claim of the 1790s about 'the state not needing scientists'.[51] The 'state does need scientists, of course', Salomon insists, 'but at the same time scientists need the state. How would they survive today without governmental financing?' See the views advanced in this respect by biophysicist Adriano Buzzati-Traverso, in Chapter 14.

NOTES

1 Some of the material presented here is taken from a descriptive folder, *X 94: Bicentenaire de l'Ecole Polytechnique*, Paris (1994).
2 According to Christian Marbach, organizer of Ecole Polytechnique's bicentennial year of 1994, speaking on 13 January 1994 at La Maison des Polytechniciens, Paris.
3 Albert E. Moyer, 'Simon Newcomb: Astronomer with Attitude', *Scientific American*, October 1998, pp. 62–7.
4 Alan Lightman, 'The Contradictory Genius', review of Albrecht Fölsing, *Albert Einstein: A Biography*, trans. Ewald Osers (New York, Viking, 1997) in the *New York Review of Books*, 10 April 1997, p. 19.
5 This airplane, powered by a Nakajima engine, was known as the *Reisen kanjikisen*, or Celebration Carrier-based Fighter. The Celebration was the year 1940, when the aircraft was introduced, or year 2600 of the Japanese calendar. The Zero reached its operational optimum in 1943; in the final months of the war, many exemplars were converted into one-way kamikaze missiles with young ensigns aboard as guidance system.
6 David, Ian, John and Margaret Millar (eds), *The Cambridge Dictionary of Scientists* (Cambridge, Cambridge University Press, 1996), p. 180.
7 Sakamoto Osamu, 'It's a Sony Recipe for Success', *Asahi Evening News*, 26 October 1999, p. 6.
8 James Burke, 'Sound Ideas' (Connections), *Scientific American*, August 1999, p. 81.
9 Kenneth Macksey, *Technology in War: The Impact of Science on Weapon Development and Modern Battle* (London, Arms & Armour, 1986), p. 163.
10 Bomber Command's file number of the document was BC/S.30314/Ops.
11 Martin Middlebrook, *The Peenemünde Raid, Night of 17–18 August 1943* (London, Penguin, 1988), Appendix I, p. 235.
12 Ibid., p. 78.
13 Quoted in ibid., p. 142.
14 Ibid., p. 151.
15 Ibid., pp. 229–30.
16 Discussions by the author with Kholodilin and Novozhilov, 1972–94.
17 Daniel J. Boorstin, *The Creators* (New York, Random House, 1992), p. 400.
18 Ibid., p. 401.
19 Roger Masters, *Beyond Relativism: Science and Human Values* (Hanover, NH, University Press of New England, 1993), p. 16.
20 Tekla S. Perry, Careers/'Profile: Richard W. Hamming', *IEEE Spectrum*, May 1993, pp. 80–2.
21 D. E. Osterbrock, J. A. Gwinn and R. S. Brashear, 'Edwin Hubble and the Expanding Universe', *Scientific American*, July 1993, pp. 73, 75.
22 Michael D. Lemonick, 'Edwin Hubble' Time 100 series, *Time* (Europe edn), 25 March 1999, unnumbered page.
23 James Reston, Jr, 'Collision Course', *Time* (Europe edn), 23 May 1994, p. 52.

24 L. F. Haber, *The Poisonous Cloud: Chemical Warfare in the First World War* (Oxford, Clarendon, 1986), p. 44. Much of the material that follows concerning Fritz Haber is drawn from this source, a technical research effort by son Ludwig to place his father's work in perspective concerning the evolution of chemical engineering. A more comprehensive and more technical biography is Dietrich Stoltzenberg, *Fritz Haber: Chemiker, Nobel-preisträger, Deutscher, Jude* (Weinheim, VCH Verlag, 1994), in German only.

25 Both citations are taken from B. H. Liddell Hart, *Foch: The Man of Orléans*, vol. 1 (London, Penguin, 1937), p. 181.

26 Max Perutz, 'Le cabinet du Docteur Haber', *La Recherche*, April 1997, pp. 78–84. This article is a French adaptation of Perutz's article on the same subject that appeared in the *New York Review of Books*, 20 June 1996.

27 John Keegan, *The First World War* (London, Hutchinson, 1998), pp. 213–19.

28 French and Allied medical countermeasures to gas attack are documented in detail. See, e.g. Jean-Jacques Ferrandis, 'Le service de santé des Armées face aux armes chimiques durant la guerre de 1914–18' (How Military Medical Services Dealt with Chemical Weapons during the 1914–18 War), in Claude Carlier and Guy Pedroncini (eds), *L'émergence des armes nouvelles* (The Emergence of New Arms) (Paris, Economica, 1997), pp. 149–61.

29 Ibid., p. 81. Another account of Ms Haber's death is Vaclav Smil, 'Global Population and the Nitrogen Cycle', *Scientific American*, July 1997, p. 63.

30 The definitive biography of Conant is James G. Hershberg, *James B. Conant: Harvard to Hiroshima and the Making of the Nuclear Age* (New York, Alfred A. Knopf), 1993.

31 Daniel J. Kevles, 'Pax Atomica' (review), *New Yorker*, 10 January 1994, p. 86.

32 National Research Council, Board on Army Science and Technology, *The Professional Environment in Army Laboratories and its Effect on Scientific and Engineering Performamce* (Washington, DC, National Academy Press, 1983), p. xiv.

33 An example is the 'internal exile' to Gorki imposed on the antiwar physicist, Andrei Sakharov, during the Brezhnev period. See the works of Christopher Andrew and Oleg Gordievsky on the limitations of contact imposed on holders of Soviet state secrets, including scientists and engineers; note esp. their *KGB: The Inside Story of its Foreign Operations from Lenin to Gorbachev* (New York, HarperCollins, 1990), *passim; Instructions from the Centre* (London, Hodder & Stoughton, 1991); and *More Instructions from the Centre* (London, Frank Cass, 1992).

34 Raymond Bonner, 'Amid Armenia's Economic Ruin, a Software Company is Making it', *IHT*, 28 April 1994, p. 12.

35 Robert A. Burgelman and Modesto A. Maidique, *Strategic Management of Technology and Innovation* (New York, McGraw-Hill, 3rd edn, 2000). The entry on skunk works is by H. E. Riggs.

36 Andrew and Gordievsky, *KGB: The Inside Story*, p. 469.

37 Raymond Bonner, 'Libya Builds a Mysterious Pipeline', *IHT*, 5 December 1997, pp. 1, 10.

38 Bruce W. Nelan, 'Germ Warfare', *Time* (Europe edn), 1 December 1997, pp. 22–5. See also Scott Ritter, *Endgame: Solving the Iraq Problem Once and for All* (New York, Simon & Schuster, 1999), pp. 86–8, 105.

39 Judith Miller, 'Iraqis Jail "Father" of Toxic Arms Program', *IHT*, 25 March 1998, p. 1, and subsequent reporting. Khidir Hamza, head of Saddan Hussein's nuclear-bomb program until his defection in 1994, states that '[b]ehind every

closed door in Baghdad is a scientist or an official who would like to leave'. Khidir Hamza with Jeff Stein, *Saddam's Bomb Maker: The Terrifying Inside Story of the Iraqi Nuclear and Biological Weapons Agenda* (New York, Scribner/Drew, 2000).

40 See, *inter alia*, Robert Buderi, *The Invention that Changed the World* (New York, Simon & Schuster, 1996), p. 251.

41 Ibid., p. 252, citing researchers as eminent as Bernard Lovell.

42 Biographer Victor McElheny recounts Land's civil and military accomplishments in *Insisting on the Impossible: The Life of Edwin Land* (Reading, MA, Perseus Books/Sloan Technology Series, 1998).

43 NATO, Scientific Affairs Division, *NATO Science Programme 1995 Calendar of Meetings* (reference 95/2), Brussels (1995), pp. 2–4.

44 *NATO Science and Society Newsletter*, no. 50, May 1998, p. 2.

45 Ibid., No. 51, February 1999, pp. 1–2.

46 Marshall-Cornwall recounts this in a memoir that he calls 'Mad Hatter's Dinner Party', *Wars and Rumours of Wars* (London, Secker & Warburg, 1984), as cited in Max Hastings (ed.), *Military Anecdotes* (Oxford, Oxford University Press, 1987), p. 408.

47 The tale of Stemmler is told in detail by David Albright in 'Engineer for Hire', *Bulletin of Atomic Scientists*, December 1993, pp. 29–36. COCOM, the Coordinating Committee on Multilateral Export Controls, was based in Paris, 1949–94, extending its reach to all NATO members (less Iceland) and Australia and Japan. It sought to exercise, not always successfully, severe export controls on strategic designs, goods and services.

48 In a talk on relations between science and the military given 16 March 1999 at the Ecole Normale Supérieure in Paris.

49 Andrew Pollack, 'From Science to Fiction: Military and Entertainment Industries Sweep Expertise', *New York Times*, 10 October 1997, pp. D1, D4.

50 E-mail from Site Editor, Alphagalileo (scientific news service), London, 21 September 1999.

51 Salomon, who long directed CNAM's program on Science, Technology and Society, alludes here to what the state prosecutor declaimed during the trial in 1794 of chemist Antoine Lavoisier; in a talk on 'Science and Ethics' given at the Ecole Normale Supérieure, Paris, 16 November 1998. Salomon is also the author of a philosophical analysis, *Le scientifique et le guerrier* (The Scientist and the Warrior) (Paris, Belin/Débats, 2001).

14

What Role for the Scientist in Future Wars?

'The world may be on the brink of sanity.'
David Kyd, International Atomic Energy Agency

'There is no future in war, there is no future in further suffering.'
King Hussein of Jordan[1]

Our perspective on the symbiosis between science and the military has shown how complex, sometimes subtle it is, and one bearing on the future of the human race. For three generations the specter of nuclear war has been a received idea of such dismal dimensions as to obscure other, real menaces.

REFUSE THE KING'S SHILLING?

The espousal of nuclear *deterrence* found much agreement among the nations that first used science to equip themselves with super-weapons. Other countries have since clamored, 'Why not us, too?' – with every political and moral justification. In *The Mirror Maker*, scientist Primo Levi urged the world to 'choose from that field which may render less painful and less dangerous the journey' of our con-temporaries. A public response to this search for choices came from a fellow-countryman, the biophysicist Adriano Buzzati-Traverso:

> Mankind must … choose either to stop the development of scientific activities or to eliminate nation-states. Scientists, performing the imperish-able values of science as an essential part of the culture of modern man, must refuse support for their research activities, unless it comes from genuine international agencies, and become missionaries for the establish-ment of world government.[2]

When Buzzati first penned these thoughts in the 1970s, most colleagues saw his stand as unrealistic (nation-states are not about to vanish) and tried hard to dissuade him from publishing his recommendation. But as researcher, teacher, diplomat and member of an outstanding family of achievers, Buzzati was adamant. In the 1990s, another prominent scientist, Michael Atiyah, made an even more impassioned plea as he stepped down from the presidency of The Royal Society of London: scientists, he supplicated, dissociate yourselves from military research! (Sir Michael Atiyah is now president of the Pugwash Conferences.)

In the early twenty-first century Buzzati's and Atiyah's call for scientific innocence remains infertile. The international official agencies cannot meet the financial demands already made on them, so they are not a source of research funding; a few original-research laboratories – that of the International Atomic Energy Agency at Monte Carlo, for instance, concentrating on marine radioactivity – are the exceptions. It is not thinkable that large-scale research budgets could come from non-official foundations or think-tanks. Governments will need, as today, to hold the purse strings for the continued funding of most original scientific studies and and their dissemination through education.

But suppose that the Italian biophysicist's proposal were workable. What could it hope to accomplish? The head of the department of war studies at Kings College, London, Lawrence Freedman, foresaw early in the 1990s the following:

> There are … growing opportunities for precision warfare emerging as a result of the information revolution, just as the transformation of warfare in the [nineteenth] century reflected the revolutions in transport and industrialization. Yet it is hard to conduct precision warfare in imprecise situations. As much as by technology, war has been influenced by the changing character of the state system, including colonization and the rise of mass society, and then by decolonization and the integration of trade and finance in the West … [I]n a state system that is so complex and diverse, and with such inequalities in wealth and territory, stability is no more than a fond hope. Things will never settle down, and that is why we are unlikely to be able to stop worrying about war[3]

… or about the new terrorism, Freedman could have added.

THREATS TO STABILITY

Big wars or other continuing conflict might figure prominently among the major menaces to global stability during the period until 2020–25. Chief among the threats is the proliferation of weapons intended for mass destruction: if not nuclear, then biological or chemical – or any fiendish combination of these. What other developments might we envisage by 2025? The experts agree on a baker's dozen of genuine menaces.

First, there is **the now-reality of 'using a system against itself'**: the commerical airliners turned into missiles leveled at the Twin Towers of the World Trade Center and the Pentagon – a rain of death on innocents in their thousands. Once combined with the subsequent diffusion (whoever its authors) of *Bacillus anthracis* through the American postal system, the 'fiction' of science fiction evaporated.

Second, the **current industrial revolution**, based on the fast-expanding information and life-science technologies, and a genesis of the menace just mentioned. Will this growth in knowledge of applications, swelling so greatly because of evolving science and technology, wash over much of the world or simply deepen the abyss existing between rich and poor?

Third, **the possible conflict resulting from population growth** and shifting demographic distribution. The world population of 6.2 billion is expected to increase by 50 per cent in the next 50 years. More human beings will make more and more demands on resources, including energy.

Fourth, **the irreversible growth pressure on human settlements**, especially cities. This will increase the demands for services: public space, housing, rationalization of the rural–urban ('rurban') transitional zones, combined with a straitened natural environment overall.

Fifth comes **the information explosion** as a phenomenon in itself, one also dependent on advances in science and technology. The non-material or 'virtual' civilization will leave the world's 600,000 villages still lacking electricity more and more isolated: they will have little access to the information superhighways.

Sixth, **arising threats against internal stability, security and peace**. The UN foresees deaths in developing countries multiplying increasingly from societal failure, such as failed public education, health-delivery and nutritional supply.

Seventh, **inequality, marginalization, exclusion, poverty**. One-fourth of the world's population has no access, for example, to potable water. Three billion people live on less than $2 per day.[4] Will the current situation intensify?

Eighth is **the general degradation of the planetary environment** and the availability of clean air, soil, water and biological diversity – among other resources.

Ninth is **the future of the rule of law, democracy and international governance** confronting both the new industrial revolution and the globalization process. How solid these are remains enigmatic.

Tenth **continuing globalization**. How serious an impact will it have on the economic, societal, juridical, ethical, institutional and political dimensions of most countries? Significant, too, is that the globalization's dissidents were largely muted by the events of autumn 2001.

Eleventh, **the changing roles of women** will continue to redress the imbalance of the sexes in most spheres of activity. This is important in education, research and legislation; in business and world affairs; and in social matters such as juvenile delinquency, drug use and premature pregnancy. The changing roles of women will not, alas, be uniform throughout the world.

Twelfth is **the irritation possible from intercultural contact**. As civilizations are stimulated by widening technologies, information and globalization, is the increasingly 'networked' globe its own powder keg?

Finally, the anticipated continuing rise in scientific and technological expertise can be expected to make **knowledge increasingly a power in itself**, presenting new ethical challenges.[5]

Each of these factors has its own ramifications, and the hierarchy listed here is indicative rather than prescriptive. All factors can be expected to have a bearing, even if indirect, on the outbreak of war within a country's borders or with neighbors across its frontiers and occasionally well beyond.

UNEVEN, MENACES, INCLUDING HYPERTERRORISM

The strategic theory of asymmetrical threats – whether they be informational, nuclear, biological, chemical or other terrorism by parties unwilling to attack one or several powers directly – is the element of acute instability that was added in September 2001 to the above scenarios of *future possible*. Equally menacing are the dangers to stability posed by the international traffic in drugs and its affiliated criminal activities, and by the uninhibited daily financial transactions taking place throughout the world and well beyond the control of governments or groups of nations. Then, as an extension of the globalization of industry and trade that such control implies, there are foreseeable disruptive tactics concerning export standards, international free trade and futures markets – energy supplies included.

Just as guerrilla warfare and street fighting (the latter introduced by the Civil War in Spain in the 1930s) upset traditional military doctrine in the Second World War, so is the new concept of *catastrophic terrorism* supplanting the pressures exerted earlier by the Cold War. Ordinary terrorism, according to former US secretary of defense William S. Cohen, is the handiwork of cowards who 'rejoice in the agony of their victims'. Reprisal is often difficult because the assailants hole up in remote areas where it is difficult for police or military forces to strike back. With catastrophic terrorism involving biological or chemical arms, adds Cohen, 'Deterrence is not … sufficient to prevent their use in future' because determining who made use of them can be difficult.[6]

In this respect, a typical statement by the National Research Council in Washington seeks to help the non-military medical community 'respond to chemical or biological terrorist attack' via some 60 R&D projects. This is intended to minimize the damage caused by 'a terrorist attack [through the use of] new drugs and vaccines to combat anthrax and smallpox, faster and easier-to-use chemical detectors and diagnostic tests, and communications software to improve disease surveillance and to provide information' about imminent attacks.[7] Governance was not wholly unprepared, in other words, for autumn 2001, although not as fully equipped as circumstances required.

On other fronts, banks, investment institutions and insurance operations could find their electronic fund-transfers wrecked by 'sniffer' programs. *Computer worms* might wreak havoc on national-defense databases, for example, those controlling the deployment of troops and their equipment and supplies. The potential menace is under study at the National Defense University in Washington, and the director of the Central Intelligence Agency reckoned as early as 1996 that cyber assault lies 'within the capabilities of a number of terrorist groups'.[8] Other nations – France, Britain, Germany and Japan among them – are studying the same problem. Bulgarian military researchers, a small group but with much experience developing information technology for the former Soviet forces, thought enough of these and the more orthodox capabilities in the world to launch at the end of the twentieth century a new journal, *Informatsiya i Sigurnost*, or Information & Security, a bilingual review published in Sofia.[9]

UNPAID SCIENTISTS AS A DANGER TO PEACE?

In New York the financier George Soros was perhaps more alert than governments to the plight of scientists and engineers in eastern Europe and the former USSR. Hungarian by birth, Soros joined his financial forces in the early 1990s to the International Science Foundation (annual budget: $100 million). The ISF sent payments of $500 each (equal to a year's salary) to more than 30,000 scientists, shipped books and specialized journals to libraries of the ex-Soviet

Union, and offered grants enabling researchers to attend conferences abroad. Soros thus helped significantly scientists and engineers formerly associated with weapon design to pursue their research at home without being tempted to hire out as mercenaries to nations seeking to escalate their own military-industrial potential.[10]

Concurrently voices rose in post-1991 Europe to the effect that perhaps *too little* attention was given to defense and its technical preparations. In 1993, Paul Kennedy noted that the commonality of the European Union would need more than freedom of transborder movement and the removal of tax barriers. Also required, Kennedy wrote, were 'enhanced powers for the European Parliament, and co-ordinated defense policies'.[11] The European Union's EUCLID project on long-term cooperation in defense, already under way for several years, began to be strengthened in 1994. The world of research sought to reinforce its relationship with the Western European Union (WEU) and the previously mentioned Western European Armament Group. Studies have concentrated on such themes as

- intelligent work-stations for command, communication and control;
- combinatory algorithms for military application, that is, improved real-time data processing;
- rapid pattern recognition;
- 'knowledge engineering' for military applications;
- concepts and techniques of battle simulation;
- multipurpose filtration for biological and chemical defense;
- submarine detection and related technologies;
- naval hydrodynamics, as well as hydrodynamic sound and noise,

in addition to the development of novel technologies in armament, transport and communication.[12] In 1999, the EU also got its first foreign-policy and defense coordinator, Javier Solana, who was 'trained' for the job as civilian secretary-general of NATO.

Hans A. Bethe, the Nobel laureate cited earlier and a veteran of work on thermonuclear weapons, realized that a solution to the problem of lessened military-scientific employment could best be resolved by adopting a new outlook. Bethe wrote in the *New York Times* that novel departures were needed to help the defense laboratories 'develop new technologies to free us from our dependence on fossil fuel, especially for road transport'. Elaborating, Bethe explained that former defense research centers could concentrate, for example, under the tutelage of the US National Science Foundation 'on designing cells in which liquid fuel is directly converted into electricity to drive engines, greatly increasing efficiency', and at the same time reducing polluting emissions. Other projects would include 'high-temperature superconductors for industry. Microrobotics could be very useful in medicine',[13] for surgery and vascular interventions.

Bethe's perspective was reinforced by an anonymous electronics executive quoted on another occasion: 'Our [firm's] scientists have won enough Nobel Prizes', stated this industrial leader, 'to last the company for a long time … What we need now is focused research aimed at making a profit for this company.'[14] Much of the physics community, alertly conscious of the significance of the centenary in 1997 of the discovery of the atom, could rightly claim that the twentieth century had been 'theirs' – notwithstanding the public's frequent identification of physics with the emergence of superweapons. Physics may well *not* play, however, the role of leading scientific discipline in the new century. Instead, as a member of the American Institute of Physics' Education Division foresees it, the new century will probably be that of the life sciences, 'with the genome dethroning the quark'.[15]

There is another picture, that of the scientist unemployed because of reductions in defense-supported research. The end of the Cold War reduced the possibilities for employment in both firms and universities affiliated with military programs. The situation, wrote the *New York Times*, spoiled 'the lifelong dreams of some students, throwing professionals out of work and possibly dulling the cutting edge of research itself'[16] – much of this excised research being of a purely military nature.

Early in 1994, the American director of Central Intelligence, R. James Woolsey, speculating on the generic armaments that might be used in wars of the twenty-first century, cautioned the Senate Select Committee on Intelligence that biological and chemical weapons could pose the threat previously represented by nuclear arms. He specified that some two dozen countries were seeking to construct nuclear, chemical or biological weapons.[17]

NOT KEEPING UP, RESENTMENT, ANGER

A civilization, as a sociocultural force, can cross swords with others. The Christians did this against the Muslims during the unending Crusades. From the late fifteenth to the early twentieth centuries, the world's Northern whites oppressed its Southern blacks. The Cold War was a conflict between rival politico-economic beliefs. For almost 60 years North Korea positioned itself against much of the rest of the world with the largest military force *per capita*. Efforts by some in the

Arab-Islamic world today to assure fundamentalism ('integrationism') from Morocco to Indonesia include the acquisition of new arms. In 1998 Spain estimated a capability in Algeria to produce weapons-grade plutonium, according to the newspaper *El País*. Although Algeria signed the Nuclear Non-Proliferation Treaty in 1995, it proceeded with the help of Argentina and China to expand a nuclear program that 'far exceeds' the Mahgrebian country's civil needs. The Algerian nuclear complex is centered at Birine, 250km south of the capital city of Algiers. Two heavy-water reactors are functioning there, one of which yields plutonium suitable for armaments.[18]

Virulent movements such as those in Algeria, Egypt and Afghanistan have sought to emulate the basic strategy of Iranian Muslims and their overthrow of the Shah in 1979 – namely, closing their country to foreign influence. Such episodes are reminiscent of the actions of the theocrat, Girolamo Savonarola, who in fifteenth-century Florence imposed austerity and effected reforms in justice, finance, even popular customs. He managed to bring about a division of the population between those who supported him (*piangioni*, or weepers) and his opponents (*arrabbiati*, the enraged). The piangioni demanded an exclusion of foreign influence, to keep Florentine society and culture unadulterated.

A former foreign minister of France, Claude Cheysson, believes that today's integrationists massacre their non-fundamentalist neighbors for the openness of the latter to influence from the outside world, religious or otherwise. Targets of the fundamentalists are often educators, scientists and engineers, or mass-media representatives – people whose vocations require knowledge and techniques often originating outside their world. Yet even the most fundamentalist regimes in the Muslim sphere cannot survive for long without benefit of alien inputs: economic theory and practice, management methods, scientific data, electrical power, nuclear energy, modern weapon systems. An open window on the 'infidel' world must remain, therefore, a strategic option for their leaderships.[19]

A 'different civilization' may be something quite apart, indeed, as happened in the southern hemisphere where an intriguing research drama began in 1993. At nearly midnight on 28 May an unexplained atmospheric disturbance occurred in southwestern Australia. Rippling shock waves followed bright flashes in the sky. Their origin was variously summarized as seismic (in a region of rare earthquakes), a mining incident (although blasting is forbidden at night), a strike by a meteor (itself of frequent occurrence), or ... a nuclear explosion. It was only after the biochemical-warfare incidents in Tokyo in spring 1995, involving the Aum Shinrikyô sect, that an Australian geologist named Harry Mason drew official attention to a curious fact: Aum Shinrikyô had arrived in Australia in April 1993 to purchase a large ranch, with its nearby Banjawaram Station, about 700km northeast of Perth.

Mason's apprehensions were transformed by the Australian and American governments' arrangements with an investigative group, the Incorporated Research Institutions for Seismology (IRIS), to probe the matter further. IRIS manages the world's most widespread array of seismometers, more than a hundred of which are found on all the continents. These sensitive devices detect fairly faint vibrations vectored by the Earth's rock structures; they help determine whether an explosion was of seismic origin or not.

The results of the inquiry by IRIS (led by Gregory van der Vink), according to its newsletter of autumn 1996, showed that the puzzling explosion of 1993 had a force 170 times larger than any mining event recorded in the Australian region in question. This force was tantamount to as much as 2,000 TNT-equivalent tonnes: less than one-seventh the strength of the Hiroshima bomb, yet potentially that of a small nuclear weapon. Because of the differences between the 'signatures' of nuclear and non-nuclear explosives, however, the experts tended to favor the idea of a meteoric impact. The IRIS newsletter concluded that the scenario involving a strike by a meteor 'is consistent with the eyewitness observations and with the energy levels derived from seismic records'.[20] May such scientific vigilance continue, unconfined.

TO BE READY OR NOT

Roman strategic thought, one recalls, strongly favored the way to peace as a road laid out for war. The Romans anticipated worst-case scenarios: 'If you want peace, prepare for war' was virtually the Imperium's rule of governance. Long-term preparedness and its first cousin, readiness against attack at any moment, depend naturally on both knowledge of adversaries and one's own political decisions. The world saw how a fully trained and well-equipped force could check and checkmate an adversary during the Gulf conflict of 1990–91.

William Owens, a retired US admiral, construes this new potential as the successor to earlier nuclear advantage. He and other strategists apprehend a possible vulnerability, nevertheless, to electronic attack on a nation's critical systems in everyday life: electrical power and other utilities, telecommunications, air-traffic control, banks and stock exchanges, social security services, even the essential functions of internal revenue[21] as part of a modern nation's organization and operation.

(Attacks on a postal service had not been anticipated.) All such systems, whose nerve-centers and client-support points interface directly with the public, are among the vulnerabilities of the new century.

So how complete can preparedness be in realistic terms? The information technologies have become a critical sector because they span selected surveillance systems (including defense against missiles, but not yet against terrorism), the deployment of highly precise weapons, and high-performance computers for command and control – all of these intended to mastermind a 'digital battlefield'[22] in tomorrow's conflicts. Computer 'viruses' are already a form of cyber-aggression.

The so-called 'information wars' imply that some military organizations possess *information dominance*: equipment, training and limited experience in fighting and winning battles on strictly novel terms. Closely coordinated networks of computers and other information technology evolved – in theory, at least – into definitive arms for victory for their operators in *all* the military modes: air, sea, land, logistics and deep economic back-up. This became United States' strategy in the 1990s, later emulated by other nations.

In 2001, the United States began implementing a plan, conceived of by the White House's National Security Council, of encouraging university students to study information-technology security. A generous annual fellowship is awarded for the number of years each candidate is willing to serve the government after graduation. The criticality of learning information just-in-time or, better yet, well in advance, was totally inapparent when non-military attacks occurred in September 2001 in New York and Washington. Dependence on technics overwhelmed the need to know plenty about human beings, how they think, how they apportion values, how they function.

NOVEL DEPLOYMENT, A DIFFERENT READINESS

The *synthetic environment* is growing rapidly and being financed by ministries of defense and private contractors to the military, and 'warfighting' (battlefield) simulations of future conflicts are being used for *smart procurement*: logistical planning and contracting on the basis of the results of simulations – much as the supermarket manager restocks his shelves in real time as a function of his clients' selections and payment. Command, control and communication can be shared in this context through *distributed networks* at the various command levels and among different arms and services. *Tactical internets* supplement any non-classified communication that may be permitted through the Internet and World Wide Web.

These techniques are particularly applicable to the requirements of air and ground forces. For navies, strategic planners anticipate a growing trend away from the traditional open-sea engagements of flotillas or unitary vessels towards a new era of expeditionary warfare. In their book projecting doctrine and strategy in the first decades of the twenty-first century, for example, political scientist George Friedman and management analyst Alison Friedman foresee offshore staging points for navies involved in maneuvers or combat on the periphery of the Eurasian landmass.[23] This new doctrine will involve more of the deployment and sustained resupply at sea that we witnessed in the follow-up to the Gulf War and in the Bosnian and Kosovo operations of 1994–2000.

As in the case of air and ground operations, such force projection of naval components will require joint teamwork on targets and strategic aims shared not only by one country's combined forces, but by the combined services of members of alliances (NATO, for example). Improved C[4]I will be critical, together with foreign languages, in all these mixed operations; this implies ever more reliance on the computer for communication and control.

The new century will see the introduction of a new kind of computer memory, too: tunneling magnetic junction random-access memory (TMJ-RAM), based on the 'up' and 'down' aspects of the spinning of electrons within the atom. This type of microelectronics, known within the broader phenomenon of quantum tunneling, was predicted theoretically in 1975. Its application to computers was announced at a meeting of the American Physical Society in Atlanta in March 1999, already known to physicists and engineers as 'spintronics'. The new technique combines the fast but limited capacity memory-chip with computer disks and their remarkable capacity to store huge amounts of data.

Research on spintronics is financed partly with defense funds at research points belonging to IBM, Hewlett-Packard, Motorola and Honeywell. Computers using spintronics will start up immediately, operate faster than ever before, and save electricity, as well as store data permanently.[24] This new race to expand memory and expand processing power is a contest between the United States, Japan and the European Union.

IS RESEARCH PREPAREDNESS THOROUGH?

There are concerns, to be sure, about loopholes in research and development. There are likely to be more biological attacks, on several continents, to follow those of 2001. Needed rapidly are faster, more efficient and reliable means of detection of biological and chemical agents: beyond anthrax to *Variola major* (causing smallpox), *Yersinia pestis* (leading to plague), sarin, tabun and perhaps worse. 'Knowing you are under attack is half the battle', according to a prominent engineering journal,[25] so that work under way in the United States and elsewhere must take into account new possibilities offered by genetic manipulation to create 'designer' bioagents.

As to nuclear threats (they haven't disappeared), additional investigations and tests to improve the quality of analysis – did India really explode two bombs, or five, in May 1998, since there was no detection by instruments – as well as the very nature of future research based on better seismology and hydroacoustics, radionuclide detection, and extended use of infrasound. Open access to all monitoring, furthermore, is essential for the purposes of both scientists and the military.

As the twentieth century glided into the twenty-first, many of the universal problems confronting the science–defense–terror relationship seemed to punctuate a few anomalies about science and some of its societal relationships. Although these invoke the problem-analysis hierarchy detailed early in this chapter, they need emphasis as we reflect on tomorrow and humanity's relationship with all new science.

IMPERFECTIONS, TOO, ON THE SCIENTIFIC SIDE

'Since wars begin in the minds of men, it is in the minds of men that the defenses of peace must be constructed.'
Prefatory declaration, Constitution of the UN Educational,
Cultural and Scientific Organization

A few critical observations may now be made on science, its military applications, and its terroristic abuses. In the case of science we need to be concerned about, and make every effort to rectify:

- **The gap that continues to exist, even expand, between North and South**. In countries where there is little science (teaching *and* research), there can be little application of the fruits of scientific advance and no control over their relevance.
- **The schizophrenic nature of science**. Technology dominates life almost everywhere, yet much advanced technology is not integrated within modern culture, left as the monopoly of the few. Can civilization expect to benefit, in the foreseeable future, from the merging of the 'two cultures' into one? And from the point of view of the different *styles* of science, should national policy favor what

physicist Freeman Dyson terms *Napoleonic* science (of rigid organization and discipline) or else the *Tolstoyan* school (of creative chaos
and freedom)?[26]

• **Science within the context of environment**. This has multiple
aspects.
(i) *Social* What are the societal effects of a changing environment, and
who decides upon the changes? How we can we implement satis-
factorily the principle of sustainable development? What are the
impacts of expanding tourism, too, on the local culture and vice versa?
(ii) *Economic* What are the benefits of a changing environment on the
well-being of nations, of world regions, of the globalizing relationship? The problem concerning universal tourism applies here too.
• **Ethics** – how much should we be concerned about the moral/
philosophic, perhaps even psychological, significance of evolving
science, as in the case of the potentially powerful biotechnologies
and their abuse for military or terroristic ends?[27] Bioethics calls for
a technological audit of the effects of introducing new pharma-
ceuticals, of producing transgenic plants and animals. In biomedicine,
reflection is needed on the use of test animals, the treatment of persons afflicted with retroviruses, the application of *in vitro* fertilization
or the administration of fertility stimulators, and the withdrawal of
life support from dying human beings.

In matters of defense applications, a special report prepared in
Washington previews potential military operations other than combat
(OOC) – since war operations are automatically assumed by the very
existence of ministries of war. OOC fall into four groups, each with a
scenario of its own:

• *A turbulent third wave*, with new technologies emerging and both
markets and environmental menaces spreading. Scientists work
together everywhere, and the military are called on to be constructive, not destructive.
• *A dark side*, whereby global trade 'melts down' and is replete with
crises of many kinds. Here the military, together with the scientific
and technical world, are expected to use OOC to the optimum.
• *Global mind change*, with countries making a concerted effort to head
off or minimize economic, environmental and mass-destruction
crises. The OOC approach becomes supportive of such efforts.
• *Technology transformation*, a synergetic interaction between fast-
emerging technologies in many fields including nanotechnology –
capable of assembling new machines and other products from the
atom and molecule upwards. Nations, their military forces and

scientific and technical communities cooperate and collaborate 'dramatically' on the OOC mission.

The primary author of this study is Robert L. Olson, who recapitulated in 1999 its main thrusts as 'The US Military's Future in Operations Other than War'.[28]

Many of us consider ourselves modern, even postmodern. Our professionalism keeps us aware of the evolution in science and technology, and today's ministries of defense are acutely aware of the value of this irreversible progress. Yet few such ministries are proactive in fomenting armed conflict – and, in tight spots, even cautious enough to restrain leaders and adversaries bent on hostilities. Most, however, exercise their professionalism by a conscientious monitoring of all conditions that might induce them to lower their guard and thus imperil their national populations.

As for terrorism,

> Science and technical progress constitute a [universal value]. Beyond current debates on unemployment and ... globalization, it remains generally admitted that advances in knowledge contribute to social progress, that research and development are criteria of a society's good health. A question that emerges from the backdrop, to be sure, is the general acceleration of science and its destabilizing nature. In changing our life styles, albeit progressively, science sunders cultural models and contributes indirectly to the 'clash of civilizations' described by [Samuel] Huntington. So if one thinks about the scientific progress achieved over the past fifty years, especially during the last twenty years, and the resulting societal transformations, one can only wonder about what awaits us in the [twenty-first] century ...[29]

especially after the violent taste some of us had in this century's first year. Recourse to the UN and its instruments is essential, as only a concert of nations can cope with international crime. The Biological and Toxic Weapons Convention (1972), for example, needs expansion and reinforcement; procedures are needed for complete investigation of abuse, for extradition of guilty parties, and for investigation and prosecution of alleged violators.

François Heisbourg, a former director of the International Institute for Strategic Studies in London, anticipated in 1997 four types of war during the twenty-first century's first quarter:

- Rogue elements intent on exploiting arms of mass destruction; most likely to happen in the 'crescent of crisis' extending from Afghanistan to North Africa.

- Wars of hatred, violence and secession by minorities seeking full power in the former USSR and Yugoslavia, elsewhere in the Balkans, in South Asia and the sub-Sahara.
- Conflicts of disruption in the industrialized countries, triggered by domestic or foreign agitators, with various forms of terror: extreme violence, even 'virtual destruction' via cyberwar.
- Traditional, Clausewitzian struggles using new-century tools to gain nineteenth-century goals: in East Asia, where the nation-state underwent the least changes in power by the end of the twentieth century.[30]

In relatively small and technologically lingering countries, wars fundamentally internecine in origin can be expected to flare across borders. An instance is that of Iraq's Saddam Hussein and his Takriti clan. This wing of the Ba'ath political party took power in 1968 and has since made every effort to suppress the country's Kurds and Shi'ites and its Sunni dissidents, a stand leading to external conflicts with Israel, Iran, Kuwait, the Coalition of 1990–91 and, in the background, the United States (together with Great Britain) via the UN's arms inspectors. Saddam effectively turned arms-control pressures on Iraq to his own purposes, a perilous rivalry that may continue as conflict beyond Iraq for years to come.

War should not be inevitable. Yet with the frenzied pace at which strategists and scientists continue their collaboration, one wonders if such efforts can be constrained within the bounds of *defense*? The logic of *Realpolitik* translates itself in the modern age into a comprehending and facile collaboration: even terrorism helps itself to what scientists and engineers have cooked up. It is the scientists, therefore, who have shown beyond doubt that war and other organized violence are extensions of science, at the behest and in the service of those who want power at any price. This combination is likely to continue making potentially violent conflict a continuation of today's and tomorrow's research. It is for the rest of us to monitor this conjunction closely and minimize its threat.

NOTES

1 Abu Abdullah Hussein, also known as Hussein Ibn Talal, King of Jordan, interviewed on 3 December 1996 by Israeli political scientist Avi Shlaim, 'His Royal Shyness: King Hussein and Israel', *New York Review of Books*, 15 July 1999, pp. 14–19.
2 Adriano Buzzati-Traverso, *La sfida della scienza* (Milan, Edizioni Scientifiche e Techniche Mondadori, 1976), p. 368; *Scientific Enterprise, Today and Tomorrow* (Paris, Unesco, 1977), p. 426.

3 Lawrence Freedman, 'Weak States and the West: Warfare Has A Future', *The Future Surveyed* (special supplement), *The Economist*, 11 September 1993, p. 44.

4 According to James Wolfensohn, president of the World Bank.

5 There are a number of concordant sources for these dilemmas. See esp. Analysis and Forecasting Office, '21st Century: Trial Identification of Several Major Trends', report), (Paris, Unesco, 10 February 2000); also Allen Hammond, *Which World? Scenarios for the 21st Century: Global Destinies, Regional Choices* (Washington, DC, World Resources Institute, and Covelo, CA, Island Press/Shearwater, 1998); International Energy Agency, *World Energy Prospects to 2020* (Moscow, G8 Energy Ministers' Meeting, 31 March 1998); National Research Council, *Global Environmental Change: Research Pathways for the Next Decade (Overview)*, (Washington, DC, National Academy Press, 1998); *The World in 2020: Towards a New Global Age* (Paris, Organization for Economic Cooperation and Development, 1997); Gérard de Bernis, Susan George *et al.*, *La mondialisation* (Paris, Association Science, Technologie et Société, 1998); National Research Council, *Global Economy, Global Technology, Global Corporations* (Washington, DC, National Academy Press, 1998); Jacques Hallak, *Education and Globalization* (Paris, International Institute for Educational Planning, 1998).

6 Cohen is quoted by Flora Lewis, 'The New Anti-Terrorism is Scary', *IHT*, 29 December 1998, p. 4.

7 Institute of Medicine and National Research Council, *Chemical and Biological Terrorism: Research and Development to Improve Civilian Medical Response* (Washington, DC, National Academy Press, 1998). The citations are from a media release (1 December) announcing the publication.

8 Steve Lohr, 'Waging Cyberwar: Is the World Ready?', *IHT*, 1 October 1996, pp. 1, 6. Norman Levin at RAND and John Arquilla of the US Naval Postgraduate School are among those weighing the menace: private communications with the author of October 1995.

9 *Informatsiya i Sigurnost*, Mladost 4, PO Box 16, 1715 Sofia, Bulgaria, published in Bulgarian and English. The managing editor is Todor Tagarev.

10 James O. Jackson, 'Master Giver', *Time* (Europe edn), 10 July 1995, p. 38. Viktor Soloviev, a former employee of the Academy of Sciences of the USSR, told the author that in his 13 years of experience with the Academy his superiors had always resisted accepting military contracts 'because, if you did, the military would "eat" you, gaining control of your research activity'. Private communication, Paris, 26 March 1996.

11 Paul Kennedy, *Preparing for the 21st Century* (London, HarperCollins/Fontana, 1993), p. 260.

12 See, for example, *Euclid Information*, the French-language periodic newsletter published by the French national coordinator for the European Union's Euclid program, Xavier Lebacq.

13 As published in *IHT*, 6 December 1993, p. 6.

14 Malcolm W. Browne, 'For Scientists, End of Cold War Brings A Chill', appearing in *IHT*, 22 February 1994, p. 1.

15 P. W. 'Bo' Hammer, 'Physics [ ] Society: Replacing the Ampersand', *Physics & Society*, October 1997, p. 10.

16 Browne, 'For Scientists'; Hammer, 'Physics [] Society', pp. 10–11, 12.

17 Tim Weiner, *IHT*, 27 January 1994, p. 1. It is a coincidence that a book published at the same time, Richard Preston's *The Hot Zone* (New York, Random House, 1994), is a terrifyingly true account of research on a violent

micro-organism that gets beyond control in a laboratory in the United States. The experience projects what might happen if antisocial elements put to work a devastating germ such as the one causing hemorrhagic or Ebola fever.

18 Reuters,'Spanish Reports Says Algeria Could Make Nuclear Arms Fuel', *IHT*, 24 August 1998, p. 4.

19 Claude Cheysson in a discussion with another former foreign minister, Jean-François Poncet, Radio France Internationale, 8:30 a.m., 7 January 1995.

20 The IRIS newsletter is cited by William J. Broad, 'Seismic Blast: Bomb or Quake?' *IHT*, 23 January 1997, p. 10.

21 As summarized by Joseph Fitchett,'US Military Draws Up Plans to Win an "Info War"', *IHT*, 19 March 1998, p. 11.

22 Bruce Clark and Bernard Gray, 'US Seeks to Modernize Armed Forces', *Financial Times*, 20 May 1997, p. 1.

23 See George and Meredith Friedman, *The Future of War: Power, Technology and American World Dominance in the 21st Century* (New York, St Martin's Griffin, 1998).

24 John Markoff, '"Spintronics" Puts New Spin on PC Building Blocks', *IHT*, 8 April 1999, p. 7.

25 Christopher Aston, 'Biological Warfare Canaries', *IEEE Spectrum*, October 2001, pp. 35–40; Kenneth Chang, Andrew Pollock, 'Early Warning of Toxic Strike Not Easy', *New York Times*, 28 October 2001, pp. B1–2.

26 Freeman J. Dyson, *Imagined Worlds* (Cambridge, MA, Harvard University Press, 1997), p. 54 *ff*.

27 Many scientists, such as the French physicist Gérard Toulouse, believe that a scientist's first concern today is a moral one. See his *Regards sur l'éthique des sciences* (Glimpses on the Ethics of Science) (Paris, Hachette/Littératures, 1998).

28 The article appeared in 1, No. 1, of *Foresight: The Journal of Future Studies, Strategic Thinking and Policy* (1999), pp. 35–47.

29 Michel Tatu's final report,'War and Peace in the 21st Century' (theme and proceedings of an international symposium organized by the Fondation pour les Etudes de la Défense, Paris), *Défense nationale*, April 1996, p. 211.

30 François Heisbourg, *The Future of Warfare*, Predictions Collection, vol. II (London, Orion/Phoenix, 1997), pp. 17–18.

Afterword

'History consists of the struggle of mind against nature; it begins at the point where the intellect emerges from the state of nature and challenges nature. But the end-result of the historical process is a return to the natural condition, for the mind never tires "of casting its terrible 'Why?' in the face of all that exists ..."'

Felix Gilbert, historian[1]

'The military, much as the merchants and bankers, are pragmatic people, used to dealing with figures, measurement, verification and computation. Their growth in influence prepares, as does the world of business, an environment favorable to science – and impedes the "dark forces" of superstition, magic and dogmatism.'

David Cosandey, physicist and historian[2]

WAR AS AN AGENT OF CULTURAL CHANGE

How does the atmosphere of wartime or globalized terrorism impinge on society, including its cultural-scientific ambience? We know that such disturbances incite profound philosophical and even psychological enquiry, generating their own artistic forms. They breed music and literature special to the times, and add introspection and high drama to the stage, films and television. Millions upon millions of people are affected. The sensation of overwhelming pressure – often that of individual and national survival – is an inevitable result of war or other hostilities.

Extreme conflict is thus an agent of change well beyond the range of armed violence. Together with conflict, concomitant events bestow, in the words of the economic historian David Landes, 'a long experience of technology in the service of violence and oppression, as well as in that of improvement and progress. We understand that techniques are two-edged instruments, available for both good and evil.'[3] But where, other than by creating new weapons and techniques with which to kill more people faster and more massively, have times of armed struggle led basic science?

We saw in Chapter 11 how an inquisitive battlefield surgeon developed, as a result of his wartime service, the cardiac regulator known commercially as the Pacemaker. We might add that the freeze-drying, or lyophilization, of blood plasma for emergency transfusions was invented by the military only a few years before. This is high technology, founded on scientific knowledge. Can we conclude that there is a direct, causal relationship between war's influences and the development of new knowledge? One impressive reply comes to mind, although there are others.

As the mechanics of the observable universe unfolded over the centuries, humankind began to understand how the universe is built and how nature works. With the explosion of the physical sciences in the nineteenth century, philosophers of science and philosophizing researchers began wondering why we could not explain – trace more accurately – the origins, and perhaps even the meaning, of life. We grasped the notions of conservation of energy, entropy, the unification of electricity and magnetism, and quantum physics. Einstein, Bohr, Hubble and other twentieth-century physicists and astronomers provided us with a brand-new view of the cosmos through the equivalence of mass and energy, wave mechanics, quantum electrodynamics, and expansion of the universe. The life sciences, however, lagged far behind.

It was in a thoroughly wartime setting that biology began to catch up with physical science. The Viennese Erwin Schrödinger was one of the founders of the new physics. He was much influenced by Einstein and Louis de Broglie, and yet we have mentioned his work in physics only in passing (Chapter 4). With the political events unfolding during the Third Reich, Schrödinger found himself suddenly in voluntary exile from his native surroundings. The Second World War saw him contemplating both his plight and the universe, while teaching at Trinity College in the neutral capital of Dublin.

Schrödinger was, quite intentionally, gliding from physics to life-science meditations. He wondered if the laws of physics and chemistry might possibly explain the fundaments of biology. In 1944, at the moment when a final attempt was made by Germans inside Germany to do away with Hitler, Schrödinger published a longish essay called 'What Is Life?' In it, the rigorous physicist posed the basic question of whether life in the cell is controlled by something he called a *code-script* to be found in the genes.

Schrödinger's probing coincided with the biological curiosity shown by another scientist, Max Delbrück, also a refugee from Hitler's Germany, and the American biochemist Linus Pauling (the only individual ever to win two unshared Nobel Prizes). Delbrück's concern lay specifically in the genetics of viruses commonly infecting certain bacteria: the bacteriophages, or bacteria eaters. His explorations in biophysics during the final year of the Second World War began to lead in the direction of biochemistry. After the conflict, Max Perutz and John Kendrew, and later Francis Crick, Rosalind Franklin, James Watson and Maurice Wilkins, made further investigations in the newly emerging field of molecular biology. Discovery of deoxyribonucleic acid's double helix resulted.

HOW INEVITABLE MIGHT BE THE INFLUENCE OF HOSTILITIES?

Would these scientific events have occurred had there been no Second World War? Possibly, but not necessarily when they did, where they did, or with the same actors.

Research costs money, a good bit of it, as our testimonial (among others) makes clear. In sustaining their investigations, the molecular biologists in Europe were reinforced psychologically from across the Atlantic by Vannevar Bush's exhortation to governments: Provide financial support for basic science, for it is to a country's long-term advantage. This was the key theme in Bush's own *Science – The Endless Frontier* (1945), and both governments and scientists took note. Material support from the state made it possible, therefore, for the new breed of researchers to perceive that the sequence of nucleotides, or biochemical building-blocks, in DNA is interpretable in terms of the sequence of amino acids within proteins: *new* knowledge.

Molecular biology's great achievement supplied detail to earlier knowledge that DNA was a carrier of genetic information. This discovery merited the Nobel Prize in physiology for 1962, which went to the Crick–Watson–Wilkins team.[4] So again the question, what if physicist Schrödinger had not plumbed biology when he did, where he did, the way he did? It may be excessive to credit the Austrian with enabling the discovery of the DNA molecule, yet it remains a fact that the gathering clouds of war offered new orientations to the seminal work of physicist Schrödinger in biology, and how this effort would be taken up by others.

Decades later, the DNA molecule is recognized in several forms. DNA-B is the most common, conforming to the double-helix hypothesis. In 1999 biochemists identified the DNA-P molecule, with a somewhat different alignment of its atoms along the lines suggested originally by Pauling. DNA-P may be accessible to enzymes, but its true role in cellular life remains to be determined. Meanwhile, Olivier Postel-Vinay, the chief editor of the journal *La Recherche* warns that 'the exploitation by certain states of progress in molecular biology to create new arms of war is preoccupying'.[5]

SEEKING THE VERY ROOTS OF CONFLICT

Since new keys were found to open intellectual locks, we have also learned considerably about how people act and react *en masse*. Think-tanks and peace-research institutes have multiplied and flourished. We believe that we understand, ever better, the roots and compulsions leading to conflict. James Schellenberg produced a history-making analysis in 1982 with *The Science of Conflict*, but we need to proceed further, much further, and this is where the social sciences should again be of value.

Stephen Peter Rosen, in his *Winning the Next War* (1991), cautions that the powerful and rich countries must develop means for managing uncertainty, so as to understand the strategic perspectives of many emerging nations. He stresses that Western countries ignore much of the political and cultural history of Japan, India or China. Such study should reduce non-Asian incertitude about how these countries might use their new power. To this one might add that Westerners should thereby better understand their own cultures of strategy, since the large and wealthy countries remain assailable as practitioners of imperialism and colonialism merely dressed in new clothing. Therein lie some of the causes of the international terrorism that punctuated the month of September 2001.

As the twenty-first century began, allocations for military research were down 20 per cent since 1990 throughout the European Union – one of the anticipated peace dividends – almost as much in the United States, and more so in Russia.[6] The new terrorism and its costs now falsify the American, Russian, British and probably French and German figures. But perhaps a new strategic culture is taking form, after all, in these nations, most of whom represent (together with China) the permanent members of the UN's Security Council.

In the continuing military–scientific partnership research may demand, anew, levels of funding that most economies cannot afford to maintain because of other societal obligations. In both the world of new science and that of quick-fix military technology we need, more than ever, to be on perpetual guard against the Dr Strangeloves of the future. We must trust, as John Keegan has urged in his incisive *The First World War*, that goodwill as well as prudence will prevail. How the future unfolds will be the deciding factor.

Philippe Delmas, a French war-and-peace expert cited in Chapter 7, explained to the author in 1996 that how and when new conflicts emerge will depend in part on:

- **the legitimacy of a possible armed conflict**, which a state will be obliged to pre-assess, contrary to the compulsions that once drove a Metternich or a Churchill. The nature of war has changed since their times so that today conflict stems, insists Delmas, from the characteristics of the state *thinking* about making war.
- **governmental breakdown** (*la panne de l'Etat*), 'which will force a state to engage in *limited wars*' (Somalia and ex-Yugoslavia, in the 1990s; who after Afghanistan?). Even internal conflicts now have a tendency to internationalize themselves (Bosnia, Burundi, later Zaire, Chechnya, Kosovo, East Timor, Ethiopia–Eritrea). Only a really strong state, Delmas maintains, can envisage *winning* a war.[7]

Former Soviet Army General Makhmut Gareev has expressed the military mirror-thought to Delmas's observations in his *If War Comes Tomorrow? The Contours of Future Armed Conflict* (1998). One needs to consider, he says, contradicting tendencies in the evolution of military affairs, drawing one's conclusions from the many, complex potential used of military power. Good reasons to think differently about one's neighbors emerged, indeed, from the Oslo process between Israel and Palestine in 1993 – only to be dashed to pieces again in 2002 by both parties' recalcitrance and renewed hostility, as terror and warlike actions again prevailed almost daily.

CAN THERE BE A FINAL WORD?

Such compulsions and rethinking are cause for science and technology to continue to find their extensions in the arenas of premeditated fighting, here and there on the planet. Much in the manner that technology has been the handmaiden of research, so science is today a powerful adjunct in the making of armed mischief. It is only good, common sense – rather than *better science, less science* or *no science* – that will prevent new abuses of the formidable and growing power of scientific knowledge in governance worldwide.

As George Friedman of Stratfor, the 'global intelligence company', says, 'The manner in which each war is fought and concluded lays the groundwork for the next conflict. There are no wars to end all wars. Conflict and warfare are a permanent part of the human condition. It is far more useful to think of war as a single, inseparable thread running throughout the fabric of human history than as separate, disconnected episodes.'[8]

NOTES

1   Felix Gilbert, *History, Choice and Commitment* (Cambridge, MA, Harvard University Press/Belknap, 1977), p. 25.
2   David Cosandey, 'Les causes du succès scientifique de l'Occident' (The Causes of the West's Scientific Success), *Sciences*, No. 2001–1, pp. 16–20. Cosandey is the author of *The Rise of the West*, found on www.riseofthewest.net
3   David S. Landes, *Revolution in Time: Clocks and the Making of the Modern World* (Cambridge, MA, Harvard University Press, 1993), p. 45.
4   But not, in this otherwise enlightened age, to the woman member, Rosalind Franklin.
5   Olivier Postel-Vinay, 'Le dossier du bioterrorisme', *La Recherche*, December 2001, p. 70.
6   According to figures published periodically by the Western European Union, Paris and Brussels.
7   Talk on future wars by Delmas at the Association Futuribles, Paris, 4 April 1996.
8   George Friedman, reporting on current geopolitics, 2 October 2001, on http://www.stratfor.com.

Select Bibliography

Note: titles listed here are mostly in addition to those in the notes.

GENERAL

Bailey, George, *Galileo's Children – Science, Sakharov, and the Power of the State* (New York, Little, Brown/Arcade, 1990; published originally in German (1988) as *Sacharow: Der Weg zur Perestroika*.)

Benton, Barbara (ed.), *Soldiers for Peace: Fifty Years of United Nations Peacekeeping* (New York, Facts on File, 1996).

De Cerreño, A. C., and A. Keynan, 'Scientific Cooperation, State Conflict: The Roles of Scientists in Mitigating International Discord' *Annals of the New York Academy of Sciences*, 10 December 1998, 866.

Fisher, David E., *A Race on the Edge of Time: Radar, the Decisive Weapon of World War 2*, (New York, Paragon House, 1989).

Fuller, J. F. C., *The Decisive Battles of the Western World*, vol. I (London, Eyre & Spottiswoode, 1954).

Goldberg, Andrew C., Debra van Opstal and James H. Barkley, *Avoiding the Brink: Theory and Practice in Crisis Management* (London, Brassey's, 1990).

Hershberg, James G., *James B. Conant: Harvard to Hiroshima and the Making of the Nuclear Age* (New York, Knopf, 1993).

Jungk, Robert, *Heller als tausend Sonnen* (Berne, Alfred Scherz Verlag, 1956); *Brighter than a Thousand Suns: A Personal History of the Atomic Scientists*, trans. James Cleugh (New York, Harcourt, Brace, 1958).

Keegan, John, *War and Our World* (London, Hutchinson, 1998).

Mayor, Federico, *et al.*, with intro. by Ilya Prigogine, *Science and Power* (Paris, UNESCO Publishing/Challenges, 1995).

Paret, P., *The Makers of Modern Strategy from Machiavelli to the Nuclear Age* (Oxford, Oxford University Press, 1986).

Parker, Geoffrey, *The Military Revolution: Military Innovation and the Rise of the West,1500–1800* (Cambridge, Cambridge University Press, 1988).

Snyder, Craig A. (ed.), *Contemporary Security and Strategy* (London, Macmillan, 1999).

PREPARATION FOR CONFLICT

Duffy, Christopher, *Fire and Stone: The Science of Fortress Warfare 1660–1860* (Mechanicsburg, PA, Stackpole, 1997, 2nd edn).

Francart, Loup, *Maîtriser la violence: Une option stratégique* (Mastering Violence: A Strategic Option), with the collaboration of Jean-Jacques Patry and intro. by André Glucksmann (Paris, Economica, 1999).

Gusterson, Hugh, *Nuclear Rites: A Weapons Laboratory at the End of the Cold War*, (Berkeley, CA, University of California Press, 1996).

Hilborn, Robert C., *Chaos and Nonlinear Dynamics: An Introduction for Scientists and Engineers* (New York and Oxford, Oxford University Press, 1994).

Horgan, John, '"Bang! You're Alive": An Unusual Trio Wins Support for "Nonlethal"Weapons', *Scientific American*, April 1994, pp. 11–12.

Leslie, Stuart W., *The Cold War and Military Science: The Military–Industrial Complex at MIT and Stanford* (New York, Columbia University Press, 1993).

Naveh, Shimon, *In Pursuit of Military Excellence: The Evolution of Operational Theory* (London, Frank Cass, 1997).

Sakharov, Andrei, *Memoirs,* trans. Richard Lourie (New York, Knopf, 1990).

WARFARE AND ITS MANAGEMENT

Abt, Clark C., *Serious Games* (New York, Viking, 1970).

Aston, Christopher, 'Biological Warfare Canaries', *IEEE Spectrum*, October 2001, 35–40.

Druzhinin, V. V., *Concept, Algorithm, Decision – Decision-Making and Automation (A Soviet View)* (Moscow, 1972; Engl. trans., Washington, DC, General Printing Office, 1975).

Fermi, Rachel, and Esther Samra, with intro. by Richard Rhodes, *Picturing the Bomb* (New York, Harry Abrams, 1995).

Lanier-Graham, Susan D., *The Ecology of War: Environmental Impacts of Weaponry and War* (New York, Walker and Company, 1993).

Rapoport, Anatol, *Fights, Games, and Debates* (Ann Arbor, MI, University of Michigan Press, 1960).

Ritchie, David, *Space War* (New York, Atheneum, 1982).

BEHIND THE ACTION, AND WARS TO COME

Adams, James, *The Next World War: Computers Are the Weapons & the Front Line is Everywhere* (New York, Simon & Schuster, 1998).

Alexander, Bevin, *The Future of Warfare* (New York, W. W. Norton, 1995).

Bowonder, B. 'Globalization of R&D: The Indian Experience and Implications for Developing Countries', *Interdisciplinary Science Review*, 26 (2001), pp. 191–203.

Lemonick, Michael, *Other Worlds: The Search for Life in the Universe* (New York, Simon & Schuster/Touchstone, 1989).

Miller, Judith, Steven Engelberg and William Broad, *Germs: Biological Weapons and America's Secret War* (New York, Simon & Schuster, 2001).

Naím, Moisés. 'Reinventing War', interview of three retired generals and an admiral by the editor-publisher of *FP-Foreign Policy*, (November/December 2001), 31–47.

Ramana, M. V. and A. H. Nayyar, 'India, Pakistan and the Bomb', *Scientific American*, December 2001, 60–71.

Solomon, Jean-Jacques, *Le scientifique et le guerrier* (The Scientist and the Warrior) (Paris, Belin/Débats, 2001).

Index